D0455013

Advances
in
Fingerprint
Technology

SECOND EDITION

CRC SERIES IN FORENSIC AND POLICE SCIENCE

BARRY A. J. FISHER, Series Editor
L.A. County Sheriff's Department

TECHNIQUES OF CRIME SCENE INVESTIGATION
Sixth Edition
Barry A. J. Fisher

SCIENTIFIC EXAMINATION OF QUESTIONED DOCUMENTS
Revised Edition
Ordway Hilton

ADVANCES IN FINGERPRINT TECHNOLOGY
Second Edition
Henry C. Lee
R. E. Gaensslen

INSTRUMENTAL DATA FOR DRUG ANALYSIS
Second Edition, Volumes 1–4
Terry Mills, III
J. Conrad Roberson

INSTRUMENTAL DATA FOR DRUG ANALYSIS
Second Edition, Volume 5
Terry Mills, III
J. Conrad Roberson
H. Horton McCurdy
William H. Wall

INSTRUMENTAL DATA FOR DRUG ANALYSIS
Second Edition, Volumes 6-7
Terry Mills, III
J. Conrad Roberson
William H. Wall
Kevin L. Lothridge
William D. McDougall
Michael W. Gilbert

Advances in Fingerprint Technology

SECOND EDITION

EDITED BY

Henry C. Lee and R. E. Gaensslen

CRC Press

Boca Raton   London   New York   Washington, D.C.

Library of Congress Cataloging-in-Publication Data

Advances in fingerprint technology / edited by Henry C. Lee, R.E. Gaensslen.--2nd ed.
    p. cm -- (CRC series in forensic and police science)
    Includes bibliographical references and index.
    ISBN 0-8493-0923-9 (alk. paper)
    1. Fingerprints. 2. Fingerprints--Data processing. I. Lee, Henry C. II. Gaensslen, R. E.
(Robert E.) III. Series.

    HV6074 .A43 2001
    363.25'8--dc21

                                             2001025816

Visit the CRC Press Web site at www.crcpress.com

© 2001 by CRC Press LLC

No claim to original U.S. Government works
International Standard Book Number 0-8493-0923-9
Library of Congress Card Number 2001025816
Printed in the United States of America 1 2 3 4 5 6 7 8 9 0
Printed on acid-free paper

Preface

The first edition of this book was published as a volume in the Elsevier Series in Forensic and Police Science. Elsevier's book business has since been acquired by CRC Press LLC and CRC has supported and extended their forensic science program. We thank CRC for the opportunity to revise *Advances in Fingerprint Technology* to this second edition.

Fingerprints is an area in which there have been many new and exciting developments in the past two decades or so, although advances in DNA typing have tended to dominate both the forensic science literature and popular information about advances in forensic sciences. Particularly in the realm of methods for developing latent prints, but also in the growth of imaging and AFIS technologies, fingerprint science has seen extraordinary breakthroughs because creative applications of principles derived from physics and organic chemistry have been applied to it.

Fingerprints constitute one of the most important categories of physical evidence. They are among the few that can be truly individualized. Fingerprint individuality is widely accepted by scientists and the courts alike. Lately there have been some modest challenges to whether a firm scientific basis exists for fingerprint individuality, based on the U.S. Supreme Court's 1993 *Daubert v. Merrell Dow Pharmaceuticals, Inc.* decision [113 S.Ct. 2786 (1993)] in which new standards for the admissibility of scientific evidence were articulated for the first time. The issues underlying these challenges are treated in Chapters 9 and 10. A perspective on the history and development of fingerprinting and the fundamentals of latent print identification are treated in Chapters 1 and 2, revised from the first edition. Latent fingerprint residue chemistry, on which every latent print detection technique is ultimately based, is covered in detail in a new Chapter 3. Chapter 4, the survey of latent print development methods and techniques, has been revised and updated. Chapter 5 on ninydrin analogues has been revised and updated. New chapters on physical developers (Chapter 7) and photoluminescent nanoparticles (Chapter 6) are added. AFIS system technology and fingerprint imaging are now widespread and may be considered mature. They are covered in a new Chapter 8.

The first edition of this volume was dedicated to the memory and lifetime work of Robert D. Olsen, Sr., who wrote the original Chapter 2, but passed away unexpectedly before the book could be published. That chapter has been revised and retained in this edition.

We want to thank all the contributors to this revised edition for their outstanding work and cooperation in bringing this work to completion. We also thank the staff at CRC, especially our acquisitions editor, Becky Mc Eldowney, for making the task comparatively painless. Again we thank our wives, Margaret and Jacqueline, for their continued love and patience with us and our work habits.

Acknowledgments

We gratefully acknowledge the assistance of Ms. Nancy Folk, Ms. Cheng Sheaw-Guey, Mr. Hsieh Sung-shan, and Mr. Kenneth Zercie in the preparation of the original Chapter 3 of the first edition. We particularly thank Ms. Erin Gould, a M.S. graduate of the University of Illinois at Chicago forensic science program, for her significant help with revised Chapter 4 for this present edition. We also thank Robert Ramotowski of the U.S. Secret Service Forensic Services Division for helpful commentary on and additional information for the revised Chapter 4.

Contributors

Joseph Almog, Ph.D.
Casali Institute of Applied Chemistry
Hebrew University of Jerusalem
Jerusalem, Israel
almog@vms.huji.ac.il

John Berry, FFS, BEM
Fingerprint Examiner and Historian
  (Retired)
South Hatfield, Hertfordshire, England

Antonio Cantu, Ph.D.
Forensic Services Division
U.S. Secret Service
Washington, D.C.
acantu@usss.treas.gov

R. E. Gaensslen, Ph.D.
Forensic Science, College of Pharmacy
University of Illinois at Chicago
Chicago, Illinois
reg@uic.edu

Robert J. Hazen
Spotsylvania, Virginia

Anil K. Jain, Ph.D.
Department of Computer Science
  and Engineering
Michigan State University
East Lansing, Michigan
jain@cse.msu.edu

James L. Johnson
Forensic Services Division
U.S. Secret Service
Washington, D.C.

Henry C. Lee, Ph.D.
Connecticut State Police Forensic
  Science Laboratory
Meriden, Connecticut

E. Roland Menzel, Ph.D.
Center for Forensic Studies
Texas Tech University
Lubbock, Texas
menzel@tomserver.phys.ttu.edu

Sharath Pankanti
IBM T. J. Watson Research Center
Hawthorne, New York
sharat@watson.ibm.com

Clarence E. Phillips

Robert Ramotowski
Forensic Services Division
U.S. Secret Service
Washington, D.C.
rramotowski@usss.treas.gov

David A. Stoney, Ph.D.
McCrone Research Institute
  Chicago, Illinois
and Clinical Professor Forensic Science
University of Illinois at Chicago
Chicago, Illinois
dstoney@mcri.org

Table of Contents

History and Development of Fingerprinting

1

JOHN BERRY
DAVID A. STONEY*

Contents

* Update.

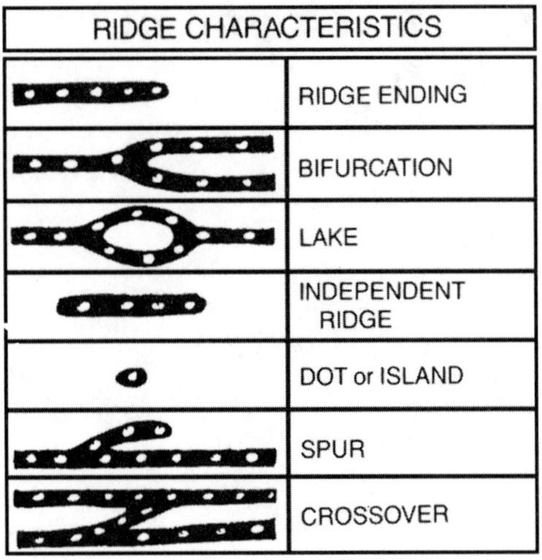

RIDGE CHARACTERISTICS	
	RIDGE ENDING
	BIFURCATION
	LAKE
	INDEPENDENT RIDGE
	DOT or ISLAND
	SPUR
	CROSSOVER

Figure 1.1 Ridge characteristics. (Drawn by John Berry.)

Introduction

The fascinating story of the development and use of fingerprints in the last hundred years will only be properly appreciated if the reader is acquainted with some knowledge of dactyloscopy; therefore I will briefly outline the basic details of this science. The inside surfaces of the hands from fingertips to wrist and the bottom surfaces of the feet from the tip of the big toe to the rear of the heel contain minute ridges of skin, with furrows between each ridge. A cross section of a finger would look exactly like the cross section of a plowed field. Whereas on a plowed field the ridges and furrows run in straight parallel lines, on the hands and feet the ridges and furrows frequently curve and, especially on the fingertips and toe ends, the ridges and furrows form complicated patterns. The ridges have pores along their entire length that exude perspiration; hence, when an article is picked up, the perspiration runs along the ridges and leaves an exact impression of the ridges, just as an inked rubber stamp leaves its impression on a blank sheet of paper.

Ridges and furrows have evolved on the hands and feet to fulfill three specific functions:

1. Exudation of perspiration
2. Tactile facility
3. Provision of a gripping surface

The ridges and furrows form seven basic characteristics, as shown in Figure 1.1. Some authorities consider that only two types of characteristics

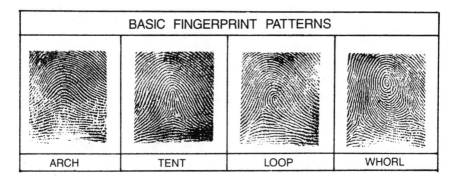

Figure 1.2 Basic fingerprint patterns.

are present, a ridge ending and a bifurcation, all other characteristics being variations of the two basic forms. I consider that my illustration defines the most important varieties of ridge detail, also known as ridge characteristics.

The ridges and furrows form patterns on the last joint of the fingers and toes, forming four basic types, as shown in Figure 1.2. There are variations of these patterns, especially with whorls, but these are the province of the fingerprint expert. Every person in the world shares these patterns — a person can have all of one type or even a mixture of all of them. The everyday use of fingers as an identification method and the production of finger and palm evidence in courts of law are based on one magnificent premise: no one has ever been found who has a sequence of ridge detail on the hands and feet that is identical to the ridge detail of any other person.

Evolution and the Elliptical Whorl (1976)

Before I researched the history of fingerprints in 1975, the earliest evidence of ridge detail on the hands and feet of humans was seen in the 4000-year-old mummies of ancient Egypt. The hands and feet of mummies have been examined on numerous occasions, and I can confirm the presence of ridge detail on the mummies' digits. Before 1975, the only other evidence reported was the presence of a small portion of palm imprint on hardened mud found in Egypt on a paleolithic site at the Sebekian deposit, Kom Ombo plain, on the east bank of the river Nile, dated around 10,000 years ago. The fact that primates have ridge detail was announced for the first time, as far as I can discover, by Joannes Evangelista Purkinje in his thesis (discussed later) published on December 22, 1823. He wrote:

> In the hands of the monkeys, as well as in their prehensile tails, similar lines occur, the distinction of which adds to the knowledge of the characteristics

of all species. Zoologists, unless they consider them unimportant, will add further details.

Purkinje illustrated a palm impression and a small portion of the prehensile tail of a spider monkey.

In 1975–1976, I and my colleagues in the Fingerprint Office in Hertfordshire, U.K. — Roger Ball, David Brooker, Nicholas Hall, Stephen Haylock, and Martin Leadbetter — commenced protracted research to confirm that all species of primates have ridge detail on their hands and feet in patterns and toe ends that conform to human patterns (see Figure 1.2). We prepared a list of over 180 species of primates from the tree shrews (family Tupaiidae) to the gorilla (family Pongidae) and prepared a roster whereby, in small groups, we visited zoos and private collections, examining and in many cases taking impressions of the hands and feet of primates. This research engendered publicity in the press and television; one sarcastic writer commented in a national newspaper that Stephen Haylock was fingerprinting monks.

Eventually, Leadbetter and I contacted Professor and Mrs. Napier, who have now retired to a Scottish island. Professor Napier was a professional writer and a world-renowned expert on the hand; his wife Prue was also a writer and worked in the British Natural History Museum on Cromwell Road, London. We discovered that her terms of reference covered a section of the museum denied to ordinary visitors where thousands of deceased primates, many of them stuffed with straw, were placed in wide receptacles in an air-conditioned hall. Mrs. Napier explained that a "rule" existed whereby when a primate died in England, the skin was sent to the museum. This "rule" has been in existence for many years. For example, Roger Ball and I used a fingerprint-lifting technique to obtain the entire length of ridge detail from the prehensile tail of a red howler monkey that had died in 1829. Figure 1.3 shows an enlarged section of the lift.

The museum authorities gave permission for Roger Ball, Stephen Haylock, Martin Leadbetter, and me to examine all the stuffed primates in the huge collection. Working in pairs and using our vacation days, we eventually examined the hand and foot surfaces of all the primates. In a few instances we lifted ridge details from the hands and feet of selected specimens. This was done by carefully smoothing several layers of acrylic paint over the surfaces and waiting for each layer to dry before peeling it off. When we returned to the Fingerprint Office in Hertfordshire, the acrylic lifts were dusted with aluminum powder and then lifted with transparent tape and placed on transparent Cobex, forming a negative duly processed in the Camtac machine, producing a positive impression, i.e., ridges were black and furrows and pores were white. After 18 months of research, we had become

Figure 1.3 Portion of the prehensile tail of a red howler monkey (1829).

the first researchers, as far as I can ascertain, to examine and record the hands, feet, and prehensile tails of every species of primate.

In a later section, I shall discuss the fingerprint pioneer Dr. Henry Faulds (pronounced "folds") in some detail; but in the present context I believe it is enormously interesting to report that on February 15, 1880, Faulds wrote to evolutionist Charles Darwin requesting his aid in obtaining the finger impressions of lemurs, anthropoids, etc. "with a view to throw light on human ancestry." On April 7, 1880, Darwin replied to Faulds:

Dear Sir,

The subject to which you refer in your letter of February 15th seems to me a curious one, which may turn out interesting, but I am sorry to say that I am most unfortunately situated for offering you any assistance. I live in the country, and from weak health seldom see anyone. I will, however, forward your letter to Mr. F. Galton, who is the man most likely that I can think of to take up the subject and make further enquiries.

Wishing you success,
I remain, dear Sir,
Yours faithfully,
Charles Darwin

The "Mr. F. Galton" referred to in the letter from Darwin in due course became an authority on fingerprint matters in England and was part of an establishment clique that sought to revile Faulds (to be described later). However, note the amazing chain of events: ... fingerprint pioneer Faulds ... primates' fingerprints ... Charles Darwin ... Mr. F. Galton (later Sir Francis Galton) ... fingerprint pioneer!

During the summer of 1976, I was, as always, fully occupied in my work as a fingerprint expert in Hertfordshire, specializing in searching for the ownership of finger imprints found at crime scenes, known in the U.S. by the particularly apt expression "cold searching." Many identifications are made as the direct result of suspects being named by investigating police officers, but it is thrilling for a fingerprint expert, even a grizzled veteran like myself working with fingerprints for 37 years, to delve into the unknown and give the police a named person for the crime they are investigating, a name completely fresh and unknown to them, which we refer to as being "out of the blue." Some astute detectives, when given the name as the result of a successful search, attempt to give the impression that somehow "they had an idea" that the name supplied to them was at that time under serious review. Fingerprint experts do not like this because the identification might have been made after laboriously searching perhaps thousands of fingerprint forms.

So in 1976 my position was that I had been scanning hundreds, possibly thousands, of fingerprints every working day for almost 22 years and at the back of my mind was the ever-present thought that all primates have "human type" finger impressions — after all, we are all primates — and, prompted by the letter from Faulds to Darwin, some original thoughts occurred to me.

I had recently read Prue Napier's book *Monkeys and Apes,* wherein she illustrated every primate, describing the physical similarities and differences that occur in geographically separate areas, such as South America (only South American primates have ridge detail on their prehensile tail strip), Japan, Africa, Sumatra, Gibraltar, India, and Madagascar. I perused books on plate tectonics, averaging the estimated dates of the separation of Madagascar from the East African coast, and calculated that this occurred 50,000,000 years ago. Madagascan primates, I mused, differ physically from African primates, but they also bore ridge detail on their hands and feet. One fingerprint pattern that frequently occurs on primates in all geographical areas is the elliptical whorl (Figure 1.4), which is also found on human finger impressions. I must stress that arches, tents, loops, and whorls (see Figure 1.2) are also found on primates, but I "latched onto" the elliptical whorl as the basis for my sudden inspiration. Surely, if East African and Madagascan primates have elliptical whorls (among other patterns), only two theories could account for this phenomenon:

Figure 1.4 Elliptical whorl.

> ***Theory 1:*** Before the distribution of certain land masses between 50,000,000 and 100,000,000 years ago, ridge detail was present on the hands and feet of our subprimate ancestors.
>
> ***Theory 2:*** At some undetermined moment in time, perhaps allied with the emergence of *Homo sapiens,* primates all over the world suddenly developed ridge detail on their hand and foot surfaces, all species having associated patterns.

I submit that Theory 2 does not even require the remotest consideration, unless one is prepared to put forward a subtheory of Divine Intervention; but even then, cynically, why would God suddenly decide to gratuitously hand out ridge detail? I forwarded details of Theory 1 to Professor Napier and to Professor Beigert, Zurich, Switzerland, for their consideration. I met with Professor Napier, who kindly presented copies of his relevant publications.

In *Monkeys Without Tails,* Professor Napier considers that the development of tree climbers like Smilodectes required, among other physical developments, "replacement of sharp claws by flattened nails associated with the development of sensitive pads on the tips of the digits." He wrote to me:

> I am quite sure that fingerprints are as old as you suggest, particularly if the evolution of the monkeys is put back to the Eocene. The chances of evolving the "human" primate pattern are very high by means of the simple process of evolutionary *convergence* which your thesis strongly suggests … it is obviously a basic pattern of Nature.

For many years Professor Beigert has published numerous books concerning ridge detail on the hand and foot surfaces of selected primates. He also forwarded to me copies of his literature and wrote, making the following observations:

> I agree with you that dermatoglyphics on palma and planta of primates have to be dated very early. In my opinion in the Paleocene, 50,000,000–60,000,000 years ago.

In his book *The Evaluation of the Skull, Hands and Feet for Primate Taxonomy* (1963), Professor Beigert writes:

> Much less attention has been given to the fact that among the other sense organs, the touch receptors underwent a significantly higher development.

My thesis was published in *Fingerprint Whorld* (July 1976) and in my esoteric annual publication *Ridge Detail in Nature* (1979); both publications were circulated to fingerprint bureaus, universities, and museums all over the world. No one has claimed prior publication of my theory regarding the fact that subprimates bore ridge detail before the separation of land masses.

I therefore submit that ridge detail appeared on the hands and feet of our subprimate ancestors over 100,000,000 years ago (a new 1987 estimate for the separation of Madagascar from Africa is closer to 200,000,000 years) and that our subprimate ancestors developed ridge detail on their hands and feet to facilitate the evolutionary requirement for grip, tactile facility, and the exudation of perspiration.

Neolithic Bricks (7000 B.C.)

Dame Kathleen Kenyon carried out excavations in the ancient city of Jericho, and in her book *Archaeology of the Holy Land,* referring to houses dated between 7000 B.C. and 6000 B.C., she reported

> The bricks of which the walls were constructed were made by hand (not in moulds, as is usual later), in shape rather like a flattened cigar, with the surface impressed with a herringbone pattern by pairs of prints of the bricklayer's thumbs, thus giving a keying such as is provided by the hollow in modern bricks.

In *Paphos — History and Archaeology* by F. G. Maier and V. Karageorghis, dealing with excavations in Paphos, birthplace of Aphrodite, reference is made to the walls of the ancient city, eighth century B.C.

The bricks, carefully laid and accurately jointed, are of near uniform size and of dark brown clay. A distinctive bright red-clay mortar was used. Many bricks have impressed fingerprints on their lower side.

Prehistoric Carvings (3000 B.C.)

Recently I discovered details on two archaeological items that proved to my entire satisfaction that early humans were cognizant of patterns on their fingertips. However, before discussing them, I wish to report on the work of "a distinguished fingerprint authority," a certain Mr. Stockis, who published a treatise in the early 1920s in which he attempted to justify his claims that persons who carved patterns on standing stones in dolmen on Goat Island, Brittany, France, were aware of ridge detail on their digits. The carvings he illustrated depicted symbolic arches, tents, loops, and whorls.

The so-called Stockis theory was investigated by the eminent fingerprint expert Professor Harold Cummins, from the U.S., who reported

> If it be true that Neolithic men really noted fingerprint patterns, and with the attention to minute detail which is claimed, credit is due to them for a spontaneous interest and keenness in such observation hardly matched by the average man of the present day.

In his critique of the Stockis theory, Professor Cummins acknowledges that pottery making could have revealed ridge detail to Neolithic humans and accepts that the carvings are "highly suggestive" of fingerprints; he even concedes that this could have been associated with hand worship. However, he concludes that although ridge detail can be noted in the carvings, there are other features included that definitely do not refer to dermatoglyphics. He concluded that "sound evidence that the carved designs had their origin in fingerprints appears to be wanting."

The first of my discoveries concerns a national monument at New Grange, Republic of Ireland (Eire), that I wrote about in the 1984 edition of *Ridge Detail in Nature*:

> The national monument at New Grange dates from around 3,000 B.C. and features a huge man-made mound with a narrow passage leading to an inner burial chamber. An opening is located above the entrance so that for just a few moments at dawn on 21st December each year the rays of the rising sun penetrate along the passage to illuminate the burial chamber. A postage stamp issued on 4th May 1983 depicts patterns at the monument incised in stone. I note that the four basic fingerprint patterns are shown, together with numerous deltas. Is it mere coincidence that these patterns

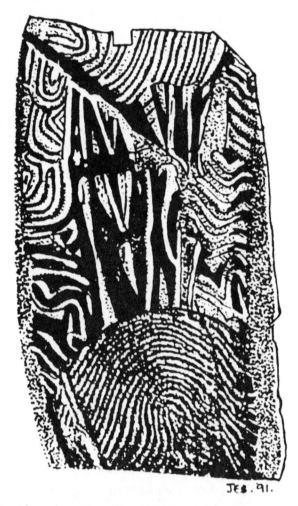

Figure 1.5 Standing stone, Goat Island. (Redrawn by John Berry, from *The Megalithic Builders of Western Europe*, Glyn Daniel, 1963.)

are found on the design, or was the interest of a pre-Celtic artist kindled by a perusal of his fingerprint patterns?

In *Ridge Detail in Nature* (1986) I illustrated and described for the first time in a ridge detail context a carving on a standing stone on Goat Island (Figure 1.5). I wrote:

Megalithic tombs and architectural monuments were built in Western Europe around 4,000 years ago, and the richest carvings are found in Brittany, north western France. It is thought that inspiration for the remarkably decorated tombs came from Spain and Southern France. A dozen characteristic symbols on the tombs represented important items in the lives of the megalithic builders, including axeheads, horns, yokes, the sun, etc. This photograph of carvings from Gavrinnis is covered with symbolic representations, and the seemingly superimposed shape at the bottom of the carving shows a tent pattern. Ridge detail is scarce, but pores are quite clear on the ridges, being especially noticeable on the ridges draped over the central spine. I have no doubt that this particular carver was aware of patterns on finger tips, possibly superimposing one of his own patterns, as clear and precise as any of English wood-carver Thomas Bewick's fingerprint representations. (Bewick is discussed later.)

I do accept there is the slight possibility that the New Grange designs could be coincidental, although I do believe that the artist was conversant with patterns plainly visible on the ends of his fingers or the fingers of his associates; but I certainly do not have any doubts whatsoever that the person who carved the tent pattern (see Figure 1.5) was aware of fingerprint patterns. This megalithic monument, carved in France at about the same time as the pyramids were being built, convinces me that the artisan knew of this pattern, and possibly, to accord individuality to one of his designs, he incorporated one of his digit patterns, perhaps carved from a mud impression purposely made. The tent pattern is "squared-off" at the base. The sweat pores are pronounced, equally spaced on the ridges; I regard this as being a most significant pointer. This carving of a tent pattern was not a coincidence: it was carved from direct observation. I unhesitatingly align myself with, and fully support, the Stockis theory.

Mummies

As I have stated, the examination and recording of ridge detail on the hands and feet of mummies has been reported. I have visited museums in several countries, always specifically seeking out the Egyptian sections, and although many of the mummies were wrapped, I have been able to scrutinize ridge detail on the hands and feet of embalmed bodies on display and confirm the presence of fingerprint patterns similar to those shown in Figure 1.2.

In 1977, the mummy Asru, from the Temple of Karnak, was fingerprinted by experts in Manchester under the direction of Detective Chief Inspector Thomas Fletcher, head of the Fingerprint Bureau of the Greater Manchester Police. He kindly sent me a report and illustrations that were subsequently published in *Fingerprint Whorld*. Mr. Fletcher utilized the technique I have already described when the Hertfordshire personnel fingerprinted primates: the application of layers of acrylic paint on the digits. (This technique was invented by Roger Ball and was revealed for the first time in *Fingerprint Whorld*, January 1976.) Mr. Fletcher used his experience as a detective to discover the occupation of Asru in the Temple of Karnak; she was either a dancer or a chantress:

> Three thousand years ago Egyptian temple dancers performed their ritual dances barefoot, the foot being used as part of the body's expression. The sole was in constant contact with the ground and even on the smoothest of flooring there would be friction and consequent wearing of the ridges on the underside of the toes and balls of the feet. Asru's feet did not show any traces of this constant contact with the floor, the depth of the furrows and the clarity of the characteristics were not consistent with her having been a dancer, and the alternative of her being a chantress was much more acceptable.

Finger Imprints on Artifacts in Antiquity (circa 3000 B.C.)

In *Fingerprint Whorld,* October 1976, I published my research on this subject under the rather facetious title "Potter Throws Light on Prints." I consider that I covered the subject quite fully and wrote:

> Research into finger imprints in antiquity is a fascinating subject, because references occur of fingerprints on pottery and figurines in many parts of the world, even in pre-history. The scope for detailed research by the fingerprint expert is considerable, because my initial source material (quoted later) reveals authorities finding fingerprints on Neolithic vases, Bronze Age cooking pots, Assyrian clay tablets, ancient Mexican pottery and Aztec clay figures. Obviously, many of these instances occurred in the manufacture of articles where the manipulation of the basic clay into utensils indirectly left fingerprints. I write here detailing examples which suggest that the fingerprints were purposely indented into the clay. The earliest trace of finger imprints being purposely impressed occurred in Mesopotamia and dates from circa 3,000 B.C. where an authority asserts that a "digital impression" was placed on each brick used in the construction of the king's storehouse. This method of making identifying marks is also found on bricks used in the construction of the "royal buildings" in Ancient Egypt. It is pertinent to note that in these two examples the buildings were for kings or pharaohs, suggesting the importance placed in the craftsmanship which was confirmed by the finger impressions of the masons.

William Frederick Bade, once director of the Palestine Institute of Archaeology, conducted excavations at various sites in Palestine and at one place found finger imprints on many pieces of broken pottery. The chaotic state of this scene caused initial difficulty in dating artifacts, but it transpired that a study of the imprints on the numerous shards indicated that one potter made most of them. These "identifications" permitted the confused debris to be dated accurately; in fact, this particular excavation was dated to the fourth century A.D. Commenting on this case, *Fingerprint Magazine* (1937) stated that "these impressions were obviously intentional, and, no doubt, represented the workman's individual trade mark."

A Chinese clay seal, dated before the third century B.C., has been the focus of considerable research and speculation for many years. A left thumb imprint is deeply embedded in the seal, and on the reverse side is ancient Chinese script representing the name of the person who made the thumb imprint. The mark is so specific in pressure and placing that there can be no doubt that it was meant as an identifying mark. If this is so, there is the strong inference that the Chinese were aware of the individuality of fingerprints well over 5000 years ago.

According to Mr. Laufer, a famous researcher who worked at the Field Museum of Natural History in the U.S., before the first century B.C., clay seals were used extensively in sealing documents such as official letters and packages. Of the superb left thumb imprint mentioned above, he stated:

> It is out of the question that this imprint is due to a mere accident caused by the handling of the clay piece. This impression is deep and sunk into the surface of the clay seal and beyond any doubt was effected with intentional energy and determination. In reasoning the case out logically, there is no other significance possible than that the thumb print belongs to the owner of the seal who has made his name on the reverse side. This case is therefore somewhat analogous to the modern practice of affixing on title deeds the thumb print to the signature, the one being verified by the other. This unique specimen is the oldest document so far on record relating to the history of the fingerprint system.

There is no evidence to conclude that the ancient Chinese were aware of the individuality of fingerprints on a universal basis. However, the care taken to impress the clay seals suggests that the persons utilizing this form of signature (even should they only be symbolic tokens, as suggested) were aware that the design on their fingers or thumbs so applied constituted individuality. This must represent, even at its crudest level, the local recognition that the person who impressed a digit on a seal was permanently bound to the contents of the documents so certified.

A researcher who dedicated many years of work in this direction, although he was not a fingerprint expert, stated:

> Fingerprint identification in our usage of the term appears to have been practiced in a simple form in times long past ... but the history of fingerprint identification becomes shadowy as it is traced backwards.

I have examined Roman pottery and noted that finger imprints are sometimes present; one example in my possession shows three whorl types (twin loops) on the semismoothed underside. Yet when I was in Romania in 1985, I visited the ruins of a Greek settlement at Hystria, on the western coast of the Black Sea, and found shards of pottery completely devoid of finger imprints. I was extremely pleased to find the handle and part of the side of a Getic earthenware vessel among the rubble on the site. It was made during the first century B.C., and under examination with my fingerprint magnifying glass, I could see that the handle and side had been smoothed with fingers so finely that I believe every endeavor had been made to avoid leaving finger imprints on the finished product. I visited museums in Hystria, Constantsa, and Bucharest, especially looking for finger imprints on pottery, and did not even find a lone example. Ergo, it is reasonable to assume that the potters in this area at least decided it was worthwhile removing offending imprints, *which they had noted,* in order to obtain an unsullied surface, a rather civilized artistic appreciation of subtlety of form.

Grauballe Man (A.D. 400)

On Saturday, April 26, 1952, a body was discovered in the Nebelgard Fen near Grauballe, in Jutland, and ^{14}C dating revealed that the body had been in the bog between A.D. 1 and A.D. 400. The skin had been tanned like leather owing to the preservative qualities of the bog water. The cause of death was a deep incision across the throat, and it was presumed that the man had been ritually sacrificed to a fertility god to ensure the survival of his fellows. Two members of the staff of the police laboratory at Aarhus were entrusted with the examination of the Grauballe man's hands and feet. They found the ridge detail was excellent and were able to take impressions from the body. The right thumb was "a double curve whorl," a twin loop, and the right forefinger was an ulnar loop.

Philosophical Transactions (1684)

The first person to study and describe ridges, furrows, and pores on the hand and foot surfaces was English plant morphologist Nehemiah Grew (Figure 1.6), born in Warwickshire in 1641. He was the first fingerprint pioneer; besides writing on the subject, he also published extremely accurate drawings of finger patterns and areas of the palm. In the 1684 publication he described, in the most beautiful phraseology, descriptions and functions of ridge detail:

Figure 1.6 Nehemiah Grew. (Drawn by John Berry.)

For if any one will but take the pains, with an indifferent Glass, to survey the Palm of his Hand very well washed with a Ball; he may perceive (besides those great Lines to which some men have given Names, and those of middle size call'd the Grain of the skin) innumerable little Ridges, of equal bigness and distance, and everywhere running parallel with one another. And especially, upon the ends and first Joynts of the Fingers and Thumb, upon the top of the Ball, and near the root of the Thumb a little above the Wrist. In all which places they are regularly disposed into Spherical Triangles, and Ellipticks. Upon these Ridges and Pores, all in Even Rows, and of that magnitude, as to be visible to a very good Eye without a Glass. But being viewed with one, every pore looks like a little Fountain, and the sweat may be seen to stand therein, as clear as rock water, and as often as it is wiped off, to spring up within them again. That which Nature intends in the position of these Ridges is, That they may the better suit with the use and motion of the Hand: those of the lower side of every Triangle, to the bending in or clutching of the Fingers: and those of the other two sides, and one of the Ellipticks to the pressure of the Hand or Fingers ends against any body, requiring them to yield to the right and left. Upon these Ridges, the Pores are very providently placed, and not in the furrows which lie between them; that so their structure might be more sturdy, and less liable to be depraved by compression; whereby only the Furrows are dilated or contracted, the Ridges constantly maintaining themselves and so the Pores unaltered. And for the same reason, the Pores are also very large, that they may be still better preserved, tho the skin be never so much compressed and condens'd by the constant use and labour of the Hand. And so those of the Feet, notwithstanding the compression of the skin by the weight of the whole body.

Grew died suddenly on March 25, 1712. He is buried at Cheshunt Parish Church, Hertfordshire.

De Externo Tactus Organo (1686)

Grew's contemporary, Marcello Malpighi (1628–1694), also a plant morphologist, researched the functions of the human skin, and the "Malpighian layers" were named for him. He worked at the University of Bologna, Italy, and in his publication he mainly dealt with the skin, although he did briefly mention ridge detail. It is believed that Grew and Malpighi corresponded to a degree, but the differences in language were a frustration, strangely because Grew was more adept at Latin usage than the Italian.

William of Orange (1690)

I am sure that the reader will think this section is a hoax, but I report herewith one well-known historical fingerprint landmark, and the latest tremendous 1987 discovery, both having a direct connection with the expatriate Dutch monarch William of Orange. The city of Londonderry (now in Northern Ireland) was under siege until relieved by forces under the command of William of Orange, and in 1691, 225 citizens of Londonderry, who had suffered damage and loss during the siege, made a representation to London for compensation. The claimants appended digit impressions on the document, adjacent to their signatures, obviously considering the individuality of their fingers as being inviolable. I have examined a photograph of the document (and have tried really hard but unsuccessfully to trace the original) and report that the imprints are unfortunately of poor quality, but it must be remembered that they were made 300 years ago.

An accidental fire occurred at the historic building Hampton Court, west of London, causing considerable damage; early in 1987, workmen removed some warped wooden panels in The Little Oak Room, Fountain Court, and found that the plaster underneath bore 17 complete handprints. I immediately visited the site with Martin Leadbetter and Nicholas Hall, a Hertfordshire Constabulary photographer, and we made a detailed examination, including measurements, photography, and an abortive attempt at lifting.

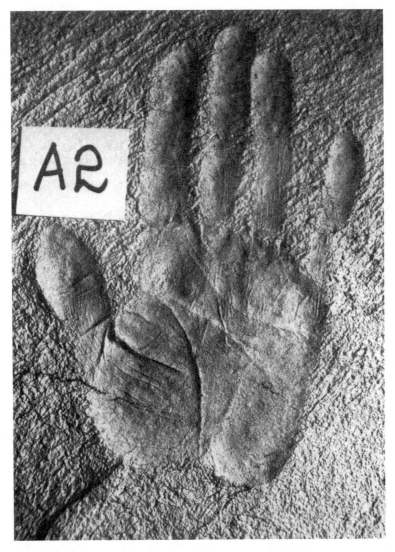

Figure 1.7 Right palm imprint in plaster, Hampton Court, London, 1689–1690. (Figure supplied by Nicholas John Hall, M.F.S., Hertfordshire.)

Most of the handprints were excellent, revealing clear ridge detail; photograph A2 (Figure 1.7) shows the finest example. The plaster was made of lime, sand, and animal hairs. Archaeologists told us that The Little Oak Room had been redecorated in 1689–1690 for King William III and his queen. The hands had been impressed in the plaster before it had hardened. We found that three different people had made the imprints. I do not believe that the plasterers

Figure 1.8 Thomas Bewick. (Drawn by John Berry.)

would desecrate their handiwork; perchance the vagrant handprints were made by carpenters, soldiers, or servants who would be aware that large wooden panels of oak would speedily be placed atop the plaster. It was a fascinating experience to have the opportunity to examine the handprints on the wall, albeit the results of our examination were officially handed to the Hampton Court authorities as part of the records of the archaeological and other finds before refurbishment; also, our work was featured in an official Home Office film that is scheduled for television broadcast and publication in book form.

Thomas Bewick (1753–1828)

Thomas Bewick (Figure 1.8) is mentioned quite frequently in fingerprint publications simply because in a few books he used an engraving of his fingerprints as a signature. The importance of this fact is that he did this almost 200 years ago, and authorities such as Sir William Herschel have credited Bewick with stimulating their initial interest in the study of fingerprints.

He was born in Ovingham, Northumberland, England, on August 12, 1753, the son of a farmer. His early school career was marred by his absence from classes and disinterest in Latin, English grammar, and arithmetic, although he was eventually constrained to study them to a reasonable standard, as one contemporary writer put it:

By kindly words of persuasion a reformation was at length affected that severe discipline and punishment had failed to accomplish.

He used all the spaces in his school papers to draw murals, and when he used these up he continued his artistic progress by chalking designs on gravestones and the church porch. He became famous in the rural community as an artist, and he decorated the walls of their cottages "with an abundance of my rude productions at a very cheap rate."

While still a child, his head was scalded and thereafter his crown had no hair, necessitating, when he grew older, the application of a brown silk cap. When he was 14 years old, he became an apprentice to an engraver in Newcastle, and after 5 years he completed his apprenticeship; the first book with a Bewick woodcut was published in 1774.

As the years progressed, Bewick became famous throughout England, and ultimately his fame became worldwide. Without doubt he was England's finest engraver. He invented the "white line" wood-engraving technique, "thus paying attention, not to what he left, but what he cut away from the block." Most of his famous wood engravings featured animals and birds. His *A General History of the Quadrupeds* ran to eight editions, as did his monumental *History of British Birds*. The finger imprint in Figure 1.9, showing the cottage and trees etched faintly in the background, is from *History of British Birds 1797–1804*. His love of the countryside and nature must have caused him to note ridge detail on his hands. It has not been possible to find out how he concluded that ridge detail was unique, but it is obvious from his carved imprint superimposed with *Thomas Bewick his Mark* that he was utterly satisfied that his imprint denoted individuality. One of his contemporaries observed that "Bewick's signature is sometimes written, a genuine autograph, but generally printed; the quaint conceit of his thumb print is amusing." Bewick died on November 8, 1828, at Gateshead, and he was buried in Ovingham churchyard, in the parish where he was born.

Concerning the External Physiological Examination of the Integumentary System (1823)

Joannes Evanelista Purkinje was a Bohemian, and part of his thesis published on December 22, 1823, dealt in considerable detail with the functions of ridges, furrows, and pores; additionally, he illustrated and described nine fingerprint patterns: one arch, one tent, two loops, and five types of whorl. In 1985 my Hertfordshire colleague Martin Leadbetter optimistically wrote to the Burser of Wroclaw University, Poland, asking for photographs and part of the original thesis dealing with fingerprints. In 2 months, to our considerable

Figure 1.9 Trademarks of Thomas Bewick. (From the publications of Thomas Bewick. With permission.)

surprise, a 35-mm film arrived with negatives of all the pertinent pages in Latin (Martin has entrusted the film to me to retain in my capacity as Historian of The Fingerprint Society). Professor Harold Cummins and Rebecca Wright Kennedy, of the U.S., translated the thesis in 1940, and The Royal Society of London obtained the translation and duly gave permission for it to be published in *Fingerprint Whorld,* April 1987.

These are some of the interesting observations Purkinje made regarding the four basic patterns (Figure 1.2) and also a most detailed description of a palm impression:

> **Arch:** From the articular fold, rugae and sulci first course in almost straight lines transversely from one side of the phalanx to the other; then little by little they become more curved in the middle, until they are bent in arches which are nearly parallel with the periphery of the phalanx.
>
> **Tent:** This is almost the same conformation as the above, the only difference being that the transversely coursing ridges are wrapped over a little perpendicular stria, as if it were a nucleus.

Loop: Now if this oblique stripe by a simple curve returns to the side from which it came and follows many others in a similar curve, an oblique loop is formed which may be more or less erect or may bend forwards. Near its base, on one side or the other, a triangle is formed from the different directions of the rugae and sulci. Their configuration in the form of the oblique loop is the commonest, and I may almost say, typical of man.

Whorl: The circle, where in the ellipse a simple line occupies the center, there is a small tubercle (island); it is surrounded with concentric circles which reach the rugae of the semicircular space.

Palm: From the space between the index finger and the thumb, great numbers of parallel lines run which pass in diverging directions across the palm, next to the linea palmiformis, into the margins of the metacarpals of the thumb and little finger. Thus triangles are formed with the vertices at the wrist. This is their most common conformation. Other parallel lines from the roots of the fingers meet and accompany the lines running across from the interval of the thumb and the index finger toward the external margin of the fifth metacarpal. Running out from these intervals, loops and whorls are interposed; but it would take too long to explain in this chapter the many varieties of these. On the thenar eminence, a trapezoidal region occurs where the rugae and sulci are set transversely to the circles. On the hypothenar eminence, toward the radial margin of the metacarpal, a larger loop is often observed where the rugae and sulci going out from the margin are again reflected onto it. Sometimes an elliptical whorl is seen on this eminence.

Fingerprint Classification

A major step forward in the use of fingerprints was a method of classification that enabled fingerprint forms bearing differing patterns to be placed in a certain order, thus enabling the search area to be minimized. If a classification system did not exist, and a person gave a wrong name, each set of fingerprint forms would have to be examined to discover the correct identity of the offender; the person would obviously not be traced by doing an alphabetical check. Many countries in the world now use the "Henry System," the brainchild of Sir Edward Henry (Figure 1.10), an Englishman who served in India toward the end of the nineteenth century. His system became operational at Scotland Yard in 1901, but I must point out that a European who emigrated to Argentina in 1884 caused the world's first fingerprint bureau to be instituted in 1896.

Figure 1.10 Sir Edward Henry. (Drawn by John Berry.)

Dr. Ivan Vucetich (1858–1925)

Dr. Ivan Vucetich (Figure 1.11) was employed in the Central Police Department, La Plata, Argentina, and was ordered to install the French Bertillon Anthropometric Identification System, which used a number of body measurements and was in extensive use in European countries. Vucetich obtained a copy of the journal *Revue Scientific* which contained an article on English fingerprint pioneer Francis Galton, who had formulated his own classification system. Dr. Vucetich became extremely interested in fingerprints and within a year had worked out his own unique system for classifying them. This became known as *"vucetichissimo,"* and it utilized four fingerprint patterns as described in his book *Dactilospia Comparada*. In 1893, the Rojas murder was solved by fingerprints, proving their effectiveness, and Vucetich was enthusiastically operating a fingerprint office built at his own expense. In 1893, he was suddenly ordered to abandon his fingerprint system and revert to bertillonage. Of course, he realized that this was a retrograde action,

Figure 1.11 Dr. Ivan Vucetich. (Drawn by John Berry.)

and he tried unsuccessfully to explain to the police authorities how superior fingerprint usage was to the measurement system. Fortunately in 1896, Argentina abandoned bertillonage and began to use *vucetichissimo*. (I possess a U.S. FBI "flyer" for someone who absconded from a state camp at Davenport, Iowa, in 1929, and although the card shows his photograph and rolled finger impressions, it also gives numerous Bertillon measurements.) The Vucetich system is not in use outside South America.

The Henry System

The FBI, with its huge collection of fingerprint forms, uses the basic Henry system, amended to the FBI's requirements. I have visited fingerprint bureaus in Australia, South Africa, Greece, Canada, and the U.S., and they all use the Henry system, which is extremely ingenious.

On British fingerprint forms, the fingers are numbered from 1 to 5 on the right hand and from 6 to 10 on the left hand (see below).

1	2	3	4	5
RT	RF	RM	RR	RL
6	7	8	9	10
LT	LF	LM	LR	LL

Whorl patterns *only* have values, as shown below. Even numbers on the form constitute the numerator, odd numbers provide the denominator.

RT · 1	RF · 2	RM · 3	RR · 4	RL · 5
16	16	8	8	4
LT · 6	LF · 7	LM · 8	LR · 9	LL · 10
4	2	2	1	1

The finger numbers are not used in the system; totaled whorl patterns only apply. Therefore, if a person does not have any whorl patterns on the fingers, the classification would be

$$\frac{0}{0}$$

This is a negative symbol, and therefore Sir Edward decided to *always* add "1" to both the numerator and denominator. Hence, a fingerprint classification without whorls would be

$$\frac{1}{1}$$

This section has the largest number of fingerprint forms, as loops constitute 63% of all fingerprint patterns.

If all fingerprint patterns were whorls, the classification would be

$$\frac{32}{32}$$

The Henry system therefore divided all fingerprint forms into 1024 bundles. It is quite obvious that if fingerprint forms are filed according to this system, the searcher chooses the bundle bearing the appropriate Henry fraction and merely searches this one bundle.

There are further subclassifications, which mean that every bundle can be further divided for searching. Unfortunately, some fingerprint patterns merge their characteristics and have to be searched as alternatives, meaning that additional bundles have to be examined in order to positively conclude a search. It must also be remembered that missing or bandaged digits have to be further searched to cover all possibilities. Some examples of the Henry system classification are shown in the following table.

W	W			W
	W	W	W	

$= \dfrac{19}{24}$

W			W	
W			W	

$= \dfrac{13}{18}$

Sir Edward Henry and Sir William Herschel

In England, an "Establishment" controversy has existed since the end of the nineteenth century concerning the merits of British fingerprint pioneers. Although the Henry system is a superb achievement, Sir Francis Galton and Sir William Herschel (Figure 1.12) also worked out classification systems, and these knights, with Sir Edward predominating, were considered to be very nice chaps. Herschel was an important figure in fingerprint pioneering because he was the first person to confirm ridge persistency, which states that the formation of ridge detail that develops on the hands and feet in the womb does not change, except as a result of serious injury to the digits or decomposition after death. This is the major requirement for a fingerprint system. I have seen the originals of Herschel's experiments, during which he took his own palm impressions in 1860 and again in 1890. The ravages of time had caused creases to flourish across his fingers and palms, and the ridges were somewhat coarser, but the sequences of ridge detail remained exactly the same. The German anthropologist Welker also took his own palm impressions in 1856 and again in 1897, just before he died. He did not envisage any criminal application to his recognition that the ridge detail present on his fingers and palms did not change with time.

Herschel wrote the famous "Hooghly letter" on August 15, 1877, to the Inspector of Jails in Bengal, India, in which he propounded the idea that persons committed to prison should be fingerprinted to confirm their identities. Herschel had been experimenting with fingerprints for 20 years before 1877 and during this time had taken thousands of fingerprints. Like Welker, he had never associated fingerprints with the identification of finger imprints found at crime scenes.

Edward Henry must receive due credit for his practical interest in fingerprints in the latter part of the nineteenth century in India as a means of identifying workers to ensure that the payment of wages was not duplicated. However, legend and myth have arisen around Sir Edward Henry, perpetuated by writers who have produced this giant among fingerprint pioneers;

Figure 1.12 Sir William Herschel. (Drawn by John Berry.)

his name even now is mentioned many times daily in most fingerprint bureaus in the world. After all, didn't Henry, while traveling in a train in India, suddenly have a flash of inspired genius whereby he quickly worked out the system of 1024 groups utilizing whorl patterns, as I have already described? In order to record this magnificent mental feat, I have read, Henry hastily scribbled the essential equations on his stiff and clean white shirt cuff. I embellish the legend every day: "I'm going to search in the 'A' Division Henry collection," I announce. If I manage a successful "cold search" from finger imprints found at a crime scene, I complete a register in the office and under the heading Method of Identification, I write "A" Henry. I should know better, but habit makes a slave of thoughtlessness. It just is not true: Sir Edward Henry shrewdly gave his name to the classification system worked out by his Indian employees Khan Bahadur Azizul Haque and Rai Bahadur Hem Chandra Bose. Haque is alleged to have muttered to confidants that Henry could not even understand the system when it was patiently explained to him.

There are always two versions to a controversy. Henry appeared before the Belper Commission in 1900. Lord Belper had been asked to chair a committee to decide what identification system should be used in Great Britain. Henry was asked point blank if the 1024 bundle system was his own invention, and he firmly announced that it was; in the past, writers have tended to support Henry's claim. They point out that as the English official in charge he undoubtedly supported and encouraged his staff and should therefore be responsible for the innovation they suggested. In a letter dated May 10, 1926, Henry wrote to a correspondent concerning Haque:

> I wish to make it clear that, in my opinion, he contributed more than any other member of my staff and contributed in a conspicuous degree to bringing about the perfecting of a system of classification that has stood the test of time and has been accepted in most countries.

The Belper Commission, aware that Henry's book was due to be published, recommended the use of the Henry Classification System, which was introduced at Scotland Yard in 1901. Police forces from all over the world duly sent their officers to learn this new fingerprint system.

The maintenance of a fingerprint collection serves the primary function of causing a file to be associated with each person whose finger impressions appear in the collection. When fingerprint sets are received at police headquarters, the person is allocated a number; in Great Britain this is known as the Criminal Record Office Number (CRO No.). This number always remains the same for the individual, and as the individual ages and collects convictions, the file accordingly gets thicker, all convictions in the file being confirmed by fingerprints taken at the time of arrest. It does happen that a person gives a fictitious name when fingerprinted, and if dealt with expeditiously at court, previous convictions will not be cited and punishment will be dealt out as if for a first-time offender. In the meantime, the routine is inexorably taking place: the fictitious name with the associated fingerprint classification is not found after a name search, and so the fingerprint form is then searched through the fingerprint collection. The true name will certainly be discovered, the alias and conviction will be added to the file, and the next time that person appears in court on another charge, they will discover, to their chagrin, that they did not beat the system.

The secondary use of a fingerprint collection is to provide a catchment area for identifying offenders who leave their fingerprints at crime scenes, and this has been my special province for the last 37 years. For the initial suggestion associating the identification of finger imprints found at crime scenes with finger impressions in the collections, we owe a quite considerable debt of gratitude to Dr. Henry Faulds.

Dr. Henry Faulds (1843–1930)

Henry Faulds (Figure 1.13), the son of Scottish parents, was born in Beith, Ayrshire, Scotland, on June 1, 1843. He became a medical missionary for the Church of Scotland and spent a year in India; however, because of a clash of personalities with the clergy in charge, he returned to Scotland the following

Figure 1.13 Dr. Henry Faulds. (Drawn by John Berry.)

year. He joined the United Presbyterian Church of Scotland and married Isabella Wilson before sailing to Japan as a medical missionary. He arrived on March 5, 1874, and set up a hospital at Tsuki, in Tokyo, that was the first of its kind in Japan. While walking along the beach of the Bay of Yedo, he found ancient shards of pottery bearing the finger imprints of the potters (obviously not using the Getic technique of smoothness of surface). He became extremely interested in fingerprints. In one classical experiment, he removed the skin from the fingers of his patients after fingerprinting them; when the skin regrew on the fingertips he fingerprinted them once more, noting that the ridge detail was exactly the same as it was before the skin was removed. He recognized that fingerprint patterns were variable, but concluded that ridge detail was immutable. I believe Faulds was the person to identify finger imprints at crime scenes; the Japanese sought his assistance twice to compare scene imprints with suspects; the people he identified subsequently admitted to the crimes.

I have already mentioned the amazing letter Faulds sent to Charles Darwin in 1880 and Darwin's reply mentioning Mr. F. Galton, later Sir Francis Galton. However, Faulds' letter to *Nature* on October 28, 1880, was a most staggering document, and I dearly wish there was sufficient space to reprint the letter in full. It covered the following points:

1. Finding finger imprints on prehistoric Japanese pottery
2. Comparing skin furrows on humans
3. Studying fingertips of monkeys
4. Collecting the finger impressions of persons of various nationalities "which I hope may aid students of ethnology in classification"
5. Using "an ordinary botanical lens" to examine fingerprints
6. Describing ridge characteristics
7. Taking finger impressions with printer's ink, with hints on removing the ink afterward
8. Discussing fingerprints of mummies
9. Describing ancient Chinese fingerprint usage
10. Describing the Egyptian method of thumbnail printing of criminals

The article contained the first and most important sentence ever written regarding crime investigation from a fingerprint standpoint:

> When bloody finger marks or impressions on clay, glass, etc., exist, they may lead to the scientific identification of criminals.

Sir William Herschel responded to Faulds' letter by writing to *Nature*; his letter was published on November 25, 1880, and the controversy in British fingerprint circles dates from this time. Faulds could not possibly be privy to Herschel's fingerprint experiments since he was in Japan for some of the time. In *Fingerprint Whorld,* in conjunction with Martin Leadbetter, I published eight chapters of *The Faulds Legacy*, and regarding Herschel's letter in *Nature,* I commented that

> ... in Herschel's own words he was working with fingerprints for twenty-three years prior to Faulds' *Nature* letter, consequently it was surely his responsibility to publicly announce his researches at a time convenient to himself.

Very belatedly, in *Nature* January 18, 1917, Herschel wrote:

> His [Faulds'] letter of 1880 announced ... that he had come to the conclusion, by original and patient experiment, that fingerprints were sufficiently personal in pattern to supply a long-wanted method of scientific identification, which would enable us to fix his crime upon any offender who left finger marks behind him, and equally well to disprove the suspected identity of an innocent person. (For which I gave him, and I still do so, the credit due for a conception so different from mine.)

However, the battle lines had been drawn 30 years before this: the Establishment view in Scotland Yard circles was that Faulds had preempted Herschel's decades of research. As recently as 1977, a senior police officer at New Scotland Yard told me firmly that Faulds was a charlatan.

Frederick Cherrill was the senior officer in charge of the New Scotland Yard Fingerprint Bureau for many years and was a hard-working and skilled fingerprint expert, visiting scenes and making identifications in major crimes even when of senior rank. However, in his *Cherrill of the Yard* (1955), he does not even mention Faulds in his chapter on the history of fingerprints. However, a year previously in *The Fingerprint System at New Scotland Yard* (1954), he wrote the following on page 6:

> The value of Henry Faulds' (1843–1930) contribution to fingerprint science has been much discussed, but it is beyond question that Herschel was in the field many years before Faulds; in fact there is incontrovertible proof that Herschel was experimenting with finger, palm and sole prints when Faulds was but 16 years old. Faulds, in his letter to *Nature* 28th October 1880, entitled *On the Skin Furrows of the Hand,* did, however, anticipate any public declaration on the part of Herschel. Faulds made reference in his letter to the use of "nature prints" for the purpose of tracing criminals, but such prints were confined to visible marks made in blood, etc., and he did not suggest the development of latent sweat deposits from the fingers which now plays such an important part in modern criminal investigation.

Faulds was annoyed when knighthoods were granted to Galton, Herschel, and Henry because he believed that he was the originator of the scenes-of-crime aspect of fingerprint identification. Indeed, Faulds was even more piqued when the fingerprint bureau was formed at the Yard in 1901, because between 1886 and 1888 he had called at the Yard and offered to organize a fingerprint bureau at his own expense, a suggestion which allegedly caused a police officer to rebuke him and make insinuations regarding his sanity.

Faulds' obsession, even hatred, of the Yard was revealed in 1905 when he allied himself with the defense at the trial of the Stratton brothers, charged with a double murder at Deptford, London. A thumb imprint on a cash box found opened at the crime scene was identified as having been made by Alfred Stratton. It was a good clear imprint with ample ridge detail to afford a positive identification, but Faulds considered it to be a "smudge" and cast doubts on its status. The Strattons were convicted of the murder and duly hanged. There was a great deal of circumstantial evidence in the case, perhaps strong enough to have gained a conviction without the fingerprint evidence, but this was the first time fingerprints had been used in a murder trial in England, and experts at the Yard were extremely delighted: the marvelous system initiated in 1901 was vindicated in this glorious triumph. Faulds was not amused.

Faulds edited seven issues of a fingerprint journal *Dactylography* in the early 1920s that contained much original thought but in which he continually carped about "the worthy baronets"; he suffered from ill health and died in Wolstanton, Staffordshire, on March 19, 1930.

The Japanese regarded Faulds with great reverence and placed a commemorative stone on a tree-lined pavement in Tokyo with Japanese and English inscriptions. It reads:

DR. HENRY FAULDS
PIONEER IN FINGERPRINT IDENTIFICATION
LIVED HERE
FROM 1874 TO 1886.

The Faulds family gravestone in Wolstanton was in a sorry state early in 1987, with a dirty chipped headstone with weeds and grass covering it. Two American fingerprint men, James Mock, F.F.S., California, and Michael Carrick, Hon. M.F.S., Salem, Oregon, paid for it to be refurbished. This was done and completed in April 1987. A plaque states:

IN MEMORY OF
DR. HENRY FAULDS
MEDICAL MISSIONARY
IN RECOGNITION OF HIS WORK
AS A PIONEER IN THE SCIENCE
OF FINGERPRINT IDENTIFICATION
1843–1930
THE FINGERPRINT SOCIETY
QUAERITE ET INVENIETIS.

This was a wonderful gesture, belatedly bequeathing to Faulds the accolade he deserved throughout his life but which was denied him.

His two daughters died without having their lifelong ambition fulfilled — to have a bronze bust of their father placed inside Reception at New Scotland Yard. Strangely enough, in the corridors of the sixth floor at the Yard are a number of large framed aspects of fingerprints, and on one of them Faulds is credited with being a "Sir" — Sir Henry Faulds! Obviously, the researcher was confused with Sir Edward Henry. Fate indeed moves in a mysterious way.

Sir Francis Galton (1822–1911)

Sir Francis Galton's (Figure 1.14) interest in fingerprints should have been alerted by Dr. Henry Faulds' letter to Charles Darwin in 1880; the letter was passed to Galton as promised, but he reposited it in the Anthropological

Figure 1.14 Sir Francis Galton. (Drawn by John Berry.)

Institute where it stayed until 1894. Galton was an authority on bertillonage, but it was in 1888 that he commenced his enthusiastic foray into dactyloscopy. Initially, he collected only thumb impressions, but in 1890 he commenced to collect full sets of finger impressions. He worked out a fingerprint classification system and was duly called before the Asquith Committee on December 18, 1893; the committee was considering the Bertillon measuring system and pondering over a replacement. It was considered that the scope of Galton's classification system was limited when a large collection was envisaged, but the committee ordered that Galton's primary classification should be added to Bertillon cards. It is noteworthy that when Galton gave evidence before the Asquith Committee, he had 5 years of experience in the study of fingerprints, which accords with the present minimum standard requirement in order to give evidence of identity before courts of law in Great Britain.

    I have twice visited the Galton Laboratory in London and have had the extreme good fortune to examine one of the world's most precious early fingerprint documents, Galton's *Photography III*, a large album containing much of his inspired research. For example, he pondered on the possibility of an intellectual aspect of fingerprint pattern distribution, and accordingly in one experiment he filed fingerprints into three categories:

1. Titled persons
2. Idiots
3. Farm laborers from Dorset and Somerset

He also fingerprinted a large family that included twin children.

On one of the last pages in *Photography III* is a monument to early American fingerprint lore; a receipt reading:

> 8th August 1882
> Mr. Jones, Sutler, will pay to
> Lying Bob seventy dollars.
>
> Gilbert Thompson.

Written at the bottom left of the document is an arch pattern, in purple ink, with 75 00/100 written across the top. Sir Francis Galton was a great fingerprint pioneer as well as a man of considerable talent in many other areas. However, British fingerprint experts do not use the expression "Galton Ridges," which is much in vogue in the U.S.

Early Fingerprint Usage in Other Countries

Germany

From the first thesis by Hintz in 1747, in which spiral shapes on the skin of the hands and feet were discussed, numerous German researchers noted papillary ridges, including Schroeter, Huschke, Welker, Kollman, and Eber. In 1902, while studying law in Munich, Robert Heindl (1883–1958) read in an English magazine about the use of a fingerprint classification system and wrote to India for details. He stressed to German police authorities that they should use fingerprints for identifying people, and the first fingerprint bureau in Germany was set up in Dresden on April 1, 1903. However, Heindl still met resistance because many German police forces still thought the Bertillon system was superior. Nevertheless, in 1903, three other German police forces commenced fingerprinting: Augsburg, Hamburg, and Nuremburg. In 1912, a conference of all German police forces took place in Berlin, at which it was concluded that identification by fingerprints was superior to identification by the Bertillon system, and in 1911 the transition took place.

Figure 1.15 Juan Steegers. (Supplied by the Cuban Ministry of Communications. With permission.)

Cuba

Juan Francisco Steegers y Perera (1856–1921) was the foremost Cuban pioneer in fingerprint identification; his name has been perpetuated by the issue of two postage stamps on April 30,1957 (Figure 1.15). Details of his life were presented in a philatelic commemorative booklet issued by the Cuban Ministry of Communications on March 1, 1957, and the details of the pioneering aspect of his fingerprint achievements are presented in this translation:

> In 1904 he was elected photographer of the National Presidium, entailing immense work dealing with all media within his reach in order to raise the quality of the department; he introduced the system of utilising fingerprints for the identification of delinquents, thus achieving the honour of having introduced in Cuba the first dactyloscopic information, addressed to the judge of Law Instruction of the Centre. This happened on 28th November 1907. By means of intense and constant studies Steegers created a new dactyloscopic-photographic medium, thus joining together dactyloscopy and photography and obtaining a complete result with his new discovery; the greatest achievement is that this same result and method are being used in several countries, having been given the name "Sistema Steegers." Thanks

to the unrelenting efforts of Steegers and his great technical ability the "Gabinete Nacional de Idenficacion" was created in 1911 and Steegers became its first director under whom the continuous technical work of scientific production was raised to its high level. This went on until his death on the 22nd March 1921.

Canada

Edward Foster (1863–1956) is known as the "Father of Canadian Fingerprinting." On July 21,1910, an Order of Council was passed sanctioning the use of the fingerprint system in Canada. The first set of fingerprints identified by the Royal Canadian Mounted Police fingerprint bureau was received by that bureau on September 20, 1911, and was taken by Inspector Edward Foster. As in most parts of the world, the Canadian bureau grew daily, and after 9 years of operation, Foster had reportedly received more than 11,000 sets of fingerprints that resulted in more than 1,000 identifications. By comparison, in 1959, 220,000 sets had been received, giving more than 77,000 identifications of previous convictions.

Australia and New Zealand

I have mentioned that Dr. Henry Faulds attempted to organize a fingerprint bureau at the Yard, between 1886 and 1888, at his own expense. One of the Scotland Yard officers he contacted was Inspector Tunbridge; although Tunbridge gave the impression that he thought there was potential in a fingerprint system, it has been suggested that behind the scenes he was not satisfied that it was a workable proposition.

In 1897, Tunbridge went to New Zealand to become Commissioner of Police; he retired in 1903 and returned to England. In 1907, he wrote the following letter to Faulds:

> I have a most distinct and pleasant recollection of our interview, and, since the F.P. system has been adopted as a means of identification of criminals with such marked success, have often wondered how it was that you have not been more actively connected with the carrying out of the system. When the Home Authorities recognised the value of the system, I was Commissioner of Police in New Zealand, and it was owing mainly to my recommendation that the system was introduced into New Zealand prisons, although the prison Authorities were somewhat opposed to it. Some of the Australian States also adopted the system, with the result that an interchange of prints took place, and soon manifested its value. The system is now in full working order in Australia, and is carried on by the police, of course, with the assistance of the prison Authorities.

United States of America

The February 1972 edition of the most excellent U.S. publication *Finger Print and Identification Magazine* mentions that a certain Thomas Taylor gave a lecture, some time before July 1877, stating that there was

> ... the possibility of identifying criminals especially murderers, by comparing the marks on the hands left upon any object with impressions in wax taken from the hands of suspected persons. In the case of murderers, the marks of bloody hands would present a very favourable opportunity. This is a new, system of palmistry.

The report was published in the July 1877 issue of *The American Journal of Microscopy and Popular Science,* and its implicit suggestion of identifying scenes of crime imprints of bloody hands predates a similar statement in Faulds' *Nature* letter of 1880. The publication of the report in 1972 represented a sensational revelation by author Duayne J. Dillon, Martinez, California, but it certainly does not seem to have merited the attention it mightily deserves.

In 1881, Surgeon John S. Billing, U.S. Army, attended the International Medical Congress in London; he has been credited with making the following statement:

> Just as each individual is in some respects peculiar and unique, so that even the minute ridges and furrows at the end of his forefinger differ from that of all other forefingers and is sufficient to identify him ...

As previously stated, Galton reported the use of fingerprints by Gilbert Thompson in 1882 in recording the payment of wages to Lying Bob; this is the first instance of fingerprint usage in the U.S.

Four years later, Taber, a San Francisco photographer, noted ridge detail while doodling on a blotting pad with inky thumbs; he duly photographed and enlarged these images. He fingerprinted his friends and associates, including some Chinese. At this time, large numbers of Chinese workers were immigrating to the U.S., and Taber wrote to the U.S. House of Representatives to suggest the use of thumbprints as an identification method; however, on the advice of experienced detectives, the idea was turned down in favor of facial photography, which was considered to be a sufficient means of identification.

Sergeant John K. Ferrier of the Scotland Yard Fingerprint Bureau visited the World's Fair Exposition in St. Louis, Missouri, in 1904 and is credited with giving the first lecture on fingerprints in the U.S. His message was somewhat messianic: he was preaching authoritatively on a new "revelation" and gathered around him a nucleus of "disciples" (not quite a dozen) who caught his every word and duly spread the "gospel according to Henry" all over the U.S. It is certainly no coincidence that the first U.S. police force to adopt fingerprinting was in St. Louis.

The first American fingerprint lecturer was Mary K. Holland, one of Ferrier's students. Gradually the use of fingerprints spread all over the U.S., resulting in the first conviction based on fingerprint evidence taking place in the state of Illinois in 1911.

The International Association for Identification (IAI) was formed in 1915, and, being a member, I was extremely proud to have assisted Martin Leadbetter in organizing the Annual Educational Conference of this august body in London in 1986. The IAI has been the backbone of fingerprint usage in the U.S. for over 74 years, and its monthly journal, *Identification News,* has always been vitally important because its contents cover all aspects of identification, fingerprints being merely one of the disciplines discussed in its pages.

I have already rightly praised the *Finger Print and Identification Magazine,* which started in July 1919; it always contained important articles on fundamental aspects of fingerprints, but also included little extracurricular gems. One of these had a tremendous influence on me! An article was written by PJ Putter, a fingerprint officer in the South Africa Police, in which he reported finding fingerprint-type ridge detail on obscure items, illustrating the article with photographs of cactus and mushroom peelings. I had already obtained a copy of *Fingerprint, Palms and Soles* by Cummins and Midlo, which had a chapter entitled "Other Patternings in Nature" (the zebra is an excellent and obvious example of their research into other areas where ridge detail is present). I became obsessed with these revelations in American publications of ridge detail on other items and in 1979 published the first edition of *Ridge Detail in Nature,* which consisted of 12 pages. Whereas the total number of examples of ridge detail was previously around one dozen, in the 1979 issue I quoted 44 examples. I now publish issues annually, and in the 1991 issue the total number of examples is 813 and requires 150 pages for their description. The 2001 issue had a total number of 1402 examples.

I have also edited 64 quarterly issues of *Fingerprint Whorld* since July 1975 and have always strived to follow the precepts of the *Finger Print and Identification Magazine* policy of being educational, but not inhibited by orthodox doctrine. For decades, fingerprint experts all over the world have received excellent support from the two American publications I have mentioned. *Finger Print and Identification Magazine* ceased publication some years ago, but resumed in 1987, later folding. The IAI publication *Identification News* changed its size and format on January 1, 1988, and is now known as the *Journal of Forensic Identification.* Together with *Fingerprint Whorld,* these journals must continue to monitor and report on the many new developments and innovations that, before the turn of the century, will revolutionize every aspect of crime investigation.

Developments to Date

I vividly recall my early days visiting scenes of crimes in the mid-1950s with my small black case that contained a mercury-based white powder (dangerous to my health), a coarse graphite-based black powder, and two stunted squirrel-hair brushes. If I found finger or palm marks, I had to telephone HQ to arrange for a photographer to visit the scene by appointment.

Suddenly there seemed to be a burst of innovation concerning fingerprint evidence as part of the crime investigation. First there appeared ninhydrin, which was extremely efficient on paper items, especially if the stock solution is added to fluorisol (Freon in the U.S.), which prevents writing on the paper from smudging. Ninhydrin reacts with the amino acids in perspiration, producing red, brown, or purple imprints; this is a most successful method of investigating check fraud. Photography has been largely replaced by lifting imprints with clear tape; in Great Britain, the Camtac machine is used which, using the lift as a negative, produces a positive print in 90 sec with marks that are correct for size, color, and direction.

During the last decade, other techniques for discovering latent imprints have appeared, including Super Glue, physical developer, small particle reagent, lasers, metal deposition, Sudan black, amido black, and radioactive sulfur dioxide; also, excellent powders are available with vastly improved fingerprint brushes. DFO is a recent improvement on ninhydrin, providing up to 300% more finger and palm imprints.

Computers are now used throughout the world for the twin purposes of maintaining and searching files of fingerprints of offenders in "Henry" order and searching imprints found at crime scenes. Computer searches of crime scene imprints provide excellent results, but the computers are certainly not 100% efficient. Therein lies the dichotomy. An experienced fingerprint expert will manually search the crime scene imprints in moderately small collections and will consider himself or herself to perform with 100% accuracy, stating categorically that the offender is *not* among the fingerprint forms that have been searched. The computer will blast through complete collections at fantastic speed, possibly scanning millions of digits, but there is no promise that the offender who made the imprints is not in the collection if an identification is not made. Computer firms who promise that their machine is totally efficient in this respect are knowingly prevaricating: 100% coverage without error will not be possible for some years.

I find that portions of palm imprints and flexure surfaces (the inside lengths of the fingers) are frequently found at crime scenes, possibly in three out of every five crimes, and yet I am not aware of any computer developments to search these valuable clues. Palms and flexures are extremely difficult to search manually.

Nevertheless, during the last 100 years, particularly since the start of its operational use in 1901, the fingerprint system of identification has maintained its infallible status, permitting the identification of countless offenders but protecting millions of innocent citizens. I feel proud to have spent over half of my life making perhaps thousands of decisions every day with the knowledge that every one of the thousands of identifications I have made since 1955 (including identifications at 40 murders) has been error-free based on one implicit factor: no person has ever been found to have ridge detail that matches the ridge detail on the hands and feet surfaces of any other person.

Reference

Napier J. *Monkeys Without Tails.* London: British Broadcasting Corporation, 1976.

Addendum to the First Edition

Regarding my paragraph suggesting lack of computer searching for palm imprints at crime scenes, I am delighted to report that my friend and colleague Martin Leadbetter B.A.(Hons), FFS, who is in charge of the Cambridgeshire Constabulary Fingerprint Bureau, has evolved a searching system which has proven highly successful in the last three years. Since 1998, computer searching at his bureau has revealed the magnificent total of 344 cold identifications. This was the world's first truly successful computer searching system. It is in use in the Miami-Dade Bureau, Florida, USA, and in the Garda Siochana Bureau, the Republic of Ireland, and they are delighted with the results. Martin can be contacted at the Cambridgeshire Constabulary HQ, Fingerprint Bureau, Hinchingbrooke Park, Huntingdon, Cambridgeshire PE 29 8NP, Great Britain.

Update*

In the years since this chapter was written, there has been a continuation of the changes that John Berry has referred to: innovations in fingerprint development,

* By David A. Stoney, Ph.D., Director, McCrone Research Institute, Chicago, and Clinical Professor of Forensic Science, University of Illinois at Chicago.

recovery, and AFIS technology. These changes are included and reviewed as part of this revised edition. They are important and often remarkable improvements in our technology. The more fundamental changes during this time, however, have been in our profession. We have a well-established certification program, growing in its recognition and its adoption as a job requirement. We are actively debating and working to achieve standardization in our practices and in our educational programs. We have a professional journal, where there once was a newsletter, and in that journal we are seeing open discussions, new ideas, frequent consensus, and occasional controversy. These are all exceptionally good things, hallmarks of an ethical and open profession.

As we progress into this next century, we also face two substantial challenges. The first is to reexamine our premises and justify our practices before a new, Daubert-driven, legal ideology. The challenge is to recognize and appreciate this newfound scrutiny, to grow with it, and to help find our new place within it. We simply won't be able to do our work the way we have and retain the respect that we feel entitled to. We will need to earn this respect by finding ways to *measure* the suitability of prints for comparison, to *measure* the amount of correspondence between prints, and to *test* the meaning of a given degree of correspondence.

The other challenge is a related one. It is full integration into the forensic laboratory sciences. This is not a superficial, physical change in the location of our practice, but a conceptual and perceptual change, one that is already well underway. It is a movement away from dogma and toward science. It means letting go of some of our absolutes and opening our minds a little further to embrace the realities of fingerprint identification as it must become: less subjective, less absolute, and more correct. This transition may not be a comfortable one, but as we confront our fears and apply ourselves to the solutions, we will find that the profession will become stronger than ever before.

Identification of Latent Prints

2

ROBERT D. OLSEN, SR.*
HENRY C. LEE

Contents

Introduction

The efforts of latent print examiners are directed toward two ultimate goals: one is the successful developing or enhancing of a latent print, and the other is identification or elimination based upon the developed latent print. The purpose of this chapter is to define the principle and logic processes involved in the development and comparison of latent prints for the purpose of identification.

The first mission of any latent print examiner is to recognize the potential areas which may contain latent prints and then to utilize one or more tech-

---

* The original edition of this volume was dedicated to the memory and lifetime work of Robert D. Olsen, Sr., the original author of this chapter. He passed away unexpectedly before the first edition of the book could be published. The chapter has been updated for this edition by Dr. Henry C. Lee.

0-8493-0923-9/01/$0.00+$1.50
© 2001 by CRC Press LLC

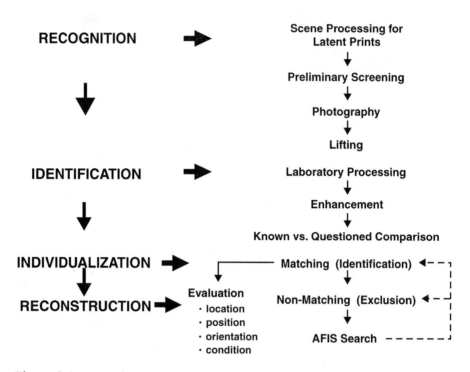

Figure 2.1 Latent fingerprint examination.

niques to process such an area with the objective of developing those latent prints and making them visible. A latent print examiner can then evaluate each print and make a judgment as to whether or not there are sufficient ridge characteristics for identification. If there are insufficient ridge characteristics present, then one has to determine what other methods could be applied to the developed print for further enhancement of the print. Once a positive decision is made, the second mission is to compare the developed latent print with a known print, with the objective of either positive identification or elimination.

Although there have been tremendous advances in fingerprint technology during recent years, the basic principle and logic of these two missions have remained the same. In fact, the latent print examination process is the same as in any other type of forensic examination. The process is concerned with recognition, examination, identification, individualization, and evaluation (Figure 2.1).

Recognition and Examination

Recognition of the areas where one is most likely to find latent prints is probably the most important step in the examination of latent print evidence.

Without it, no amount of further laboratory examination or automated fingerprint identification systems (AFIS) searches are likely to shed much light on the case, with regard to fingerprint evidence. If crucial latent print evidence is not recognized, developed, collected, and preserved, it will be lost, and the potential important links between a suspect and a crime may never be known or established.

A latent print examiner has to possess the ability to recognize the potential evidence that may bear latent prints. Training and experience are critical to the determination of what is likely to be of importance among the various possibilities. The recognition process involves basic principles of forensic examination: logical analysis of human behavior, physical examination of the area, surface property observation, field and laboratory processing, pattern enhancement, and information evaluation.

Once the potential area which is most likely to yield fingerprint evidence is selected, a variety of techniques, such as physical, chemical, and instrumental methods, can be used to process the surface and to develop fingerprints.[1] The method of choice should not be based on convenience or the preferences of the latent examiner. The selection of methods should rest on the nature of the surface, the type of matrix of the print, and the condition of the print. Chapter 4 covers all the major techniques currently available and the respective procedures for processing. The determination of whether to process an item of evidence for latent fingerprints at the crime scene or to package that item and submit it to the laboratory for further analysis is largely dependent on the object and surface involved (movable and immovable) and the technical availability at the scene (such as reagents, instruments, and personnel).

A latent print examiner should have the ability to utilize the best methods, or combination of techniques, for the systematic processing of a latent print. This also requires the examiner to possess an important additional form of recognition skills. The latent examiner has to have the ability to separate potentially important and informative ridge patterns on the developed surface from all the background and other unrelated materials.

Identification and Individualization

Identification is a process common to all the sciences and, in fact, to everyday life. It may be regarded as a classification scheme, in which items are assigned to categories containing like items, and given names. Different items within a given category all have the same generic name. In this way, mineralogists will identify rocks by categorizing them and naming them. Likewise, botanists identify plants and chemists identify chemical compounds. A latent print examiner will identify fingerprints by comparing ridge characteristics.

Objects are identified by comparing their class characteristics with those of known standards or previously established criteria. Comparing the class characteristics of the questioned evidence with those of known standards or control materials leads to identification. If all the measurable class characteristics are the same between the questioned sample and the known control, then these two samples could have come from the same source or origin. If there are significant differences in some of the class characteristics measurements, then the questioned sample can be absolutely excluded as coming from the particular source. In other words, the exclusionary value of comparison in the forensic field is considered absolute. Depending on the nature and type of the physical evidence, no further analysis can be made beyond the comparison step with many types of physical evidence due to inherent limitations.

Two approaches have been used for latent print identification and individualization: systems engineering and human problem-solving techniques. They have both been modified to stress the decision-making requirements essential for effecting identification. This chapter is an effort to describe and define the identification methodology as practiced by a human latent print examiner and not the various algorithms employed in automated fingerprint identification systems (AFIS).[2]

All training programs for latent print examiners place great emphasis on practical experience during the phases of instruction regarding the evaluation and comparison of latent prints. This emphasis is well founded and has considerable merit, but it has been stressed so heavily that little written information exists regarding the methodologies and procedures for making a comparison of two prints. This lack of information has resulted in a failure to adequately define the many tasks involved in the evaluation and identification processes and the subsequent failure of many persons to recognize the scientific nature of latent print identification.

A description of the problem-solving techniques employed in each task in the evaluation and identification processes is essential for an understanding of the scientific methodology of this forensic discipline: the conceptualization of the problems encountered, the formulation of the data observed, and the logic that must be applied to make the decisions necessary in solving each problem encountered in establishing identity.

Many experienced latent print examiners may scoff at any attempt to thoroughly examine the thought processes involved in the evaluation and identification of latent prints. They may believe that such processes are merely common sense observations of physical phenomena, i.e., friction ridge characteristics. "Common sense, however, is based on common experience, supported and elaborated by the logic we apply to the explanation of that experience."[3] Forensic scientists who fail to understand the scientific methodology involved in their work will quite often fare badly under rigorous cross-examination when defending their findings in a court of law.

Individualization is unique to forensic science; it refers to the demonstration that a particular sample is unique, even among members of the same class. It may also refer to the demonstration that a questioned piece of physical evidence and a similar known sample have a common origin. Thus, in addition to class characteristics, objects and materials possess individual characteristics that can be used to distinguish members of the same class. The nature of these individual characteristics varies from one type of evidence to another, but forensic scientists try to take advantage of them in an effort to individualize a piece of physical evidence. Not all evidence can be truly individualized, but with some kinds, an approach to the goal of individualization is possible. We refer to those as partial individualization, and in some cases they are nothing more than refined identifications, such as conventional genetic marker determination of a bloodstain, microscopical fiber evidence comparison, or trace elemental analysis of paint chips. The term identification is sometimes used to mean personal identification (the individualization of persons). Fingerprints, for example, are often used to "identify" an individual. The terminology is unfortunate, since this process is really individualization. Likewise, dental evidence and dental records may be used by a forensic odontologist in making personal individualization in situations where dead bodies cannot otherwise be readily identified, such as mass disasters and cases involving fire or explosions.

The little information that is available in the identification literature regarding the processes of evaluation and individualization usually covers only the numbers of points required for an identification or the methods of demonstrating an identification in legal proceedings. The methods of courtroom presentation of fingerprint evidence may provide a clue as to the rationale of some examiners when making an identification in as much as these presentations may be viewed as models of the methodology of these examiners in arriving at their conclusions. In review of the available literature and training manuals, there are eight models currently used by latent print examiners for the evaluation and individualization of latent fingerprints.

Osborn Grid Method

The Osborn grid method (Figure 2.2) consists of photographing the latent and inked prints and making photographic enlargements of each.[4] A nonstandard grid of equally sized squares is superimposed on each enlargement with the squares of each grid occupying identical positions on each print. Both prints are examined, square for square, and the points of identity in each are noted. If all the available points in each square are identical between the latent and the known print, then an identification (individualization) is declared.

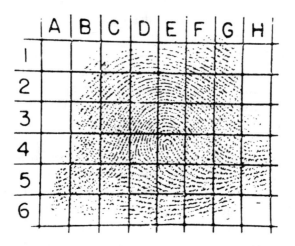

Figure 2.2 Osborn grid method.

Seymour Trace Method

In the Seymour trace method, the latent and inked prints are both copied on tracing paper.[5] The two tracings are then compared by superimposing one over the other and viewing them with backlighting. By tracing each point between the latent and the known print, a comparison is made.

Photographic Strip Method

The photographic strip method also involves the use of photographic enlargements.[6] The positioning and alignment of both prints in the enlargements must be in as close agreement as possible. The enlargement of the inked print is secured to a rigid mount. The enlargement of the latent print is then cut in lateral strips and placed over the enlargement of the inked print. The two enlargements must be fastened together in perfect conjunction. The identity is then demonstrated by removing the strips of the latent enlargement one at a time, exposing the inked print below.

Polygon Method

The polygon method (Figure 2.3), also called the "pincushion" method, of demonstrating identity also requires photographic enlargements of the latent and inked prints; both must be made at the same scale.[7-9] Small pinpoint holes are punched in each enlargement at the corresponding ridge characteristics. The enlargements are then reversed and straight lines are drawn connecting the points punched. The geometric configuration of each print is then compared. If the polygon of pin holes between the latent and the ink print matches, the identity is declared.

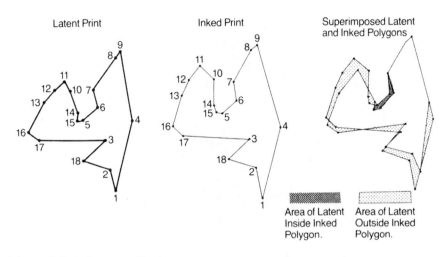

Figure 2.3 Polygon method.

Overlay Method

The overlay method is often suggested by some examiners to demonstrate identity or nonidentity.[10] One approach is to place a transparent overlay over an enlargement of the latent print and mark the ridge characteristics with a suitable writing instrument. The same overlay is then placed over an enlargement of the inked print, which must be to the same scale as the latent print, and the corresponding ridge characteristics are noted.

A variation in this method is to make transparent photographic enlargements of the latent and inked prints in two different colors, e.g., the ridge details of the latent may be yellow and those of the inked print may be blue. The latent print is then superimposed over the inked print, and matching ridges will appear green while nonmatching ridges will appear either yellow or blue. Of course, other colors have been used.

Osterburg Grid Method

The Osterburg grid method (Figure 2.4) is, in part, similar to the Osborn grid method.[11] A transparent grid is superimposed over the latent and inked prints, but whereas the Osborn grid has no specific measurements, the grid lines of the Osterburg grid are at 1-mm intervals. The Osterburg method, however, goes beyond simply matching characteristics in corresponding grid cells. Each type of characteristic is weighed according to a purported order of frequency, and weights are also assigned to cells without a characteristic. Determination of identity is made by the total value of the weighed characteristics found in a given area. No agency has officially adopted this method for establishing the identity of latent prints. Its application in latent print comparisons is entirely theoretical at this time.

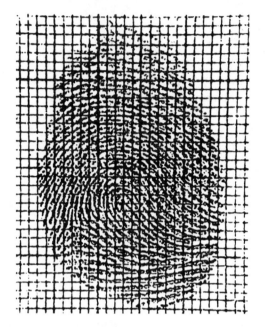

Figure 2.4 Osterburg grid method.

Microscopic Triangulation Method

The microscopic triangulation method is basically a combination of the grid and polygon methods of comparison.[12,13] A microscope is used to view the latent and inked prints at magnifications between 10× and 25×. A reference grid of hairlines in the microscopic field is used during the preliminary stage of the examination to scan the prints for similarities and dissimilarities. To establish identity, imaginary vertical and horizontal axes are drawn between arbitrarily selected ridge characteristics; the other characteristics are then plotted with respect to their relationship to the axes. This method has been soundly discredited and has no practical use in latent print identification.

Conventional Method

The conventional method is the oldest and surest method of demonstrating the identity of latent prints.[14,15] Identification is based on the ridge characteristics and their unit relationship to one another. Unit relationship, in this context, is not the spatial positioning of the characteristics as indicated by all the other demonstrative models. It is the relationship between the characteristics and all the other ridges in the print. The models that rely on spatial positioning do not take into consideration the influence of distortion in the print; it takes considerable experience to fully comprehend this influence.

Experience and Skill

Although the techniques used to process latent prints are well documented and most reagents are commonly available, these techniques require practice and training. Self-instruction in latent processing procedures and identification methodology without adequate guidance from a qualified instructor could prove disastrous. In addition, none of the methods of demonstrating identity attempt to define each separate task involved in the evaluation and comparison of latent prints. Above all, they do not explain the logical decisions that are required throughout the entire identification processes.

Some forensic scientists consider latent print processing to be a purely mechanical application of a standard set of powders and chemicals onto a suspected surface or that latent print comparison is only a method of demonstration. Still others consider that establishing identity is merely an observation of the spatial positioning of ridge characteristics and, therefore, that latent print identification is a simple procedure requiring little experience and that there is no need for any formal training.

Clear and distinct prints can be demonstrated so easily that untrained people will fail to understand the reasons why considerable experience is needed to identify other latent prints. Such persons usually regard all anomalies in a latent print as dissimilarities and fail to understand the natural effects of distortion and other adverse influences. To understand the role of experience in latent print identification, it is necessary to understand the relationship between experience and the tasks and problem-solving techniques employed in the evaluation and comparison of latent prints. A task may be defined as a process that is required to accomplish a measurable objective. A problem-solving technique is the application of certain principles and/or methodologies to the fulfillment of a task.

Problem-solving, perceptual motor skills involve responses to real objects in the spatial world; therefore, skilled performance is usually connected with perceptual discrimination. There are three overlapping stages in the acquisition of perceptual skills: cognition, fixation, and automation. Cognitive processes involve the conceptualization, understanding, and recognition of the problem encountered. The fixation stage is the longest and most difficult stage. During this stage the problem is fully analyzed and solutions are sought. The automation stage is characterized by rapid, automatic performance of the problem-solving skills with a minimum of errors.

Problem-solving ability, performance, or skill in latent print identification may be viewed with respect to the individual's position in the spectrum of expertise.[16] An individual enters the profession as a lay person and progresses to novice, professional, expert, and ultimately, master by virtue of education, research, and experience. Experience is a requirement for advancement throughout the spectrum. Experience is the foundation for superior problem-solving ability in all professions; in latent print identification, it is the hone for sharpening all essential skills.

As individuals progress from one level to another along the spectrum of expertise, they also progress up the phylogenic scale of problem-solving development.[17] Experience is a vital factor in problem-solving ability because the greater the individual's experience, the greater the likelihood that the same set of circumstances has been previously encountered and that previous solutions can be applied to the problem at hand.

Superior problem-solving ability may, however, present a false impression to lay persons and novices. They may observe only the rapidity of the problem-solving processes. To such persons, the evaluation and comparison tasks may appear to have been too easily performed and without complete analysis of the empirical data. Such false impressions usually give rise to the term "art" in describing the identification processes, a term that readily identifies its source as lacking an understanding of the scientific methodologies and logical reasoning processes required in this forensic science discipline.

Latent print processing and visualization procedures require logical decision making based on past knowledge. Selection of a target area to process is based on the principles of transfer theory and human behavior. Selection of a correct technique to process the target surface is based on the training and experience.

Identification Protocol

Figure 2.5 presents a problem-solving protocol and flowchart for the evaluation and comparison required in the examination of a latent print. To limit the description, the area for examination has been restricted to those ridge characteristics depicted in Figure 2.6(b). Figure 2.6(a) depicts the fingerprint from which the area of ridges was selected. Figure 2.6(c) is an illustration of how the area being examined would appear if only the spatial positions of the ridge characteristics were to be considered. Figure 2.6(d) is a conceptual enhancement of Figure 2.6(c). These last two illustrations are included to show the limitations of any protocols that take into consideration only the spatial positions of the ridge characteristics.

Several decisions that are based mostly on experience must be made before comparing a latent print with an inked impression. Was the impression made by friction ridge skin? Is there color reversal in the image of the latent print? What area of friction skin made the impression? Is it possible to determine pattern type or ridge flow? Are there sufficient ridge characteristics present for comparison with an inked print?

The initial identification of the latent print is made by comparing it with the inked print using 4× or 5× magnifiers. After determining the general pattern area of the latent print, a reference point is selected by the examiner to begin the search for matching characteristics in the inked print. The reference point may be one of the focal points of the pattern, core or delta, or several ridge characteristics that are near each other. After locating similar characteristics in the inked print, the examiner again observes the latent print for additional ridge characteristics that are near those previously selected and that match. This process is repeated until the examiner is satisfied that there is sufficient agreement between the two prints to form a conclusion as to identity.

In addition to locating points of similarity and establishing their unit relationship, the examiner must also search both prints for ridge characteristics that may appear in one impression, but not the other: in other words, dissimilarities between the two prints. If the "apparent" dissimilarity can be explained by the examiner as the result of natural phenomena, it is not a dissimilarity insofar as identity is concerned. If, however, no explanation can be found for the dissimilarity, the examiner cannot conclude a positive identification. This rule is often referred to in identification literature as the "one-dissimilarity doctrine."

Color reversal of latent prints is not an uncommon occurrence, and it is a possibility that an examiner must always consider. Color reversal occurs when the color of the ridges is the opposite of that expected. For example, a black powder is applied to a surface, but the ridges appear white against a black background. Color reversal may also occur when excessive pressure is applied, pushing the latent print residue between the ridges for final deposit on the receiving surface.

If pore details are present in the print, color reversal is apparent by the presence of the pores in what may at first appear to be the furrows of the print. In some instances, the ridge characteristics may be present, but the ridge count between some of the characteristics may be off by one ridge. Generally, when there has been a color reversal of the ridges, characteristics such as an enclosure may appear as a short ridge. However, this is not always the case and it is possible to have a latent print in which the ridge events are the same regardless of how the color of the ridges is viewed. In instances such as the latter, any arguments regarding the color of the ridges would be superfluous and would distract from the real issue of identity.

Distortions may be found in a fingerprint as a result of pressure applied to the finger or because of the curvature of the receiving surface. Failure to understand the effects of distortion and the techniques for resolving such problems has been a handicap to many inexperienced examiners. Figure 2.7 is an example of pressure distortion in known fingerprints from the same

Flowchart   Protocol

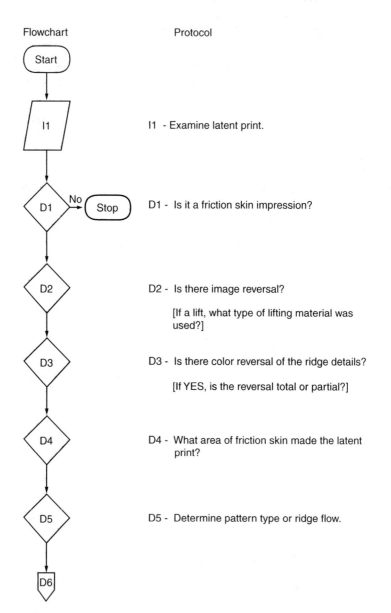

I1 - Examine latent print.

D1 - Is it a friction skin impression?

D2 - Is there image reversal?

      [If a lift, what type of lifting material was used?]

D3 - Is there color reversal of the ridge details?

      [If YES, is the reversal total or partial?]

D4 - What area of friction skin made the latent print?

D5 - Determine pattern type or ridge flow.

Figure 2.5 Flowchart. Problem-solving protocol and flowchart for the examination of a latent print.

finger. Note that in the core of the print on the left, there is a ridge ending, whereas in the print on the right, that same ridge is part of a recurring ridge. The examiner can readily understand and conclude that the "apparent" dissimilarity has been caused by pressure distortion by establishing the proper relationship of the ridges in the core to other ridge characteristics in the print and by tracing the ridges involved with a pointer.

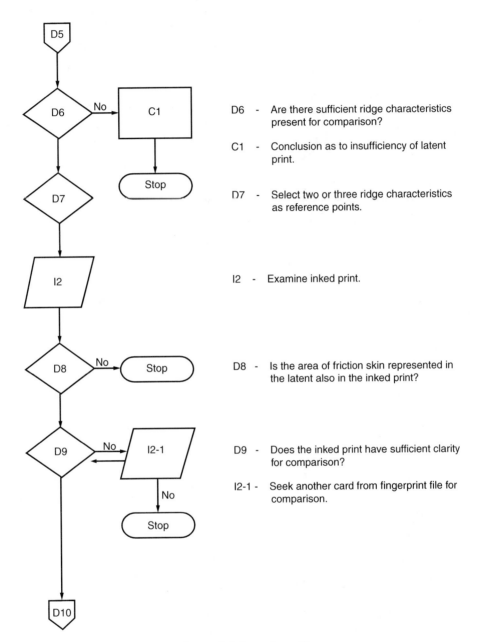

Figure 2.5 (continued)

Reconstruction

Reconstruction of fingerprint evidence is based on the results of crime scene processing of latent fingerprints, laboratory examination of physical evidence,

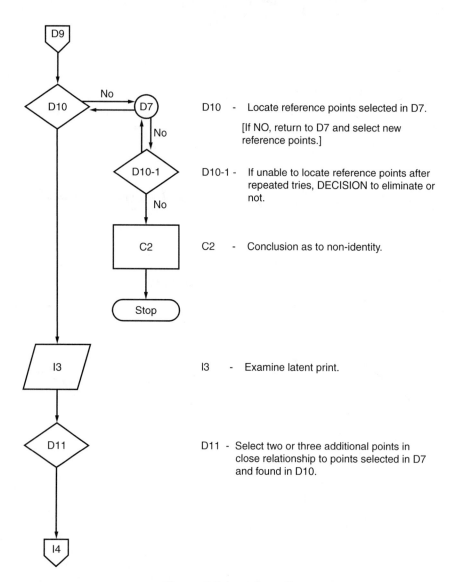

D10 - Locate reference points selected in D7.

[If NO, return to D7 and select new reference points.]

D10-1 - If unable to locate reference points after repeated tries, DECISION to eliminate or not.

C2 - Conclusion as to non-identity.

I3 - Examine latent print.

D11 - Select two or three additional points in close relationship to points selected in D7 and found in D10.

Figure 2.5 (continued)

comparison and identification of fingerprints, and other available data, records, and information to reconstruct case events.

Reconstruction often involves the use of both inductive and deductive logic, statistical data, and information from the crime scene such as the location of the latent print, the orientation of those fingerprints, and the position of each print. Reconstruction can be a very complex task, linking many types of physical evidence, pattern information, analytic results, investigative information, and other documentary and testimonial evidence into

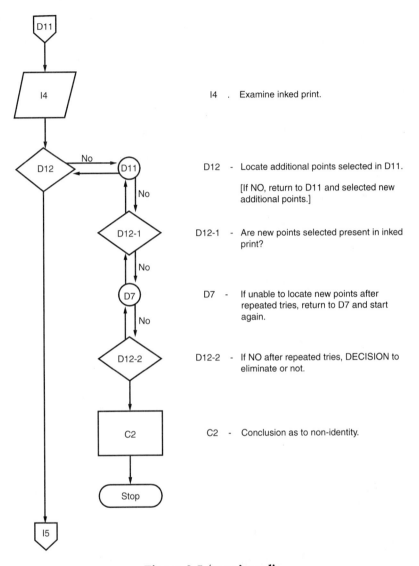

I4 . Examine inked print.

D12 - Locate additional points selected in D11.

[If NO, return to D11 and selected new additional points.]

D12-1 - Are new points selected present in inked print?

D7 - If unable to locate new points after repeated tries, return to D7 and start again.

D12-2 - If NO after repeated tries, DECISION to eliminate or not.

C2 - Conclusion as to non-identity.

Figure 2.5 (continued)

a complete entity.[16] Latent print identification generally follows the same type of reasoning. The latent print examiner will identify the print by categorizing it based on morphological pattern recognition, physical properties of finger prints and palm prints, physical characteristics of ridge patterns, and spatial relationships of fingers on the hand.

Latent print evaluation and comparison is primarily a visual information processing system. It is visual discrimination based on geometrical data and pattern recognition and the application of cognitive analysis. Experience provides a long-term data reference bank for correlation with current data

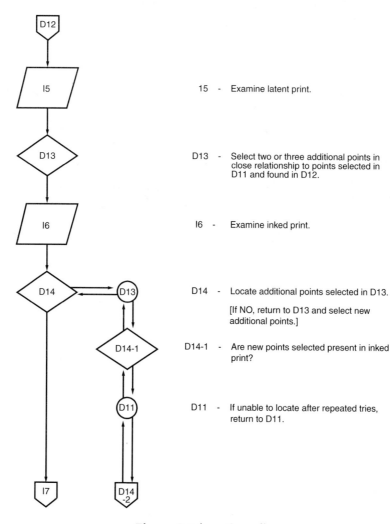

15 - Examine latent print.

D13 - Select two or three additional points in close relationship to points selected in D11 and found in D12.

16 - Examine inked print.

D14 - Locate additional points selected in D13.

[If NO, return to D13 and select new additional points.]

D14-1 - Are new points selected present in inked print?

D11 - If unable to locate after repeated tries, return to D11.

Figure 2.5 (continued)

in the latent print under examination. To understand the role of experience in latent print identification, it is necessary to understand the relationship between experience and the tasks and problem-solving techniques employed throughout the process of establishing identity.

The process of identification may be separated into separate and distinct tasks, which, in application, an examiner would perform so automatically that their existence is almost undetectable. Each separate task throughout the identification process requires decisions that must be made regarding the empirical data observed and correlation of this data with previously observed empirical data and with experience to comprehend its significance.

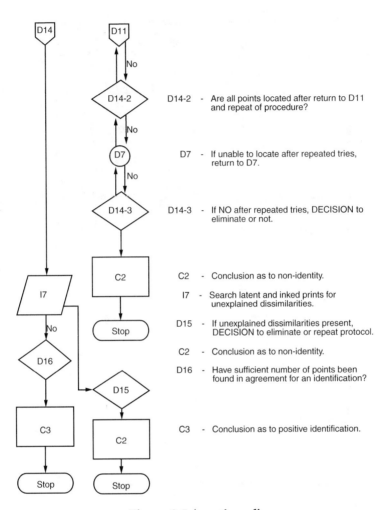

D14-2 - Are all points located after return to D11
          and repeat of procedure?

D7 - If unable to locate after repeated tries,
       return to D7.

D14-3 - If NO after repeated tries, DECISION to
          eliminate or not.

C2 - Conclusion as to non-identity.

I7 - Search latent and inked prints for
       unexplained dissimilarities.

D15 - If unexplained dissimilarities present,
        DECISION to eliminate or repeat protocol.

C2 - Conclusion as to non-identity.

D16 - Have sufficient number of points been
        found in agreement for an identification?

C3 - Conclusion as to positive identification.

Figure 2.5 (continued)

Deductive reasoning is used for making decisions throughout the identification process, as it is essential to the methodology of all scientific disciplines. In instances where the decision-making process involves retrieval of
data from experience (long-term memory storage), the reasoning is still
deductive if the decision is based on past observations of empirical data.
Reliance on experience is valid because the data can be verified.

Deductive reasoning is the process of deriving the logical consequences
of propositions. The propositions may be based on current observations
(empirical data from the prints being examined) and on experience (long-
term memory storage regarding past observations). Many people are often
unaware of the rules of inference that they employ in making deductions and

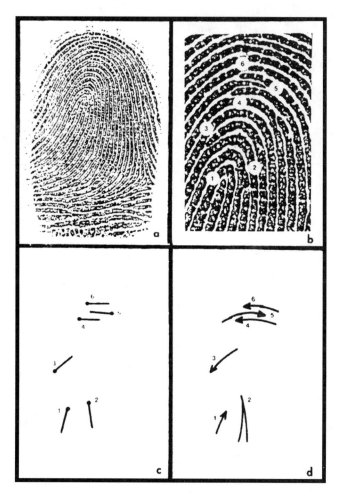

Figure 2.6 Examination of ridge characteristics. (a) Fingerprint from which the area of ridges was selected; (b) area of examination was restricted to the ridge characteristics depicted; (c) how the area being examined would appear if only spatial position of ridge characteristics were considered; (d) conceptional enhancement of (c).

derive their conclusions from premises simply by recognizing intuitively the connection between the familiarity of the data observed.

　　Logic, in general, is the science of right thinking; it prescribes the rules and procedures by which conclusions can be demonstrated to be valid or invalid. A very brief description of deductive reasoning is necessary to comprehend its role in latent print identification. In deduction, two propositions, which between them have a common term, are so related that from their combination a judgment, the conclusion, necessarily follows. The arrangement of the two propositions, termed the major and minor premises, followed by the

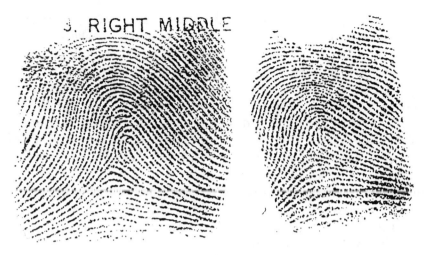

Figure 2.7 Example of pressure distortion. (left) Core of print with a ridge ending; (right) same ridge is part of a recurving ridge.

conclusion into full logical form constitute a mathematical formula termed a syllogism. Valid reasoning from true premises must lead to a true conclusion.

The premises used throughout the decision-making processes involved in the tasks of the evaluation and comparison processes are true if they are based on visual data and experience regarding the analysis of similar data, both of which are verifiable facts.

Conclusion

It has been suggested by some lay people that latent print identification may not be scientific because there is no minimum standard regarding the total number of ridge characteristics required for a positive identification. This belief reflects a simplistic view that the identification process is merely the totaling of clearly defined ridge characteristics to obtain an arbitrary number, a task that may be easily performed by marginally trained technicians.

Latent print identification is more than simply counting ridge characteristics. It involves many factors, including the skill gained only through experience. Latent print identification is a visual information-processing system employing scientific methodologies and human problem-solving techniques and requiring considerable experience for their proper employment. Experienced examiners, consciously or unconsciously, will consider, in addition to the number of characteristics, the overall quality and clarity of the impression, the rarity of the pattern type or ridge flow, and the uniqueness of the ridge characteristics.

Above all, the experienced examiner knows that the validity of the identification can be demonstrated to the satisfaction of other qualified examiners. The validity of fingerprint identification is best demonstrated using the conventional method. In preparing a chart of the latent and inked prints for demonstration purposes, photographic enlargements of the prints are marked by drawing numbered lines from selected ridge characteristics to the margins of the enlargements. The examiner demonstrates points of identity by using essentially the same methodology that was used in making the initial identification.

The flowchart and protocol presented in this chapter represent one algorithm for comparing the fingerprint depicted in Figure 2.6. It must be recognized that there can always be several algorithms for solving any problem, and the briefness of the algorithm presented is dictated by the limited purpose of this chapter: to merely acquaint the reader with the principles involved.

Latent print examiners must be cognizant of and understand the tasks involved and the decisions required throughout the processes of establishing identity. Fingerprint identification is a science, and as such, it must have well-defined principles and procedures for its application. The developing fields of artificial intelligence and expert systems have opened up a new dimension in reconstruction. These systems enable the latent print examiner to model and make representations of laboratory analysis results, allow reasoning and enacting of a crime scene, and aid in making logical decisions concerning the case. Advances in hardware and software have added systematic problem solving to the forensic scientist's repertoire. Computer technology allows communication between the user and the expert system — in a sense each is helping the other to solve a specific forensic problem.

References

1. Lee, H. C. and Harris, H. A., *Physical Evidence in Forensic Science*, Lawyer & Judges, Tucson, AZ, 1999.

2. Lee, H. C. and Gaensslen, R. E., Editors, *Advances in Fingerprint Technology*, CRC Press, Boca Raton, FL, 1991 (see also Chapter 8 of this volume).

3. Halle, L. *Out of Chaos*, Houghton Mifflin, Boston, 1977, 15.

4. Osborn, A. *Questioned Documents*, Lawyers Co-operative, Rochester, NY, 1910, 479–481.

5. Seymour, L. *Finger Print Classification*. Los Angeles (privately printed by author), 1913, 72–79.

6. Bridges, B. *Practical Fingerprinting*. Funk & Wagnalls, New York, 1942, 335–336.

7. Brown, W., Here we go again! *Finger Print Mag.*, 28, 5, 1947.

8. Davis, J., Pressure distortion in latent prints. *Finger Print Mag.*, 28, 3, 1946.

9. Mairs, G., Novel method of print comparison. *Finger Print Mag.*, 28, 20, 1946.

10. Wohlfeil, P., Fingerprints in color. *Tech. Photogr.*, 16, 28, 1984.

11. Osterburg, J., Parthasarathy, T., Raghavan, T. et al. Development of a mathematical formula for the calculation of fingerprint probabilities based on individual characteristics. *J. Am. Statistical Assoc.*, 72, 772, 1977

12. Morfopoulos, V., Anatomy of evidence. *Ident. News*, 20, 10, 1970.

13. Hoover, J., Fingerprints do not lie. *FBI Law Enforcement Bull.*, 38, 20, 1969.

14. Cowger, J. *Friction Ridge Skin: Comparison and Identification,* Elsevier, New York, 1983, 129–189.

15. Dondero, J. *Comparing Finger Prints for Positive Identification*, Faurot, New York, 1944.

16. Olsen, R., Cult of the mediocre. *Ident. News,* 32, 3, 1982.

17. Newell, A. and Simon, S. *Human Problem Solving,* Prentice-Hall, Englewood Cliffs, NJ, 1972.

Composition of Latent Print Residue

3

ROBERT S. RAMOTOWSKI

Contents

0-8493-0923-9/01/$0.00+$1.50
© 2001 by CRC Press LLC

Introduction

The composition of human perspiration has been studied and reported extensively in the medical literature. The medical community has analyzed sweat for many purposes, including attempts to diagnose certain diseases, such as cystic fibrosis, and studies of skin conditions, such as acne. Even the perfume and cosmetics industry has an interest in determining the precise chemical nature of perspiration and how it might interact with their personal hygiene products. However, the information ascertained in these studies does not begin to address the issue that is most critical for forensic scientists. Knowing the precise contents of the various skin glands does not accurately represent the nature of what is actually secreted onto substrates from the fingers and palms. In operational scenarios, numerous contaminants are present in the fingerprint deposit, including material from other glands, cosmetics, perfumes, and food residues. In addition, the secreted material is almost immediately altered by oxidative and bacterial degradation mechanisms. These factors are particularly important since crime scene technicians seldom encounter latent print deposits immediately after they are deposited by a perpetrator. However, there is little information available that describes how a latent print deposit changes with time. Thus, a more thorough understanding of these transformations would allow forensic scientists to develop specific reagents for visualizing compounds known to be stable for long periods of time.

Skin Anatomy

Skin serves several functions, including regulation of body temperature, water retention, protection, sensation, excretion, immunity, blood reservoir, and synthesis of vitamin D (except where noted, the information in this section was obtained from Odland[1]). The skin of an average adult exceeds 2 m^2 in area; yet, in most places it is no more than 2 mm thick. While the average thickness of epidermal skin varies little over most of the body, the thickness on the palms and soles can be as much as 0.4 to 0.6 mm. The skin is usually divided into two distinct layers. The outer layer is a stratified epithelium called the epidermis, which has an average thickness of 75 to 150 μm. The underlying layer of skin is called the dermis, a dense fibroelastic connective tissue that constitutes the primary mass of the skin. This portion of the skin contains most of the specialized excretory and secretory glands that produce sweat. Although the dermis constitutes between 90 to 95% of the mass of human skin, the epidermis accounts for the major proportion of the biochemical transformations that occur in the skin (although structures that extend into the dermis, such as the various sweat glands and hair follicles, are also metabolically important).

The Epidermis

The epidermis (Figure 3.1) consists of several cell layers.[2] The innermost is known as the stratum germinativum (basal cell layer). It consists of one layer of columnar epithelial cells, which upon division push into the stratum spinosum. The stratum spinosum (prickle cell layer) consists of several layers that are held together by intercellular fibrils. The combined stratum spinosum and stratum germinativum are often referred to as the Malpighian layer (named in honor of Marcello Malpighi, a 17th century Italian professor and fingerprint science pioneer who first used high magnification to detail the fine structure of ridges and pores).

As these cells approach the skin surface, they begin to grow larger and form the next layer, the stratum granulosum (granular layer). Keratohyalin granules (the precursor of keratin, a fibrous, insoluble protein found in skin) are formed in this layer, which is approximately two to four cells thick. The nuclei are then either broken up or dissolved, resulting in the death of the epidermal cell and an increase in the number of cytoplasmic granules. The penultimate layer, the stratum lucidum (clear layer), is ill-defined and consists primarily of eleidin, which is presumed to be a transformation product of the keratohyalin present in the stratum granulosum. In the outermost layer, the stratum corneum (cornified layer), the eleidin is converted to keratin, which is the ultimate fate of the original epidermal cell. Keratin, which is continually sloughed off, must continuously be replaced by cells beneath it. It has been estimated that a typical individual will shed approximately 0.5 to 1 g of dead skin cells per day.[2] The total cell cycle in the epidermis is estimated to take approximately 28 days. Figure 3.2 is a stained skin section showing all of the layers of the epidermis.

The Dermis

The dermis is a moderately dense fibroelastic connective tissue composed of collagen (a fibrous protein composed of primarily glycine, alanine, proline, and hydroxyproline), elastin fibers (a fibrous protein containing primarily

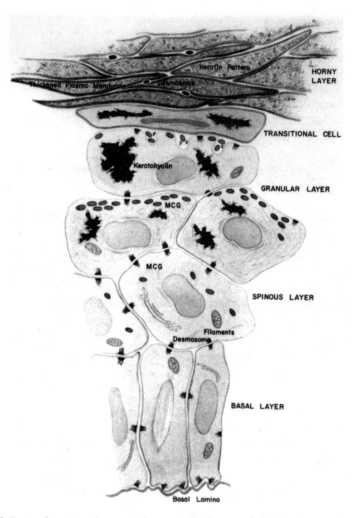

Figure 3.1 A schematic diagram showing the layers of the epidermis. (From *The Structure and Function of Skin, 3rd Edition*, Montagna, W. and Parakkal, P.F., Eds., Academic Press, 1974. With permission.)

glycine, alanine, valine, and lysine), and an interfibrillar gel of glycosamin-proteoglycans, salts, and water. This layer contains up to five million secretory glands, including eccrine, apocrine, and sebaceous glands.[2] Collagen fibers form an irregular meshwork that is roughly parallel to the epidermal surface and provides skin tensile strength and resistance to mechanical stress. Elastin gives skin its elasticity and its ability to resume its natural shape after deformation. Fibrous mats of elastin are intermeshed with collagen to give skin its tension. This tension is greatest over body areas where the skin is thin and elastin is abundant (e.g., the scalp and face). Fibroblasts, which form elastin and collagen, and histiocytes, which form interferon for protection against

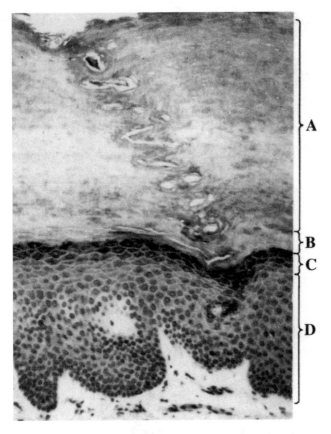

Figure 3.2 A stained section of the epidermis from the palm showing all of the layers. Section A is the stratum corneum, section B is the stratum lucidum, section C is the stratum granulosum, and section D is the stratum malpighii. The structure evident in the stratum corneum is the duct of an eccrine sweat gland. (From *The Structure and Function of Skin, 3rd Edition*, Montagna, W. and Parakkal, P.F., Eds., Academic Press, 1974. With permission.)

viral infections, are present in this layer. A system of blood, lymphatic, and nerve vessels is also present.

The dermis is divided into two anatomical regions, the pars papillaris and the pars reticularis. The papillary dermis is the outermost portion of the dermal layer and contains smaller and more loosely distributed elastin and collagen fibrils than does the reticular dermis. The papillae are supplied by numerous capillaries, which ultimately supply nourishment to the epidermis via diffusion. The second region, the reticular dermis, lies beneath the papillary dermis and comprises the bulk of this layer. It is characterized by dense collagenous and elastic connective tissue. These collagen bundles are arranged predominately in interwoven strands that are parallel to the skin surface, although some tangentially oriented bundles are present.

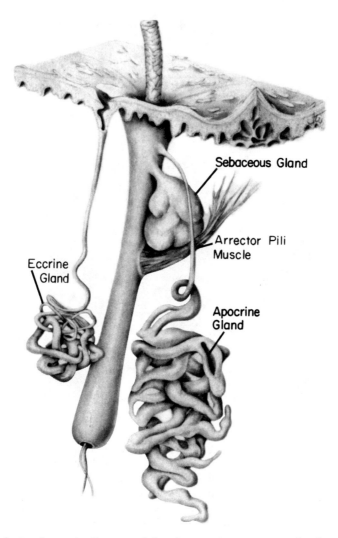

Figure 3.3 A schematic diagram of the three major secretory glands in relation to other cutaneous appendages. (From *The Structure and Function of Skin, 3rd Edition*, Montagna, W. and Parakkal, P.F., Eds., Academic Press, 1974. With permission.)

Secretory Glands

The three major glands (eccrine, apocrine, and sebaceous) responsible for the secretion of "sweat" are shown in Figure 3.3. The eccrine glands are usually found throughout the body, but the highest densities are found in the palms and soles. The sebaceous glands are typically localized to regions containing hair follicles, as well as the face and scalp. The apocrine glands are found primarily in the axillary regions (e.g., armpits and genital areas). However, in most instances, only the eccrine and sebaceous glands contribute significantly to the latent print deposit. Although the composition of sweat is approximately 99% water,[3] studies have shown that a considerable variety of chemical compounds are present. A recent study found approximately 346 compounds (303 of which were positively identified) present in surface skin residues.[4,5]

Eccrine Glands

There are between two and four million eccrine sweat glands distributed throughout the human body surface (except where noted, the following information was obtained from Quinton[6]). Each gland has been calculated to have an estimated weight of 30 to 40 µg, for an aggregate weight of about 100 g. In normal individuals, these glands are capable of secreting as much as 2 to 4 L of fluid per hour. The evaporation of this quantity of sweat requires approximately 18 kcal/min, which affords humans an ability to dissipate heat faster than any other animal. Sweat glands are most abundant on the soles of the feet ($620/cm^2$) and least abundant on the back ($64/cm^2$).[7] Gland formation begins around the third fetal month on the palms and soles and at about 5 months for the rest of the body. Typically, the glands have fully matured by the eighth fetal month. The eccrine gland is essentially a tubular shaped structure with a duct portion that coils in helical fashion down deep into the dermis layer. The function of the distal half of the sweat gland tubule is to reabsorb sodium, chloride, bicarbonate, glucose, and several other small solutes. Under normal conditions, this allows water to be evaporated from the skin surface without the loss of essential solutes.

Inorganic Compounds

Although eccrine sweat is usually in excess of 98% water, it also contains numerous organic and inorganic constituents. The presence of these solutes on the skin surface causes a reduction in sweat vapor pressure. These effects have been modeled and quantified.[8] Excess secretion of certain chloride salts has been reported to be a cause for increased rates of corrosion of metal surfaces by particular individuals.[9] This effect was particularly pronounced in patients suffering from hyperhidrosis, a condition which causes excess sweat production. The rate of eccrine sweating has been shown to depend on the amount of water ingested, but does not appear to exert an independent effect on the relationship of sweat composition to sweat rate.[10] Sweat has been reported to contain 0.5 to 8 mM total ammonia,[11] which is 20 to 50 times higher than plasma levels. In addition, trace amounts of the following inorganic substances have also been detected in sweat: magnesium, iodide

(5 to 12 µg/L), bromide (0.2 to 0.5 mg/L), fluoride (0.2 to 1.18 mg/L), phosphate (10 to 17 mg/L), sulfate (7 to 190 mg/L), iron (1 to 70 mg/L),[12] zinc, copper, cobalt, lead, manganese, molybdenum, sulfur, tin, and mercury.[13-15]

Interestingly, the eccrine gland is one of the target organs for cystic fibrosis. Historically, this condition has been diagnosed on the basis of elevated sodium chloride concentration in sweat. In general, the sweat sodium ion concentration appears to be isotonic to that of human plasma, although significant variations can be obtained depending on the method of collection (e.g., thermal vs. pharmacologically induced sweat).[16] One study found that the sodium concentration varied over a rather large range, from 34 to 266 mEq/L. Others reported the average concentration at 140 ± 1.8 mEq/L[7] and 60 mEq/L.[17] The latter source reported that the chloride concentration is generally lower than that of sodium, averaging around 46 mEq/L, and that the potassium level ranged from 5 to 59 mEq/L. In general, chloride levels are isotonic with those in plasma.[18] Other studies have determined the potassium levels to be between 4.9 to 8.3 mEq/L[16] and 8.8 mEq/L.[19] The amount of calcium in sweat was found to be about 3.4 mEq/L and the amount of magnesium was 1.2 mEq/L.

The HCO_3^--CO_2 buffer system appears to play a critical role in maintaining sweat pH. The pH of sweat isolated from human secretory coils (in the dermis) is approximately 7.2, while the pH of sweat secreted from the gland can vary from as low as 5.0 (at a low sweat rate) up to 6.5 to 7.0 (at a high sweat rate). This indicates that the duct itself acidifies the sweat, presumably by reabsorbing bicarbonate and/or secreting H^+ in exchange for a Na^+ ion.[20] At low sweat rates, this mechanism can conserve bicarbonate (and other solutes) efficiently and thus maintain a slightly acidic sweat pH. At higher sweat rates, the mechanism is overwhelmed and cannot reabsorb solutes effectively. This results in secreted sweat containing higher amounts of bicarbonate and thus it has a higher pH. The typical bicarbonate concentration has been reported to be between 15 to 20 mM.

Amino Acids

Of critical importance to latent print visualization with ninhydrin is the concentration of amino acids and proteins. The total amount of amino acids present in a print has been reported to be between 0.3 to 2.59 mg/L.[14] The first amino acid found in eccrine sweat was serine, isolated as β-naphthalinesulfoserine by using a microbiological method, and was reported by Embden and Tachau in 1910. A study of samples of pharmacologically induced sweat (using pilocarpine hydrochloride) collected after a hygienic bath yielded 22 amino acids.[21] Amino acid amounts in sweat have been reported to be several times higher than corresponding values in plasma.[22] One study found the most abundant amino acids to be serine and alanine,

Table 3.1   A Summary of the Relative Abundance (Serine Ratio) of Amino Acids in Fingerprint Deposits

	Hamilton[28]	Hadorn et al.[27]	Oro and Skewes[29]
Serine	100	100	100
Glycine	67	54	59
Ornithine	32	45	45
(Ornithine, lysine)	42	47	45
Alanine	27	35	28
Aspartic acid	22	11	22
Threonine	17	9	18
Histidine	17	13	14
Valine	12	10	9
Leucine	10	7	10
Isoleucine	8	6	8
Glutamic acid	8	12	5
Lysine	10	5	—
Phenylalanine	7	5	5
Tyrosine	6	3	5

15.44 and 14.63 mg%, respectively. Another study of both active and inactive participants found that in both cases, serine, glycine, and alanine were the most abundant amino acids.[23] A similar trend was also reported by several others.[24-26]

Quantitatively, amino acid concentrations can vary as much as 2 to 20 times depending on collection methods (e.g., thermally induced sweat vs. exercise-induced sweat) and by sample location on the body. A study comparing sweat samples obtained from the back and hands of subjects found some significant differences.[27] The samples from the backs of subjects showed higher amounts of amino acids involved in the urea cycle. These and other differences appeared to be independent of plasma and urine amino acid levels, suggesting that amino acids do not appear in sweat as a result of filtration from the blood plasma. Table 3.1 summarizes the relative amino acid abundance values from several different studies. One study reported a series of ninhydrin positive substances, in addition to amino acids, in human eccrine sweat.[30] Some of these substances include o-phosphoserine, methionine sulfoxide, α-amino-isobutyric acid, glucosamine, α-amino-n-valeric acid, cystathionine, β-amino-isobutyric acid, ethanolamine, γ-aminobutyric acid, and carnosine.

Proteins

The total protein content in sweat has been determined to range between 15 to 25 mg/dL. One study using two-dimensional electrophoresis and ultrasensitive silver staining found over 400 polypeptide components.[31] Some specific examples determined by sodium dodecyl sulfate polyacrylamide gel electrophoresis (SDS-PAGE) include albumin, Zn-α_2-glycoprotein, lysozyme, and the α_1-acid glycoprotein orosomucoid.[32] An agarose gel iso-tachophoresis analysis of thermally induced sweat detected transferrin, fast-migrating γ-globulins, α- and β-lipoproteins, and several glycoproteins.[33] It has been determined by size fractionation HPLC that the bulk of the peptides in sweat are in the low end of the molecular weight range. Secretion of higher molecular weight proteins (i.e., in excess of 10,000 Da) has been reported to increase as the rate of sweating increases.

Lipids

The lipid content of secretions from the eccrine gland has also been investi-gated.[34] Contamination of samples by lipids of sebaceous and epidermal origin is a major consideration in these analyses. In this particular study, thin layer chromatography was used to separate the lipid fraction collected from both "clean" and "scraped" sweat samples. Results indicated that the "scraped" samples contained a significant amount of lipids that were consis-tent with those found in the stratum corneum. In contrast, the "clean" sam-ples collected using the method described by Boysen et al.[35] contained only one significant lipid band, which corresponded to the cholesterol/fatty acid standard. In the samples collected, fatty acid concentrations ranged from less than 0.01 to 0.1 µg/mL and sterol concentrations ranged from less than 0.01 to 0.12 µg/mL. These results would indicate that "scraped" samples were contaminated by lipids from the epidermis, while "clean" samples gave a more realistic characterization of eccrine lipids.

Miscellaneous Constituents

Lactate and urea have been reported at significant levels in perspiration. The amounts of these compounds can vary from 30 to 40 mM at low sweat rates to as low as 10 to 15 mM at higher rates.[13] Other miscellaneous components of eccrine sweat include creatine, creatinine,[36] glucose (0.2 to 0.5 mg/dL), pyruvate (0.2 to 1.6 mM), cAMP, phenobarbitone, and immunoglobulins.[37] Numerous enzymes have also been detected in dissected sweat glands, includ-ing alkaline phosphatase, acid phosphatase, Na/K ATPase, phosphatidic acid phosphatase, monoamine oxidase, acetyl cholinesterase, and lactic, malic, glucose-6-phosphate, isocitric, and succinic dehydrogenases.

Drugs have also been found in eccrine sweat.[38] Sulfonamides, antipyrine, and aminopyrine were found to exhibit sweat concentrations that were directly proportional to plasma levels. Simple diffusion, aided by the relatively low ionization of the drugs studied within the physiological pH range, was assumed to be the mechanism by which these drugs entered the sweat glands. Another study found that L-dimethylamphetamine as well as its metabolite L-methamphetamine were found to be excreted in sweat.[39] After taking 25 mg

Table 3.2   A Summary of the Composition of Eccrine Sweat

Inorganic (major)		Inorganic (trace)	
Sodium	34–266 mEq/L	Magnesium	
Potassium	4.9–8.8 mEq/L	Zinc	
Calcium	3.4 mEq/L	Copper	
Iron	1–70 mg/L	Cobalt	
Chloride	0.52–7 mg/mL	Lead	
Fluoride	0.2–1.18 mg/L	Manganese	
Bromide	0.2–0.5 mg/L	Molybdenum	
Iodide	5–12 µg/L	Tin	
Bicarbonate	15–20 mM	Mercury	
Phosphate	10–17 mg/L		
Sulfate	7–190 mg/L		
Ammonia	0.5–8 mM		
Organic (general)		**Organic (lipids)**	
Amino acids	0.3–2.59 mg/L	Fatty acids	0.01–0.1 µg/mL
Proteins	15–25 mg/dL	Sterols	0.01–0.12 µg/mL
Glucose	0.2–0.5 mg/dL		
Lactate	30–40 mM		
Urea	10–15 mM		
Pyruvate	0.2–1.6 mM		
Creatine			
Creatinine			
Glycogen			
Uric acid			
Vitamins			

Miscellaneous
Enzymes
Immunoglobulins

Note: Some compounds and species were only listed as present in sweat in the literature. No concentrations were specified for these components.

of the L-dimethylamphetamine, the maximum concentration in sweat was found to be approximately 2 to 4 µg/mL, within a few hours after ingestion. Unlike the urine concentration, L-dimethylamphetamine levels in sweat were found to be independent of pH. Ethanol has also been detected. Several relatively rapid, noninvasive methods have been proposed to examine the ethanol (as well as other volatile organics) present in perspiration.[40] The composition of eccrine sweat is summarized in Table 3.2.

Sebaceous Glands

The second major class of secretory glands, sebaceous glands, are located throughout the body, except for the palms and dorsum of the feet (except where noted, the information in this section was obtained from Strauss

Table 3.3   Anatomical Variation in the Amount and Composition of Human Sebum Collected After 12 hr of Accumulation (in Weight Percent)

Site	Total lipid (μg/cm²)	CH	CE	TG	DG	FA	WE	SQ	TG+DG+FA
Forehead	288	1.1	2.7	29.6	3.5	27.2	25.9	10.1	60.3
Cheek	144	1.1	3.4	39.4	2.7	15.4	26.9	11.2	57.5
Chest	122	1.3	2.6	29.7	5.4	24.9	25.7	10.3	60.0
Back	84	2.2	2.0	35.9	4.5	17.4	27.4	10.6	57.8
Arm	76	4.8	4.3	34.3	2.4	18.4	27.7	8.1	55.1
Side	57	4.3	4.5	47.1	1.9	7.6	24.9	9.6	56.6
Leg	57	6.3	6.0	44.6	1.5	10.2	23.1	8.1	56.3

Note: CH = cholesterol; CE = cholesterol esters; TG = triglycerides; DG = diglycerides; FA = free fatty acids; WE = wax esters; SQ = squalene; and TG + DG + FA = total glycerides plus free fatty acids.

Source: Greene, R. S., Downing, D. T., Pochi, P. E., and Strauss, J. S., Anatomical variation in the amount and composition of human skin surface lipid. *J. Invest. Dermatol.,* 54(3), 246, 1970. With permission.

et al.[41]). Gland density is greatest around the face and scalp, where as many as 400 to 800 glands per cubic centimeter may be found. The sebaceous glands are generally associated with hair follicles and open inside the hair shaft canals. Unlike eccrine secretions, which empty directly onto the skin surface, the sebum produced by sebaceous glands first travels into the follicular canal and then onto the skin surface. The lipid is produced by a holocrine mechanism, whereby lipid-laden cells disintegrate and empty their contents through the sebaceous duct onto the skin surface.[42] These glands develop during fetal life between weeks 13 and 15 and have achieved a nearly full size by the time of birth.[43] The glands are fully developed and functioning before birth, probably due to stimulation by maternal hormones. At birth, with the termination of the source of these hormones, the glands soon become mostly inactive. Table 3.3 summarizes sebum production and composition for various anatomical regions.[44]

Sebaceous gland activity appears to be controlled by a somewhat complex process. It appears that mid-brain dopamine stimulates the anterior and intermediate lobes of the pituitary gland to release various hormones via certain glands (e.g., thyroid, adrenals, and gonads).[45] In turn, these glands secrete additional hormones that stimulate sebum production. Several androgens have been found to stimulate sebum production.[46] Testosterone is an especially potent stimulator of sebum production in humans. It has been reported that sebum production levels in castrated males are considerably lower than in intact men.[47] The administration of testosterone to castrated males has been reported to result in a significant increase in sebaceous gland activity.[48] However, administration of testosterone to the normal adult male does not lead to an increase in sebum production. This would indicate

Table 3.4 The Approximate Composition of Sebum and Surface Epidermal Lipids

Constituent	Sebum (wt%)	Surface epidermal lipid (wt%)
Glyceride/free fatty acids	57.5	65
Wax esters	26.0	—
Squalene	12.0	—
Cholesterol esters	3.0	15
Cholesterol	1.5	20

Source: Downing, D. T. and Strauss, J. S., Synthesis and composition of surface lipids of human skin, *J. Invest. Dermatol.*, 62, 231, 1974. With permission.

that maximum stimulation of the sebaceous glands is accomplished by endogenous testosterone. Other studies have found slight increases in skin surface lipids after administering testosterone.[49] Testosterone given to children also produced a significant increase in sebum production.[50] Metabolism and elimination of these compounds in human skin samples has been reported.[51] It appears that excretion of C_{19}- and C_{18}-steroids through the skin may exceed their urinary elimination.

Lipid Origin and Breakdown

Radioactive labeling studies have illuminated the formation and origin of lipids.[52] Autoradiograms from one study showed that radioactivity (from incubating samples of subcutaneous fat from scalp biopsies with [14C] acetate) found in total lipid extracts was confined to squalene, wax esters, triglycerides, and phospholipids. It is significant to note that cholesterol, cholesterol esters, and free fatty acids did not contain any significant amount of radioactivity. That would imply that these compounds are of epidermal origin rather than being produced in the sebaceous gland. The differences in lipid classes between lipids of sebaceous and epidermal origin are listed in Table 3.4. Another study proposed that sebaceous lipids are derived from two different sources, the body's circulation (exogenous lipid) and from *de novo* synthesis (endogenous lipids).[53] They assumed that the composition of both of these sources remained constant, but that their relative contribution to sebum was variable. Examples of possible exogenous lipids would include linoleate (an essential fatty acid), cholesterol, cholesterol esters, and triglycerides. However, the fact that circulating cholesterol esters and triglycerides have different fatty acid compositions than their sebaceous counterparts makes it unlikely that they are incorporated directly into sebum. Examples of endogenous lipids that are not available from blood include Δ6 fatty acids, squalene, and wax esters.

Various oxidative and bacteriological changes occur after sebum is excreted. Lipolysis by enzymes derived from the epidermis or bacteria present in skin surface debris from human skin has a tendency to break down triglycerides and methyl esters.[54] That particular study reported that, in ether, triolein and tristearin were converted primarily to free fatty acids and 1,2-diglycerides and only trace amounts of 1,3-diglycerides and monoglycerides. This evidence leads to the conclusion that the majority of free fatty acids present in sweat originate from the hydrolysis of sebum triglycerides. Evidence of varying degrees of bacterial lipolysis has been offered for *Corynebacterium acnes*,[55,56] staphylococci,[57] *Pityrosporum ovale*,[58] *Pityrosporum acnes, Pityrosporum granulosum*,[59] Micrococcaceae, and propionibacteria.[60] Several studies have shown that treatment of skin with antibiotic compounds (e.g., clindamycin) reduced bacterial populations and led to a concurrent decrease in free fatty acids.[61-63] However, one study found that treatment with neomycin failed to affect the *C. acnes* population.[64] It is likely that certain bacteria, such as *C. acnes*, are present within the hair follicles and would be inaccessible to topical antibiotics.

Chemical Composition of Sebum

There is a considerable variety of organic compounds present in sebum. Several factors can influence a particular individual's sebum profile, including diet and genetics. It is possible that each person may have a unique scent signature, as demonstrated by the ability of certain breeds of dogs to track humans over wide areas. In addition, in animals, certain lipids may function as a means of communication. One study determined that in certain species, short-chained aliphatic acids were found to act as pheromones.[65] These compounds also allow animals to recognize members of their own social group. It is possible that a similar situation was once present in humans; however, modern hygiene practices may have diminished our ability to recognize the signals. In fact, in humans, sweat has to be broken down bacterially before it acquires a detectable, characteristic odor. A summary of sebum composition by lipid class is presented in Table 3.5.

Fatty Acids

Hydrolysis of human sebum results in the formation of a mixture of fatty acids. The amount of free fatty acids in sebum shows considerable variation, but averages between 15 to 25%. They are derived primarily from the hydrolysis of triglycerides and wax esters. It has been proposed that as the amount of liberated free fatty acids increases to a certain concentration, the pH drops sufficiently to inhibit bacterial lipases responsible for their production.[64] It has been reported that patients with acne have elevated levels of free fatty acids, typically greater than 30%.[71] It has also been observed that free fatty

Table 3.5 Summary of Sebum Composition

	Downing et al.[66]	Lewis and Hayward[67]	Haahti[68]	Nicolaides and Foster[69]	Felger[70]	Nordstrom et al.[71]	Goode and Morris[3]	Darke and Wilson[72]
Glycerides	43.2	46.4	42.6	31.7	35.4[b]	16.1	33	30.2[c]
Fatty acids	16.4	16.0	16.2	29.6	27.2[b]	33.0	30	22.0
Wax esters	25.0	21.5	24.2[a]	21.8	22.6	25.3	22	29.3[d]
Cholesterol esters	2.1	2.9	—	3.3	2.5	2.0	2	—
Cholesterol	1.4	1.8	1.4	2.4	0.7	3.8	2	1.1
Squalene	12.0	11.4	15.6	12.8	11.6	19.9	10	17.4

[a] This value is for both wax and cholesterol esters.
[b] The differences between these and other values listed are more than likely caused by individual differences in the degree of lipolysis of triglycerides by bacterial lipases.
[c] This value includes cholesterol esters.
[d] This value includes a minor contribution from diglycerides.

acid content can change with time in the same individual. One study found that certain fatty acids from the same donor taken once a week for 7 weeks showed significant variation in concentration with time.[73] The study also reported significant differences between male and female fatty acid composition. In addition, minor differences were observed between fatty acids isolated from wax esters and cholesterol esters. However, it is difficult to draw conclusions from this data since only two subjects were involved in the study.

Approximately 50% of the fatty acids in sweat are saturated, with straight chain C_{16} and C_{14} being the dominant acids.[74] Monoenes typically constitute 48% of fatty acids, with straight chain C_{16} and C_{18} being the most prominent. The structures of unsaturated fatty acids have been reported to vary with age and sex.[75] The amounts of Δ9-type unsaturated fatty acids (in triglycerides, wax esters, and sterol esters) were always higher in females than in males. The amount of Δ9-type unsaturated fatty acids reaches a maximal value during the prepubertal years, decreases to a minimum from adolescence to middle age, and then begins to increase again with advancing age. In nature, Δ9-type monounsaturated compounds are the most common and Δ6-type are relatively rare. Interestingly, the presence of Δ6-type fatty acids in humans appears to be virtually unique among species studied.[76] Also, Δ6-type unsaturated fatty acids are almost exclusively derived from sebaceous glands, whereas Δ9-type acids appear to be primarily of epidermal origin. Dienoic fatty acids comprise about 2 to 3% of samples, with major isomers being 18:Δ5,8 and 18:Δ9,12.[77] Increased levels of the 18:Δ5,8 diene have been reported in acne patients.[78]

Several branched chain fatty acids have been detected in humans. The largest variation occurred with iso-even fatty acids. One study found significant variations (10- to 20-fold) in the amounts of iso-branched acids having an even number of carbons.[74] Odd-carbon iso- and anteiso-branched acids showed only a threefold variation among individuals tested. Another study examined the possibility that genetics controls the proportions of iso-even fatty acids by analyzing the sebaceous wax esters of twins.[79] While the general population has large variations in the proportions of iso-even fatty acids, intrapair differences in 13 pairs of identical twins were found to be very small. It has been suggested that slight differences in the overall composition of the sebaceous fatty acid mixture could lead to unique, individual odors in humans.[76] Another study found that certain short chain fatty acids, such as iso-valeric acid (iso C_5), are responsible for "offensive" human odors.[80]

Phospholipids

Phospholipids, which are present in the membranes of sebaceous cells, are typically not found in surface sebum. Although epidermal cells have phospholipids, the stratum corneum is virtually devoid of them. This is most likely due to their degradation in the granular layer, a process that allows for re-absorption of essential nutrients, such as phosphorus and choline. In the epidermis, fatty acids liberated by this degradation process remain in the keratinizing cells and become partly esterified with cholesterol. A similar mechanism has been proposed for fatty acids liberated in the sebaceous glands. However, the lack of cholesterol diminishes the probability of fatty acid esterification. Likewise, a lack of glycerol limits the formation of tri-glycerides. The study concluded that these fatty acids are most likely reduced to fatty alcohols and then esterified to form wax esters.

Wax Esters

On average, wax esters comprise approximately 20 to 25% of adult skin surface lipids. Wax esters are compounds that contain a fatty acid esterified with a fatty alcohol. Free fatty alcohols have not been found in human skin surface lipids, possibly due to the inability of bacterial or epidermal lipases to hydrolyze wax esters.[80] A study of the fatty alcohol profile derived from wax esters reported a considerable variety of compounds, ranging from C_{18} to C_{27}, with the C_{20} chain being the most abundant.[81] Both iso- and anteiso-branched chain fatty alcohols were also found. In adult wax esters, the most common positional isomer was the Δ6-type, comprising 98.28% of detected mono-unsaturated acids.[82] Since wax esters are known to be of sebaceous origin, this evidence would indicate that fatty acids with the Δ6 double bond position are also of sebaceous gland origin, whereas those with Δ9-type are of epidermal origin. It was also reported that 26.7% of adult wax ester fatty acids were of a branched chain type. It is rare to find a wax ester that contains two fully saturated straight chain fatty acid components. One possible reason would be that the presence of unsaturation or branching makes it more likely that the resulting wax ester would be liquid at skin temperature.

Sterols

Sterol esters comprise approximately 2 to 3% of adult skin surface lipids. It has been proposed that sterol esters are not synthesized directly but rather are secondary products.[82] Two strains of bacteria, staphylococci and propi-onibacteria (minimally), have been found to esterify cholesterol.[83] There is also evidence that a major proportion of cholesterol esterification occurs on the skin surface.[84] Two to three times more sterols were found esterified on the skin surface than in the epidermis or in isolated stratum corneum. Free sterols are built up in the living portion of the epidermis and are then esterified primarily with sebum fatty acids, but also with some acids released from the epidermis during the late stages of keratinization. The fact that a high percentage of sterol esters (88.92%) have fatty acids with Δ6-type unsat-uration lends support to the hypothesis that the fatty acids comprising them are of sebaceous origin.[82] Approximately 20% of the fatty acids in sterol esters were reported to be of a branched chain type. Also, the levels of sterols and sterol esters have been reported to be higher in women than men. Cholesterol, cholest-5-en-3β-ol, is approximately 1 to 2% of adult surface lipids. Cholesterol, which is the most abundant steroid in animal tissues, is not believed to be synthesized in the sebaceous glands. It may be incorporated into sebum from the body's circulation (e.g., blood, plasma, etc.).

Squalene

Squalene comprises approximately 11 to 12% of adult lipids. Squalene, 2,6,10,15,19,23-hexamethyl-2,6,10,14,18,22-tetracosahexaene, cyclizes readily to form steroids in the body, including the steroid alcohols lanosterol and cholesterol. Squalene levels have been reported to be elevated in acne patients.[85,86] Patients with acne were reported to have a mean squalene content of 19.9%.[71] Squalene production in sebaceous glands has been found to vary depending on the gland size, with larger glands producing greater amounts of the lipid.

Miscellaneous Organic Compounds

A recent study of sweat collected from glass beads using cryofocusing GC/MS revealed a considerable number of trace organic compounds.[5] Most of the ketones detected were between butanone and decanone. However, trace amounts of the following were also found: 2-nonen-4-one, 2-decanone, 2-methoxy-2-octen-4-one, 6,10-dimethyl-5,9-undecadien-2-one, and possibly 3-hydroxyandrostan-11,17-dione. Numerous aldehydes were also detected, with the most prevalent being in the series between propanal and nonanal. Alkanes and alkenes below decane were not detected because of high volatility and amounts below instrument detection limits. Few amides were reported. However, a series of tertiary amines was detected ranging from N,N-dimethyl-1-dodecanamine to N,N-dimethyl-1-octadecanamine. Several heterocyclic compounds were detected, including substituted pyrroles, pyridines, piperidines, pyrazines, and furans. Nicotine was also detected in some samples. A number of haloalkanes were reported, including an incomplete series from chlorohexane to chlorohexadecane. Carbon disulfide and dimethyl sulfide and a few mercaptans, including thiomethane and 2-thiopropane, were also present. The chemical composition of secretions from the sebaceous gland is summarized in Table 3.6.

Apocrine Glands

The apocrine glands are another class of secretory glands. These glands are large coiled structures that are located close to hair follicles and their associated sebaceous glands (except where noted, the information in this section was

Table 3.6   A Summary of the Composition of Sebaceous Secretions

Organic (major)		Organic (trace)
Triglycerides	30–40%	Aldehydes
Free fatty acids	15–25%	Ketones
saturated	50%	Amines
monounsaturated	48%	Amides
polyunsaturated	2%	Alkanes
Wax esters	20–25%	Alkenes
Squalene	10–12%	Alcohols
Cholesterol	1–3%	Phospholipids
Cholesterol esters	2–3%	Pyrroles
		Pyridines
		Piperidines
		Pyrazines
		Furans
		Haloalkanes
		Mercaptans
		Sulfides

obtained from Robertshaw[87]). They are localized primarily in the axillary and perineal areas. The excretory portion of these glands takes the form of a huge intertwined coil that can extend well into the sub-dermal fatty layer.[2] The duct leaving the coil takes a more or less vertical path parallel to an adjacent hair follicle into which it opens at a point above the hair's sebaceous gland.

Few studies have been made to analyze the secretions emanating from the apocrine glands. Detailed analysis of apocrine secretions is complicated by contamination from eccrine and sebaceous glands. One of the few studies done on human apocrine secretions found a substance that was milky in appearance and dried to a plastic-like solid.[88] This material fluoresced and had a variable odor. One source reported several substances isolated from apocrine secretions, including proteins, carbohydrates, cholesterol, and iron.[89] C_{19}-steroid sulfates and $\Delta 16$-steroids (e.g., 5α-androst-16-en-3α-ol and 5α-androst-16-en-3-one) have also been reported.[90,91]

Variation of Sebum Composition with Age of Donor

It has been well established that the chemical content of sweat changes from birth to puberty and up through old age. Rates of sebum excretion, amounts of certain fatty acids, the ratio of wax esters to cholesterol, and cholesterol esters have been found to change.[92] Some components do not show any significant difference with age. Table 3.7 compares the variation in surface lipid composition by age group.[93]

Table 3.7   Changes in Surface Lipid Composition with Age

Age	Free Fatty Acids	Triglycerides	Wax Esters	Cholesterol	Cholesterol Esters	Squalene
5 days	1.5	51.9	26.7	2.5	6.1	9.9
1 month–2 years	20.8	38.4	17.6	3.7	10.3	9.4
2–4 years	22.9	49.6	8.0	4.2	8.9	6.2
4–8 years	15.9	45.6	6.9	7.2	14.6	7.7
8–10 years	17.8	47.4	17.8	3.2	5.7	8.3
10–15 years	18.8	42.9	23.6	1.8	4.2	8.4
18–45 years	16.4	41.0	25.0	1.4	2.1	12.0

Source: Ramasastry, P., Downing, D. T., Pochi, P. E., and Strauss, J. S., Chemical composition of human skin surface lipids from birth to puberty, *J. Invest. Dermatol.,* 54(2), 143, 1970. With permission.

Newborns

One study[94] of neonatal skin surface lipids (from vernix caseosa, a grayish-white substance that covers the skin of the fetus and newborn) reported the following lipid classes and amounts: sterol esters, 35%; triglycerides, 26%; wax esters, 12%; squalene, 9%; free sterols, 9%; diesters, 7%; and miscellaneous lipids, 4%. These values show more similarity to adult sebum profiles than to young children. The composition of wax ester fatty acids (with regard to the chain type and the amount of saturated and unsaturated) in vernix caseosa has been found to be quite similar to that of adults.[82] However, the amount of sterol esters showed considerable difference. In adults, sterol esters constituted approximately 2.81% of the skin surface lipids, whereas vernix caseosa contained 25.4%. The large percentage of high molecular weight sterol esters in vernix caseosa probably helps to provide a waxy coating of low water solubility that prevents excessive wetting of fetal skin. Fatty acids in vernix caseosa were predominantly saturated (65%) while adult samples were primarily mono-unsaturated (54%). A study of vernix caseosa by Miettienen and Lukkäinen found at least eight additional sterols besides cholesterol, including lanosterol.[95]

The vernix caseosa of male fetuses contained much more sebum than those of female fetuses, which had a higher proportion of epidermal lipids.[75] The differences were significant enough to be able to distinguish the sex of the fetus based on the thin layer chromatogram of lipids extracted from the vernix caseosa. Although androgen levels are high in newborns, the level of hormones (as well as sebum production) drops rapidly during subsequent months.[96] This leads to a dramatic change in the amount and composition of excreted lipids.

Young Children

The sebum composition of children aged 2 to 8 years old is dominated by epidermal lipids (e.g., cholesterol and its esters).[93] Typically, the amounts of wax esters and squalene in young children were measured to be approximately one third and one half of adult levels, respectively. By the ages of 8 to 10 years, the levels rose to about two thirds of adult levels. Adult levels were reached between the ages of 10 to 15 years. Median wax ester secretion rates were found to be between 10 to 50 µg/10 cm^2 per 3-hr collection period.[97] Levels of cholesterol and cholesterol ester secretion were found to vary little between children, with the average amount secreted being 11.0 ± 4.5 and 16.6 ± 8.7 µg/10 cm^2 per 3-hr period. Another study measured the total sebum production rate in children.[43] The rates varied in females from 0.60 mg lipid (per 10 cm^2 area per 3-hr period) for 7 year olds to 1.29 mg for 14 year olds. For males the values varied between 0.58 mg for 9 year olds to 2.17 mg for 16 year olds. However, in late childhood, as sebum secretion begins to increase, the amount of wax esters (which are of sebaceous origin) increased relative to cholesterol and cholesterol esters (which are of epidermal origin).

There are significant changes in the relative concentrations of the major fatty acids constituting the triglyceride and wax ester fraction of children's sebum.[98] The levels of C_{15} fatty acids increased from 3% in the pre-pubertal group to 9% in the pubertal group. The levels of $C_{16:1}$ fatty acids increased to between 20 to 40% while C_{18}, $C_{18:1}$, and $C_{18:2}$ sharply declined. Also, the ratio of wax esters to cholesterol and cholesterol esters begins to increase between the ages of 7 and 8 and reaches a more "adult" profile by age 10 or 11.[99] Sebum secretion rates continue to increase during adolescence until about age 17 or 18, when a relatively stable phase is achieved.[100] Once maturity has been achieved, it appears that little changes occur in sebaceous gland activity until middle age.

Adolescents

At the onset of puberty, hormone-mediated sebaceous gland enlargement occurs and sebum production increases significantly. It has been suggested that during puberty the proportion of endogenously synthesized sebaceous lipids (characterized by squalene, wax esters, and Δ6 fatty acids) increases while the proportion of exogenous-type (characterized by cholesterol, Δ9 fatty acids, and linoleic acid) decreases. This may be explained by the fact that sebaceous cells have a relatively constant amount of exogenous-type lipid, but they synthesize variable amounts of the endogenously synthesized sebaceous-type lipids. The amount synthesized is directly related to the gland's activity. The more active the gland, the more dilute the exogenous lipids become due to excess production of sebaceous-type lipids.

In one study, the levels of sebum production (measured as milligrams of lipid collected on a 10-cm^2 patch of skin over 3 hr) of subjects of varying age were measured.[43] The values obtained for adolescent males and females were 2.35 mg and 2.17 mg (per 10-cm^2 area per 3-hr period), respectively. The largest jump in sebum production occurred between the ages of 12 and 13 in both males and females. The mean sebum levels differed significantly in certain age cohorts for subjects with and without acne. In addition, patients suffering from acne vulgaris were found to possess a greater amount of lipolytic agents than those patients without acne, which might explain the reported elevated fatty acid levels.[101] The difference between subject males aged 15 to 19 with and without acne was 2.80 mg and 1.73 mg. For females 15 to 19, the values were 2.64 mg and 1.85 mg. In the 20 to 29 age cohort, the values for males were 2.87 mg and 2.37 mg; for females the values were 2.58 mg and 1.77 mg.

Post-Adolescence

Sebum production continues with age, peaking during the mid thirties and then begins to decline in middle age. In old age, levels of sebum may drop to near pre-puberty levels. One study of sebaceous wax esters found that secretions decreased about 23% per decade in men and about 32% in women.[102] This is in contrast to some findings that show the rates remain somewhat stable.[43,103] Overall, it appears that no significant changes occur in sebum composition until much later in life. A study of sebum secretion rates of four adult males by gravimetry found a range of rates from 2.15 to 4.47 mg/10 cm^2 per 3-hr period.[104] In another study, the sebum production rates for males and females were reported for 20 to 29 year olds, 2.48 mg and 2.03 mg; 30 to 39 year olds, 2.52 mg and 2.04 mg; 40 to 49 year olds, 2.39 mg and 1.86 mg; and 50 to 69 year olds, 2.42 mg and 1.10 mg.[43]

The principal cause for the decrease in sebum gland activity with age is diminished hormonal stimulation.[100] Testosterone levels in men begin to decrease significantly between the age of 50 to 60 years. Sebaceous gland activity typically does not decrease until a decade or so later. In women, the decrease is observed a decade or so sooner than in men. The sebum production rates for males and females have been reported to be 1.69 mg and 0.85 mg, respectively, for subjects over age 70.[43] Interestingly, some studies have shown that, although sebaceous gland activity decreases with age, the glands themselves become larger rather than smaller.[105] It also appears that with advancing age, the proportion of Δ9-type unsaturated fatty acids increases.[75]

The Composition of Latent Print Residue

Although considerable research has been conducted on sweat samples, comparatively little data are available on the content of latent print residues. The components of sweat transferred to different surfaces may differ from that found on the surface of skin. The law enforcement community began to examine latent print residues critically and scientifically in the late 1960s. The foundation work in this area was sponsored by the United Kingdom Home Office and conducted by the Atomic Weapons Research Establishment (AWRE) and the Atomic Energy Research Establishment (AERE). These research efforts concentrated on analyzing the chemical components of latent print deposits.

United Kingdom Home Office

The United Kingdom Home Office sponsored a considerable number of research projects over the past 35 years. These projects were carried out in cooperation with the Central Research Establishment (CRE) and the Police Scientific Development Branch (PSDB), which was formerly known as the Scientific Research and Development Branch (SRDB). These efforts represented, in many cases, the first attempt to perform a detailed study and analysis of visualization methods as well as the composition of print residue.

During the mid to late 1960s, a series of projects were done to investigate the organic and inorganic substances present in a latent print. One study examined the water soluble components and reported the following substances (and approximate amounts): chloride, 1 to 15 µg; calcium, 0.03 to 0.3 µg; sulfur, 0.02 to 0.2 µg; urea, 0.4 to 1.8 µg; lactic acid, 9 to 10 µg; amino acids, 1 µg; phenol, 0.06 to 0.25 µg; sodium, 0.2 to 6.9 µg; potassium, 0.2 to 5.0 µg; and ammonia, 0.2 to 0.3 µg.[106] A subsequent study examined the change in chloride content in fingerprints as a factor of the donor's age.[107] Results indicated that the chloride content decreased with advancing age. In addition, the donor's occupation also appeared to be a factor. Office workers were found to have the highest amounts of chloride followed by laboratory workers and persons employed in workshops. Differences were also found between left and right hands as well for individual fingers. Statistically, digits on left hands were found to have a higher chloride content, presumably because most of the donors were right handed. Thumbs had the lowest amount of chloride while little fingers had the highest. However, because of a significant variation present within the same individual, these trends were not always observed.

The Home Office also conducted detailed studies of the lipid (or water-insoluble) portion of latent prints, with an emphasis on the free fatty acid content.[108] Palmitic acid was found to be the most abundant fatty acid. In general, the most abundant acids were $C_{18}/C_{18:1}$ + squalene followed by $C_{16}/C_{16:1}$, $C_{14}/C_{14:1}$, C_{15}, and $C_{12}/C_{12:1}$. Another study confirmed that palmitic, stearic, and palmitoleic acids were the most abundant fatty acids.[72] This study also addressed the contribution of cosmetics present in samples from female volunteers. They found that the presence of cosmetics might introduce peaks in the early portion of the chromatogram (e.g., decanoic acid). The mean values obtained for the amounts of the various lipid classes found in forehead samples are reported in Table 3.5.[72] Those values can be compared with the following average values obtained from fingers: squalene, 14.6%; cholesterol, 3.8%; free fatty acids, 37.6%; wax esters (with diglycerides), 25%; and triglycerides (with monoglycerides and cholesterol esters), 21%. Although some differences are to be found in the free fatty acid and glyceride values, these discrepancies can be attributed to individual variations in bacterial lipase activity. Additional studies, using gas-liquid chromatography, detected over 40 different organic constituents in sebaceous secretions. The results, expressed as general lipid classes, are reported in Table 3.5.[3] The report stressed that the sebaceous secretions are very important with regard to fingerprint visualization because they are more stable to water than the principal components of eccrine sweat.

Oak Ridge National Laboratory

A 1993 child abduction case in Tennessee inspired a local police criminalist and a chemist from the Oak Ridge National Laboratory (ORNL) to team up and analyze fingerprint residues.[109-111] Knoxville Police criminalist Art Bohanan observed that children's fingerprints left on nonporous surfaces (such as a vinyl car seat) did not seem to last for more than a day or two. Subsequent analyses performed by Buchanan et al. at ORNL indicated a significant difference in the chemical composition of children's and adults' print residues.[112,113] Children's prints contained more volatile components that would not remain in the deposit for more than a couple of days (depending on the environmental conditions). In both children and adults, fatty acids (as methyl esters) in the C_{12} to C_{24} range were detected. Although cholesterol was found in prints from children and adults, the amount was significantly higher in children. There were differences detected between samples from male and female children, although these compounds were not identified. The most abundant compound detected in the isopropyl alcohol extracted material of adults was squalene. In addition, several long chain fatty acid esters were identified, including pentadecanoic acid dodecyl ester, and the undecyl, tridecyl, pentadecyl, heptadecyl, and octadecyl esters of hexadecanoic acid.

Subsequent studies conducted at the ORNL yielded some unusual results.[114] Nicotine was detected in some of the adult samples. Although initially dismissed as environmental contamination caused by handling tobacco products or exposure to second-hand tobacco smoke, a subsequent analysis of a sample obtained from an individual who had quit smoking several weeks before (but had been chewing nicotine gum) showed traces of nicotine. While unexpected, this result is not unprecedented. Robinson et al. reported the presence of nicotine, as well as morphine and alcohol, in sweat in 1954.[115] Traces of steroids were also observed in some of the fingerprint samples. ORNL plans to direct future efforts toward the ability to detect trace amounts of special target compounds (e.g., illegal drugs and their metabolites) in latent print residues to provide investigative leads for law enforcement purposes. If successful, such noninvasive methods could potentially eliminate the need to obtain biologically hazardous samples such as blood or urine.

Pacific Northwest National Laboratory

With funding obtained from the Technical Support Working Group (TSWG is an interagency working group that funds counter terrorism projects), the U.S. Secret Service (USSS) teamed up with the Pacific Northwest National Laboratory (PNNL) to conduct a research project to investigate the composition of latent print residue. The most critical aspect of this project was to investigate how latent print residue changes over a period of time. Fingerprint samples from 79 volunteers, ranging in age from 3 to 60 years old, were analyzed. Volunteers placed fingerprints on filter paper samples. The samples were then stored at ambient conditions before being extracted. After derivatization, the samples were analyzed by gas chromatography/mass spectrometry.

The results of this study were in agreement with the data obtained at the ORNL.[116] Several samples analyzed appeared to be contaminated by external sources of lipids, such as hand lotions, cosmetics, and soaps. Removing all traces of these contaminants proved difficult. The data obtained from the aging of fingerprint residues were also reported. As expected, most of the unsaturated lipids (e.g., squalene and fatty acids such as oleic and palmitoleic) tended to diminish substantially within the 30-day period, with significant losses during the first week noted. Since lipids like squalene and oleic acid are liquid at room temperature, they provide an environment suitable for partitioning of certain lipid-specific visualization reagents. Once they have been modified and the majority of the water content of the print has evaporated, the print dries out and is no longer amenable to lipid partitioning reagents. For example, reagents like Nile red, which partition into the lipid layer, are generally ineffective on prints more than a few days old.

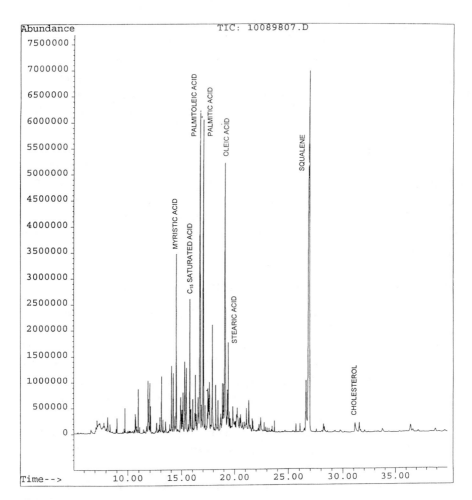

Figure 3.4a A chromatogram of a fingerprint deposit extracted and analyzed shortly after deposition.

In contrast, saturated compounds (e.g., palmitic and stearic acids) remained relatively unchanged during the same time period. Wax esters also remained relatively stable. Overall, as the sample fingerprint aged, compounds in the low molecular weight range began to form. These compounds would be consistent with lighter molecular weight saturated acids (e.g., nonanoic acid) and diacids (e.g., nonandioic acid). Figures 3.4a and 3.4b are chromatograms of samples taken from the same donor and analyzed initially and 60 days later. Overall, the results of the study indicate that saturated compounds dominate aged samples. Unfortunately, these compounds do not make good targets for chemical reagents.

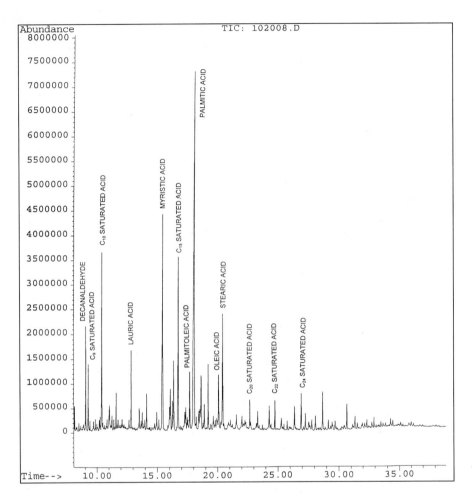

Figure 3.4b A chromatogram of the same fingerprint deposit extracted and analyzed 60 days after deposition.

Savannah River Technical Center Research

Another project was recently begun at the Savannah River Technical Center (SRTC) in cooperation with the USSS to analyze latent print residue and how it changes with time. With funding from both the TSWG and Department of Energy, the SRTC is looking into characterizing the degradation products formed as the latent print residue ages to determine if any of these compounds may be suitable for chemical visualization reagents. The SRTC is focusing on the formation of hydroperoxides, one class of breakdown products formed as lipids oxidize. A series of standard lipids representative of the various lipid classes found in a latent print was used. These included compounds typically found in print residue, including cholesterol, triglycerides, fatty acids, wax esters, cholesterol esters, and catalyze the reaction between triplet a sensitizer (protoporphyrin IX dimethyl ester, 0.01% of the overall mixture). The sensitizer was added to oxygen and light to form singlet oxygen (a highly reactive species). These compounds were placed on a glass slide and aged in various conditions (e.g., light/no light and/or indoors/outdoors). Like PNNL, the SRTC found that unsaturated compounds are rapidly depleted from samples even in cool, dark storage conditions. An experiment involving the aging of squalene on a glass slide found that after one month of exposure to ambient conditions, 10% of the sample was composed of hydroperoxides. The SRTC is looking into chemiluminescent methods for visualizing the hydroperoxides formed as fingerprints age.

Forensic Science Service

Recent work done at the Home Office Forensic Science Service (FSS), Metropolitan Laboratory, London, England, involved the use of thin layer chromatography (TLC) to directly separate sebum-rich fingerprints from five donors left on TLC plates.[117] The FSS has recently updated this work.[118,119] Although the use of TLC to analyze latent print residues is not new,[120,121] the direct separation and characterization of a deposited print was unique. The ultimate goal of these experiments was to react the separated classes of latent print residue with different chemical reagents. Additional studies are being planned in cooperation with the Police Science and Criminology Institute, University of Lausanne, Switzerland. In addition, the FSS has been working on trying to identify the compound(s) responsible for inherent luminescence observed in some latent prints. Efforts using TLC, GC/MS, and Raman spectroscopy have not provided a definitive answer, but one leading candidate is bilirubin. The FSS suggested that bacteria, present on the skin, might be involved. Bacteria are known to produce porphyrins (intermediates in the synthesis of heme), which fluoresce in the visible region. The most likely candidate for inherent luminescence, bilirubin, is the breakdown product of heme.

Currently, a collaborative effort, funded by the TSWG, is underway between the USSS and FSS to investigate the effect of light conditions on the aging of print residues. The project will analyze samples from five male donors, aged 24 to 34, at a sampling interval of 0 (shortly after deposition), 3, 7, 9, 10, 15, and 20 days. The samples will also be cut in half and then subjected to different lighting conditions while at constant temperature and humidity. Although the study is not complete, some of the initial results are consistent with data generated by PNNL. There appear to be significant differences in decomposition rates for samples in the different lighting conditions. It would be of interest, if future funding is available, to evaluate the impact of other environmental conditions on latent print decomposition products and rate.

DNA From Latent Prints

Another important component of latent print residue is deoxyribonucleic acid (DNA). It is not surprising that a significant amount of DNA is often present in visible blood prints. However, it can also be deposited in non-blood latent print residue from the epidermal cells that are continuously sloughed off the skin surface through rubbing of the skin or through direct contact with a substrate. In the past, an examiner was often forced to decide what evidence is more important, the DNA or the ridge detail. Advances in DNA technology have made this decision easier since fewer latent print visualization processes inhibit sample analyses. The use of polymerase chain reaction (PCR) analysis has allowed subnanogram quantities of DNA to be detected, amplified, and analyzed. In addition, "lab on a chip" technology will soon allow for extremely fast analysis and identification at the crime scene.[122-125] Examiners are now also able to extract DNA in situations previously considered improbable. Sweet et al. reported that identifiable DNA was obtained from a bite mark on skin from a victim who had been drowned.[126] Such advances will begin to highlight the need to rapidly and reliably extract, analyze, and identify DNA recovered from latent prints.

DNA From Blood Prints and Stains

The recovery of DNA from visible blood prints and latent blood prints developed by chemical reagents has been well documented. Most studies found that only a few visualization reagents inhibit DNA analysis. A study of envelopes, stamps, and cigarette butts by Presley et al. using Chelex extraction and PCR HLA DQ alpha typing found negative DNA results after processing with PD.[127] A subsequent study by Walls also found that physical developer adversely affected DNA analysis.[128] However, it was reported that the problem with PD could be overcome by using organic extraction rather than Chelex. Stein et al. studied the effect of black powder, ninhydrin, cyanoacrylate fuming, and gentian violet on 1-, 14-, and 56-day-old bloodstains and saliva samples. They found that none of the latent print visualization treatments adversely affected DNA extraction, quality, or typing using restriction fragment length polymorphism (RFLP) or PCR-short tandem repeat (STR).[129] Another study examined the effects of cyanoacrylate (CA) fuming and forensic light sources on bloodstains with subsequent analysis of DNA using RFLP.[130] No adverse effects were reported. Newall et al. investigated the effect of CA fuming on blood prints and also found no inhibition.[131] Another light source study was conducted by Andersen and Bramble.[132] They found that exposure of DNA to 255-nm shortwave UV radiation (1 mW/cm^2 at a distance of 25 to 35 cm) for as little as 30 sec could drastically reduce the chances of recovering and identifying DNA using PCR-STR analysis.

A study of the effect of seven different blood reagents (amido black, DFO, ninhydrin, Hungarian Red, Crowle's Double Stain, luminol, and Leucomalachite Green) on DNA recovered from diluted blood prints on several porous and nonporous substrates and analyzed using the PCR-STR/Profiler Plus multiplex system found no adverse results.[133] Miller reported success with these reagents with a blood dilution factor of up to 1:10,000.[134] The report also mentioned that as the length of exposure to the reagents and the extent of dilution of the blood sample increased (beyond 1:10,000), the possibility of recovering DNA diminished significantly. A similar result for luminol was reported by Gross et al.[135] Champod reported on PCR-STR analysis work done by Brignoli and Coquoz that found difficulties with LMG and o-tolidine, but not with MMD.[136] Hochmeister et al. reported a similar result for LMG and o-tolidine using RFLP analysis.[137] Roux et al. also looked at the effect of visualization reagents on blood prints.[138] MMD, magnetic fingerprint powder, and UV radiation were found to interfere with PCR DNA analysis. The study also found that DFO, Sticky-side powder, ninhydrin with secondary metal salt treatment, amido black, diaminobenzidine, luminol, CA with rhodamine 6G, and black powder could adversely affect recovery and analysis of DNA using the D1S80 system primers. Most of these problems were resolved by using CTT system primers. Their study also indicated problems with the blood reagent benzidine dissolved in glacial acetic acid.

DNA From Developed Latent Prints

Very few studies have been published that examine the possibility of recovering DNA from treated latent prints (rather than treated bloodstains or blood prints). Recently, Zamir et al. investigated the effect of DFO treatment of latent prints on DNA analysis and found that it had no adverse effect.[139] Another related issue involves the possibility of recovering DNA from undeveloped fingerprints left on commonly handled objects. This issue was highlighted by van Oorschot and Jones in the journal *Nature* in 1997.[140] The quantity of DNA recovered from objects like a car key, briefcase handle, and a telephone handset was found to be sufficient to identify the person who had handled the item. In some cases DNA transferred from another source (a secondary transfer) was detected and identified. However, a similar study done by the Royal Canadian Mounted Police (RCMP) found that such secondary transfers can occur but are rare.[141] Another study by Ladd et al. found that primary transfer was not always detected and that no secondary transfer occurred with their samples.[142]

A subsequent letter in *Nature* reported success in using PCR-STR to obtain profiles from single cells using six forensic STR markers.[143] DNA was successfully amplified in 91% of the cells tested and a full DNA profile was obtained in 50% of those cases. This sort of success ultimately leads to the question of whether DNA could be recovered from a smeared or partial, developed print that was not of identification value. Two issues are critical. Do latent prints contain a sufficient number of cells and what effect do all of the latent print visualization techniques have on DNA analysis? Two projects funded by the TSWG in cooperation with the USSS are currently underway to begin exploring both concerns. Dr. Mark Batzer, from The Louisiana State University Medical Center (LSUMC), New Orleans, LA, is working on quantifying the amount of cellular material present in a latent print as well as using nuclear DNA methods to analyze and identify it. Dr. Robert Bever, of the Bode Technology Group, Springfield, VA, is working on optimizing mitochondrial DNA (mtDNA) techniques for partial latent prints. Since there are inherently several orders of magnitude more copies of mtDNA present in a cell, the likelihood of finding it is better in very small or degraded samples.

DNA is also capable of yielding more than just a strict identification or elimination of a suspect. The sex and geographic origin of the individual can now be determined from DNA.[144-146] DNA markers that can yield information about hair color, height, and other morphological characteristics are also being explored. This was evident at the recent Millennium Conference on Forensic Human Identification sponsored by the Forensic Science Service, which was held in London in October 1999.[147-150] Interestingly, this technology is likely to be involved in settling a controversy surrounding Beethoven's origin.[151]

Miscellaneous Compounds and Contaminants

Many environmental contaminants have been detected both in analyses of sweat and fingerprint residues. Caution must be exercised in determining whether such compounds might indeed be contaminants or as compounds derived from an endogenous source. There may be some overlap between compounds present in the contaminant and ones from an endogenous source, which could lead to overestimates of the quantity of such compounds. Bernier et al. reported a significant amount of glycerol in one sample.[5] This was later found to be caused by the use of hair gel by one of the volunteers. Benzene, toluene, styrene, and alkyl substituted benzenes were also detected but considered as exogenous contaminants. A number of siloxanes, believed to be related to the column stationary phase, and phthalates were also detected. Hexamethylcyclotrisiloxane and octamethylcyclotetrasiloxane were the two primary siloxane compounds. In addition, 1,1-difluoroethane was one of the most intense peaks detected. This compound is a component of Dust-Off, a product used to cool the glass injection port liner between runs.

The study by PNNL also detected several exogenous contaminants, including acetaminophen and n-butylphenylsulfonamide, a detergent found in gasoline. A number of hydrocarbons and glycerol esters were detected and attributed to contamination by cosmetics or other personal hygiene products. Typical examples of contaminant hydrocarbons include a series from tricosane to nonacosane, eitriacontane, and dotriacontane. Examples of esters include the 3,4-methoxyphenyl-2-ethylhexyl ester of propenoic acid and glyceryl trioctyl ester.

Conclusions

Latent print residue is a complex mixture of many different types of substances. Derived primarily from the three major secretory glands, sweat is deposited on virtually every surface touched by hands. Future efforts must continue to focus on determining how latent print residue adheres to, interacts with, and changes with time on different surfaces. This information is critical to understanding not only how reagents used to visualize latent prints work, but also to provide better guidance in modifying existing reagents and developing new ones.

Interestingly, there have been efforts in this past decade by several laboratories to produce "artificial sweat." Both the German Bundeskriminalamt (BKA) and the FSS have worked on creating a way of reproducibly creating a standard latent print. The applications for such a "standard latent print" are numerous. With the advent of laboratory accreditation guidelines established by organizations such as the American Society of Crime Laboratory Directors (ASCLD-LAB) and the International Organization for Standardization (ISO), the use of a "standard latent print" becomes critical in evaluating the effectiveness of visualization reagents that are routinely used in the evidence processing laboratory, as well as in the area of comparative testing and evaluation of new reagents worldwide. In the near future, the TSWG will be providing funding to build upon the groundwork established by the BKA and FSS. This project will also take advantage of the knowledge gained by the recent research efforts that have examined the chemical composition of recent and aged latent print residues.

References

1. Odland, G. F., Structure of the skin. In Goldsmith, L. A., Ed. *Physiology, Biochemistry, and Molecular Biology of the Skin. 2nd ed.* New York: Oxford University Press, 1991.

2. Vincent, P. G., Skin. A brief look under the surface. *Fingerprint Whorld,* 11(41), 8-12, 1985.

3. Goode, G. C. and Morris, J. R., Latent fingerprints: a review of their origin, composition and methods for detection. *AWRE Report No. 022/83,* 1983.

4. Bernier, U. R., Booth, M. M., and Yost, R. A., Analysis of human skin emanations by gas chromatography/mass spectrometry. 1. Thermal desorption of attractants for the yellow fever mosquito (*Aedes aegypti*) from handled glass beads. *Anal. Chem.,* 71, 1-7, 1999.

5. Bernier, U. R., Kline, D. L., Barnard, D. R., Schreck, C. E., and Yost, R. A., Analysis of human skin emanations by gas chromatography/mass spectrometry. 2. Identification of volatile compounds that are candidate attractants for the yellow fever mosquito (*Aedes aegypti*). *Anal. Chem.,* 72(4), 747-756, 2000.

6. Quinton, P. M., Sweating and its disorders. *Annu. Rev. Med.,* 34, 429-452, 1983.

7. Sato, K. and Dobson, R. L., Regional and individual variations in the function of the human eccrine sweat gland. *J. Invest. Dermatol.,* 54, 443-449, 1970.

8. Berglund, L. G., Gallagher, R. R., and McNall, P. E., Simulation of the thermal effects of dissolved materials in human sweat. *Comput. Biomed. Res.,* 6, 127-138, 1973.

9. Jensen, O., Nielsen, E., Rusters. The corrosive action of palmar sweat. II. Physical and chemical factors in palmar hyperhidrosis. *Acta Dermatovener (Stockholm),* 59, 139-143, 1979.

10. Cage, G. W., Wolfe, S. M., Thompson, R. H., and Gordon, R. S., Effects of water intake on composition of thermal sweat in normal human volunteers. *J. Appl. Physiol.,* 29, 687-690, 1970.

11. Brusilow, S. W. and Gordes, E. H., Ammonia secretion in sweat. *Amer. J. Physiol.,* 214, 513-517, 1967.

12. Mitchell, H. H. and Hamilton, T. S., The dermal excretion under controlled environmental conditions of nitrogen and minerals in human subjects, with particular reference to calcium and iron. *J. Biol. Chem.,* 178, 360, 1949.

13. Sato, K., The physiology, pharmacology, and biochemistry of the eccrine sweat gland. *Rev. Physiol. Biochem. Pharmacol.,* 79, 52-131, 1979.

14. Bayford, F., Sweat. *Fingerprint Whorld,* 1, 42-43, 1976.

15. Olsen, R. D., The chemical composition of palmar sweat. *Fing. Ident. Mag.,* 53(10), 4, 1972.

16. Sato, K., Feibleman, C., and Dobson, R. L., The electrolyte composition of pharmacologically and thermally stimulated sweat: a comparative study. *J. Invest. Dermatol.,* 55, 433-438, 1970.

17. Seutter, E., Goedhart-De Groot, N., Sutorius, H. M., and Urselmann, E. J. M., The quantitative analysis of some constituents of crude sweat. *Dermatologica*, 141, 226-233, 1970.

18. Schultz, I. J., Micropuncture studies of the sweat formation in cystic fibrosis patients. *J. Clin. Invest.*, 48, 1470–1477, 1969.

19. Verde, T., Shephard, R. J., Corey, P., and Moore, R., Sweat composition in exercise and in heat. *J. Appl. Phys. Respir. Environ. Exerc. Phys.*, 53, 1540–1545, 1982.

20. Kaiser, D. and Drack, E., Diminished excretion of bicarbonate from the single sweat gland of patients with cystic fibrosis of the pancreas. *Eur. J. Clin. Invest.*, 4, 261-265, 1974.

21. Miklaszewska, M., Free amino acids of eccrine sweat. Method. *Pol. Med. J.*, 7, 617-623, 1968.

22. Miklaszewska, M., Comparative studies of free amino acids of eccrine sweat and plasma. *Pol. Med. J.*, 7, 1313–1318, 1968.

23. Liappis, N., Kelderbacher, S. D., Kesseler, K., and Bantzer, P., Quantitative study of free amino acids in human eccrine sweat excreted from the forearms of healthy trained and untrained men during exercise. *Eur. J. Appl. Physiol.*, 42, 227-234, 1979.

24. Gitlitz, P. H., Sunderman, F. W., and Hohnadel, D. C., Ion-exchange chromatography of amino acids in sweat collected from healthy subjects during sauna bathing. *Clin. Chem.*, 20, 1305–1312, 1974.

25. Coltman, C. A., Rowe, N. J., and Atwell, R. J., The amino acid content of sweat in normal adults. *Am. J. Clin. Nutr.*, 18, 373-378, 1966.

26. Jenkinson, D., Mabon, R. M., and Manson, W., Sweat proteins. *Br. J. Dermatol.*, 90, 175-181, 1974.

27. Hadorn, B., Hanimann, F., Anders, P., Curtius, H-Ch, and Halverson, R., Free amino acids in human sweat from different parts of the body. *Nature*, 215, 416-417, 1967.

28. Hamilton, P. B., Amino-acids on hands. *Nature*, 205, 284-285, 1965.

29. Oro, J. and Skewes, H. B., Free amino-acids on human fingers: the question of contamination in microanalysis. *Nature*, 207, 1042–1045, 1965.

30. Liappis, N. and Hungerland, H., The trace amino acid pattern in human eccrine sweat. *Clin. Chim. Acta*, 48, 233-236, 1973.

31. Marshall, T., Analysis of human sweat proteins by two-dimensional electrophoresis and ultrasensitive silver staining. *Anal. Biochem.*, 139, 506-509, 1984.

32. Nakayashiki, N., Sweat protein components tested by SDS-polyacrylamide gel electrophoresis followed by immunoblotting. *J. Exp. Med.*, 161, 25-31, 1990.

33. Uyttendaele, M., De Groote, M., Blaton, V., and Peeters, H., Analysis of the proteins in sweat and urine by agarose-gel isotachophoresis. *J. Chromatogr.*, 132, 261-266, 1977.

34. Takemura, T., Wertz, P. W., and Sato, K., Free fatty acids and sterols in human eccrine sweat. *Br. J. Dermatol.*, 120, 43-47, 1989.

35. Boysen, T. C., Yanagawa, S., Sato, F., and Sato, K., A modified anaerobic method of sweat collection. *J. Appl. Physiol.*, 56, 1302–1307, 1984.

36. Lobitz, W. C., and Mason, H. L., Chemistry of palmar sweat. VII. Discussion of studies on chloride, urea, glucose, uric acid, ammonia nitrogen, and creatinine. *Arch. Dermatol. Syph.*, 57, 908, 1948.

37. Förström, L., Goldyne, M. E., and Winkelmann, R. K., IgE in human eccrine sweat. *J. Invest. Dermatol.*, 64, 156-157, 1975.

38. Johnson, H. L. and Maibach, H. I., Drug excretion in human eccrine sweat. *J. Invest. Dermatol.*, 56, 182-188, 1971.

39. Vree, T. B., Muskens, A. T. J. M., and van Rossum, J. M., Excretion of amphetamines in human sweat. *Arch. Int. Pharmacodyn.*, 199, 311-317, 1972.

40. Naitoh, K., Inai, Y., and Hirabayashi, T., Direct temperature-controlled trapping system and its use for the gas chromatographic determination of organic vapor released from human skin. *Anal. Chem.*, 72(13), 2797–2801, 2000.

41. Strauss, J. S., Downing, D. T., Ebling, F. J., and Stewart, M. E., Sebaceous glands. In Goldsmith LA, Ed. *Physiology, Biochemistry, and Molecular Biology of the Skin, 2nd ed.* New York: Oxford University Press, 1991.

42. Nikkari, T., Comparative chemistry of sebum, *J. Invest. Dermatol.*, 62, 257-267, 1974.

43. Pochi, P. E. and Strauss, J. S., Endocrinologic control of the development and activity of the human sebaceous gland. *J. Invest. Dermatol.*, 62, 191-201, 1974.

44. Greene, R. S., Downing, D. T., Pochi, P. E., and Strauss, J. S., Anatomical variation in the amount and composition of human skin surface lipid. *J. Invest. Dermatol.*, 54, 246, 1970.

45. Shuster, S. and Thody, A. J., The control and measurement of sebum secretion. *J. Invest. Dermatol.*, 62, 172-190, 1974.

46. Ebling, F. J., Hormonal control and methods of measuring sebaceous gland activity. *J. Invest. Dermatol.*, 62, 161-171, 1974.

47. Hamilton, J. B. and Mestler, G. E., Low values for sebum in eunuchs and oophorectomized women. *Proc. Soc. Exp. Biol. Med.*, 112, 374-378, 1963.

48. Pochi, P. E., Strauss, J. S., and Mescon, H., Sebum excretion and urinary fractional 17-ketosteroid and total 17-hydroxycorticoid excretion in male castrates. *J. Invest. Dermatol.*, 39, 475-483, 1962.

49. Jarrett, A., The effects of progesterone and testosterone on the surface sebum of acne vulgaris. *Br. J. Dermatol.*, 67, 102-116, 1959.

50. Strauss, J. S. and Pochi, P. E., The human sebaceous gland: its regulation by steroidal hormones and its use as an end organ for assaying androgenicity *in vivo*. *Recent Progr. Horm. Res.*, 19, 385-444, 1963.

51. Oertel, G. W. and Treiber, L., Metabolism and excretion of C_{19}- and C_{18}-steroids by human skin. *Eur. J. Biochem.*, 7, 234-238, 1969.

52. Downing, D. T., Strauss, J. S., Norton, L. A., Pochi, P. E., and Stewart, M. E., The time course of lipid formation in human sebaceous glands. *J. Invest. Dermatol.*, 69, 407-412, 1977.

53. Stewart, M. E., Steele, W. A., and Downing, D. T., Changes in the relative amounts of endogenous and exogenous fatty acids in sebaceous lipids during early adolescence. *J. Invest. Dermatol.*, 92, 371-378, 1989.

54. Downing, D. T., Lipolysis by human skin surface debris in organic solvents. *J. Invest. Dermatol.*, 54, 395-398, 1970.

55. Reisner, R. M., Silver, D. Z., Puuhvel, M., and Sternberg, T. H., Lipolytic activity of *Corynebacterium* acnes. *J. Invest. Dermatol.*, 51, 190-196, 1968.

56. Marples, R. R., Downing, D. T., and Kligman, A. M., Control of free fatty acids in human surface lipids by *Corynebacterium* acnes. *J. Invest. Dermatol.*, 56, 127-131, 1971.

57. Holt, R. J., The esterase and lipase activity of aerobic skin bacteria. *Br. J. Dermatol.*, 85, 18-23, 1971.

58. Weary, P., Comedogenic potential of the lipid extract of *Pityrosporum ovale*. *Arch. Dermatol.*, 102, 84-91, 1970.

59. Puhvel, S. M., Reisner, R. M., and Sakamoto, M., Analysis of lipid composition of isolated human sebaceous gland homogenates after incubation with cutaneous bacteria. Thin layer chromatography. *J. Invest. Dermatol.*, 64, 406-411, 1975.

60. Cove, J. H., Holland, K. T., and Cunliffe, W. J., An analysis of sebum excretion rate, bacterial population and the production rate of free fatty acids on human skin. *Br. J. Dermatol.*, 103, 383-386, 1980.

61. Marples, R. R. and Kligman, A. M., Ecological effects of oral antibiotics on the microflora of human skin. *Arch. Dermatol.*, 103, 148-153, 1971.

62. Cunliffe, W. J., Coterill, J. A., and Williamson, B., The effect of clindamycin in acne: a clinical and laboratory investigation. *Br. J. Dermatol.*, 87, 37-41, 1972.

63. Shalita, A. R., Wheatley, V. R., and Brind, J., Clinical and laboratory evaluation of antibacterial agents in the treatment of acne vulgaris (abstract). *J. Invest. Dermatol.*, 60, 250, 1973.

64. Marples, R. R., Kligman, A. M., Lantis, L. R., and Downing, D. T., The role of the aerobic microflora in the genesis of fatty acids in human surface lipids. *J. Invest. Dermatol.*, 55, 173-178, 1970.

65. Mykytowycz, R. and Goodrich, B. S., Skin glands as organs of communication in mammals. *J. Invest. Dermatol.*, 62, 124-131, 1974.

66. Downing, D. T., Strauss, J. S., and Pochi, P. E., Variability in the chemical composition of human skin surface lipids. *J. Invest. Dermatol.*, 53, 322-327, 1969.

67. Lewis, C. A. and Hayward, B., Human skin surface lipids. In Borrie P, Ed. *Modern Trends in Dermatology. Vol. 4.* London: Butterworths, 1971.

68. Haahti, E., Major lipid constituents of human skin surface with special reference to gas chromatographic methods. *Scan. J. Clin. Lab. Invest.*, 13(Suppl. 59), 1961.

69. Nicolaides, N. and Foster, R. C., Esters in human hair fat. *J. Am. Oil Chem. Soc.*, 33, 404-409, 1956.

70. Felger, C. B., The etiology of acne. I. Composition of sebum before and after puberty. *J. Soc. Cosmet. Chem.*, 20, 565, 1969.

71. Nordstrom, K. M., Labows, J. N., McGinley, K. J., and Leyden, J. J., Characterization of wax esters, triglycerides, and free fatty acids of folicular casts. *J. Invest. Dermatol.*, 86, 700-705, 1986.

72. Darke, D. J. and Wilson, J. D., The total analysis by gas chromatography of palmar and forehead lipids. *AERE Report No. G 1528*, 1979.

73. Boniforti, L., Passi, S., Caprilli, F., and Nazzaro-Porro, M., Skin surface lipids. Identification and determination by thin-layer chromatography and gas-liquid chromatography. *Clin. Chem. Acta*, 47, 223-231, 1973.

74. Green, S. C., Stewart, M. E., and Downing, D. T., Variation in sebum fatty acid composition among adult humans. *J. Invest. Dermatol.*, 83, 114-117, 1984.

75. Nazzaro-Porro, M., Passi, S., Boniforti, L., and Belsito, F., Effects of aging on fatty acids in skin surface lipids. *J. Invest. Dermatol.*, 73, 112-117, 1979.

76. Nicolaides, N., Skin lipids: their biochemical uniqueness. *Science*, 186, 19-26, 1974.

77. Nicolaides, N. and Ansari, M. N. A., The dienoic fatty acids of human skin surface lipid. *Lipids*, 4, 79-81, 1968.

78. Krakow, R., Downing, D. T., Strauss, J. S., and Pochi, P. E., Identification of a fatty acid in human surface lipids apparently associated with acne vulgaris. *J. Invest. Dermatol.*, 61, 286-289, 1973.

79. Stewart, M. E., McDonnell, M. W., and Downing, D. T., Possible genetic control of the proportions of branched-chain fatty acids in human sebaceous wax esters. *J. Invest. Dermatol.*, 86, 706-708, 1986.

80. Kanda, F., Yagi, E., Fukuda, M., Nakajima, K., Ohta, T., and Nakata, O., Elucidation of chemical compounds responsible for foot malodour. *Br. J. Dermatol.*, 122, 771-776, 1990.

81. Nicolaides, N., The monoene and other wax alcohols of human skin surface lipid and their relation to the fatty acids of this lipid. *Lipids*, 2, 266-275, 1966.

82. Nicolaides, N., Fu, H. C., Ansari, M. N. A., and Rice, G. R., The fatty acids of wax esters and sterol esters from vernix caseosa and from human skin surface lipid. *Lipids*, 7, 506-517, 1972.

83. Puhvel, S. M., Esterification of [4-^{14}C]cholesterol by cutaneous bacteria (*Staphylococcus epidermis, Propionibacterium acnes,* and *Propionibacterium granulosum*). *J. Invest. Dermatol.*, 64, 397-400, 1975.

84. Freinkel, R. K. and Aso, K., Esterification of cholesterol in the skin. *J. Invest. Dermatol.*, 52, 148-154, 1969.

85. Summerly, R., Yardley, H. J., Raymond, M., Tabiowo, A., and Ilderton, E., The lipid composition of sebaceous glands as a reflection of gland size. *Br. J. Dermatol.*, 94, 45-53, 1976.

86. Cunliffe, W. J., Cotterill, J. A., and Williamson, B., Skin surface lipids in acne. *Br. J. Dermatol.*, 85, 496, 1971.

87. Robertshaw, D., Apocrine sweat glands. In Goldsmith LA, Ed. *Physiology, Biochemistry, and Molecular Biology of the Skin. 2nd Ed.* New York: Oxford University Press, 1991.

88. Shelley, W. B., Apocrine sweat. *J. Invest. Dermatol.*, 17, 255, 1951.

89. Knowles, A. M., Aspects of physiochemical methods for the detection of latent fingerprints. *J. Phys. E. Sci. Instrum.*, 11, 713-721, 1978.

90. Toth, I. and Faredin, I., Steroid excreted by human skin. II. C_{19}-steroid sulfates in human axillary sweat. *Acta Med. Hung.*, 42, 21-28, 1985.

91. Labows, J. N., Preti, G., Hoelzle, E., Leyden, J., and Kligman, A., Steroid analysis of human apocrine secretion. *Steroids*, 34, 249-258, 1979.

92. Yamamoto, A., Serizawa, S., Ito, M., and Sato, Y., Effect of aging on sebaceous gland activity and on the fatty acid composition of wax esters. *J. Invest. Dermatol.*, 89, 507-512, 1987.

93. Ramasastry, P., Downing, D. T., Pochi, P. E., and Strauss, J. S., Chemical composition of human surface lipids from birth to puberty. *J. Invest. Dermatol.*, 54, 139-144, 1970.

94. Kärkkäinen, J., Nikkari, T., Ruponen, S., and Haahti, E., Lipids of *vernix caseosa*. *J. Invest. Dermatol.*, 44, 333-338, 1965.

95. Miettienen, T. A. and Lukkäinen, T., Gas-liquid chromatographic and mass spectroscopic studies on sterols in vernix caseosa, amniotic fluid and meconium. *Acta Chem. Scand.*, 22, 2603–2612, 1968.

96. Forest, G. M. and Bertrand, J., Sexual steroids in the neonatal period. *Steroid Biochem.*, 6, 24-26, 1975.

97. Stewart, M. E. and Downing, D. T., Measurement of sebum secretion rates in young children. *J. Invest. Dermatol.*, 84, 59-61, 1985.

98. Sansone-Bazzano, G., Cummings, B., Seeler, A. K., and Reisner, R. M., Differences in the lipid constituents of sebum from pre-pubertal and pubertal subjects. *Br. J. Dermatol.*, 103, 131-137, 1980.

99. Pochi, P. E., Strauss, J. S., and Downing, D. T., Skin surface lipid composition, acne, pubertal development, and urinary excretion of testosterone and 17-ketosteroids in children. *J. Invest. Dermatol.*, 69, 485-489, 1977.

100. Pochi, P. E., Strauss, J. S., and Downing, D. T., Age related changes in sebaceous gland activity. *J. Invest. Dermatol.*, 73, 108-111, 1979.

101. Kellum, R. E., Strangfeld, K., and Ray, L. F., Acne vulgaris. Studies in pathogenesis: triglycerides hydrolysis by *C. acnes in vitro*. *Arch. Dermatol.*, 101, 41-47, 1970.

102. Jacobsen, E., Billings, J. K., Frantz, R. A., Kinney, C. K., Stewart, M. E., and Downing, D. T., Age-related changes in sebaceous wax ester secretion rates in men and women. *J. Invest. Dermatol.*, 85, 483-485, 1985.

103. Cunliffe, W. J. and Schuster, S., Pathogenesis of acne. *Lancet*, 1 (7597), 685-687, 1969.

104. Strauss, J. S. and Pochi, P. E., The quantitative gravimetric determination of sebum production. *J. Invest. Dermatol.*, 36, 293-298, 1961.

105. Plewig, G. and Kligman, A. M., Proliferative activity of the sebaceous glands of the aged. *J. Invest. Dermatol.*, 70, 314-317, 1978.

106. Cuthbertson, F., The chemistry of fingerprints. *AWRE Report, SSCD Memorandum SAC/8/65*, 1965.

107. Cuthbertson, F., The chemistry of fingerprints. *AWRE Report No. 013/69*, 1969.

108. Wilson, J. D. and Darke, D. J., The results of analyses of the mixtures of fatty acids on the skin. Part 1. commentary. *AERE Report No. G 1154*, ca. 1978.

109. Noble, D., Vanished into thin air: the search for children's fingerprints. *Anal. Chem.*, 67, 435A-438A, 1995.

110. Witze, A., Scientists do detective work on kid's fingerprints. *Dallas Morning News.* 21 April 1997, pp. 8D, 10D.

111. Noble, D., The disappearing fingerprints. *Chem Matters.* February, 9-12, 1997.

112. Fletcher, J. A., Gas Chromatography-Mass Spectrometry Identification of the Chemical Composition of Fingerprints, unpublished report, 1994.

113. Schultz, C. S., Determining the Chemical Composition of Children and Adult's Fingerprints Using Gas Chromatography-Mass Spectrometry, unpublished report, 1994.

114. Buchanan, M. V., Asano, K., and Bohanon, A., Chemical characterization of fingerprints from adults and children. *SPIE Photonics East Conf. Proc.*, 2941, 89-95, 1996.

115. Robinson, S. and Robinson, A. H., Chemical composition of sweat. *Physiol. Rev.*, 34, 215, 1954.

116. Mong, G. M., Petersen, C. E., and Clauss, T. R. W., Advanced fingerprint analysis project. Fingerprint constituents. *PNNL Report 13019*, 1999.

117. Bramble, S. K., Separation of latent fingermark residue by thin-layer chromatography. *J. Forensic Sci.*, 40, 969-975, 1995.

118. Jones, N. E., Davies, L. M., Brennan, J. S., and Bramble, S. K., Separation of visibly-excited fluorescent components in fingerprint residue by thin-layer chromatography. *J. Forensic Sci.*, 45, 1286–1293, 2000.

119. Davies, L. M., Jones, N. E., Brenna J. S., and Bramble, S. K., A new visibly-excited fluorescent component in latent fingerprint residue induced by gaseous electrical discharge. *J. Forensic Sci.*, 45, 1294–1298, 2000.

120. Duff, J. M. and Menzel, E. R., Laser-assisted thin-layer chromatography and luminescence of fingerprints: an approach to fingerprint age determination. *J. Forensic Sci.*, 23, 129-134, 1978.

121. Dikshitsu, Y. S., Prasad, L., Pal, J. N., and Rao, C. V. N., Aging studies of fingerprint residues using thin-layer and high performance liquid chromatography. *Forensic Sci. Int.*, 31, 261-266, 1986.

122. Lloyd, R., Lab on a chip may turn police into DNA detectives. *Washington Post*, 1 March 1999, A9.

123. Wu, C., Device eliminates wait for DNA results. *Sci. News*, 27 March 1999, 155, 199.

124. Bredemeier, K., In Virginia, freedom from fear for crime victims, relief for families. *Washington Post*, 7 July 1999, A14.

125. Morrison, R. D., E-gels allow DNA results in 35 minutes. *Law Enforcement Tech*, 1999 August, 88-89.

126. Sweet, D. and Shutler, G. G., Analysis of salivary DNA evidence from a bite mark on a body submerged in water. *J. Forensic Sci.*, 44(5), 1069–1072, 1999.

127. Presley, L. A., Baumstark, A. L., and Dixon, A., The effects of specific latent fingerprint and questioned document examinations on the amplification and typing of the HLA DQ alpha gene region in forensic casework. *J. Forensic Sci.*, 38(5), 1028–1036, 1993.

128. Walls, C., Effects of latent print technology on PCR DNA analysis. *CBDIAI Examiner.* Fall, 17-18, 1997.

129. Stein, C., Kyeck, S. H., and Henssge, C., DNA typing of fingerprint reagent treated biological stains. *J. Forensic Sci.*, 41(6), 1012–1017, 1996.

130. Shipp, E., Roelofs, R., Togneri, E., Wright, R., Atkinson, D., and Henry, B., Effects of argon laser light, alternate source light, and cyanoacrylate fuming on DNA typing of human bloodstains. *J. Forensic Sci.*, 38(1), 184-191, 1993.

131. Newall, P. J., Richard, M. L., Kafarowski, E., Donnelly, W. J., Meloche, G. E., and Newman, J. C., Homicide case report: successful amplification and STR typing of bloodstains subjected to fingerprint treatment by cyanoacrylate fuming. *Can. Soc. Forensic. Sci. J.*, 29(1), 1-5, 1996.

132. Andersen, J. and Bramble, S., The effects of fingermark enhancement light sources on subsequent PCR-STR DNA analysis of fresh bloodstains. *J. Forensic Sci.*, 42(2), 303-306, 1997.

133. Fregeau, C. J., Germain, O., and Fourney, R. M., Fingerprint enhancement revisited and the effects of blood enhancement chemicals on subsequent profiler plus fluorescent short tandem repeat DNA analysis of fresh and aged bloody fingerprints. *J. Forensic Sci.*, 45(2), 354-380, 2000.

134. Miller, K., Blood reagents — their use and their effect on DNA. *FIRRS Bulletin No. 42*, November 1998.

135. Gross, A. M., Harris, K. A., and Kaldun, G. L., The effect of luminol on presumptive tests and DNA analysis using the polymerase chain reaction. *J. Forensic Sci.*, 44(4), 837-840, 1999.

136. Brignoli, C. and Coquoz, R., DNA compatibility with fingerprint detection techniques and blood reagents, paper presented at the International Fingerprint Research Group Meeting, 25-28 May 1999.

137. Hochmeister, M. N., Budowle, B., and Baechtel, F. S., Effects of presumptive test reagents on the ability to obtain restriction fragment length polymorphism (RFLP) patterns from human blood and semen stains. *J. Forensic Sci.*, 36(3), 656-661, 1991.

138. Roux, C., Gill, K., Sutton, J., and Lennard, C., A further study to investigate the effect of fingerprint enhancement techniques on the DNA analysis of bloodstains. *J. Forensic Ident.*, 49(4), 357-376, 1999.

139. Zamir, A., Oz, C., and Geller, B., Threat mail and forensic science: DNA profiling from items of evidence after treatment with DFO. *J. Forensic Sci.*, 45(2), 445-446, 2000.

140. Van Oorschot, R. A. H. and Jones, M. K., DNA fingerprints from fingerprints. *Nature*, 387, 767, 1997.

141. Bellefeuille, J., Bowen, K., Wilkinson, D., and Yamishita, B., Crime scene protocols for DNA evidence. *FIRRS Bulletin No. 45*, April 1999.

142. Ladd, C., Adamowicz, M. S., Bourke, M. T., Scherczinger, C. A., and Lee, H. C., A systematic analysis of secondary DNA transfer. *J. Forensic Sci.*, 44(6), 1270–1272, 1999.

143. Findlay, I., Taylor, A., Quirke, P., Frazier, R., and Urquhart, A., DNA fingerprinting from single cells. *Nature*, 389, 555-556, 1997.

144. Batzer, M. A., Arcot, S. S., Phinney, J. W., Alegria-Hartman, M., Kass, D. H., Milligan, S. M., Kimpton, C., Gill, P., Hochmeister, M., Ioannou, P. A., Herrera, R. J., Boudreau, D. A., Scheer, W. D., Keats, B. J. B., Deininger, P. L., and Stoneking, M., Genetic variation of recent alu insertions in human populations. *J. Mol. Evol.*, 42, 22-29, 1996.

145. Harpending, H. C., Batzer, M. A., Gurven, M., Jorde, L. B., Rogers, A. R., and Sherry, S. T., Genetic traces of ancient demography. *Proc. Natl. Acad. Sci.*, 95, 1961–1967, 1998.

146. Saferstein, R., DNA: a new forensic science tool. In *Criminalistics — An Introduction to Forensic Science, 7th edition.* Upper Saddle River: Prentice-Hall, 2000.

147. Lowe, A., DNA based predictions of physical characteristics. First International Conference on Forensic Human Identification in the Millenium, 1999, http://www.forensic.gov.uk/conference/papers_list.htm.

148. Jobling, M. A., The Y chromosome as a forensic tool: progress and prospects for the new millennium. First International Conference on Forensic Human Identification in the Millenium, 1999, http://www.forensic.gov.uk/conference/papers_list.htm.

149. Kloosterman, A., Application of Y-chromosome specific STR-typing in forensic stains. First International Conference on Forensic Human Identification in the Millenium, 1999, http://www.forensic.gov.uk/conference/papers_list.htm.

150. Van Oorschot, R. A. H., Szepietowska, I., Scott, D. L., Weston, R. K., and Jones, M. K., Retrieval of genetic profiles from touched objects. First International Conference on Forensic Human Identification in the Millenium, 1999, http://www.forensic.gov.uk/conference/papers_list.htm.

151. Claiborne, W., Beethoven: a life undone by heavy metal? *Washington Post*, 18 October 2000, A3.

Methods of Latent Fingerprint Development

4

HENRY C. LEE
R.E. GAENSSLEN

Contents

Introduction

Fingerprints have often been and still are considered one of the most valuable types of physical evidence in identification. A complete discussion of the history and development of fingerprints and their use in identification is presented in Chapter 1. There are, in general, three forms of fingerprint evidence that may be found at a crime scene: visible (or patent) prints, impression (or plastic) prints, and latent prints. This chapter is mainly concerned with latent prints, which, as the name suggests, are ordinarily invisible or less visible and thus require some means of development or enhancement for their visualization. Over time, many investigators have explored new and improved techniques for the development and recovery of latent prints. In more recent years, new dimensions have been opened in latent print processing techniques, revolutionizing the field of fingerprint identification. New techniques have been developed not only for latent fingerprint detection, but also for fingerprint identification. These developments have significantly improved the efficiency of criminal investigation and personal identification.

In the past, powder dusting, ninhydrin spraying, iodine fuming, and silver nitrate soaking were the four most commonly used techniques of latent print development.[1-4] These conventional techniques are quite effective in the recovery of latent prints under many ordinary circumstances. However, latent prints can be deposited on objects or surfaces with unique characteristics: wet surfaces, surfaces with multicolored backgrounds, surfaces contaminated with blood or other body fluids, objects with unusual shapes or contours, waxed surfaces, fabrics or untreated wood, varnished surfaces, human skin, cardboard boxes, and other porous or nonabsorbent surfaces. Under these conditions, traditional methods of latent print detection are often ineffective. At times, application of the wrong techniques may even result in the destruction of potential latent print evidence.

For years, fingerprint scientists have sought new methods or tried to improve existing methods for the visualization of latents. At an overall level, all successful methods of latent print enhancement are targeted toward some known component of latent print residue (see Chapter 3). Although a complete understanding of all individual components in latent print residue and their quantities has not been attained, many of the compounds present are known. Some methods target water-soluble components while others target lipids. The best method, then, depends on the latent, the surface, and any environmentally induced changes. At another level, enhancement methods exploit the chemistry of latent residue components and their potential reactions and interactions. Efforts have focused on the development of techniques that may be successfully applied to unique and difficult surfaces and that offer increased sensitivity over conventional techniques. The newer procedures can be divided into three major categories: (1) new chemical reagents for latent print visualization; (2) optical and illumination methods for the development or enhancement of latent prints; (3) combinations of chemical and illumination methods. Finally, there are systematic approaches, involving not only combinations of methods, but careful consideration of their order of application. Some of these areas have been periodically reviewed, e.g., by Pounds,[5] Goode and Morris,[6] Hazen,[3] Lee and Gaensslen,[7] and Lennard and Margot.[8,9] In this chapter, we discuss the various physical, chemical, and illumination methods and systematic approaches for the enhancement and visualization of latent fingerprints, and also provide some of the reagent formulations and procedures used.

Powder Dusting

The simplest and most commonly used procedure for latent fingerprint development is powder dusting. Powder dusting is a "physical" method of enhancement that relies on the mechanical adherence of fingerprint powder particles to the moisture and oily components of skin ridge deposits. Application of powder to latent prints by brushing is a simple technique and yields instantly apparent prints, but it also has disadvantages. Contact of the brush with the fingerprint ridges has an inevitably destructive effect. The use of fingerprint powders dates back to the early nineteenth century. In general, there are four classes of fingerprint powders: regular, luminescent, metallic, and thermoplastic.

Regular Fingerprint Powders

Traditional Fingerprint Powders

Regular fingerprint powders consist of both a resinous polymer for adhesion and a colorant for contrast. Hundreds of fingerprint powder formulas have been developed over the years. A detailed discussion of fingerprint powder formulas and their preparations can be found in the first edition of *Scott's Fingerprint Mechanics*[1] and in the report by Goode and Morris.[6] Following are some of the most commonly used fingerprint powder formulas:

Black Fingerprint Powder Formulas:

Ferric oxide powder

Black ferric oxide	50%
Rosin	25%
Lampblack	25%

Manganese dioxide powder

Manganese dioxide	45%
Black ferric oxide	25%
Lampblack	25%
Rosin	5%

Lampblack powder

Lampblack	60%
Rosin	25%
Fuller's earth	15%

White Fingerprint Powder Formulas

Titanium oxide powder

Titanium oxide	60%
Talc	20%
Kaolin lenis	20%

Chalk-titanium oxide powder

Chalk	15%
Kaolin lenis	15%
Titanium oxide	70%

Gray Fingerprint Powder Formulas

Chemist gray powder

Chemist gray	80%
Aluminum powder	20%

Lead Carbonate Powder

Lead carbonate	80%
Gum arabic	15%
Aluminum powder	3%
Lampblack	2%

In addition, there are many different types of colors or metallic fingerprint powders commercially available. Some of the chemical substances used in fingerprint powders are toxic or pose other potential health hazards, including antimony trisulfide, antimony powder, cobalt oxide, copper powder, cupric oxide, lead carbonate, lead iodide, lead oxide, lead sulfide, manganese dioxide, mercuric oxide, mercuric sulfide, tin powder, and titanium dioxide. Safety procedures and caution should be exercised when preparing or using powders containing these chemicals.

In recent years, researchers have further improved the mechanism and technique of powder dusting latent fingerprints by coating the fingerprint powder onto fine quartz powder and/or small plastic particles. Different sizes of fingerprint powder-coated particles can be used for different purposes in processing. The following are some of the basic formulations used by BVDA Inc., The Netherlands, in their particle-coated fingerprint powders:

Silver powder	Aluminum flake, quartz powder
Gold powder	Bronze flake, quartz powder
Black powder	Iron oxide, quartz powder, kaolin, carbon soot

| White powder | Dolomite, starch powder |
| Gray powder | Kaolin, aluminum flake powder |

The following factors should ordinarily be considered in the selection of a fingerprint powder:

1. The surface should be suitable for powder dusting and not itself attractive to fingerprint powder (such as polyethylene).
2. The color of the fingerprint powder should be selected to give maximum contrast with the surface on which the latent print was deposited.
3. The powder must adhere well to the deposits left by the friction skin ridges of a finger or palm.
4. The particle size of the powder should be fine enough to yield good, clear ridge patterns.

Generally, fingerprint powder is applied to the surface bearing the latent print with a fingerprint brush. These brushes are distinguished according to the types of fibers used to make them. Occasionally, powder can be applied to the surface by means of an atomizer, aerosol spray, or electrostatic apparatus.

When applying powder with a fingerprint brush, extreme care should be taken to avoid damaging the latent print. Valuable fingerprint evidence is occasionally destroyed by carelessness in the application of powder. James et al. have looked carefully at this problem and recommended techniques and types of brushes for best avoiding it.[10] The following is a generalized procedure for developing latent prints with fingerprint powder:

1. Visually search the surface to identify possible latent print deposits.
2. If a fingerprint is found, it should be photographed using an appropriate photographic technique.
3. Select an appropriate fingerprint powder and brush. When in doubt, make a test print to help in choosing the best powder and brush for the circumstances.
4. Carefully apply the powder to the surface with a light brushing action.
5. Remove the excess powder by dusting the surface with a gentle, smooth motion until the best fingerprint image has been developed.
6. Photograph useful fingerprints *in situ*. The photograph should contain all the necessary case information and the latent print number.
7. Apply a suitable fingerprint lifting tape and carefully lift the powdered latent print from the surface.
8. Examine the latent lift and if necessary reprocess or relift the original latent print.

An alternative technique was proposed by Barron, Haque, and Westland[11] in which a freeze and thaw method was used before dusting with fingerprint powder. James et al. milled aluminum-based and other powders to determine the optimal particle size (5 to 10 μm long and 0.5 μm thick) and stearic acid content (3 to 5%) for latent fingerprint development.[12]

A variation on the usual powder dusting procedures, but which can nevertheless be considered a kind of "powder" development technique, was described by Waldock.[13] A camphor candle was used to produce soot that could "coat" the latent print.

Organic Fingerprint Powders

Many commercial fingerprint powders contain toxic inorganic chemicals such as lead, mercury, cadmium, copper, silicon, titanium, and bismuth. Long-term exposure to them may present a health hazard. The use of organic fingerprint powders for latent print dusting was suggested by Kerr, Haque, and Westland.[14] A typical powder formula consists of the following:

Potassium bromide	1 g
Cornstarch	35 g
Distilled water	25 mL

The procedure that was used to prepare the organic fingerprint powder was as follows:

1. Dissolve 1 g potassium bromide in 25 mL distilled water.
2. Slowly dissolve 35 g cornstarch in the above solution with constant stirring.
3. Dry the cornstarch mixture at room temperature for 7 days.
4. The solid mass is periodically ground with a mortar and pestle over the drying period to produce a finer powder.
5. The powder is stored in a tightly stoppered container containing anhydrous calcium sulfate as a desiccant.

It was reported that cornstarch-based fingerprint powders yielded excellent results in developing latent prints on nonporous surfaces. In addition to regular cornstarch fingerprint powders, the same research group also reported on the use of organic-based fluorescent powders for latent print detection.[15] The following are several organic-based fluorescent fingerprint powders as reported by Kerr et al.:[15]

| Calcium sulfate | 5–10% |
| Dihydrate cornstarch | 90–95% |

Fluorescein solution (in methanol/water)	1%
Barium sulfate	5%
Flour	5%
Titanium dioxide	0.5%
Cornstarch	89.5%
Fluorescein solution (in methanol/water)	1%
Gum arabic	2%
Cornstarch	98%
Rhodamine B (aqueous solution)	2%
Cornstarch	100%
Fluorescein solution (in methanol water)	1%

Luminescent (Fluorescent and Phosphorescent) Fingerprint Powders

Many types of powders contain natural and/or synthetic compounds that fluoresce or phosphoresce upon exposure to ultraviolet (UV) light, laser light, and other light sources. These types of fingerprint powders are useful for the visualization of latent prints deposited on multicolored surfaces that would present a contrast problem if developed with regular fingerprint powder. Luminescent fingerprint powders have rarely been used in the field. With the advent of laser detection, however, it was found that dusting the latent prints with fluorescent or phosphorescent powders greatly enhanced laser examination. Acridine yellow, acridine orange, coumarin 6, crystal violet, p,p'-dichlorodiphenylmethyl carbinol, 3,3'-diethyloxadicarbocyanine iodide, 3,3'-diethylthiotricarbocyanine iodide, merocyanine 540, Nile Blue perchlorate, Rhodamine B, Rhodamine 6G, phenothiazine, and many other luminescent dyes and pigments have been reported to be useful as luminescent dusting powders for laser examination. Selection of the most satisfactory powder is largely dependent on the background colors and their luminescent properties. Good results have been reported with several formulations.[16-20]

Metallic (Magnetic, Fine Lead, and Metal Evaporation) Fingerprint Powders

Magnetic powders are fine ferromagnetic powders that are applied by use of a magnetic applicator. This method was first reported by MacDonell.[21] It was found that magnetic powders are particularly successful in the recovery of latent prints from surfaces such as leather, plastics, walls, and human skin. The magnetic powder process has also been widely used for processing latent prints on vertical surfaces. The basic materials used in magnetic powder are iron oxide and iron powder dust along with other coloration compounds. Magnetic flake powders developed by James and collaborators[22] have been shown to be equal or superior to classical "magna" powders in developing latent fingerprints.[23] The new powders no longer contain magnetic particles to serve as the "brush" and nonmagnetic particles to adhere to the print residue. In addition, fine lead powder has been used for latent print detection with X-ray electronography and autoelectronography.[24] Cadmium, zinc, and gold/zinc metals have also been used in vacuum metal deposition techniques for latent print detection.[25,26] These procedures are discussed below.

Thermoplastic Fingerprint Powders

Thermoplastic powder-dusting techniques involve powders such as photocopier toners or dry inks.[27,28] Latent fingerprints developed with such materials become fused to the surface upon exposure to heat.

Casting of Plastic Fingerprints/Recovery by Casting Methods

Stimac[29] noted that the processing of plastic (or "indentation") prints is not commonly discussed. He described a casting method similar to what might be used for fine tool marks, followed then by the use of the resulting cast to make an inked impression for comparison. Feucht[30] described the use of polyvinylsiloxane dental impression materials to recover latent prints from rough surfaces including ceiling tiles, safes, and paper currency.

Small Particle Reagent and Variants

The small particle reagent technique relies on the adherence of fine particles suspended in a treating solution to the fatty or oily constituents of latent fingerprint residue. Accordingly, it may be regarded as belonging to the same family of methods as powder dusting. Small particle reagent (SPR) consists of a suspension of fine molybdenum disulfide particles in detergent solution. The particles adhere to the fatty constituents of latent print residues and form a gray molybdenum disulfide deposit. This method was first reported by Morris and Wells.[31] A detailed procedure and formulation were described later by Goode and Morris.[6] Pounds and Jones[32] reported that choline chloride was not an essential component of the formulation. They recommended the use of molybdenum disulfide dispersed in Manoxol OT.

The following is one formulation and procedure used for developing latent prints with small particle reagent:

Reagents

Molybdenum disulfide (MoS_2)	30 g
Distilled water	1 L
Photo Flo 200	see below

Notes: *Dissolve the MoS_2 in the distilled water. Add 3 drops of the Photo Flo 200 and shake the solution well to ensure that the molybdenum disulfide has gone into solution. This solution has a shelf life of about 6 to 8 weeks.*

Spraying Procedure:

1. Shake the reagent solution thoroughly and fill a spray bottle with it.
2. Spray the SPR onto the area to be searched for latent prints. Shake the bottle between sprayings to prevent the molybdenum disulfide from settling to the bottom.
3. Using a separate spray bottle with clean water, rinse the searched area to remove the excess SPR reagent.

Dipping Procedure:

1. Mix the reagent solution thoroughly and fill a photographic processing tray with it.
2. Rock to mix the solution thoroughly, and immerse the evidence item in it. Particles of MoS_2 will settle on the surfaces where latent prints are likely to be located.
3. Repeat the treatment with the other side of the evidence item.
4. After 2 min, carefully remove the evidence item and rinse gently with clean water.

The developed latent print appears as a dark to light gray color. The SPR solution has been successfully used to develop latent prints on paper, cardboard, metal, rusty metal, rocks, concrete, plastic, vinyl, wood, and glass. Similarly, latent prints have been developed on sticky surfaces, such as soda cans and candy wrappers. SPR reagent-developed latent prints can be lifted with clean lifting tape.

Margot and Lennard found that the crystalline structure of the MoS_2 used in the recipe can have a significant effect on latent print development results.[9] They recommended using ROCOL™ AS powder, made up as 10 g with 0.8 mL Tergitol 7 in a 100-mL stock solution. This stock is then diluted 1:10 for dipping and 1:7 for spraying. They further noted that substituting iron oxide as the powder component, as suggested by Haque et al.,[33] proved less effective in their experience than the molybdenum disulfide.

Ishizawa and collaborators reported testing both white and black suspended particle mixtures in several "fixer" solutions.[34] The white particle mixture consisted of 80% agalmatolite, 10% lithopone, and 10% zinc oxide, all w/v in the fixer. Black particle mixture was 45% carbon black and 55%

carbon graphite. The best "fixer" was a proprietary silicone-based, water-soluble coating named SP-F (Taiho Kogyo Co. Ltd.). Frank and Almog[35] tested particles other than MoS_2 in suspension, including barium sulfate, titanium dioxide, talc, zinc oxide, zinc carbonate, and basic zinc carbonate to look for a suitable lighter colored entity to interact with the fingerprint residue. Best results were seen with 0.66 g zinc carbonate, 20 mL water, 0.06 g Tergitol 7, and 55 g dimethyl ether. They further noted that particles of 2-μm average size adhered better than those of 6-μm average size. Springer and Bergman[36] have described the preparation of SPR containing the fluorescent dyes Rhodamine 6G and Brilliant Yellow 40 (BY40). The basis for using these dyes is more fully developed below under post-treatment of cyanoacrylate latent prints. The preparations all worked initially, but the R6G reagent had poor shelf life. A BY40 suspension of 100 mL of 0.1% BY40 in ethanol mixed with 100 mL stock SPR showed consistently good results.

Chemical Fuming and Enhancement

Iodine Fuming

The iodine fuming technique has been used for latent print development for at least a century. Several variations of the fuming procedure have been proposed over the years.[1,37-39] The mechanism of the iodine fuming reaction was initially thought to involve the reversible addition of iodine to the double bonds of the unsaturated fatty acids in fingerprint residue by the process of halogenation. More recent research by Almog, Sasson, and Anah[40] suggests that the mechanism of interaction involves physical absorption rather than a chemical reaction. When iodine crystals are warmed, they produce a violet iodine vapor by sublimation. The iodine fumes are absorbed by the fingerprint secretion residues to give yellowish brown latent prints. The iodine color is not stable, however, and is short-lived unless the iodine is chemically fixed (see below). There are four ways to develop latent prints with iodine.

Iodine Fuming Gun Method

An iodine fuming gun can be made from either a glass or hard plastic tube. Fresh calcium chloride crystals should be used as a drying agent.

1. Place 0.5 g iodine crystals into the fuming gun.
2. To fume a surface containing latent prints, the nozzle of the fuming gun is moved slowly over the surface at close range, approximately 0.5 in. away.
3. Blow air into the mouthpiece of the fuming gun (the end containing the calcium chloride crystals) through a connecting tube.

4. Avoid inhaling any iodine fumes or allowing any contact of the vapors with skin. Iodine crystals and vapors are toxic and corrosive.
5. Concentrate the fumes in areas where latent prints begin to appear.
6. Photograph the developed fingerprint as soon as possible or, alternatively, fix the developed latent print with iodine fixing chemicals.

Iodine Fuming Cabinet Method

1. Suspend specimens or articles to be treated in the upper portion of the fuming cabinet.
2. Place approximately 1 g iodine crystals in a clean evaporating dish in the cabinet.
3. Close the fuming cabinet door.
4. Heat the iodine crystals slowly and gently to about 50°C with a heating block or other appropriate heat source apparatus.
5. Observe the development of latent prints. When maximum contrast has been achieved between the latent print and the background, remove the remaining iodine crystals from the cabinet.
6. Remove the specimens from the cabinet.
7. Photograph the developed fingerprint as soon as possible or, alternatively, fix the developed print with fixing chemicals.

Iodine Dusting Method

Iodine crystals are ground into a fine powder and dusted onto the surface containing latent fingerprints with a fingerprint brush in the same manner as that used with regular fingerprint powder.

Iodine Solution Method

Haque, Westland, and Kerr[41] reported that, by dissolving iodine in the 7,8-benzoflavone fixation reagent, fingerprints that were several weeks old could be developed on various porous surfaces. Compared with the iodine fuming techniques, this technique showed improved convenience and sensitivity. Pounds and Hussain[42] have noted that a working solution consisting of 2 mL of 10% 7,8-benzoflavone in dichloromethane and 100 mL of 0.1% iodine in cyclohexane can be painted onto large surfaces at a crime scene to reveal latent prints. The technique was particularly effective in revealing freshly deposited latent fingerprints. The technique of adding the 7,8-benzoflavone to the iodine reagent for either spraying or solution application is described by Margot and Lennard as well.[9]

Although the iodine fuming technique is simple to use, it suffers from several disadvantages: the vapors are toxic and corrosive, iodine-developed latent fingerprint images fade away rapidly upon standing in air, and old latent prints are difficult to develop. Almog, Sasson, and Anah[40] reported a method in which controlling the addition of water vapor to the iodine fumes solved the problem of recovering aging latent prints. They showed that latent prints up to 110 days old could be developed on paper by this method.

Methods exist for fixing iodine-developed fingerprints. These methods include starch spray,[43] silver plate transfer,[44] tetrabase solution,[45] and benzoflavone reagents.[41,46] The best results are usually produced by treating the iodine-developed fingerprint with 7,8-benzoflavone (α-naphthoflavone) reagent. The following is a commonly used formula:

1. Dissolve 1 g α-naphthoflavone in 50 mL acetic acid.
2. Add 300 mL 1,1,2-trichlorotrifluoroethane to the above solution. A clear, yellow iodine fixing solution is produced.
3. Store the solution in a brown glass bottle; it will be stable indefinitely.

Midkiff, Codell, and Chapman described an iodine fuming procedure followed by benzoflavone fixation that performed well on clear and light-colored tapes.[47]

Cyanoacrylate (Super Glue) Fuming

In 1982, latent fingerprint examiners working at the U.S. Army Criminal Investigation Laboratory in Japan (USACIL-Pacific) and in the Bureau of Alcohol, Tobacco and Firearms (BATF) laboratory introduced a novel procedure to the U.S. that used alkyl-2-cyanoacrylate ester (Super Glue) as a means of developing latent prints. The method was first devised by the Criminal Identification Division of the Japanese National Police Agency in 1978. Since its introduction into the U.S., the method has received much attention from researchers who have evaluated it and attempted to improve its sensitivity and extend its range of application.[48-51] The principles underlying the cyanoacrylate fuming method and its reaction have also been discussed.[52] The structure of 2-cyanoacrylate ester and the mechanism of its polymerization are shown in Figure 4.1.

Cyanoacrylate fuming has been successfully used for the development of latent prints on surfaces as diverse as plastics, electrical tape, garbage bags, Styrofoam, carbon paper, aluminum foil, finished and unfinished wood, rubber, copper and other metals, cellophane, rubber bands, and smooth rocks. The cyanoacrylate fuming procedure and several modifications of it that accelerate the development of latent prints are given below.

Cyanoacrylate Fuming Procedure

The equipment and materials required include cyanoacrylate and a fuming tank, cabinet, or other suitable container with a proper ventilation system.

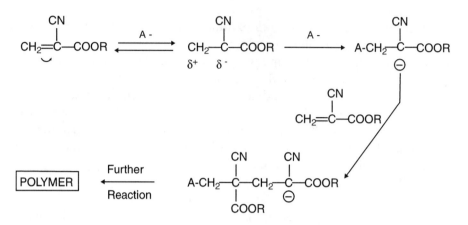

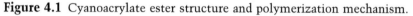

Figure 4.1 Cyanoacrylate ester structure and polymerization mechanism.

1. Place the specimens or items on which latent prints are to be developed into the cabinet. They should be suspended from the upper portions of the cabinet if possible to allow their surfaces to be exposed to the cyanoacrylate fumes.
2. Place 2 or 3 drops of liquid cyanoacrylate into a small porcelain dish, and place the dish into the fuming cabinet.
3. Allow the items to be exposed to the fumes for at least 2 hr until whitish-colored fingerprint patterns appear.

The cyanoacrylate-developed print may be further enhanced by dusting with regular or magnetic fingerprint powder.

Fume Circulation Procedure

In addition to the equipment required for the regular cyanoacrylate fuming procedure, the fume circulation technique requires a small battery-operated fan or air-circulating pump.

1. Place the specimens and Super Glue in the porcelain dish into the cabinet as in the regular procedure.
2. Turn on the fan. Its motion will circulate the fumes and increase the surface contact between latent print residues and cyanoacrylate vapors. Alternatively, a small circulating motor, such as a fish tank water pump, can be used to force the cyanoacrylate vapors to circulate in the fuming tank.
3. Allow the item to fume for 1 to 2 hr until a whitish-colored print appears.

The developed prints may be enhanced by dusting as noted above or by other methods discussed below.

Heat Acceleration Procedure

In addition to the equipment required for the general procedure, the heat acceleration procedure requires a heating apparatus, such as a light bulb, portable heater, hot plate, hair dryer, or alcohol lamp.

1. Place the specimens and Super Glue in the porcelain dish into the cabinet as in the regular procedure.
2. Place the heating apparatus under the porcelain dish or arrange for the heat to contact the dish. The heat accelerates the polymerization process in the cyanoacrylate and increases monomer volatility, resulting in faster vapor release and thus faster development of the latent print.
3. Allow the item to fume for 20 to 40 min, until a whitish-colored print appears.

The developed prints may be enhanced by dusting as noted above, or by other methods discussed below.

Chemical Acceleration Procedure

In addition to the equipment and reagents required for the general procedure, the chemical acceleration procedure requires 0.5 N sodium hydroxide and cotton pads or other absorbent media.[53]

1. Prepare 0.5 N sodium hydroxide by dissolving 2 g solid NaOH in 100 mL distilled water.
2. Place a clean cotton pad, cotton ball, or other absorbent medium into the dish.
3. Place 2 or 3 drops of liquid cyanoacrylate onto the absorbent medium.
4. Add 2 drops of 0.5 N sodium hydroxide solution to the absorbent medium.
5. Allow the item to fume for 30 min to 1 hr until a whitish-colored print appears.

The developed print may be enhanced by dusting as noted above, or by other procedures discussed below.

Vacuum Acceleration Procedure

Not long ago, a new vacuum acceleration technique was developed by Watkin of the Royal Canadian Mounted Police (RCMP) Identification Division.[54,55] It was found that cyanoacrylate is easier to vaporize and the vapor is more effective using this procedure. In a limited comparison study, a majority of latent examiners preferred prints developed by the vacuum procedure.[56]

Large vacuum chambers for processing a variety of objects are available commercially. Margot and Lennard[9] generally agree on the usefulness of this procedure.

Other Acceleration Procedures

Many other acceleration procedures have been used, including heating combined with circulation, intense heating combined with the addition of polymerization retardant to the cyanoacrylate, moist vapor combined with heating, cyanoacrylate in gel media, and combinations of chemical accelerators. All these techniques have the same two basic objectives: (1) accelerate the polymerization process and (2) prolong the volatilization. Grady[57] described good results from a combination of heating within a vacuum chamber. He noted that although development could not be monitored, overfuming was rare and that background dye stain fluorescence was reduced.

Cyanoacrylate ester has been incorporated into a gel matrix that is placed in a foil pouch that is reusable and has wide applications for processing latent prints. In 1985, Gilman, Sahs, and Gorajczyk[58] also reported a similar method in which a mixture of cyanoacrylate and petroleum jelly are sandwiched between acetate sheets. It has also been found that cyanoacrylate fuming is an excellent method for processing latent prints in motor vehicles and in small enclosed spaces at crime scenes. Olenik[59] has described another sandwich technique in which a thin film of cyanoacrylate is placed between aluminum foils by the use of a fingerprint roller.

Even when care is exercised, fingerprints can be overdeveloped with cyanoacrylate. Springer[60] noted that carefully controlled heating of the overdeveloped print at 70 to 80°C can selectively remove enough cyanoacrylate polymer to render the print identifiable. However, one cannot re-fume the latent after this procedure has been used. The technique was based on the observation by Almog and Gabay,[61] later confirmed by Davis, McCloud, and Bonebrake,[62] that polymerized (solidified) Super Glue produces fumes, i.e., monomeric vapor, upon heating. Geng described several methods of applying organic solvent mixtures (such as spraying, dipping, etc.) to overdeveloped Super Glue prints to render them more suitable.[63] The composition of the treating solvent and method of application depended on the surface.

Though not an "acceleration" procedure, Zhang and Gong[64] described a cyanoacrylate ester dry transfer method that placed test objects in contact with neutral filter paper that had been pre-treated with Super Glue, then dried. Additionally, various applications to special situations or conditions, such as large or immovable objects, plastic bags, leaves, surfaces contaminated by cigarette smoke residues, etc., have been noted periodically.[65-70]

Further Enhancement and Post-Treatment Procedures after Cyanoacrylate Processing

Although cyanoacrylate fuming is an excellent method for processing, the latent prints developed by this procedure often lack contrast and are difficult to visualize. Over the years, several methods for enhancing cyanoacrylate-developed prints have been reported. The most common one is simply to dust the developed print with fingerprint powder. In addition, cyanoacrylate-developed latent prints may be further enhanced by staining with any of several histological dyes in solution, mixtures of them, or other compounds that luminesce or fluoresce under UV, laser, or other illumination. Treatment with visible or luminescence-inducing dyes is commonly called "dye staining." These post-treatments are particularly useful on multicolored or other surfaces that do not contrast well with directly developed cyanoacrylate prints, and that are not highly luminescent themselves. Either gentian violet or coumarin 540 laser dye,[71] staining with Ardrox dye and examining with a UV light source,[9,72-74] by staining with Rhodamine 6G and examining with a laser,[75] by dusting with fluorescent powder,[76] and by combining acrylate fuming with the ninhydrin/zinc chloride method with laser examination[77] have all been described. Weaver and Clary[78] described a one-step procedure using the Super Glue "fuming wand" with various cyanoacrylates into which had been incorporated several proprietary fluorescent dyes, followed by examination with the argon laser. Some of the reagents and procedures are given below.

Gentian Violet Solution — Phenol Containing Formulation.

Stock solution

Gentian violet	5 g
Phenol	10 g
Ethanol	50 mL

Working solution

Stock solution is diluted to 150 mL with water.

Cyanoacrylate-developed prints are immersed in the working gentian violet solution for about 1 min with gentle rocking. The article bearing the latent print is then removed and excess dye is removed with running water. For larger articles, a pipette or syringe can be used to cover the developed print areas with an excess of the reagent.

Gentian Violet Solution — Non-Phenol Formulation.   Phenol is very caustic, and correspondingly hazardous. The FBI Laboratory procedures[79] and those of some other U.S. laboratories[80] call for preparing the solution by dissolving 1 g dye in 1 L distilled water. The item is treated by dipping or painting for 1 to 2 min and then rinsed off under cold water. The solution has a long shelf life when stored in a dark bottle.

There is some indication[81] that the phenol-containing formulation may perform better than the strictly aqueous solution. Margot and Lennard[9] describe a solution made from 0.1 g dye in 10 mL acetonitrole and 5 mL methanol and brought to 100 mL with "Arklone" (trichlorotrifluoroethane). Bramble et al.[82] recently reported optimizing the absorption and emission wavelengths for latent viewing after gentian violet development. It may also be noted that gentian violet processing has been commonly used for processing sticky tape surfaces (see below) and for more common surfaces with no preceding cyanoacrylate treatment.[83]

Coumarin 540 Dye Staining Method.   The reagent is made by dissolving 0.01 g coumarin 540 in 150 mL ethanol. The item can be immersed in the solution, or the solution can be applied to the latent print areas with a suitable device as in the gentian violet procedure above. Excess reagent is removed by overlaying the treated area with absorbent paper or similar material.

Ardrox Dye Staining Method.   In 1986 Vachon and Sorel[73] first reported the Ardrox dye staining technique. Ardrox is an industrial dye manufactured in Canada, and it is reported to be noncarcinogenic and nonhazardous; however, it may dry the skin. Miles reported an improved-staining Ardrox solution using 1,1,2-trichlorofluoroethane (Freon 113) as the main carrier.[72] McCarthy[74] has suggested the following modified procedure:

1. Mix 1 mL of Ardrox P133D in 60 ml of methanol.
2. Mix the Ardrox-methanol solution with 40 ml of Freon.
3. Immerse the object into the solution for 1 min.
4. Rinse the object with tap water and air dry.
5. Examine the object under a UV light source.

Margot and Lennard[9] use 1 mL Ardrox 970-P10 in 8 mL methyl ethyl ketone and bring this up to a final volume of 100 mL with petroleum ether. Another variation consists of 1 mL Ardrox in 9 mL isopropanol and 15 mL methyl ethyl ketone (MEK) to which is added 75 mL distilled water.[84] The more recent formulations represent attempts to find substitutes for the now banned Freon solvents (see further below).

Other Dyes and Dye Mixtures. Several other dyes have been used for the post-treatment of cyanoacrylate-developed fingerprints. These include Rhodamine 6G (R6G), basic yellow 40 (BY40), basic red 28 (BR28), and styryl 7 (S7). Mazzella and Leonard[85] looked at Rhodamine 6G, basic yellow 40, basic red 28 and styryl 7 separately and in various combinations. Formulations were: for R6G, 20 mg R6G in 60 mL propanol and 40 mL acetonitrile stock, and 5 mL of this stock to 100 mL petroleum ether for working solution; for BY40, 100 mg in 60 mL propanol and 40 mL acetonitrile stock, and 5 mL of this stock to 100 mL petroleum ether for working solution; for BR28, 200 mg BR28 in 60 mL propanol and 40 mL acetonitrile stock, and 5 mL of this stock to 100 mL petroleum ether for working solution, and for styryl 7, 100 mg styryl 7 as for the others. Dye mixtures were prepared as: for BY40 + BR28, 3 mL BY40 stock and 2 mL BR28 stock in final volume of 100 mL petroleum ether; for BR28 + S7, 3 mL BR28 stock and 2 mL S7 stock in final volume of 100 mL petroleum ether; and for BY40 + BR28 + S7, 2 mL BY40 stock + 2 mL BR28 stock and 2 mL S7 stock to a final volume of 100 mL with petroleum ether. These formulations appear in Margot and Lennard[9] as well. BR28 was an excellent enhancement dye. S7 was found not to be especially stable. Olenik[86] described a simple three-dye blend consisting of Ardrox P133D, R6G, and BY40: 1 L of the solution was made by adding 1 g BY40, 0.1 g R6G, and 8 mL Ardrox to 940 mL isopropanol or denatured ethanol. Adding an additional 50 mL acetonitrile enhanced the luminescence effects.

Various different dyes are used to post-treat cyanoacrylate-developed prints because they have different absorption and emission maxima and thus offer versatility in enhancing latent fingerprints on various types of surfaces that can themselves be multicolored and have varying luminescence characteristics. Dye mixtures increase versatility through intermolecular energy transfers that enable the examiner to take advantage of one dye's absorption maximum while monitoring luminescence at another dye's emission wavelength.

Cummings, Hollars, and Trozzi[87] did similar studies on a number of dye mixtures for the treatment of cyanoacrylate-developed latents. Some of their stock and working solution recipes differ slightly from those above. Two mixtures are of interest. So-called RAM is Rhodamine 6G, Ardrox, and MBD. MBD is 7-(p-methoxybenzylamino)-4-nitrobenz-2-oxa-1,3-diazole. Stock solutions are

R6G: 100 mg in 100 mL methanol
MBD: 100 mg in 100 mL acetone

RAM is then made using 3 mL R6G stock, 2 mL Ardrox P133D, and 7 mL MBD stock in 20 mL methanol, 10 mL isopropanol, 8 mL acetonitrile, and

Table 4.1   Approximate Absorption and Emission
Maxima of Dyes and Dye Mixtures Used to Visualize
Cyanoacrylate-Developed Latent Prints

Dye/Dye Mixture	Absorption Max (nm)	Emission Max (nm)
Rhodamine 6G	525	555
Ardrox	380	500
MBD	465	515
RAM	460	555
Basic Yellow 40 (BY40)	440	490
Basic Red 28 (BR28)	495	585
Styryl 7 (S7)	555	680
BY40 + BR28	445	590
BR28 + S7	510	680
BY40 + BR28 + S7	445	680

950 mL petroleum ether (in order). A "modified" RAM consisted of 30 mg
MBD, 25 mL acetone, 40 mL ethanol, 15 mL 2-propanol, and 950 mL petroleum ether, 1 mL Ardrox P133D, 5 mL R6G stock, and 20 mL acetonitrile
(combined in order).

A second mixture formulation, called "MRM 10," requires another dye,
Yellow 40 (Maxilon Flavine 10GFF). The Yellow 40 (Y40) stock is 2 g Yellow
40 on 1 L methanol. MRM 10 is then 3 mL R6G stock, 3 mL Y40 stock, 7 mL
MBD stock, 20 mL methanol, 10 mL 2-propanol, 8 mL acetonitrile, and
950 mL petroleum ether (combined in order).

Morimoto, Kaminogo, and Hirano subjected cyanoacrylate-developed
prints to sublimates of 1-amino-2-phenoxy-4-hydroxy-anthraquinone and
1,4-bis(ethylamino)-anthroquinone.[88] Sublimation was achieved by incorporating the dyes into incense sticks. Kempton and Rowe[89] dye-stained
cyanoacrylate-developed prints with several histological stains as well as with
commercial "Rit" dyes. Generally, methanolic solutions were superior to
aqueous ones on most tested surfaces. Prints treated with gentian violet,
diamond fuchsin, and "safranin bluish" fluoresced under 312 nm light (safranin the strongest). Day and Bowker[90] reported good results with Nile Red
as a post-cyanoarylate dye stain. Table 4.1, modified from Margot and Lennard,[9] shows absorption and emission maxima and is helpful in understanding the reasons for choosing these various cyanoacrylate-developed print
post-treatment dyes and dye mixtures.

Rare Earth Complexes.   Wilkinson and Watkin reported good results in
enhancing cyanoacrylate-developed prints with a aryl diketone chelate of
europium (Eu), called TEC.[91] The idea for this enhancement technique was
based on the fact that rare earths like europium have narrow emission bands

and long excited state lifetimes (see below for further development of the origins of using rare earth complexes). However, Eu is a poor light absorber, so the organic ligand functions as an efficient absorber and intramolecular energy transfer entity, resulting in characteristic Eu fluorescence at 615 nm. The reasoning behind the method is similar to that underlying the metal ion enhancement of ninydrin-developed latent prints.

Lock et al. tested several Eu complexes and reported good results after treating cyanoacrylate-developed prints with europium thenoyltrifluoroacetone ortho-phenanthroline (EuTTAPhen).[92] The stock solution was 0.5 g EuTTAPhen in 60 mL propanol and 40 mL acetonitrile. A working solution was made by diluting 5 mL of this stock to 100 mL final with petroleum ether. Effectiveness was assessed by comparison with TEC. Generally, the formulation was said to behave similarly to TEC, but gave better luminescence yields.

Fluorescent and Other Chemical Fuming/Treatment Procedures

Some fluorescent reagents have low sublimation temperatures, i.e., as with iodine, these chemicals will vaporize appreciably at temperatures below their melting point. The fluorescent reagent vapors can thus be used for developing and visualizing latent fingerprints in a manner similar to that of iodine fuming. Almog and Gabay[61] tested eight fluorescent chemicals (anthracene, anthranilic acid, perylene, Rhodamine B, Rhodamine 6G, 7-diethylamino-4-methylcoumarin, triphenylcarbinol, and antimony trichloride) that sublime readily. They found that all eight chemicals produced clear impressions of the latent prints under UV light. The best results for fresh fingerprints were obtained with anthranilic acid. For older prints, anthracene produced somewhat better results. The results with Rhodamine B and Rhodamine 6G were less satisfactory.

Other fluorescent chemicals such as 8-hydroxyquinoline and dimethoxycoumarin have also been reported to be useful fuming reagents for latent fingerprint detection (Forensic Science Institute, People's Republic of China, personal communication, 1989.). 8-Hydroxyquinoline has been used as a field fuming reagent in searching for latent prints at crime scenes.

The fumes of many other materials, such as camphor, pine tar, nitrocellulose, magnesium, and titanium tetrachloride, can be generated by heating the materials and used for the detection of latent fingerprints.[1,93,94] However, the means by which the fumes are formed is different from that of iodine fuming, and most of these fuming techniques have only historical interest. Radioactive sulfur dioxide gas fuming has also been reported to be a useful technique for the detection of latent fingerprints on a variety of surfaces, including paper, adhesive tapes, and fine fabrics.[95] After an exhibit has been exposed to radioactive $^{35}SO_2$, the presence of fingerprints may be detected and recorded by autoradiography. Nitric acid fumes have been used for the detection and visualization of latent fingerprints on brass casings and metal objects under special conditions.[96]

Sodhi and Kaur[97] reported good results in the detection of latent prints with eosin blue dye in the presence of *t*-tetrabutyl ammonium iodide, referred to as a "phase transfer catalyst." No illumination or luminescence techniques were used.

It has been clear for a long time that dimethylaminocinnamaldehyde (DMAC), which reacts with urea, a component of eccrine sweat and thus of eccrine fingerprint residue, can be used to enhance latent prints.[6,98] Fingerprint examiners have long assumed that the DMAC reacts exclusively with urea in latent residue because of its established reaction with urea. For example, DMAC has been used for years by biological evidence analysts as the basis for a presumptive test for urine. DMAC can also react with primary and secondary amines, and the basis for its reaction with latent residue has recently been questioned.[99] An earlier common formulation used a 35% ethanol, 65% Freon solvent. Ramotowski[99] noted that the following formulation gave good results:

Solution A

DMAC	0.25 g
Ethanol	50 mL

Solution B

Sulfosalicylic acid	1 g
Ethanol	50 mL

Solutions A and B are mixed together in equal proportions just before use. Solution A may require a quick filtration to remove particulates prior to mixing it with Solution B. Margot and Lennard noted that the reaction product is unstable and that DMAC-developed prints should be photographed immediately.[9] Sasson and Almog also noted some of the limitations of this reagent.[98] More recently, Brennan et al. reported fairly good results with a DMAC fuming technique.[100] DMAC did not interfere with the subsequent use of DFO or PD on paper substrata, but was not compatible with cyanoacrylate processing. It was said to give good fluorescent results with latents on fax-type papers. Both Menzel[20] and Katzung[101] previously described the luminescent properties of the DMAC-urea complex, and the best results from this study took advantage of luminescence using narrowband illumination. Ramotowski[99] said that use of a vapor contact procedure significantly reduced background fluorescence.

A method involving immersion or spraying with ruthenium tetroxide (RTX) was described by Mashito and Miyamoto.[102] It has been noted that RTX may be exceptionally toxic.[103]

Wilkinson described a Eu-(TTA)3·2TOPO chelate formulation for latent fingerprints with significant lipid content.[104] This procedure was based on the principles discussed above as the basis of TEC processing of cyanoacrylate-developed latents.

A method based on similar principles but arrived at independently was described by Allred and Menzel.[105] They used 1,10-phenanthroline and theonyltrifluoroacetone as secondary complexing agents for the Eu ion after an EDTA-Eu ion chelate had reacted with the lipid residues in the latent residue.

Murphy et al.[106] described a newly synthesized porphyrin derivative whose chemical properties would suggest it might be suitable for reaction/interaction with either lipid or water-soluble components of latent print residue. Formulations of the compound were compared with PD and with ninhydrin and DFO in test latents. DFO generally performed better with fresher prints but the converse was true with older ones. With latents on thermal fax paper, the compound performed better than ninhydrin or DFO.

Ninhydrin and Chemical Alternatives

Ninhydrin

As early as 1910, Ruhemann in England and Abderhalden and Schmidt in Germany reported that alpha amino acids, polypeptides, and proteins formed color products upon reaction with ninhydrin. In 1954, the Swedish scientists Oden and von Hofsten advocated the use of ninhydrin for developing latent fingerprints.[107] In 1955, Oden patented the process as a latent fingerprint techinque. Various concentrations of the ninhydrin solution have been suggested, the concentration of ninhydrin varying from 0.2 to 1.5%.[39,108-110] Various types of solvents, such as acetone, methanol, ethanol, ethyl ether, ethylene glycol, petroleum ether, naphtha, Freon 113 (trichlorotrifluoroethane), and combinations of solvents,[111-115] have been used for ninhydrin. Although differences still exist over the optimal concentration of ninhydrin and the ideal solvent, the best results may ordinarily be obtained with concentrations ranging from 0.6 to 1.0% in Freon 113. The selection of the appropriate concentration and solvent for latent fingerprint detection depends on the type of material being processed and whether or not there is any writing on the material. The so-called NFN (nontoxic, nonflammable) formulation that is made up in Freon, as well as its variations which have been widely used, originated with Morris and Goode.[115]

Ninhydrin solutions may be applied by spraying, swabbing, or dipping. Post-processing treatment by the application of heat can be used to accelerate the reaction. Various temperatures and equipment (such as ovens, irons, steam irons, hair dryers, or microwave ovens) have been suggested for post-processing heating. Optimal results have been obtained when ninhydrin-treated documents were heated to 80°F in 80% relative humidity.[1] The following recipes are CFC free (see below) and represent recent efforts to reformulate a number of fingerprint reagents because of the probable unavailability of the chlorofluorocarbon (CFC) solvents. The original ninhydrin formulation involved making 15 g up in 30 mL glacial acetic acid and 60 mL absolute ethanol, then diluting 3 mL of this stock with 100 mL fluorisol.

Reagents

According to Watling and Smith:[116]

1. Prepare a stock ninhydrin solution with either:

Ninhydrin	33 g
Absolute anhydrous ethanol	225 mL

   or

Ninhydrin	30 g
Absolute anhydrous ethanol	225 mL

2. Remove 400 mL heptane from a 4-L bottle and reserve.
3. Add the ninhydrin-ethanol solution to the bottle; shake vigorously; top off with the reserved heptane.

Note: *Crystals may form in the alcohol solution, that may be helped into solution by gentle warming.*

According to Hewlett, Sears, and Suzuki:[117]

Ninhydrin	5 g
Absolute anhydrous ethanol	75 mL
Ethyl acetate	25 mL
Glacial acetic acid	3 mL
Heptane	1 L

Another recipe for ninhydrin spray solution consists of 25 g ninhydrin in 4 L acetone, stirred well and stored in a dark bottle.

Procedure

1. Fill the spray unit with the working ninhydrin solution and spray the surface containing the latent print from a distance of about 6 in.
2. Allow the solvent to evaporate and then repeat the spraying process.
3. After spraying, the surface can be heated with an infrared lamp or steam iron for a short period. Be careful not to overheat the surface and do not allow the heat source to come into direct contact with the surface.
4. Alternatively, leave the specimen at room temperature until the latent print fully develops. It may take quite a bit longer to develop prints at room temperature than it would if the development is heat enhanced. However, it often yields more satisfactory results.

As just noted in connection with the ninhydrin solution formulation, a number of latent print investigators have recently focused attention on reformulating ninhydrin, its analogues, and other chemicals that are commonly sprayed (such as DFO) in solvents/vehicles other than Freon 113. Freon 113 (CFC 113, 1,1,2-trichlorotrifluoroethane) was included in the "Montreal Protocol" signed in 1987 which banned CFCs in most of the industrialized countries because of concerns about the ozone layer. It appears likely that CFCs will not be available for this purpose. It should be noted that Watling and Smith[116] and Hewlett, Sears, and Suzuki[117] used heptane as the solvent because of the resulting reagent's performance; heptane is extremely flammable. Margot and Lennard[9] noted that they have substituted mainly petroleum ether, even though care and attention are necessary because of the potential fire hazard. Jungbluth[118] explored an industrial solvent called Genesolv 2000 for both ninhydrin and DFO and found it to be satisfactory, and Hewlett et al.[117,119] found the hydrofluorocarbons (HFCs) HFC4310mee and HFE7100 to be promising ninhydrin solvents, but not as good overall as the heptane based formulation.

Marquez described a modified ninhydrin development procedure applicable to carbonless form documents.[120] Here, the ninhydrin solution was prepared in ethanol and heptane. Filter paper pieces the size of the document were saturated with the ninhydrin solution and then allowed to dry. The document was then sandwiched between the filter papers and heat applied for 30 min, after which the document was placed in a humid chamber. This method was said to prevent the ninhydrin solvent from causing running of the writing on the carbonless document. Pressly described the successful processing of latent prints on latex gloves using a ninhydrin dipping procedure, but with no heating.[121] Margot and Lennard said that heat acceleration of development of ninhydrin-treated latent prints should be avoided, but especially avoided if any post-treatment with metal salts is to be effective.[9]

Pre-Treatment and Post-Treatment Techniques for the Enhancement of Ninhydrin-Developed Latent Prints

Ninhydrin-developed fingerprints often lack contrast because of the color of the background surface. In 1981, German[122] reported the utilization of lasers to examine ninhydrin-treated latent prints. Kobus, Stoilovic, and Warrener[123] described a simple post-ninhydrin treatment technique using zinc chloride and xenon arc light to yield luminescent latent print images. They found that this method improved the visualization of latent prints on paper where ninhydrin alone gave poor results.

Herod and Menzel found that latent prints that did not develop well with ninhydrin could be brought out if examined under dye laser light.[124] Subsequently, they suggested two modified treatments for using ninhydrin to develop latent fingerprints:[77,125] pre-treatment with trypsin and post-treatment with metal salts. In the first modification, latent prints were treated either by spraying with a methanol solution containing both ninhydrin and trypsin or by spraying first with a water solution of trypsin and then with ninhydrin under room light. The samples sprayed first with trypsin and then with ninhydrin showed a somewhat better development than those treated either by the combined solution or by ninhydrin alone. Results under dye laser examination showed no dramatic improvement. In the second modification, ninhydrin-developed latent prints were sprayed with solutions of nickel nitrate, zinc chloride, and cadmium nitrate and then examined by argon laser light. It was found that a combination of the ninhydrin-zinc chloride procedure and 488-nm argon laser light yielded the most promising results by far.

Stoilovic et al. reported a method for improving the enhancement of ninhydrin-developed fingerprints by cadmium complexation using a low-temperature photoluminescence technique.[126] Everse and Menzel further reported that there was a pronounced enhancement of the detectability of latent prints by combining pretreatment with trypsin or pronase with post-treatment with zinc chloride followed by examination by argon laser light.[127]

Recently, researchers in Australia have found that metal complexes formed by using group IIb transition metals show favorable luminescent properties at low temperatures (77°K) and that ninhydrin-treated fingerprints can be enhanced considerably.[128] The structure of the metal complexes formed between Ruhemann's purple and group IIb metal salts was also studied.

Goode and Morris[6] reported that treating ninhydrin-developed fingerprints with metal solutions improves the contrast between the background and the print. Treatment with zinc chloride solution changes the purple color to orange. Treatment with nickel chloride solution produces an orange-red color.

Use of metal ions to form luminescent complexes with the Ruhemann's purple (RP) formed by the reaction of amino acids in the fingerprint residue and ninhydrin (or its analogues) has become a routine practice in developing latents on porous surfaces. Understanding the rather complicated chemistry underlying formation of these complexes also laid the groundwork for more recent work on the use of rare earth ions to induce luminescence[129,130] (and see below). This material has also been reviewed by Menzel.[20,131] Liberti, Calabro, and Chiarotti[132] have studied the stability of the zinc RP complexes.

Ninhydrin/Zinc Chloride Procedures Without Freon:[118]

Ninhydrin solution

Ninhydrin	6 g	
Glacial acetic acid	10 mL	
Methanol	20 mL	

Note: *Stir the above until completely dissolved, then:*

Genesolv 2020	100 mL

Zinc chloride solution

Zinc chloride	6 g
Glacial acetic acid	10 mL
Ethanol	50 mL
Propanol	10 mL

Note: *Stir the above until completely dissolved, then:*

Genesolv 2020	200 mL

Notes: *Fingerprints developed first with cyanoacrylate are immersed in the ninhydrin solution, air dried, and then treated with the zinc chloride solution. The Super Glue treatment stabilizes inks on paper substrata so that they do not run when treated with the ninhydrin.*

Chemical Alternatives to Ninhydrin

Ninhydrin has traditionally been the most common reagent employed for processing latent prints on paper. There are, however, several limitations to the ninhydrin method, such as the sensitivity of the ninhydrin reaction, background colors of the matrix surface, background coloration after ninhydrin treatment, and certain nonreactive surface materials. Numerous compounds have been reported as potential substitutes for ninhydrin in the detection of latent fingerprints. They can be divided into two categories: reagents for amino acid detection and ninhydrin analogues. This area has been thoroughly reviewed by Almog[133] and is the subject of Chapter 5 of this volume.

Reagents for Detection of Amino Acids

In the 1970s and 1980s, fluorescamine,[134] o-phthalaldehyde[135] and NBD-chloride (7-chloro-4-nitrobenzo-2-oxa-1,3-diazole),[136,137] NBD-fluoride (7-fluoro-4-nitrobenzo-2-oxa-1,3-diazole) (Criminal Investigation Bureau, Taiwan, Republic of China, personal communication, 1989), and dansyl chloride[138] had been suggested as substitute reagents for ninhydrin. These reagents react with amino acids in the fingerprint residues to produce fluorescent products that render the latent print pattern visible.[139] Studies have shown that these reagents not only have a greater sensitivity than ninhydrin but also work well for the detection of latent fingerprints on multicolored materials. An additional advantage of the treatment of latent prints with fluorescamine, o-phthalaldehyde and NBD-chloride (NBD-Cl) is that they can subsequently be further enhanced with laser light, xenon arc light, or other light sources.[140] The principal disadvantages of these fluorigenic reagents are that they are not too stable in solution and sometimes produce interfering background luminescence. The procedures for preparing these reagents are as follows:

Fluorescamine reagent

Fluorescamine	20 mg
Acetone	100 mL
20% triethylamine-methylene chloride solution	4 mL

Note:	*Fluorescamine is dissolved in acetone, the 20% triethylamine-methylene chloride solution is added, and the pH is then adjusted to 9 to 11.*

o-Phthalaldehyde reagent

Boric acid	2.5 g
Water	95 mL
4 N KOH	See below
30% Brij 35 solution	0.3 mL
2-Mercaptoethanol	0.2 mL
o-Phthalaldehyde	0.5 g
Methanol	1 mL

Notes: *Boric acid is dissolved in the distilled water, and the pH is adjusted to 10.4 with 4 N KOH. This solution is then stabilized with the addition of the Brij 35 solution and then reduced with the addition of 2-mercaptoethanol. The o-phthalaldehyde dissolved in the methanol is added last.*

Formulations available for the NBD-chloride, NDB-F, and dansyl chloride reagents were provided in the previous edition of the chapter, but all of them are based on Freon. We are not aware of any substitute, CFC-free recipes that have been tested or validated for the development of latents.

Almog et al.[141] have reported on a new series of fluorigenic reagents. Five nitrobenzofurazanyl ethers, 4-methoxy-7-nitrobenzofurazan (NBD-OCH$_3$), 4-ethoxy-7-nitrobenzofurazan (NBD-OCH$_2$CH$_3$), 4-(2-hydroxy)-7-nitrobenzofurazan (NBD-OCH$_2$CH$_2$OH), 4-(methoxy-ethoxy)-7-nitrobenzofurazan (NBD-OCH$_2$CH$_2$OCH$_3$), and 4-phenoxy-7-nitrobenzofurazan (NBD-OC$_6$H$_5$), have been prepared and examined as potential reagents for the detection of latent fingerprints on paper. It was found that all five reagents developed latent prints with high sensitivity, similar to that of the parent compound NBD-Cl. These reagents can also be used in vapor phase development. The study indicates that vapor phase development techniques have advantages, such as the avoidance of the use of solvents and the reduction of the background fluorescence and discoloration. Pounds[5,142] has reported on the use of 1,8-diazafluoren-9-one (DFO) for the fluorescent detection of latent prints on paper. He found that fingerprints visualized by DFO revealed more ridge detail than those developed with ninhydrin/ZnCl$_2$. DFO treatment can be used in conjunction with ninhydrin, but must precede it. DFO treated paper substrata, subsequently developed with ninhydrin, yielded more prints than those developed with ninhydrin alone.[119]

The original preparation of DFO reagent used fluorisol. Other solvent systems besides methanol-fluorisol have been reported by Masters, Morgan, and Shepp (personal communication, 1990) and by Peigare (FBI, personal communication, 1990). The following is the formulation used by them.

DFO stock solution

DFO	1 g
Methanol	180 mL
Acetic acid	20 mL

Working solution

DFO stock solution	60 mL
Acetone	50 mL
2-Propanol	10 mL

Xylene	50 mL
Petroleum ether	830 mL

Procedure

1. Dip the paper containing latent prints into the freshly prepared solution for 5 sec.
2. Allow the paper specimen to dry for 30 sec.
3. Repeat the dipping for another 5 sec (some indicate this step can be omitted)
4. Heat the paper to 100°C for 10 min.
5. View the surface under alternative light sources as follows:
   a. Video spectral comparator (VSC-1) using blue-green light excitation — Fluorescence can be observed through a 610-nm filter.
   b. A 12-W argon laser operated at 514 nm — Fluorescence can be observed through a 550- or a 610-nm filter.
   c. A mercury vapor lamp — Fluorescence can be observed through a 546-nm filter.

As noted above, Jungbluth[118] formulated DFO in a Freon substitute: 50 mg DFO is dissolved in 4 mL methanol and 2 mL acetic acid; then 94 mL Genesolv 2000 is added. Geide[143] similarly formulated DFO in the Freon-substitute solvent *t*-butyl-methyl ether. He noted that the solvent is highly flammable and volatile and must be used with care in a hood. Bratton and Juhala[144] described a sandwiching procedure in which the test item was sandwiched between DFO-treated filter papers and then subjected to 5% acetic acid "steam" (from a steam iron), to get around the problem of solvent-caused ink bleed on documents.

Ninhydrin Analogues

Almog, Hirschfeld, and Klug[145] synthesized several ninhydrin analogues: benzo[e]ninhydrin (2,2-dihydroxybenz[e]-indane-1,3-dione), benzo[f]ninhydrin (2,2-dihydroxybenz[f]-indane-1,3-dione), and 2,2-dihydroxy-5-chloro-6-methoxyindane-1,3-dione. These compounds were tested for their applicability to latent print detection. It was found that the ninhydrin analogues developed latent prints with a sensitivity similar to that of ninhydrin and that the quality of development was independent of the age of the latent fingerprints. Benzo[f]ninhydrin performance in several solvent formulations was recently compared directly with ninhydrin, and found to be superior for certain surfaces, but not in the number of prints developed on actual exhibits overall.[146]

More recently, Almog et al. have synthesized and evaluated a series of both 4- and 5-aminoninhydrins.[147] Absorption and emission characteristics of the compounds were determined and part of the evaluation was based on the reaction of the compounds with alanine in solution. The 5-aminoninhydrins were superior to the 4-amino compounds. However, the 5-amino compounds gave significantly slower development than either ninhydrin or 5-methoxyninhydrin. It was noted that the 5-amino compounds might prove useful as direct fluorigenic reagents for developing latent prints on fluorescent surfaces that absorb in the 400- to 500-nm range and emit at 550 to 650 nm, precluding the use of ninhydrin or 5-methoxyninhydrin.

Menzel and Almog have studied the fluorescent properties of the fingerprints developed by ninhydrin analogues when complexed with zinc chloride. They found that only benzo[f]ninhydrin complex fluoresced as intensely as the ninhydrin complex, and its absorption maximum is 530 nm. The neodymium:yttrium aluminum garnet (Nd:YAG) laser emits light at 532 nm and is more effective than the argon ion laser, which has emission maxima at 488 nm or 514 nm.[148]

Lennard et al.[149] have synthesized methoxy, chloro, bromo, and perinaphtho derivatives of ninhydrin. They found that fingerprints developed by all of the derivatives have the same sensitivity as ninhydrin and photoluminescent complexes that were formed on addition of zinc and cadmium salts.

Almog et al.[150] synthesized 5-methylthio-ninhydrin derivatives and tested them next to other ninhydrin analogues and DFO. They showed superior luminescence properties when the reaction product was complexed with zinc. Cantu et al.[151] compared a series of ninhydrin analogues using a dried amino acid spot model and found thieno[f]ninhydrin to be superior when complexed with zinc, thus providing further evidence that the sulfur-containing ninhydrin analogues exhibit superior luminescence properties when complexed with zinc.

Ramotowski et al. reported on the effectiveness of a series of 1,2-indanediones synthesized at the University of Pennsylvania for latent print development.[152] These compounds may be regarded as ninhydrin analogues of a sort. Overall, the 5,6-dimethoxy-1,2-indanedione was the most effective.[153] The 5,6-dimethyl compound (50 mg) was dissolved in 2 mL methylene chloride and then diluted with 50 mL methanol. The zinc complex of the reaction product gave very good luminescence results with test amino acid spots and with test latent prints. Almog's group further validated 5,6-dimethoxy-1,2-indanedione as equal or superior to other ninhydrin analogues and to DFO.[154,155] Wilkinson[156] presented spectroscopic evidence that alcohols should be avoided as a solvent for the 1,2-indanedione compounds for latent print development. Recently, the Almog group reported that computational design software might be useful in modeling the potential luminescence behavior of Ruhemann's purple-metal complexes of various ninhydrin analogues.[157] As noted earlier, Joseph Almog reviewed this material in the previous edition[133] and presents the current information in Chapter 5 of this volume.

Development of Latent Prints With Metal Ions/Compounds — Physical Developers

Silver Nitrate Reagent

Silver nitrate has been used for developing latent fingerprints since 1891.[1] The basic principle of this technique is the reaction of silver nitrate with the chloride present in the fingerprint deposit. The product of this reaction, silver chloride, rapidly turns black on exposure to light. However, because the procedure is cumbersome and the background can stain, this method is principally of historical interest today.

Goode and Morris[6] have suggested using a methanolic solution instead of the conventional aqueous solution. This method works well with latent prints on newspaper and untreated wood. However, silver nitrate reagent does not work well with physical evidence that has been stored or exposed to high humidity. Under conditions of high humidity, the chloride in the latent print deposit migrates by diffusion. Researchers have shown that significant deterioration occurs after 15 days at 60% relative humidity. Prints weakly developed with silver nitrate may be enhanced by further treatment with dilute physical developer.[9]

Other Silver-Containing Compounds

Kerr, Westland, and Haque[158] have studied the perchlorate, tetrafluoroborate, and hexafluoroantimonate salts of silver as well as silver perchlorate/camphor as alternative reagents for silver nitrate solution. These compounds were effective, and the studies indicated that the silver salt reaction with the chloride in latent fingerprint residue was dependent on the microroughness of the surface.

Physical Developer

Physical developer enhancement is a photographic process based on the formation of silver onto a latent fingerprint image from a ferrous/ferric redox couple and metal salt mixture. Goode and Morris[6] have reviewed the early work on techniques using "stabilized" physical developer[31] and found that physical developer reacts with lipid material present in the fingerprint residue. The technique has been used to develop latent prints on paper, nonabsorbent surfaces, and pressure-sensitive tapes. It also can be used on objects after ninhydrin processing.[6]

Phillips, Cole, and Jones[159] reported that, in actual casework in the FBI Latent Fingerprint Section, identifiable latent prints that did not develop with ninhydrin were developed on 20% of the specimens processed with physical developer (PD). They also found latent prints on postage stamps, the adhesive strip on the closure flaps of envelopes, adhesive tapes, the emulsion side of photographs, and U.S. currency. The following is a simplified version of the procedure reported by them.

Reagents

Prewash solution

Maleic acid	25 g
Distilled water	1 L

Redox solution

Ferric nitrate	30 g
Ammonium ferrous sulfate	80 g
Citric acid	20 g
Distilled water	900 mL

Surfactant solution

n-Dodecylamine acetate	3 g
Synperonic N	4 g
Distilled water	1 L

Silver nitrate solution

Silver nitrate	10 g
Distilled water	50 mL

Note: *PD working solution: mix 900 mL redox solution, 40 mL surfactant solution, and 50 mL silver nitrate solution.*

Procedures

1. Immerse specimen in maleic acid solution for at least 5 min.
2. Transfer the specimen from the prewash solution to the PD working solution.
3. Submerge the specimen in PD working solution for approximately 5 min with a gentle rocking (as long as it takes to develop, but not overdevelop, prints).

4. Rinse the specimen in tap water.
5. Dry the specimen thoroughly with a temperature-adjustable hair dryer.
6. Reprocess weakly developed latent prints (low contrast) in PD working solution.
7. Photograph the developed latent print(s).
8. The visualization of latent prints developed on soiled and darkened surfaces can be enhanced by immersing the specimen in a 50% dilution of common household bleach.

Margot and Lennard[9] describe recipes for the original reagent mixtures and the Phillips, Cole, and Jones modification[159] just given. In addition, they mention a simplified PD, personally communicated to them by Saunders in 1993 and fully described in Chapter 7 of this volume. The Phillips, Cole, and Jones physical developer described above is more stable and produces better prints than the Saunders recipe.

Modified Physical Developer Methods

In 1989, Saunders and the U.S. Secret Service Forensic Services Division reported a new procedure involving the use of colloidal gold with PD. This technique was called "multimetal deposition" (MMD).[160] An additional colloidal gold step was used. Collodial gold at pH 3 binds to amino acids, peptides, and proteins in fingerprint residue. The bound colloidal gold provides a nucleation site around which silver precipitates in the second incubation step. The following is the procedure for the multimetal deposition method:

Reagents

Stabilized Physical Developer: Colloidal Gold

Solution A: Redox

Ferric nitrate	33 g
Ferrous ammonium sulfate	89 g
Citric acid	22 g
Tween 20	1 mL
Distilled water	1 L

Notes: *Dissolve the chemicals in the order listed in 1 L distilled water and then add the Tween 20. This solution is stable indefinitely at room temperature.*

Solution B: Silver nitrate

Silver nitrate	20 g
Distilled water	100 mL

Note: *Store in a dark bottle at room temperature.*

> Working Solution
>
> | Solution A | 99 parts |
> |---|---|
> | Solution B | 1 part |

Notes: *Make just before using: the working solution is stable for only about 15 min. Develop prints in the absence of fluorescent lights if possible.*

Preparation of Colloidal Gold

> Stock gold: Prepare a 10% (w/v) solution of tetrachloroauric acid in high-quality distilled water. This solution is stable indefinitely at room temperature.
>
> Stock sodium citrate: Prepare a 1% (w/v) solution of sodium citrate in distilled water. This solution is stable indefinitely at room temperature.

1. Add 1 mL stock gold solution to 1 L distilled water and bring to a boil.
2. Gently add 10 mL stock sodium citrate solution and boil gently for 10 min. The final solution should be the color of port wine.
3. Stir in 5 mL Tween 20 while solution is still hot and then allow to cool.
4. Adjust the pH to about 3 with 0.5 M citric acid (usually about 1 mL is required).
5. Restore the solution volume to 1 L. Some volume is lost during the boiling steps.
6. Store the solution in a scrupulously clean glass or plastic container in the refrigerator. The solution is stable for several months at 4°C.

Procedure

1. If item to be tested is paper, soak it in several changes of distilled water for 20 to 30 min. Do not use maleic acid.
2. Place the item to be tested in the colloidal gold solution for 30 to 120 min.
3. Rinse the item with distilled water.
4. Place the item in the silver developer (modified PD working solution) for 5 to 15 min.
5. Thoroughly rinse the item in distilled water.
6. Air dry the item and photograph the latent prints.

Saunders found that this procedure worked well with many surfaces and materials, such as computer floppy disks, adhesive tapes, metals, papers, Styrofoam, credit cards, and glass. It also can be used for specimens that have been treated with ninhydrin. In addition, latent prints can be first transferred from the specimen surface to a nitrocellulose membrane and then developed.

In another modification, Knowles[161] reported a radioactive visualization method. The developed latent print silver image is first converted to silver bromide, which is then reacted with radioactively labeled thiourea to produce silver sulfide, and the latent print image can then be recorded by autoradiography. Nolan et al.[162] reported a method employing scanning electron microscopy to remove interference from the background.

Recently, Ramotowski[163] compared a series of commercial and laboratory-prepared PD reagents for effectiveness in developing latents on different papers. The commercial reagents generally performed adequately, though there can be problems with the reagents on occasion. Dilute acetic acid (household vinegar) worked about as well as a pre-treatment as the usual maleic acid. Physical developers are fully reviewed and discussed by Antonio Cantu in Chapter 7.

Metal Deposition

In 1968, Theys et al.[25] reported that it was possible to detect the presence of fat films on some surfaces by the selective condensation of metals under vacuum. This is often called vacuum metal deposition (VMD). Since that time, several metals have been investigated as possible reagents for the delineation of latent fingerprints. It was reported that a combination of gold followed by cadmium treatment produced excellent results.[24] Since cadmium is toxic, zinc and the combination of gold/zinc have been suggested.[164] Kent et al.[26] reported a fairly high success rate with this technique on polyethylene bags.

Batey et al.[165] indicated the procedure worked well on nonporous paper and plastic and could be helpful with older items, such as from older cases. Kent and Stoilovic[166] reported successful development of latents with several metals using DC sputtering, a variant of VMD. Murphy[167] reported good results raising an identifiable latent on a milk carton surface where cyanoacrylate fuming alone had not sufficed.

Migron et al. evaluated a number of metal deposition and vacuum metal deposition techniques for detecting both eccrine and sebaceous latent prints deposited on cartridge cases prior to firing the cartridges in the appropriate firearm.[168] Some identifiable prints could be developed on brass cases, but generally, these were difficult surfaces.

Special Surfaces or Situations

Enhancement of Bloody Fingerprints

Special techniques are often required for successfully developing bloody latent fingerprints.[6,169-171] Bloody fingerprints can often be found deposited

on weapons, victims' bodies, and objects at crime scenes. In many c
these bloody prints require enhancement to increase contrast and make them more visible. There are two general categories of chemical reagents that can be used to enhance the bloody fingerprints.

The first category of reagents are those chemicals that react with the heme moiety of the hemoglobin molecule of the red blood cells in blood. Heme will catalyze an oxidation reaction and convert the reagent to an oxidized product that is colored. In the past, reagents prepared using benzidine were the most popular choice for bloody print enhancement. However, benzidine was found to be carcinogenic and thus extremely hazardous. Since 1974, the use of benzidine has been banned for all practical purposes by the federal Occupational Safety and Health Administration.[172] Lee[173] reported that a number of safer chemicals, including tetramethylbenzidine,[174] o-tolidine, phenolphthalin, and leucomalachite green, can be substituted for benzidine in the enhancement schemes.

The second category of reagents is general protein stains. These chemical dye solutions will bind to the protein molecules in blood and yield a colored complex. However, since most proteins are water soluble, the bloody fingerprint proteins have to be denatured and fixed onto the surface before immersion of the object into the dye solution. The commonly used protein dyes such as amido black,[175] ninhydrin, crystal violet, and Coomassie blue[176] have been reported to work very successfully in the enhancement of bloody fingerprints. The preparation of these reagents and procedures for their use with latent fingerprints are as follows:

1. Heme-reacting chemicals
   a. Tetramethylbenzidine

Reagents

Buffer solution

Sodium acetate	5 g
Glacial acetic acid	43 mL
Distilled water	50 mL

Stock solution

3,3′,5,5′-Tetramethylbenzidine	0.4 g
Buffer solution	20 mL

Colloidon-ethanol-ether solution

Collodion	30 mL
Ethanol	15 mL
Ethyl ether	120 mL

Working solution

Stock solution	6 mL
Sodium perborate	0.5 g
Colloidon-ethanol-ether solution	120 mL

Note: *Mix the stock solution and sodium perborate well, add the colloidon-ethanol-ether solution, and mix well again.*

Procedure

Spray the surface containing the bloody fingerprints two or three times from a distance of about 10 in.

> b. Phenolphthalin

Reagents

Stock solution

Phenolphthalin	2 g
Potassium hydroxide	20 g
Distilled water	100 mL
Powdered zinc	20 g

Note: *Reflux until the solution becomes colorless (typically 2 to 3 hr). Store in a dark bottle with some zinc powder at the bottom.*

Working solution

Stock solution	20 mL
Ethanol	80 mL
3% Hydrogen peroxide	5 drops

Procedure

Apply the working solution to the surface containing the bloody fingerprints and allow it to dry.

> c. Leucomalachite green

Reagents

Leucomalachite green	1 g
Ethyl ether	70 mL

Glacial acetic acid	10 drops
20 to 30% hydrogen peroxide	5 drops

Procedure

Apply the working solution to the surface containing the bloody fingerprints and allow it to dry.

2. Protein dye solutions
   a. Amido black (Naphthol blue black; naphthalene 12B)

Reagents

First solution

Amido black 10B	0.2 g
Glacial acetic acid	10 mL
Methanol	90 mL

Second solution

Glacial acetic acid	10 mL
Methanol	90 mL

Third solution

Glacial acetic acid	5 mL
Methanol	98 mL

Procedure

1. Bake article to be examined at 100°C for 30 min or immerse the item in methanol for 1 hr. If methanol immersion is likely to damage the item, use the alternative (aqueous-based) formula.
2. Immerse the article into the first solution and agitate it to ensure that the entire surface is treated.
3. Immerse the article into the second solution and agitate it.
4. Rinse the article in the third solution.
5. Allow the article to dry and then photograph the print.

   b. Amido black (alternative aqueous-based formula)

Citric acid stock:

Citric acid	38 g
Distilled water	2 L

Note: *Combine and stir until citric acid is completely dissolved.*

Developing solution:

Citric acid stock solution	2 L
Amido black	2 g
Kodak PhotoFlo 600	

Note: *Add amido black to stirred solution of citric acid stock, stir 30 min, and then add the PhotoFlo.*

c. Crystal violet

Reagent

Crystal violet	0.1 g
Distilled water	100 mL
Ammonia	

Notes: *Dissolve 0.1 g crystal violet in 100 mL distilled water. Stir until the solid is completely dissolved. Adjust pH to 7 to 8 with ammonia.*

Procedure

1. Bake the article to be examined at 100°C for 30 min.
2. Immerse the article into the solution for 3 min.
3. Rinse the article with distilled water and allow the surfaces to dry.

d. Coomassie blue

Reagents

Staining solution

Coomassie brilliant blue R250	0.44 g
Glacial acetic acid	40 mL
Methanol	200 mL
Distilled water	200 mL

Destaining solution

Glacial acetic acid	40 mL
Methanol	200 mL
Distilled water	200 mL

Procedure

1. Bake the article to be examined at 100°C for 30 min.
2. Immerse the article into the solution for 3 min.
3. Rinse the article with destaining solution and allow the surfaces to dry.

e. Crowle's reagent

Reagents

Crocein scarlet 7B	2.5 g
Coomassie brilliant blue R250	0.15 g
Glacial acetic acid	50 mL
Trichloroacetic acid	30 mL
Distilled water	920 mL

Procedure

1. Bake the article to be examined at 100°C for 30 min. This step can be omitted with some items.
2. Immerse the article into the dye solution for 5 to 30 min with constant agitation.
3. Rinse the article with Crowle's destaining solution (3 mL glacial acetic acid in a final volume of 1 L with water) until the background coloration disappears (about 1 min) and allow the surface to dry.

Note: The staining procedure can be repeated.

In addition, Whritenour reported that a method using cyanoacrylate fuming before Coomassie blue staining enhanced bloody fingerprints on plastic bag material.[177] However, McCarthy and Grieve[178] have found that no improvement was achieved with cyanoacrylate fuming in most situations. With glass and metal surfaces, cyanoacrylate preprocessing is harmful for further processing with Coomassie blue, Crowle's reagent, and amido black dye. Warrick reported good results in developing a bloody print on a cotton sheet surface with an amido black staining solution used in conjunction with digital enhancement of the resulting developed print.[179] Jaret, Heriau, and Donche[180] investigated the feasibility of transferring heme reagent-developed prints onto photographic papers or other similar media and noted that only leucocrystal violet and leucomalachite green treated prints could be transferred.

Zauner[181] noted that on a rare occasion, a friction ridge print could be developed on denim.

Lee and Gaensslen have compared all the methods available for the enhancement of bloody fingerprints.[7] It was found that the heme-reacting chemical reagents, such as tetramethylbenzidine, phenolphthalin, o-tolidine, and leucomalachite green, are extremely sensitive to the presence of blood and will yield positive results with dilutions of blood as low as 1 part in 1 million. On the other hand, general protein dye solutions, such as Crowle's reagent, amido black, crystal violet, and Coomassie blue, show a sensitivity toward blood that generally falls in the 1 part in 1 thousand dilution range. A disadvantage of techniques involving the dye solution staining technique is that articles containing latent prints have to be directly immersed in the solution. To prevent the bloodstain from dissolving in the solution, the article has to be baked in an oven at 100°C for 3 to 5 min to denature and fix the bloodstain on the surface. In addition, most dye solutions are made with organic solvents or are soluble under acidic conditions, making them unsuitable for use on certain surfaces. Hunter[182] described successful development of an identifiable print on gloves after 25 years with Coomassie blue.

Allman and Pounds communicated to Margot and Lennard[9] in 1991 and 1992 that they favored the use of diaminobenzidine (DAB) for bloody print enhancement. Treatment of the bloody latent prints is by immersion, first in a solution of 2% 5-sulfosalicylic acid for about 2 min followed by a distilled water wash. Next, the prints are treated in a solution consisting of (a) 0.1 g DAB in 10 mL distilled water; (b) 90 mL of 0.1 M phosphate buffer, pH 7.4; and (c) 0.5 mL of 30% H_2O_2 solution. Stoilovic[183] noted that blood prints on porous surfaces can be visualized using DFO and Polilight with a 590 bandpass viewing filter. Use of DFO does not preclude the subsequent use of colored protein stains.

It is known that when liquid blood coagulates (clots), the serum and blood cells separate. A straw-colored liquid, the serum fraction, forms around the solid red mass, the blood cell fraction. If a finger touches coagulated blood that has not dried and then deposits a print on a surface, the resulting "bloody" fingerprint may be composed mainly of serum, mainly of coagulated red cells, or of both. These possibilities have significant implications for choosing the optimal method of bloody fingerprint enhancement. The best method for a particular bloody print should be based on an understanding of the nature of the bloody print and the mechanism of transfer. Although not strictly having to do with latent print development, another issue that sometimes arises is the order of deposition of blood vs. fingerprints.[184,185]

Development of Latent Prints on Tapes or Sticky Surfaces

The development of fingerprints on adhesive tape has always been a challenge for latent fingerprint examiners. In 1981, Ishiyama[186] reported the successful development of fingerprints on the adhesive side of cellophane tape using Coomassie brilliant blue 250. Koemm[187] reported the use of gentian violet (crystal violet) to develop latent prints on the sticky side of tape. Arima[188] reported using aqueous solutions of crystal violet or Victoria page blue for polyvinyl chloride (PVC), cloth, Kraft paper, or cellophane tapes as long as these tapes were not of a dark color. Latent fingerprints on the sticky surfaces of adhesive tapes could be successfully developed. He also suggested the use of a fluorescent dye, Mikephor, for colored or black electrical tape. Latent prints can be visualized by treatment with Mikephor BS, a fluorescent brightener, and subsequently viewed under UV light. Arima also found that the fluorescent reagents o-phthalaldehyde and 8-anilino-1-napthalene sulfonic acid were equally effective. Martin developed identifiable prints on the sticky side of black tape by painting an ash-gray powder suspended in PhotoFlo solution onto the surface then gently rinsing with water.[189] Similarly, Sneddon[190] and Paris[191] described the successful use of mixtures of detergents and black powders for sticky tape surfaces, and Burns[192] used a product called "Sticky Side" powder (available in Japan) with PhotoFlo with good results on the items tested except the sticky side of black electric tape.

Wilson and McCleod[193] proposed an alternative method for the visualization of fingerprints on black tape using crystal violet and photographic paper. Tucker[194] described a modified crystal violet method for processing latent prints on black electrical tape. The following is the general outline of the procedure:

Reagents

Stock solution

Crystal violet	1.5 g
Ethyl alcohol	100 mL

Working solution

Stock solution	10 mL
Distilled water	500 mL

Procedure

1. Brush the adhesive side of the tape with the crystal violet working solution using a camel-hair brush.
2. Dry the tape surface with a hot hair dryer.

3. Expose the tape surface to a high-intensity photo lamp until the latent prints have developed.
4. Photograph the developed latent prints.
5. With black tape, transfer the developed latent print onto photographic paper by the following procedure.
   a. Place the developed tape between two pieces of RC photographic paper with the emulsion side of the photographic papers facing the tape to form a "sandwich."
   b. Place the sandwich between two pieces of 1/8-in.-thick blotter paper.
   c. Heat the blotter paper at low temperature using an iron.
   d. Photograph the transferred fingerprint.

Margot and Lennard[9] use a stock solution of 5 g gentian violet and 10 g phenol (very toxic) in 50 mL ethanol. The working solution is a 1:25 dilution of stock into water. The processed latents are transferred onto photographic paper. Other recipes we have seen for the phenol-based reagent use the same stock solution as Margot and Lennard, but the working solution is a 1:100 dilution of stock into water.

Teuszkowski and Loninga[195] have found that the emulsion side of photographic paper often sticks to the adhesive side of the tape and suggested an alternative procedure for processing latent prints on the sticky side of black tape. Taylor and Mankevich[196] reported using a silver protein staining procedure to develop latent prints on tape. This method was found to be very effective when used in conjunction with gentian violet. Hollars, Trozzi, and Barron described a procedure involving treatment with Ardrox in detergent solution that was said to work well on dark-colored, sticky surfaces where gentian violet worked poorly.[197] Bratton and Gregus compared gentian violet, a commercial "Sticky Side" powder, and a black powder in detergent suspension on a series of latent prints on various tapes.[198] Prints in the study were characterized as "initial," "sebaceous," and "eccrine." The black powder in detergent suspension worked best on the "eccrine" prints, that are apparently not well developed by gentian violet. Howard[199] used basic fuchsin processing on black electric tape that does not respond well to gentian violet; 20 mg basic fuchsin (Aldrich Chemical product was preferred in limited comparison study) was dissolved in 400 mL methanol or water, and the test item was immersed for 50 sec to 1 min before drying and examination under laser light.

Martin[200] reported moderate success in developing latents on smooth glossy surfaces that had been transferred there from the sticky surfaces of tapes. Frosted cellophane tape was the most efficient transfer medium.

Detection of Latent Prints on Skin

Over the years, various procedures have been suggested for the visualization and recovery of latent fingerprints on human skin. Methods such as dusting with magnetic powder,[201] Kromekote card lifting,[24] electronography,[24] iodine-silver plate transfer,[202-204] laser detection by inherent luminescence,[205] dusting with fluorescent powder or evaporative staining with fluorescent dyes followed by laser examination,[206] and Super Glue fuming have all been investigated.[207] Allman and Pounds reviewed this subject in 1991.[208]

The iodine-silver plate transfer method was at one time considered to be a practical technique for the recovery of latent prints on skin.[209] In this method, the area of skin with the suspected latent print is first fumed with an iodine fuming gun. Once the latent print image is developed, the image is transferred onto a silver plate, exposed to strong light, and evaluated.

Cyanoacrylate fuming and dusting with Mars red fluorescent powder or staining with Rhodamine 6G followed by laser examination have recently been shown to be somewhat successful. Delmas[210] studied the use of luminescent magnetic powder in conjunction with cyanoacrylate fuming and laser examination on cadavers. Five cadavers were examined after intentionally placing latent prints on body surfaces, and identifiable latent prints were recovered in four of the cases.

The following is the general procedure for processing latent fingerprints on the human body by the combination method of cyanoacrylate fuming, dusting with fluorescent powder, and laser examination:

1. Place a suitable tank, box, tent, or casket over the cadaver.
2. Put approximately 0.5 to 1.0 g Super Glue into the fuming chamber.
3. Place 500 mL hot water into a beaker and put this in the fuming chamber to increase the humidity.
4. Fume the body for approximately 30 min to 1 hr.
5. Prepare the Rhodamine 6G magnetic powder:
   a. Dissolve 0.1 g Rhodamine 6G in 50 mL methanol.
   b. Add 100 g black magnetic powder to the rhodamine solution.
   c. Heat the mixture with constant stirring until dried.
   d. Grind the dried mixture to fine powder.
6. Dust the body with the rhodamine-coated magnetic powder.
7. Examine the dusted area under laser light or any other light sources.
8. Photograph the developed latent print(s).

Sampson has described systematic methods for latent prints on skin.[211,212] The temperature differential between the lifting medium and body (10 to 16°C), where the medium is warmer, is said to be key to success. Various lifting media were used, followed by Super Glue fuming. Ruthenium tetroxide,[102] various modifications of Super Glue[64,213] (including experiments using an animal model)[214] and transfer to polyethylene terephthalate (PET) sheets,[215] and casting techniques[30] have all been mentioned.

Wilkinson and Watkin[91] described a europium chelate (TEC) designed to exploit the narrow emission band of the rare earths using intramolecular energy transfer to overcome its poor absorption characteristics and successfully applied this technique to cyanoacrylate-developed latents on cadaver skin under certain conditions. In comparing this procedure to others, however, they generally got the most consistent results with an iodine-benzoflavone technique.[216]

Generally, hairless areas of smooth skin on a fresh body are more likely to yield identifiable latent prints. However, there has yet to be a single, effective procedure developed, and success rates are very low.

Development of Latent Fingerprints on Wet Surfaces

Morris and Wells patented a technique for developing latent prints on wet surfaces, especially wet paper, that used finely divided particles in a surfactant solution.[31] This reagent is called stabilized physical developer (SPD; see Physical Developer on page 136).[217] SPD has been found to offer considerable potential for the detection of latent prints on surfaces that have been exposed to water. SPD reagent consists of a solution containing ferrous ammonium sulfate and ferric nitrate, silver nitrate, citric acid buffer, and two surfactants: laurylamine acetate and Lissapol. The development is done under tungsten light to reduce random background deposition over the entire surface.

Development of Latent Fingerprints on Other Special Surfaces

Periodically, there have been reports on special techniques or variations of existing techniques to improve development of latent prints on unusual surfaces, such as incendiary bottles,[218-220] stones,[221] firearms and firearms-related evidence,[96,168,222-225] computer components in gaming machines,[226] deer antlers,[227] and aluminum foil.[228] Levi and Leifer[229] described a procedure to create contrast between latent prints on glass bottles and the glass for photography.

Luminescence/Fluorescence — Laser and Alternative Light Source Methods for Latent Print Enhancement

Laser Light and Alternative Light Sources

The ability to use laser illumination to detect latent fingerprints is one of the most significant developments in this field ever. The routine use of laser illumination is often done in conjunction with metal salt post-treatment of ninhydrin-developed latents. Accordingly, much of the information was presented starting on page 127. Here, the underlying principles and some more recent developments are discussed further.

As early as 1937, scientists suggested that alternative light sources (other than room light) could be used for the enhancement and visualization of latent fingerprints. High-intensity lamps, UV light sources, lasers, and xenon arc lamps have been utilized in the development of latent prints[16-19,77,230,231] and have produced better latent print images than regular room light.

Dalrymple, Duff, and Menzel[230] first reported the technique of laser detection of latent fingerprints by their inherent luminescence. Subsequently, a number of alternative procedures were suggested. Various fluorescent powders such as Mars red, hi-intensity fingerprint powder, Red Lake C, and naphthol red B (2'-naphtholazo-1-bromo-2-naphthol-1'-sulfonate) have subsequently been employed to enhance the detection sensitivity of the laser procedure. Other fluorigenic dyes, such as coumarin 6, Rhodamine 6G, Rhodamine B, Aquabest orange fluorescent pigment, phenothiazine, Nile Blue A perchloride, and 3,3'-diethylthiatricarbocyamine iodine, have also been used to enhance laser light detection of latent prints.[16-20] Initially, it was recognized that inducement of the intrinsic fluorescence of latent fingerprint residue required wavelengths shorter than were available in any commercial lasers. Thus, use of compounds with desirable excitation and emission wavelengths that would also adhere to fingerprint residue or interact with ninhydrin- or cyanoacrylate-processed latent prints greatly extended the applicability of laser processing.[16,17,20,75,148,232] These chemicals react or interact preferentially with components in fingerprint residues to form luminescent reaction products. Of all the different strategies tried, post-treatment of ninhydrin-developed latent prints with zinc chloride has proved the most robust for laser processing.[77,124] Other types of lasers such as dye lasers and copper vapor lasers have also been used for latent print detection. A review of the use of lasers for the detection of latent prints can be found in the first edition of this book.[131]

Bramble et al. showed that shortwave UV illumination produced as the fourth harmonic of a Nd:YAG laser (266 nm) gave good results with a series of sebaceous prints on white surfaces, yielding more prints of good quality than several visible luminescence methods.[233] Ben-Yosef et al. reported similar results, although noting that the technique was primarily applicable to searching textiles and other substrata for biological fluids.[234] Shortwave UV illumination did not give good luminescence results with eccrine prints. These methods take advantage of the intrinsic fluorescence properties of latent fingerprint residue and may be preferable to more widespread methods under certain circumstances. The Bramble group has also used thin-layer chromatography of actual latent fingerprint residue to help identify the fluorescing species.[235] In this context, it is also of interest that high-energy discharges yield fluorescence in latent print residue[236,237] and that the responsible component may well be a lipid. Related to this is a corona discharge technique described by Halahmi et al.[238]

Menzel[131] has noted that laser detection of latent print residue can exploit three properties associated with luminescence: intensity, color, and lifetime. He and collaborators investigated the use of time-resolved imaging methods to take advantage of the fact that background luminescence is typically shorter (by orders of magnitude) than fingerprint residue signal.[239] A similar approach has been mentioned in connection with supressing background illumination when using portable laser light at crime scenes.[240]

Some trivalent lanthanides display long lifetime luminescence characteristics and will complex with Ruhemann's purple.[241] Menzel recognized in 1997 that this feature made them good candidates for latent print detection and amenable to both optical filtering and time-resolved imaging as well.[242-244] This approach in effect substitutes a lanthanide (usually Eu) for zinc in complex with Ruhemann's purple. Unlike the Zn complexes, the lanthanide ones require UV excitation, however, and the coupling of other compounds to the complex to take advatange of intramolecular energy transfer to improve the luminesence have been explored, especially by Wilkinson and her collaborators.[91,92,245,246] Allred and Menzel described a novel Eu biocomplex (with EDTA) to enhance Ruhemann's purple luminescence from latent print residues.[105]

In 1983, Kobus, Stoilovic, and Warrener at the Forensic Science Research Unit of Australia developed a modified xenon arc lamp.[123] About the same time, the "Quaser" light source was developed by the Scientific Research and Development Branch of the U.K. Home Office, and the "Lumaprint" light was designed by Watkin at the National Research Council of Canada. It was found that the modified xenon arc lamp could produce results comparable to those obtained with the laser in the detection of latent prints developed with either NBD-Cl or ninhydrin followed by zinc chloride.[140] Currently, there are several different alternative light sources commercially available under the trade names Unilite, Luma-Lite, and Polilight. In addition, some very good results have been reported by German using a reflected UV imaging system (RUVIS) originally developed by scientists at the National Police Agency of Japan and commercially available.[247] The so-called alternate or alternative light sources have sufficient versatility in their illumination bandwidth adjustments to be good alternatives to lasers when used with appropriate dyes in the various latent development techniques and with appropriate viewing filters.

The most recent developments in novel approaches to latent print development involve photoluminescent nanocrystals or nanocomposites by Menzel and collaborators.[248-250] Practical methods based on this interesting approach have yet to be fully developed. The subject is reviewed and explored in Chapter 6.

Miscellaneous Methods

Nolan et al.[251] reported that latent prints developed by small particle reagents are easily imaged by the back-scattered electron image mode of the scanning electron microscope (SEM). Low SEM magnifications have permitted the recording of single complete fingerprints on checks, newsprint, and other surfaces. In addition, X-ray radiography and infrared microscopy have also been suggested for the detection of latent fingerprints.[252,253]

Graham and Gray described an electronography technique in 1966.[24] A latent print was first dusted with fine lead powder and subsequently bombarded with X-rays from high-energy sources; the emissions were then detected by photographic emulsions. It was reported that that technique has been used successfully in developing latent print human skin.[24,254] It also worked well on multicolored surfaces, background interferences being totally eliminated.[255]

A few techniques have been proposed that were based on now dated serological techniques.[256-258] One study[259] looked at a bacteriological technique for the detection of fingerprints.

Systematic Approaches to Latent Print Processing

There have been hundreds of techniques for the development and visualization of latent fingerprints reported in the literature. Each of the methods has its advantages and performed well under certain conditions. The application of the correct technique for a particular surface or given set of conditions is extremely important. The application of more than one technique or reagent for the detection of latent prints can often increase the number of prints found or improve the quality of those already developed. However, it is imperative that reagents are applied in a systematic and correct order. Use of a wrong or inappropriate procedure might actually destroy the latent print evidence and obviate any chance for visualization by another technique.

Beginning in 1985, several investigators suggested different logical schemes for the sequential development of latent prints.[260-262] An excellent manual of fingerprint development technique was published in 1986 that contained various systematic process charts for developing latent fingerprints.[260] Lennard and Margot[8,9] conducted detailed studies of the various chemical reagents available

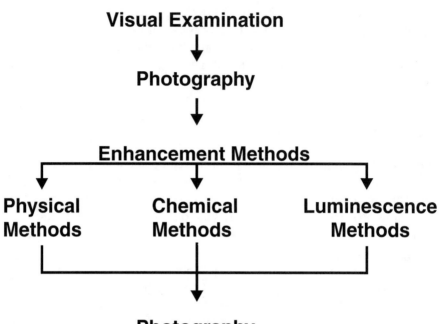

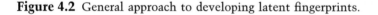

Figure 4.2 General approach to developing latent fingerprints.

and developed sequential procedures for improved visualization of latent fingerprints on porous and nonporous surfaces.

Figures 4.2 through 4.7 represent some of the systematic approaches that have been successfully employed by the Connecticut State Police Forensic Science Laboratory. Figure 4.2 represents a general approach for the detection of latent fingerprints. Figure 4.3 is a scheme for the enhancement of bloody fingerprints. Figure 4.4 shows the approach for the detection of latent fingerprints on nonporous surfaces. Figure 4.5 is the procedure used for visualization of latent fingerprints on greasy or waxed surfaces. Figure 4.6 shows the systematic approach for the detection of latent fingerprints on adhesive tape. Figure 4.7 is the procedural scheme for the development of latent fingerprints on paper products. These logical schemes serve primarily as suggested orders for the application of a series of techniques to the processing of latent prints by examiners. They are not to be regarded as complete or perfect. The systematic approaches should be continuously modified and refined as new procedures, chemical reagents, and approaches are developed.

The fingerprint field has witnessed revolutionary change in the last 30 years, especially in the development of novel methods for the development and enhancement of latents. Many of the newer methods are based on clever

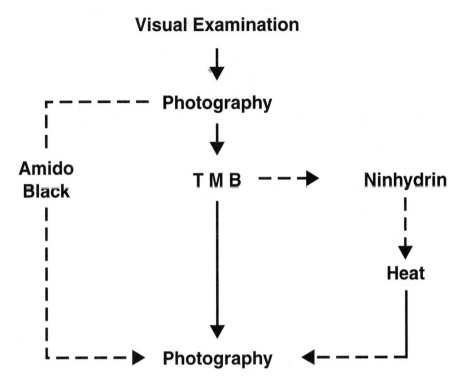

Figure 4.3 Systematic approach for developing bloody fingerprints.

applications of chemistry and physics to fingerprint science. Fingerprint examiners continue to play a primary role in crime scene and criminal investigations, but will increasingly need greater knowledge of and training in chemistry, luminescence methods, imaging, and computer technologies as the field moves forward.

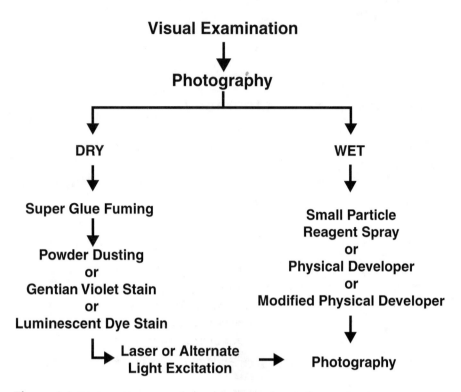

Figure 4.4 Systematic approach for developing latent fingerprints on nonporous surfaces.

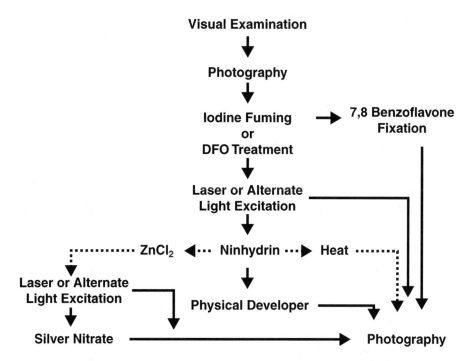

Figure 4.5 Systematic approach for developing latent fingerprints on greasy or waxy surfaces.

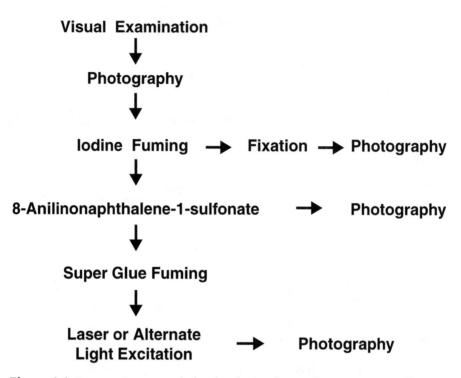

Figure 4.6 Systematic approach for developing latent fingerprints on adhesive tapes.

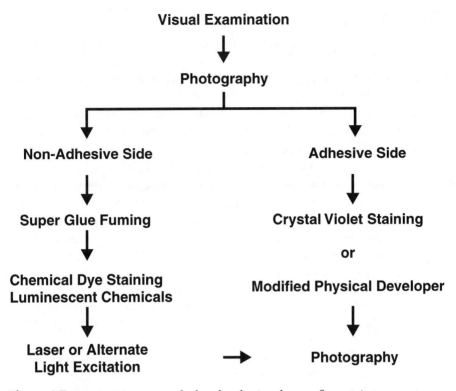

Figure 4.7 Systematic approach for developing latent fingerprints on porous surfaces, including paper.

References

1. Olsen, R. D., *Scott's Fingerprint Mechanics*, Charles C Thomas, Springfield, IL, 1978.

2. Federal Bureau of Investigation, The Science of Fingerprints, U.S. Government Printing Office, Washington, D.C., 1977.

3. Hazen, R. J., Significant advances in the science of fingerprints, in *Forensic Science*, Davies, G., Ed., American Chemical Society, Washington, D.C., 1986,

4. De Forest, P. R., Gaensslen, R. E., and Lee, H. C., *Forensic Science: An Introduction to Criminalistics,* McGraw-Hill, New York, 1983.

5. Pounds, C. A., Developments in fingerprint visualisation. *Forensic Sci. Progr.*, Maehly, A. and Williams, R.L., Eds., Springer-Verlag, Berlin, 1988, 91-119.

6. Goode, G. C. and Morris, J. R., Latent Fingerprints: A Review of Their Origin, Composition and Methods for Detection. Atomic Weapons Research Establishment, Aldermaston, England, 1983

7. Lee, H. C. and Gaensslen, R. E., Methods of latent print development, in Proceedings of the International Forensic Symposium on Latent Prints, Laboratory & Identification Divisions, Federal Bureau of Investigation FSRTC FBI Academy, Quantico, VA, U.S. Government Printing Office, Washington, D.C., 1983, 15-24.

8. Lennard, C. J. and Margot, P. A., Sequencing of reagents for the improved visualization of latent fingerprints. *J. Forensic Ident.*, 38, 197, 1988.

9. Margot, P. and Lennard, C., *Fingerprint Detection Techniques,* Universite de Lausanne, Institut de Police Scientifique et de Criminologie, Lausanne, 1994.

10. James, J. D., Pounds, C. A., and Wilshire, B. W., Obliteration of latent fingerprints. *J. Forensic Sci.*, 36, 1376, 1991.

11. Barron, I. W., Haque, F., and Westland, A. D., Rejuvenation of latent fingerprints by the freeze-thaw technique. *Ident. News*, 31, 14, 1981.

12. James, J. D., Pounds, C. A., and Wilshire, B. W., Flake metal powders for revealing latent fingerprints. *J. Forensic Sci.*, 36, 1368, 1991.

13. Waldock, T. L., The flame method of soot deposition for the development of latent prints on non-porous surfaces. *J. Forensic Ident.*, 43, 463, 1993.

14. Kerr, F. M., Haque, F., and Westland, A. D., Organic based powders for fingerprint detection on smooth surfaces, I. *Can. Soc. Forensic Sci. J.*, 16, 140, 1983.

15. Kerr, F. M., Barron, I. W., Haque, F. et al., Organic based powders for fingerprint detection on smooth surfaces, II. *Can. Soc. Forensic Sci. J.*, 16, 39, 1983.

16. Menzel, E. R. and Duff, J. M., Laser detection of latent fingerprints — treatment with fluorescers. *J. Forensic Sci.*, 24, 96, 1979.

17. Menzel, E. R., Laser detection of latent fingerprints — treatment with phosphorescers. *J. Forensic Sci.*, 24, 582, 1979.

18. Menzel, E. R. and Fox, K. E., Laser detection of latent fingerprints: preparation of fluorescent dusting powders and the feasibility of a portable system. *J. Forensic Sci.*, 25, 150, 1980.

19. Thornton, J. I., Modification of fingerprint powder with coumarin 6 laser dye. *J. Forensic Sci.*, 23, 536, 1979.

20. Menzel, E. R., *Fingerprint Detection With Laser,* Marcel Dekker, New York, 1980.

21. MacDonell, H. L., Bristless brush development of latent fingerprints. *Ident. News*, 11, 7, 1961.

22. James, J. D., Pounds, C. A., and Wilshire, B. W., Magnetic flake fingerprint technology. *J. Forensic Ident.*, 41, 237, 1991.

23. James, J. D., Pounds, C. A., and Wilshire, B., Magnetic flake powders for fingerprint development. *J. Forensic Sci.*, 38, 391, 1993.

24. Graham, D. and Gray, H. C., The use of X-ray electronography and autoelectronography in forensic investigations. *J. Forensic Sci.*, 11, 124, 1966.

25. Theys, P., Turgis, Y., Lepareux, A. et al., New technique for bringing out latent fingerprints on paper: vacuum metallisation. *Int. Crim. Police Rev.*, 217, 106, 1968.

26. Kent, T., Thomas, G. L., Reynoldson, T. E., and East, H. W., A vacuum coating technique for the development of latent fingerprints on polythene. *J. Forensic Sci. Soc.*, 16, 93, 1976.

27. Jones, R. G., Fused finger prints. *Fingerprint Ident. Mag.*, 48, 11, 1967.

28. Micik, W., Dry ink works better than toner. *Fingerprint Ident. Mag.*, 55, 11, 1974.

29. Stimac, J. T., Plastic fingerprint impressions: an inked approach. *J. Forensic Ident.*, 48, 574, 1998.

30. Feucht, D. A., The dental impression material latent print recovery method. *J. Forensic Ident.*, 45, 173, 1995.

31. Morris, J. R. and Wells, J. M. Patent 154, 147, 1979. Great Britain.

32. Pounds, C. A. and Jones, R. J. The Use of Powder Suspensions for Developing Latent Fingerprints. Home Office Central Research Establishment (HOCRE), Aldermaston, England, 1981.

33. Haque, F., Westland, A. D., Milligan, J., and Kerr, F. M., A small particle (iron oxide) suspension for detection of latent fingerprints on smooth surfaces. *Forensic Sci. Int.*, 41, 73, 1989.

34. Ishizawa, F., Takamura, Y., Fukuchi, T., Shimizu, M., Ito, M., Kanzaki, M., Hasegawa, T., and Miyagi, A., New sprays for the development of latent fingerprints. *J. Forensic Ident.*, 49, 499, 2000.

35. Frank, A. and Almog, J., Modified SPR for latent fingerprint development on wet, dark objects. *J. Forensic Ident.*, 43, 240, 1993.

36. Springer, E. and Bergman, P., A fluorescent small particle reagent (SPR). *J. Forensic Ident.*, 45, 164, 1995.

37. Rhodes, H. T. F., *Forensic Chemistry,* Chemical Publishing, New York, 1940.

38. Bridges, B. C., *Practical Fingerprinting,* Funk and Wagnalls, New York, 1963.

39. Moenssens, A. A., *Fingerprint Techniques,* Chilton, New York, 1971.

40. Almog, J., Sasson, Y., and Anah, A., Chemical reagents for the development of latent fingerprints. II. Controlled addition of water vapor to iodine fumes — a solution to the ageing problem. *J. Forensic Sci.*, 24, 431, 1979.

41. Haque, F., Westland, A., and Kerr, F. M., An improved non-destructive method for detection of latent fingerprints on documents with iodine-7,8-benzoflavone. *Forensic Sci. Int.*, 21, 79, 1983.

42. Pounds, C. A. and Hussain, J. I., Biologic and chemical aspects of latent fingerprint detection, in Proceedings of the International Forensic Symposium on Latent Prints, Laboratory & Identification Divisions, Federal Bureau of Investigation FSRTC FBI Academy, Quantico, VA, U.S. Government Printing Office, Washington, D.C., 1987, 9-13.

43. Larsen, J. K., The starch powder-steam method of fixing iodine fumed latent prints. *Fingerprint Ident. Mag.*, 44, 3, 1962.

44. Foley, J. F., Development of latent fingerprints — iodine silver transfer method. *Ident. News*, 22, 14, 1974.

45. Trowell, F., A method for fixing latent fingerprints developed with iodine. *J. Forensic Sci. Soc.*, 15, 189, 1975.

46. Mashito, K. and Makoto, I., Latent fingerprint processing: iodine 7,8 benzoflavone method. *Ident. News*, 27, 3, 1977.

47. Midkiff, C. R., Codell, D., and Chapman, J., Development of prints on tape, III. *Fingerprint Whorld*, 23, 83, 1997.

48. Kendall, F. G., Super Glue fuming for the development of latent fingerprints. *Ident. News*, 32, 13, 1982.

49. Bensonsen, J. A., Heat acceleration of the Super Glue fuming method for development of latent fingerprints. *Ident. News*, 33, 3, 1983.

50. Olenik, J. H., Super Glue — a modified method. *Ident. News*, 33, 9, 1983.

51. Kendall, F. G. and Rehn, B. W., Rapid method of Super Glue fuming application for the development of latent fingerprints. *J. Forensic Sci.*, 28, 777, 1983.

52. Lee, H. C. and Gaensslen, R. E., Cyanoacrylate fuming — theory and practice. *Ident. News*, 34, 8, 1984.

53. Shonberger, M. F., Slow-reaching catalyst for cyanoacrylate fuming. *J. Forensic Ident.*, 45, 651, 1995.

54. Watkin, J. E., La fluorescence et la lieux de crimes dans les annue 90. *Gaz. G. R. C.*, 52, 1, 1990 (as cited by Margot and Lennard, 1994).

55. Campbell, B. M., Vapeurs de cyano-acrylate dans une chambre a vide: evolution de la technique. *Gaz. G. R. C.*, 53, 12, 1991 (as cited by Margot and Lennard[9]).

56. Watkin, J. E., Wilkinson, D. A., Misner, A. H., and Yamashita, A. B., Cyanoacrylate fuming of latent prints: vacuum vs. heat/humidity. *J. Forensic Ident.*, 44, 545, 1994.

57. Grady, D. P., Cyanoacrylate fuming: Accelerating by heat within a vacuum. *J. Forensic Ident.*, 49, 377, 1999.

58. Gilman, P. L., Sahs, P. T., and Gorajczyk, J. S., Stabilized cyanoacrylate. *Ident. News*, 35, 7, 1985.

59. Olenik, J. H., Cyanoacrylate fuming: an alternative non-heat method. *J. Forensic Ident.*, 39, 302, 1989.

60. Springer, E., Two Techniques for Improving Fingerprint Yield, Almog, J. and Springer, E., Eds., Israel National Police, Jerusalem, Israel, 1995, 109-113.

61. Almog, J. and Gabay, A., Chemical reagents for the development of latent fingerprints. III. Visualization of latent fingerprints by fluorescent reagents in vapor phase. *J. Forensic Sci.*, 25, 408, 1980.

62. Davis, P. R., McCloud, V. D., and Bonebrake, J. K., Don't throw dried-up glue away. *J. Forensic Ident.*, 45, 598, 1995.

63. Geng, Q., Recovery of Super Glue over-fumed fingerprints. *J. Forensic Ident.*, 48, 17, 2000.

64. Zhang, J. and Gong, D.-A., A modified cyanoacrylate technique utilizing treated neutral filter paper for developing latent fingerprints. *Forensic Sci. Int.*, 52, 31, 1991.

65. Weaver, D., Large scale cyanoacrylate fuming. *J. Forensic Ident.*, 43, 135, 1993.

66. Goetz, M. W., Cyanoacrylate fuming precautions. *J. Forensic Ident.*, 46, 409, 1996.

67. Ruslander, H. W., Super Glue fuming of vegetation at crime scenes. *J. Forensic Ident.*, 47, 42, 1997.

68. Shonberger, M. F., A variation of Super Glue processing of small immovable, or difficult to move, items. *J. Forensic Ident.*, 47, 47, 1997.

69. McFadden, O. A. and Righi, R., Super Glue processing of small immovable, or difficult to move items. *J. Forensic Ident.*, 43, 466, 1993.

70. Moody, E. W., The development of fingerprint impressions on plastic bags over time and under different storage temperatures. *J. Forensic Ident.*, 44, 266, 1994.

71. Kobus, H. J., Warrener, R. N., and Stoilovic, M., Two simple staining procedures which improve the contrast and ridge detail of fingerprints developed with Super Glue (cyanoacrylate ester). *Forensic Sci. Int.*, 23, 233, 1983.

72. Miles, C. Analysis of Ardrox 970-P10 Liquid Penentrant. Field Identification Resource Section Report No. 001, Royal Canadian Mounted Police, Ottawa, Ontario, 1987.

73. Vachon, G. and Sorel, J., New fingerprint development process, in Proceedings of the International Forensic Symposium on Latent Prints, Laboratory & Identification Divisions, Federal Bureau of Investigation FSRTC FBI Academy, Quantico, VA, U.S. Government Printing Office, Washington, D.C., 1987.

74. McCarthy, M. M., Evaluation of Ardrox as a luminescent stain for cyanoacry-late processed latent impressions. *J. Forensic Ident.*, 38, 197, 1988.

75. Menzel, E. R., Burt, J. A., and Sinor, T. W., Laser detection of latent finger-prints: treatment with glue containing cyanoacrylate ester. *J. Forensic Sci.*, 28, 307, 1983.

76. Flynn, J., Stoilovic, M., and Lennard, C., Detection and enhancement of latent fingerprints on polymer banknotes: a preliminary study. *J. Forensic Ident.*, 49, 594, 1999.

77. Herod, D. W. and Menzel, E. R., Laser detection of latent fingerprints: nin-hydrin followed by zinc chloride. *J. Forensic Sci.*, 27, 513, 1982.

78. Weaver, D. E. and Clary, E. J., A one-step fluorescent cyanoacrylate fingerprint development technology. *J. Forensic Ident.*, 43, 481, 1993.

79. Federal Bureau of Investigation, Chemical Formulas and Processing Guide for Developing Latent Prints, Washington, D.C., 1994.

80. Gray, M. L., Sticky-side powder vs. gentian violet: the search for the superior method for processing the sticky side of adhesive tape. *J. Forensic Ident.*, 46, 268, 1996.

81. Tuthill, H., Re: "Sticky-side powder vs. gentian violet," JFI 46(3) [letter]. *J. Forensic Ident.*, 47, 4, 1997.

82. Bramble, S. K., Cantu, A. A., Ramotowski, R. S., and Brennan, J. S., Deep red to near infrared (NIR) fluorescence of gentian violet-treated latent prints. *J. Forensic Ident.*, 50, 33, 2000.

83. Stitt, W., New use for gentian violet. *J. Forensic Ident.*, 47, 274, 1997.

84. Gambue, M. and O'Daniel, L., Substitute ardrox formula. *J. Forensic Ident.*, 49, 134, 1999.

85. Mazzella, W. D. and Lennard, C. J., An additional study of cyanoacrylate stains. *J. Forensic Ident.*, 45, 5, 1995.

86. Olenik, J. H., A simple three dye blend. *J. Forensic Ident.*, 47, 530, 1997.

87. Cummings, H., Hollars, M., and Trozzi, T., Getting the most from cyanoacry-late dyes. *J. Forensic Ident.*, 43, 37, 1993.

88. Morimoto, S., Kaminogo, A., and Hirano, T., A new method to enhance visualization of latent fingermarks by sublimating dyes, and its practical use with a combination of cyanoacrylate fuming. *Forensic Sci. Int.*, 97, 101, 2000.

89. Kempton, J. B. and Rowe, W. F., Contrast enhancement of cyanoacrylate-developed latent fingerprints using biological stains and commercial fabric dyes. *J. Forensic Sci.*, 37, 99, 1992.

90. Day, K. J. and Bowker, W., Enhancement of cyanoacrylate developed latent prints using Nile Red. *J. Forensic Ident.*, 46, 183, 1996.

91. Wilkinson, D. A. and Watkin, J. E., Europium aryl-β-diketone complexes as fluorescent dyes for the detection of cyanoacrylate developed fingerprints on human skin. *Forensic Sci. Int.*, 60, 67, 1993.

92. Lock, E. R. A., Mazzella, W. D., and Margot, P., A new Europium chelate as a fluorescent dye for cyanoacrylate pretreated fingerprints — EuTTAPhen: Europium ThenoylTrifluoroAcetone Ortho-Phenanthroline. *J. Forensic Sci.*, 40, 654, 1995.

93. Corr, J. J., Flame method for the development of latent fingerprints. *Kriminalistik*, 10, 429, 1956.

94. Vandiver, J. V., Comments on smoke technique. *Ident. News*, 23, 12, 1973.

95. Spedding D.J., Detection of latent fingerprints with $^{35}SO_2$. *Nature*, 229, 123, 1971.

96. Given, B. W., Latent fingerprints on cartridges and expended cartridge casings. *J. Forensic Sci.*, 20, 587, 1975.

97. Sodhi, G. S. and Kaur, J., Fingermarks detection by eosin-blue dye. *Forensic Sci. Int.*, 115, 69, 2000.

98. Sasson, Y. and Almog, J., Chemical reagents for the development of latent fingerprints. I. Scope and limitation of the reagent 4-dimethylamino-cinnamaldehyde. *J. Forensic Sci.*, 23, 852, 1978.

99. Ramotowski, R., Fluorescence Visualization of Latent Fingerprints on Paper Using p-Dimethylaminocinnamaldehyde (PDMAC), Almog, J. and Springer, E., Eds., Israel National Police, Jerusalem, Israel, 1995, 91-94.

100. Brennan, J., Bramble, S., Crabtree, S., and Wright, G., Fuming of latent fingerprints using dimethylaminocinnamaldehyde. *J. Forensic Ident.*, 45, 373, 1995.

101. Katzung, W., New reagents for the chemical development of latent fingerprints on paper, and their possible applications. *Krim. Forensische Wiss.*, 82, 1985.

102. Mashito, K. and Miyamoto, T., Latent fingerprint processing by the ruthenium tetroxide method. *J. Forensic Ident.*, 48, 279, 2000.

103. Blackledge, R. D., Latent print processing by the ruthenium tetroxide method [letter]. *J. Forensic Ident.*, 48, 557, 1998.

104. Wilkinson, D., A one-step fluorescent detection method for lipid fingerprints; $Eu(TTA)_3 \cdot 2TOPO$. *Forensic Sci. Int.*, 99, 5, 1999.

105. Allred, C. E. and Menzel, E. R., A novel europium-bioconjugate method for latent fingerprint detection. *Forensic Sci. Int.*, 85, 83, 1997.

106. Murphy, K. A., Cartner, A. M., Henderson, W., and Kim, N. D., Appraisal of the porphyrin compound, $(TPP)Sn(OH)_2$, as a latent fingerprint reagent. *J. Forensic Ident.*, 49, 269, 1999.

107. Oden, S. and von Hofsten, B., Detection of fingerprints by the ninhydrin reaction. *Nature*, 173, 449, 1954.

108. Speaks, H. A., The use of ninhydrin in the development of latent fingerprints. *Fingerprint Ident. Mag.*, 45, 11, 1964.

109. Shulenberger, W. A., Present status of the ninhydrin process for developing latent fingerprints. *Ident. News*, 13, 9, 1963.

110. Mooney, D. G., Development of latent fingerprints and palmprints by ninhydrin. *Ident. News*, 16, 4, 1966.

111. Mooney, D. G., Additional notes on the use of ninhydrin. *Ident. News*, 23, 9, 1973.

112. Crown, D. A., The development of latent fingerprints with ninhydrin. *J. Crim. Law Criminol. Police Sci.*, 60, 258, 1969.

113. Linde, H. G., Latent fingerprints by a superior ninhydrin method. *J. Forensic Sci.*, 20, 581, 1975.

114. Mooney, D. G., Currin, T. J., and Matheny, D., Naphtha — ninhydrin method. *Ident. News*, 27, 6, 1977.

115. Morris, J. R. and Goode, G. C., NFN — an improved ninhydrin reagent for detection of latent fingerprints. *Police Res. Bull.*, 24, 45, 1974.

116. Watling, W. and Smith, K., Heptane: an alternative to the freon/ninhydrin mixture. *J. Forensic Ident.*, 43, 131, 1993.

117. Hewlett, D. F., Sears, V. G., and Suzuki, S., Replacements for CFC113 in the ninhydrin process. 2. *J. Forensic Ident.*, 47, 300, 1997.

118. Jungbluth, W., Replacement for Freon 113. *J. Forensic Ident.*, 43, 226, 1993.

119. Hewlett, D. F. and Sears, V. G., Formulation of Amino Acid Reagents — Search for Safe Effective Replacement for CFCs, Almog, J. and Springer, E., Eds., Israel National Police, Jerusalem, Israel, 1995, 99-108.

120. Marquez, H., Technique for processing carbonless documents for latent prints. *J. Forensic Ident.*, 49, 122, 2000.

121. Pressly, J., Ninhydrin on latex gloves: an alternative use for an old technique. *J. Forensic Ident.*, 49, 257, 2000.

122. German, E. R., You are missing ninhydrin developed prints. *Ident. News*, 31, 3, 1981.

123. Kobus, H. J., Stoilovic, M., and Warrener, R. N., A simple luminescent post-ninhydrin treatment for the improved visualisation of fingerprints on documents in cases where ninhydrin alone gives poor results. *Forensic Sci. Int.*, 22, 161, 1983.

124. Herod, D. W. and Menzel, E. R., Laser detection of latent fingerprints: ninhydrin. *J. Forensic Sci.*, 27, 200, 1982.

125. Menzel, E. R., Everse, J., Everse, K. E., Sinor, T. W., and Burt, J. A., Room light and laser development of latent fingerprints with enzymes. *J. Forensic Sci.*, 29, 99, 1984.

126. Stoilovic, M., Kobus, H. J., Margot, P. A., and Warrener, R. N., Improved enhancement of ninhydrin developed fingerprints by cadmium complexion using low temperature photoluminescence technique. *J. Forensic Sci.*, 31, 432, 1986.

127. Everse, K. and Menzel, E. R., Sensitivity enhancement of ninhydrin-treated latent fingerprints by enzymes and metal salts. *J. Forensic Sci.*, 31, 446, 1986.

128. Lennard, C. J., Margot, P. A., Sterns, M., and Warrener, R. N., Photoluminescent enhancement of ninhydrin developed fingerprints by metal complexation: structural studies of complexes formed between Ruhemann's purple and group IIb metal salts. *J. Forensic Sci.*, 32, 597, 1987.

129. Menzel, E. R. and Mitchell, K. E., Intramolecular energy transfer in the europium-Ruhemann's purple complex: application to latent fingerprint detection. *J. Forensic Sci.*, 35, 35, 1990.

130. Menzel, E. R., Bartsch, R. A., and Hallman, J. L., Fluorescent metal-Ruhemann's purple coordination compounds: applications to latent fingerprint detection. *J. Forensic Sci.*, 35, 25, 1990.

131. Menzel, E. R., Applications of laser technology in latent fingerprint enhancement, in *Advances in Fingerprint Technology*, Lee, H. C. and Gaensslen, R. E., Eds., Elsevier, New York, 1991, 135-162.

132. Liberti, A., Calabro, G., and Chiarotti, M., Storage effects on ninhydrin-developed fingerprints enhanced by zinc complexation. *Forensic Sci. Int.*, 72, 161, 2000.

133. Almog, J., Fingerprint development by ninhydrin and its analogues, in *Advances in Fingerprint Technology*, Lee, H. C. and Gaensslen, R. E., Eds., Elsevier, New York, 1991, 103-133.

134. Ohki, H., A new detection method of latent fingerprints with fluorescamine. *Rep. Natl. Res. Inst. Police Sci. Tokyo*, 29, 46, 1976.

135. Mayer, S. W., Meilleur, C. P., and Jones, P. F., The use of orthophthalaldehyde for superior fluorescent visualization of latent fingerprints. *J. Forensic Sci. Soc.*, 18, 233, 1978.

136. Salares, V. R., Eves, C. R., and Carey, P. R., On the detection of fingerprints by laser excited luminescence. *Forensic Sci. Int.*, 14, 229, 1979.

137. Stoilovic, M., Warrener, R. N., and Kobus, H. J., An evaluation of the reagent NBD chloride for the production of luminescent fingerprints on paper. II. A comparison with ninhydrin. *Forensic Sci. Int.*, 24, 279, 1984.

138. Lee, H. C. and Attard, A., The use of dansyl chloride in latent prints detection, in *Proc. Am. Acad. Forensic Sci. Annu. Meet.*, Atlanta, GA, 1979 (abstr.).

139. Lee, H. C. and Attard, A. E., Comparison of fluorescamine, *o*-phthalaldehyde and ninhydrin for the detection and visualization of latent fingerprints. *J. Police Sci. Admin.*, 7, 333, 1979.

140. Warrener, R. N., Kobus, H. J., and Stoilovic, M., An evaluation of the reagent NBD chloride for the production of luminescent fingerprints on paper. I. A support for a xenon arc lamp being a cheaper and valuable alternative to an argon ion laser as an excitation source. *Forensic Sci. Int.*, 23, 179, 1983.

141. Almog, J., Zeichner, A., Shifrina, S., and Scharf, G., Nitro-benzofurazanyl ethers — a new series of fluorigenic fingerprint reagents. *J. Forensic Sci.*, 32, 585, 1987.

142. Pounds, C. A., Grigg, R., and Mongkolaussavaratana, T., The use of 1,8-diaz-afluoren-9-one (DFO) for the fluorescent detection of latent fingerprints on paper. A preliminary evaluation. *J. Forensic Sci.*, 35, 169, 1990.

143. Geide, B., Detection of Latent Fingerprints — DFO without CFC, Almog, J. and Springer, E., Eds., Israel National Police, Jerusalem, Israel, 1995, 95-97.

144. Bratton, R. M. and Juhala, J. A., DFO-dry. *J. Forensic Ident.*, 45, 169, 1995.

145. Almog, J., Hirschfeld, A., and Klug, J. T., Reagents for the chemical development of latent fingerprints. Synthesis and properties of some ninhydrin analogues. *J. Forensic Sci.*, 27, 912, 1982.

146. Almog, J., Sears, V. G., Springer, E., Hewlett, D. F., Walker, S., Wiesner, S., Lidor, R., and Bahar, E., Reagents for the chemical development of latent fingerprints: scope and limitations of benzo[*f*]ninhydrin in comparison to ninhydrin. *J. Forensic Sci.*, 45, 538, 2000.

147. Almog, J., Hirshfeld, A., Frank, A., Sterling, J., and Leonov, D., Aminoninhydrins: fingerprint reagents with direct fluorogenic activity — preliminary studies. *J. Forensic Sci.*, 36, 104, 1991.

148. Menzel, E. R. and Almog, J., Latent fingerprint development by frequency-doubled neodymium:yttrium aluminum garnet (Nd:YAG) lasers: benzo(*f*)ninhydrin. *J. Forensic Sci.*, 30, 371, 1985.

149. Lennard, C. J., Margot, P. A., Stoilovic, M., and Warrener, R. N., Synthesis and evaluation of ninhydrin analogues as reagents for the development of latent fingerprints on paper surfaces. *J. Forensic Sci. Soc.*, 28, 3, 1988.

150. Almog, J., Hirshfeld, A., Frank, A., Grant, H., Harel, Z., and Ittah, Y., 5-Methylthio ninhydrin and related compounds: a novel class of fluorogenic fingerprint reagents. *J. Forensic Sci.*, 37, 688, 1992.

151. Cantu, A. A., Leben, D. A., Joullie, M. M., Heffner, R. J., and Hark, R. R., A comparative examination of several amino acid reagents for visualizing amino acid (glycine) on paper. *J. Forensic Ident.*, 43, 44, 1993.

152. Ramotowski, R., Cantu, A. A., Joullie, M. M., and Petrovskaia, O., 1,2-Indanediones: a preliminary evaluation of a new class of amino acid visualizing compounds. *Fingerprint Whorld*, 23, 131, 1997.

153. Hauze, D. B., Petrovskaia, O., Taylor, B., Joullie, M. M., Ramotowski, R., and Cantu, A. A., 1,2-Indanediones: new reagents for visualizing the amino acid components of latent prints. *J. Forensic Sci.*, 43, 744, 1998.

154. Almog, J., Springer, E., Wiesner, S., Frank, A., Khodzhaev, O., Lidor, R., Bahar, E., Varkony, H., Dayan, S., and Rozen, S., Latent fingerprint visualization by 1,2-indanedione and related compounds: preliminary results. *J. Forensic Sci.*, 44, 114, 1999.

155. Wiesner, S., Springer, E., Sasson, Y., and Almog, J., Chemical development of latent fingerprints: 1,2-indanedione has come of age. *J. Forensic Sci.*, 46, in press.

156. Wilkinson, D., Spectroscopic study of 1,2-indanedione. *Forensic Sci. Int.*, 114, 123, 2000.

157. Elber, R., Frank, A., and Almog, J., Chemical development of latent finger-prints: computational design of ninhydrin analogues. *J. Forensic Sci.*, 45, 757, 2000.

158. Kerr, F. M., Westland, A. D., and Haque, F., Observations on the use of silver compounds for fingerprint visualization. *Forensic Sci. Int.*, 18, 209, 1981.

159. Phillips, C. E., Cole, D. O., and Jones, G. W., Physical developer: a practical and productive latent print developer. *J. Forensic Ident.*, 40, 135, 1990.

160. Saunders, G., Multimetal deposition technique, personal communication. 1989.

161. Knowles, A. M., Aspects of the physicochemical methods for the detection of latent prints. *J. Phys. E*, 11, 713, 1978.

162. Nolan, P. J., Brennan, J. S., Keely, R. H., and Pounds, C. A., The imaging of developed fingerprints using the scaning electron microscope. *J. Forensic Sci. Soc.*, 1984 (abstr.).

163. Ramotowski, R., Comparison of different physical developer systems and acid pretreatments and their effects on developing latent prints. *J. Forensic Ident.*, 50, 363, 2000.

164. Kent, T. User Guide to the Metal Deposition Process for the Development of Latent Fingerprints. Home Office Scientific Research and Development Branch (HOSRDB), Aldermaston, England, 1982.

165. Batey, G. W., Copeland, J., Donnelly, D. L., Hill, C. L., Laturnus, P. L., McDiarmid, C. H., Miller, K. J., Misner, A. H., Tario, A., and Yamashita, A. B., Metal deposition for latent prints. *J. Forensic Ident.*, 48, 165, 2000.

166. Kent, K. and Stoilovic, M., Development of latent fingerprints using preferential DC sputter deposition. *Forensic Sci. Int.*, 72, 35, 2000.

167. Murphy, M. P., A vacuum metal identification. *J. Forensic Ident.*, 41, 318, 2000.

168. Migron, Y., Hocherman, G., Springer, E., Almog, J., and Mandler, D., Visualization of sebaceous fingerprints on fired cartridge cases: a laboratory study. *J. Forensic Sci.*, 43, 543, 1998.

169. Thomas, G. L., Physical methods of fingerprint development. *Can. Soc. Forensic Sci. J.*, 8, 144, 1975.

170. Jones, R. J., Chemistry of Fingerprints: A Bibliography, Home Office Forensic Science Service, Central Research Establishment, Aldermaston, England, 1983.

171. Conley, B. J. and Andes, J. F., A test for blood latent palmprints and fingerprints. *Fingerprint Ident. Mag.*, 40, 16, 1959.

172. Lee, H. C., Benzidine or *o*-tolidine. *Ident. News*, 34, 13, 1984.

173. Lee, H. C., TMB as an enhancement reagent for bloody prints. *Ident. News*, 34, 10, 1984.

174. Shipp, E., Fassett, M., Wright, R., and Togneri, E., Tetramethylbenzidine to the rescue. *J. Forensic Ident.*, 44, 159, 1994.

175. Jones, R. J. and Pounds, C. A. The Enhancement of Fingerprints Made in Blood. Home Office Central Research Establishment (HOCRE), Aldermaston, England, 1982.

176. Norkus, P. and Noppinger, K., New reagent for the enhancement of blood prints. *Ident. News*, 36, 5, 1986.

177. Whritenour, R. D., Variation to Coomassie blue blood print enhancement technique. *Ident. News*, 35, 6, 1986.

178. McCarthy, M. M. and Grieve, D. L., Preprocessing with cyanoacrylate ester fuming for fingerprint impressions in blood. *J. Forensic Ident.*, 39, 23, 1988.

179. Warrick, P., Identification of blood prints on fabric using Amido Black and digital enhancement. *J. Forensic Ident.*, 50, 21, 2000.

180. Jaret, Y., Heriau, M., and Donche, A., Transfer of bloody fingerprints. *J. Forensic Ident.*, 47, 38, 1997.

181. Zauner, D. R., Friction ridge impression in blood on blue denim. *J. Forensic Ident.*, 48, 689, 1998.

182. Hunter, J., Fingerprint evidence and Coomassie Blue — After 25 years. *J. Forensic Ident.*, 44, 619, 1994.

183. Stoilovic, M., Detection of semen and blood stains using Polilight as a light source. *Forensic Sci. Int.*, 51, 289, 1991.

184. Creighton, J. T., Visualization of latent impressions after incidental or direct contact with human blood. *J. Forensic Ident.*, 47, 534, 1997.

185. Huss, K., Clark, J. D., and Chisum, W. J., Which was first -- fingerprint or blood? *J. Forensic Ident.*, 50, 344, 2000.

186. Ishiyama, I., Rapid histological examination of trace evidence by means of cellophane tape. *J. Forensic Sci.*, 26, 570, 1981.

187. Koemm, R. M., Latent prints on sticky surfaces. *Ident. News*, 31, 14, 1981.

188. Arima, T., Development of latent fingerprints on sticky surfaces by dye staining or fluorescent brightening. *Ident. News*, 31, 14, 1981.

189. Martin, B. L., Developing latent prints on the adhesive surface of black electrical tape. *J. Forensic Ident.*, 49, 127, 2000.

190. Sneddon, N., Black powder method to process duct tape. *J. Forensic Ident.*, 49, 347, 2000.

191. Paris, K. M., Getting the most from fingerprint powders. *J. Forensic Ident.*, 49, 494, 1999.

192. Burns, D. S., Sticky-side powder: the Japanese solution. *J. Forensic Ident.*, 44, 133, 1994.

193. Wilson, B. J. and McLeod, V. D., Development of latent prints on black plastic tape using crystal violet and photographic paper. *Ident. News*, 32, 3, 1982.

194. Tucker, G., A modified crystal violet application technique for black electrical tape. *J. Forensic Ident.*, 40, 148, 1990.

195. Teuszkowski, G. and Loninga, K., A modified approach in development of latent print on black plastic tape using crystal violet and photographic paper. *Ident. News*, 34, 2, 1984.

196. Taylor, E. and Mankevich, A., A new latent print developing method for use on tape. *Ident. News*, 34, 4, 1984.

197. Hollars, M. L., Trozzi, T. A., and Barron, B. L., Development of latent fingerprints on dark colored sticky surfaces using Liqui-Drox. *J. Forensic Ident.*, 50, 357, 2000.

198. Bratton, R. and Gregus, J., Development of a black powder method to process adhesive tapes. *Fingerprint Whorld*, January, 21, 1997.

199. Howard, S., Basic fuchsin — a guide to a one-step processing technique for black electrical tape. *J. Forensic Sci.*, 38, 1391, 1993.

200. Martin, K. F., Laterally-reversed transfers of latent fingerprints upon non-porous surfaces. *J. Forensic Ident.*, 44, 530, 1994.

201. Reichardi, G. J., Carr, J. C., and Stone, E. G., A conventional method for lifting latent fingerprints from human skin surfaces. *J. Forensic Sci.*, 23, 135, 1978.

202. Adcock, J. M., The development of latent fingerprints on human skin: iodine silver plate transfer method. *J. Forensic Sci.*, 22, 599, 1977.

203. Gray, C., The detection and persistence of latent fingerprints on human skin: an assessment of the iodine-silver plate method. *J. Forensic Sci. Soc.*, 18, 47, 1978.

204. Gelinas, N. L., The iodine silver transfer method for obtaining fingerprints from skin. *Law and Order*, 1977, 72.

205. Dalrymple, B. E., Case analysis of fingerprint detection by laser. *J. Forensic Sci.*, 24, 586, 1979.

206. Menzel, E. R., Laser detection of latent fingerprints on skin. *J. Forensic Sci.*, 27, 918, 1982.

207. Hamilton, J. and Battista, J., Cyanoacrylate ester — latent print from murdered body. *Fingerprint Whorld*, 11, 18, 1985.

208. Allman, D. S. and Pounds, C. A., Detection of fingerprints on skin. *Forensic Sci. Rev.*, 3, 83, 1991.

209. Federal Bureau of Investigation. Development of Latent Prints on Human Skin. Police Instructor's Bulletin. FBI Training Division, Quantico, VA, 1976 (Ref. Type: Generic).

210. Delmas, B. J., Postmortem latent print recovery from skin surfaces. *J. Forensic Ident.*, 38, 49, 1988.

211. Sampson, W. C., Sequential applications in the development and recovery of latent fingerprint evidence from human skin. *Fingerprint Whorld*, 23, 94, 1997.

212. Sampson, W. C., Latent fingerprint evidence on human skin (Part 1). *J. Forensic Ident.*, 46, 188, 1996.

213. Hebrard, J. and Donche, A., Fingerprint detection methods on skin. *J. Forensic Ident.*, 44, 623, 1994.

214. Fortunato, S. L. and Walton, G., Development of latent fingerprints from skin. *J. Forensic Ident.*, 48, 704, 1998.

215. Guo, Y.-C. and Xing, L.-P., Visualization method for fingerprints on skin by impression on a polyethylene terephthalate (PET) semirigid sheet. *J. Forensic Sci.*, 37, 604, 1992.

216. Wilkinson, D. A., Watkin, J. E., and Misner, A. H., A comparison of techniques for the visualization of fingerprints on human skin including the application of iodine and α-naphthoflavone. *J. Forensic Ident.*, 46, 432, 1996.

217. Morris, J. R. The Detection of Latent Fingerprints on Wet Paper Samples. Atomic Weapons Research Establishment (AWRE), Aldermaston, England, 1975.

218. Shelef, R., Levy, A., Rhima, I., Tsaroom, S., and Elkayan, R., Development of latent prints from incendiary bottles. I. Development of latent fingerprints from unignited incendiary bottle. *J. Forensic Ident.*, 46, 556, 1996.

219. Shelef, R., Levy, A., Rhima, I., Tsaroom, S., and Elkayam, R., Development of latent prints from incendiary bottles. III. Recovery of latent fingerprints from soot-covered incendiarized glass surfaces. *J. Forensic Ident.*, 46, 565, 1996.

220. Elkayam, R., Rhima, I., and Shelef, R., Development of latent prints from incendiary bottles. II. Optimization of small particle reagent for the development of latent fingerprints from glass surfaces washed in accelerant fluids. *J. Forensic Ident.*, 46, 561, 1996.

221. Donche, A. and Loyan, S., Development of latent prints on stones. *J. Forensic Ident.*, 46, 542, 1996.

222. Migron, Y. and Mandler, D., Development of latent fingerprints on unfired cartridges by palladium deposition: a surface study. *J. Forensic Sci.*, 42, 986, 1997.

223. Barnum, C. A. and Klasey, D. R., Factors affecting the recovery of latent prints on firearms. *J. Forensic Ident.*, 47, 141, 1997.

224. Freeman, H. N., Magnetic fingerprint powder on firearms and metal cartridges. *J. Forensic Ident.*, 49, 479, 1999.

225. Sampson, W. C., An inquiry into the methodology of preserving and developing latent prints on expended cartridge cases. *J. Forensic Ident.*, 43, 4, 1993.

226. Shipp, E., Davenport, W., and Togneri, E., Latent print and the gaming industry. *J. Forensic Ident.*, 45, 504, 1995.

227. Otis, J. C. and Downing, A., Development of latent fingerprint impressions on deer antlers. *J. Forensic Ident.*, 44, 9, 1994.

228. Wiesner, S. and Springer, E., Improved technique for recovering fingerprints on aluminum foil. *J. Forensic Ident.*, 47, 138, 1997.

229. Levi, J. A. and Leifer, A., Improving contrast in photographs of latent finger-prints on bottles. *J. Forensic Ident.*, 50, 8, 2000.

230. Dalrymple, B. E., Duff, J. M., and Menzel, E. R., Inherent fingerprint lumi-nescence: detection by laser. *J. Forensic Sci.*, 22, 105, 1977.

231. Duff, J. M. and Menzel, E. R., Laser assisted thin layer chromatography and luminescence of fingerprints: an approach to fingerprint age determination. *J. Forensic Sci.*, 23, 129, 1978.

232. Menzel, E. R., Posttreatment of latent prints for laser development. *Forensic Sci. Rev.*, 1, 43, 1989.

233. Bramble, S. K., Creer, K. E., Gui Qiang, W., and Sheard, B., Ultraviolet lumi-nescence from latent fingerprints. *Forensic Sci. Int.*, 59, 3, 1993.

234. Ben-Yosef, N., Almog, J., Frank, A., Springer, E., and Cantu, A. A., Short UV luminescence for forensic applications: design of a real-time observation system for detection of latent fingerprints and body fluids. *J. Forensic Sci.*, 43, 299, 1998.

235. Jones, N. E., Davies, L. M., Brennan, J. S., and Bramble, S. K., Separation of visibly-excited fluorescent components in fingerprint residue by thin-layer chromatography. *J. Forensic Sci.*, 45, 1286, 2000.

236. Meylan, N., Lennard, C. J., and Margot, P. A., Use of a gaseous electrical discharge to induce luminescence in latent fingerprints. *Forensic Sci. Int.*, 45, 73, 1990.

237. Davies, L. M., Jones, N. E., Brennan, J. S., and Bramble, S. K., A new visibly-excited fluorescent component in latent fingerprint residue induced by gas-eous electrical discharge. *J. Forensic Sci.*, 45, 1294, 2000.

238. Halahmi, E., Levi, O., Kronik, L., and Boxman, R. L., Development of latent fingerprints using a corona discharge. *J. Forensic Sci.*, 42, 833, 1997.

239. Murdock, R. H. and Menzel, E. R., A computer interfaced time-resolved lumi-nescence imaging system. *J. Forensic Sci.*, 38, 521, 1993.

240. Li, W., Ma, C., Jiang, H., Wu, C., Lu, Z., Wang, B., and Lin, B., Laser finger-print detection under background light interference. *J. Forensic Sci.*, 37, 1076, 1992.

241. Alaoui, I. M. and Menzel, E. R., Substituent effects on luminescence enhance-ment in europium and terbium Ruhemann's purple complexes. *Forensic Sci. Int.*, 77, 3, 2000.

242. Mekkaoui, A. I. and Menzel, E. R., Spectroscopy of rare earth-Ruhemann's purple complexes. *J. Forensic Sci.*, 38, 506, 1993.

243. Allred, C. E., Lin, T., and Menzel, E. R., Lipid-specific latent fingerprint detec-tion: fingerprints on currency. *J. Forensic Sci.*, 42, 997, 1997.

244. Allred, C. E., Murdock, R. H., and Menzel, E. R., New lipid-specific, rare earth-based chemical fingerprint detection methods. *J. Forensic Ident.*, 47, 542, 1997.

245. Misner, A., Wilkinson, D., and Watkin, J., Thenoyl Europium Chelate: a new fluorescent dye with a narrow emission band to detect cyanoacrylate developed fingerprints on non-porous substrates and cadavers. *J. Forensic Ident.*, 43, 154, 1993.

246. Wilkinson, D. A. and Misner, A. H., A comparison of thenoyl europium chelate with ardrox and rhodamine 6G for the fluorescent detection of cyanoacrylate prints. *J. Forensic Ident.*, 44, 387, 1994.

247. German, E. R., Reflected Ultraviolet Imaging System Applications, Almog, J. and Springer, E., Eds., Israel National Police, Jerusalem, Israel, 1995, 115-118.

248. Menzel, E. R., Savoy, S. M., Ulvick, S. J., Cheng, K. H., Murdock, R. H., and Sudduth, M. R., Photoluminescent semiconductor nanocrystals for fingerprint detection. *J. Forensic Sci.*, 45, 545, 2000.

249. Menzel, E. R., Takatsu, M., Murdock, R. H., Bouldin, K., and Cheng, K. H., Photoluminescent CdS/dendrimer nanocomposites for fingerprint detection. *J. Forensic Sci.*, 45, 770, 2000.

250. Bouldin, K. K., Menzel, E. R., Takatsu, M., and Murdock, R. H., Diimide-enhanced fingerprint detection with photoluminescent CdS/dendrimer nanocomposites. *J. Forensic Sci.*, 45, 1239, 2000.

251. Nolan, P. J., Brennan, J. S., Keeley, R. H., and Pounds, C. A., The imaging of developed fingerprints using scanning electron microscopy, in *Proceedings of the 10th Meeting of the International Association of Forensic Sciences*, Oxford, England, 1984 (abstr.).

252. Wilkinson, R. D., The use of infrared microscopy in detecting latent fingerprints, personal communication, 1979.

253. Lail, H. A., Fingerprint recovery with electronography. *Police Chief*, 42, 34, 1975.

254. Mooney, D. G., Fingerprints on human skin. *Ident. News*, 27, 5, 1977.

255. Winstanley, R., Recovery of latent fingerprints from difficult surfaces by an X-ray method. *J. Forensic Sci. Soc.*, 17, 121, 1977.

256. Ishiyama, I., Orui, M., Ogawa, K., and Kimura, T., The determination of isoantigenic activity from latent fingerprints: mixed cell agglutination reaction in forensic serology. *J. Forensic Sci.*, 22, 365, 1977.

257. Okada, T. and Ohrui, M., On new method of identifying blood types from latent prints. *Acta Crim. Med. Leg. Jpn.*, 44, 94, 1978.

258. Hussain, J. I. and Pounds, C. A., The detection of latent fingerprints by biological techniques, in *Proceedings of the 10th Meeting of the International Association of Forensic Sciences*, Oxford, England, 1984 (abstr.).

259. Harper, D. R., Clare, C. M., Heaps, C. D., Brennan, J., and Hussain, J., A bacteriological technique for the development of latent fingerprints. *Forensic Sci. Int.*, 33, 209, 1987.

260. Home Office Scientific Research and Development Branch (HOSRDB). Manual of Fingerprint Development Techniques. Aldermaston, England, 1986.

261. Lee, H. C. and Gaensslen, R. E., Systematic approaches in developing finger-prints, Savannah,GA, 1985.

262. Lee, H. C. and Gaensslen, R. E., Systematic approaches in latent fingerprint examination, in *Proc. Annu. Meet. Am. Chem. Soc.,* Miami, FL, 1985 (abstr.).

Fingerprint Development by Ninhydrin and Its Analogues

5

JOSEPH ALMOG

Contents

Despite the wide variety of reagents for chemical development of latent fingerprints on paper, many of which have been reported and investigated over the past decade, none has been found with sufficient advantages to supplant ninhydrin.

Ninhydrin reacts with amino acids and other components of palmar sweat that yield amino acids when broken down. The final color of the developed prints is usually purple (Ruhemann's purple). Full development may take several days or even weeks, but the reaction can be accelerated by heat and moisture. The most recent formulation uses the solvent HFE7100 as the carrier, after the former highly successful formulation was banned by the "Montreal Protocol on Substances that Deplete the Ozone Layer."

The art of fingerprint development has made great progress since the discovery that latent fingerprints on paper can be visualized by ninhydrin.

0-8493-0923-9/01/$0.00+$1.50
© 2001 by CRC Press LLC

There were four principal milestones in this evolution: (1) the introduction of the nonflammable formulation, NFN (nonflammable ninhydrin, which is now banned); (2) the introduction to fingerprint development of lasers and alternate light sources; (3) the secondary treatment with metal salts to produce fluorescent impressions; and, (4) the preparation and examination of ninhydrin analogues, whose crowning achievements were the introduction of DFO and the recent discovery of the potential of 1,2-indanedione. These processes remarkably improved the ability of law-enforcement agencies to detect latent fingerprints on porous surfaces such as paper and cardboard. Indeed, over the past few years many reports have appeared in the forensic science literature describing actual cases of fingerprint detection that would have been impossible only a few years ago. Ninhydrin is currently used in a sequence in advanced fingerprint laboratories. To achieve best results, it is applied after DFO and before PD.

The aim of this chapter is to survey the use of ninhydrin as a fingerprint reagent, with emphasis on progress in recent years. Two sections, "Comparison with Other Reagents" and "Miscellaneous Considerations," that appeared in the previous edition of *Advances in Fingerprint Technology* do not appear separately this time.

Chemical Development of Latent Fingerprints

Latent fingerprints on porous surfaces can be visualized by numerous chemical methods. Many of these can be regarded as purely theoretical because they have no practical use in the forensic science laboratory. On the other hand, no single technique for recovering latent prints has universal applications under all circumstances, and the choice of method may vary from case to case.[1,2] In its narrow definition, the chemical development of latent fingerprints is expressed by a visual chemical reaction between the reagent and one or more of the constituents of human perspiration, to yield a colored, luminescent, or radioactive product. In this manner the ridge detail becomes visible and the prints can be photographed and further manipulated.

Amino acids are the most desirable substrate of the palmar sweat components to be developed on paper. They are always present in human perspiration and they produce colored and luminescent products with a variety of reagents. Due to their high affinity for cellulose, they do not migrate with age (like urea or inorganic salts) and can be developed even after a long period of time. Cases have been reported in which latent prints have been detected and identified on paper specimens known to have been handled several years previously.[3,4] Amino acids on paper can be visualized by a variety of chemical reagents such as fluorescamine,[5-7] alloxan,[3,8] o-phthalaldehyde[6,7]

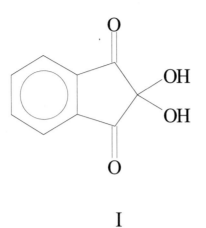

I

Figure 5.1 2,2-Dihydroxy-1,3-indanedione (ninhydrin).

and other aromatic vicinal dicarboxaldehydes,[9,10] 7-chloro-4-nitrobenzo-2-oxa-1,3-diazole (NBD-chloride) and its derivatives,[12-14] together with a long list of ninhydrin analogues, particularly 1,8-diazafluorenone (DFO) and most recently also 1,2-indanedione (see text); but from the forensic scientist's perspective, ninhydrin is undoubtedly the most important.[1,3,7,15,16]

Ninhydrin: The Universal Reagent for Fingerprints on Paper

History and General Properties of Ninhydrin

Ninhydrin (Figure 5.1) was first prepared by Ruhemann[17] in an attempt to oxidize 1-hydrindone (II) to 1,2-diketohydrindene (III, Figure 5.2)*. Instead of the expected product, he obtained another compound, triketohydrindene hydrate, known today as ninhydrin. On the basis of his experimental work, Ruhemann proposed the structure of the new substance as 2,2-dihydroxy-1,3-indanedione (Figure 5.1).[17,18]

It is interesting that Kaufmann had previously reported the preparation of a compound with the same structure, but his compound did not have ninhydrin properties.[19]

Ninhydrin is a crystalline solid that is soluble in water and other polar solvents. It crystallizes from ethanol as pale yellow prisms. When the solid is heated to 125–130°C, it changes to pink, red, or reddish brown. At 130–140°C,

---

* The more common names for these compounds are 1-indanone and 1,2-indanedione, accordingly. These names will prevail throughout this chapter.

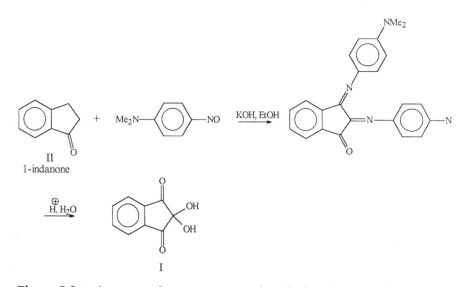

Figure 5.2 Ruhemann's first preparation of ninhydrin. (From Ruhemann, S., *J. Chem. Soc.*, 97, 2025, 1910.)

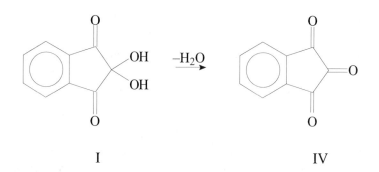

Figure 5.3 Formation of 1,2,3-indanetrione, the anhydrous form of ninhydrin.

it becomes deep purple-red and melts sharply, with decomposition at 241°C. It becomes red when exposed to sunlight and should be stored in a cool place.[20]

Upon heating in vacuum or treatment with thionyl chloride, ninhydrin loses water to give dark red needles of 1,2,3-indanetrione (IV, Figure 5.3), the anhydrous form of ninhydrin.[21] Ninhydrin reduces Fehling's solution[17] and forms phthalic anhydride upon heating in a current of air.[21] Its most important activity is obviously the reaction with amino acids to form a colored product ("Ruhemann's purple"), as explained in the next chapter section.

It is interesting that in forensic chemistry there is also a totally different use of ninhydrin — the detection of drugs on thin-layer chromatography (TLC) plates. Various drugs develop spots of different colors when TLC plates

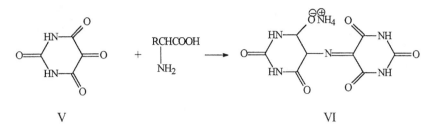

Figure 5.4 Formation of murexide (VI) in the reaction between alloxan (V) and amino acids.

are sprayed with a concentrated solution of ninhydrin. The mechanism of this reaction remains unclear.[22]

A comprehensive review of ninhydrin and its chemical and physical properties was published by McCaldin in 1960.[20] Of the two more recent reviews on ninhydrin and related compounds, the one by Joullié et al. is of particular importance because it covers not only general chemistry, but also forensic aspects.[23,24] A comprehensive review of vicinal polycarbonyl compounds has appeared very recently.[25]

Reaction with Amino Acids

Ruhemann discovered and correctly interpreted ninhydrin's most useful reaction with alpha amino acids.[18] He was impressed by the close similarity between ninhydrin and another cyclic triketone, alloxan, whose reaction with alpha amino acids gives carbon dioxide, an aldehyde, and a blue compound, murexide (Figure 5.4). Ruhemann showed that the purple product of the ninhydrin reaction (later named after him, Ruhemann's purple) was the ninhydrin analogue of murexide.[17,18,26-28]

Despite the fact that the ninhydrin reaction has been used extensively to detect and estimate amino acids, its mechanism has not been fully understood until recently; hence, it has given rise to a number of theories. There was even a controversy regarding the type of amino acids that undergo this reaction. Although Ruhemann claimed that not only alpha, but also beta amino acids, give the purple-blue color when treated with the reagent, it has been stated by others in later years that only alpha amino acids are reactive in this manner.[29,30] The general nature of the reaction, however, gave an indication of its probable course: if the reaction is as general as stated, it is likely that the purple color is the same for all amino acids and that only a fragment of the amino acid involved is contained in the colored compound.[20] A detailed discussion of the mechanism is beyond the scope of this chapter.

The currently acceptable general mechanism for the ninhydrin reaction, as suggested by Friedman and Williams in 1974,[31] is outlined in Figure 5.5. Ninhydrin (I) tautomerizes to 1,2,3-indanetrione (IV), which forms a Schiff's

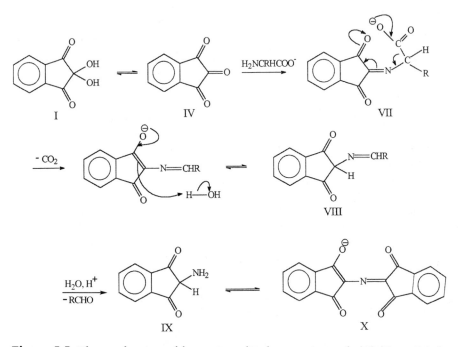

Figure 5.5 The mechanism of formation of Ruhemann's purple (X). (From Fried-man, M. and Williams, L.D., *Bioorganic Chem.*, 3, 267, 1974.)

base with the amino acid. The ketimine formed (VII) undergoes decarbox-ylation and cleavage, yielding the aldehyde and an intermediate amine (IX). Condesation of the amine (IX) with another molecule of ninhydrin (I) fol-lows to form the chromophore, Ruhemann's purple (X). A slight modifica-tion of this mechanism was suggested in 1986 by Grigg and co-workers.[32] They indicated that the intermediate imine (VIII) exists as a 1,3-dipole (XI, Figure 5.6), and that 1,3-dipole form is also the structure of the protonated form of Ruhemann's purple (XII, Figure 5.7).

The deprotonated form, which is the colored product, Ruhemann's pur-ple (X), has a highly stabilized aza-allylic chromophore that is responsible for the color (XIII, Figure 5.7). A summary of the mechanistic approaches was published by Bottom and co-workers.[33] Grigg's modification, which involves the formation of an azomethine ylide, is the currently accepted mechanism.[34]

Ninhydrin as a Latent Fingerprint Reagent

Shortly after the discovery of the ninhydrin reaction with amino acids, sci-entists noticed that many common materials form blue-colored products upon reaction with ninhydrin. In 1913, three years after the first report on ninhydrin, Abderhalden and Schmidt in Germany wrote:[35]

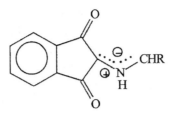

XI

Figure 5.6 The 1,3-dipole form of the intermediate imine in the ninhydrin reaction.

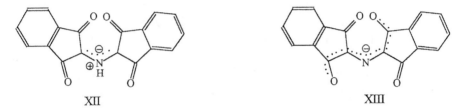

XII   XIII

Figure 5.7 Protonated (XII) and deprotonated (XIII) forms of Ruhemann's purple. (From Grigg, R., Malone, J.F., Mongkolaussavaratana, T., and Thianpatanagul, S., *J. Chem. Soc., Chem. Commun.*, 421, 1986.

> Ninhydrin is a valuable reagent for the detection of the non-biuret dialyzable amino acids. Various tissues, milk, urine, saliva, blood, plasma, serum, lymph, cyst contents, fresh eggs, albumin, fresh and boiled meat, and sweat contain substances which dialyze and react with ninhydrin. The fact that sweat gives an intense reaction is of importance in carrying out the test. Caution must be taken that nothing is touched which later comes in contact with the reagent.

In the following years, ninhydrin became a common reagent in various biochemical and medical test methods. Following the introduction of chromatographic techniques in the early 1940s, ninhydrin was routinely used to locate amino acids on chromatograms. Thus, it is somewhat surprising that despite its usage over the years and the oft-repeated admonition against touching chromatograms or other test material to be exposed to ninhydrin, only in 1954 was ninhydrin recognized as a latent fingerprint reagent. Two Swedish scientists, Oden and von Hofsten, were the first to suggest the use of ninhydrin as a means to develop latent fingerprints.[36] A year later, Oden patented the process.[37,38]

As mentioned previously, one of the outstanding features of ninhydrin compared with other chemical processes for paper is the fact that amino acids, the substrate for its action, are stable and do not appear to migrate with age. Ninhydrin is, therefore, a most suitable reagent for revealing latent prints on porous surfaces such as paper, cardboard, raw wood, and plasterboard. Its use is relatively simple, but achieving good results requires some skill and experience. The process can be carried out with no substantial hazard to health,* provided that a few straightforward precautions are observed.

Formulation Variations

The ninhydrin formulations and development conditions recommended by the first few groups of researchers varied widely and did not provide maximum detection efficiency.[42] There was no agreement on factors such as concentrations, solvents, temperatures and heating times, pH, modes of application, and humidity conditions. In 1955, Oden recommended a formulation composed of ninhydrin solution in acetone or ether that also contained acetic acid to enhance sensitivity.[37] Since then, a number of studies have been published in which one or more of the aforementioned factors were varied. Until 1974, the solvent list included acetone, diethyl ether, ethyl alcohol, isopropanol, petroleum ether, and acetone-water mixtures. Ninhydrin concentrations varied between 0.2 and 1.5%, and the concentration of acetic acid varied between 0 and 4%.[1,42] In general, little or no improvement over Oden's original formulation was achieved. Crown's formulation in 1969,[43] however, was of particular importance to questioned documents examiners. It was based on petroleum ether, which does not dissolve ink. It suffered, however, from one major disadvantage — high flammability. As a matter of fact, most other formulations were also flammable, particularly those containing diethyl ether. Indeed, fires in forensic science laboratories have been reported as a result of using these solvents.[44] Ether is also liable to explode and its use in solutions or spray is extremely hazardous!

In 1974, a most remarkable breakthrough in optimizing the formulation of the ninhydrin reagent was reported by two Englishmen, Morris and Goode. They described an improved ninhydrin reagent based on another nonpolar solvent, 1,1,2-trifluorotrichloroethane (known also as Fluorisol, Arklone P, Freon 113, or CFC113). Their formulation, which has since been named "NFN formulation" (nonflammable ninhydrin), is nonflammable, nontoxic, and does not dissolve ink on documents. It is highly sensitive and can be applied by dipping or swabbing.[42] A modified composition, containing the

---

* In 1989, it was reported that use of a surgical marking pen containing ninhydrin to indicate best areas on the skin caused eczema in three female patients.[39] More recently, a fingerprint technician developed symptoms of rhinitis as a result of handling papers immersed in a solution containing ninhydrin. Medical tests confirmed that it was an allergic reaction to ninhydrin.[40,41]

less volatile 1,1,2-trichloroethane, was recommended by J.R. Morris for spraying.[45] A standard working solution of NFN contains about 0.5% ninhydrin (w/v), 0.9% acetic acid (v/v), and 1.8% ethyl alcohol, in Fluorisol. Ethyl alcohol is required to dissolve the solid ninhydrin, and acetic acid provides the acidity required to balance the alkalinity of some papers.[46]

The authors also mentioned some disadvantages of the new formulation in their original paper. It forms background coloration on papers with a particular surface coating, such as banknotes, some checks and postal money orders, and rag-based writing papers, and on surfaces that have been exposed to high humidity. NFN reagent is not suitable for application to nonabsorbent surfaces such as plastics or ceramics.[12] An attempt to further improve the formulation was reported in 1984 by Tighe. The solution suggested, "Freon plus two," is also based on Fluorisol, but instead of ethyl alcohol it contains methyl alcohol and ethyl acetate.[47] Margot, Lennard, and co-workers reported that the addition of acetic acid improves upon the results obtained by the "Freon plus two" formulation. In 1986, they reported that the main advantage of this formulation is the ease of its preparation; however, in all other respects it resembles the original NFN reagent.[48]

NFN formulation was the recommended composition in the *Fingerprint Development Techniques Guide,* published in 1986 by the Scientific Research and Development Branch (SRDB), of the British Home Office. The editor, T. Kent, recommended the use of this reagent for paper, cardboard, raw wood, and plasterboard. In his chapter on ninhydrin, Kent surveyed all the operational aspects of this technique, including the preparation of solutions, necessary laboratory equipment, the mode of application, and safety requirements.[49]

The NFN formulation has become a general-purpose reagent, applicable to a wide range of paper and other surfaces, with minimal background effects.

The production of Fluorisol was banned within the European community, the U.S., and many other countries since the end of 1994 under the 1992 Brussels Amendment to the "Montreal Protocol on Substances that Deplete the Ozone Layer." In 1993, Watling and Smith suggested the use of heptane as an alternative carrier to Freon 113.[50] W.O. Jungbluth, of the U.S. Army Laboratory, reported in the same year that Genesolv 2000, a hydrochlorofluorocarbon, was an acceptable replacement for Freon 113, "provided the evidence does not possess ... handwriting for possible examination."[51] Good results with heptane, comparable to those obtained with Freon 113, were reported also by Hewlett and Sears, but they did not recommend its use for fingerprint development due to the high flammability of the solvent.[52] Supercritical carbon dioxide was reported as a potential substitute for Freon 113 by Hewlett et al. in 1996.[53]

A recent formulation that appears to satisfy all the requirements for fingerprint work is based on the work of Hewlett, Sears, and Suzuki from

1997, which uses the solvent HFE7100 as the carrier.[54] HFE7100 is a mixture of two hydrofluoroethers: 50 to 70% methylnonafluoroisobutyl ether and 30 to 50% methylnonafluorobutyl ether. It is a volatile, nonpolar, nontoxic, and nonflammable liquid and provides a safe and effective replacement to Freon 113 in the ninhydrin process. The working solution contains 0.5% ninhydrin in HFE7100 carrier that also contains ethanol, ethyl acetate, and acetic acid.[55]

The Influence of Temperature and Humidity: Modes of Application

Crown,[43] the 1976 FBI guide for the development of latent impression,[4] and Olsen[1] all recommend the following order for visualizing latent fingerprints on porous surfaces: treat with iodine fumes, then with ninhydrin, and finally with silver nitrate solution. This simplified procedure more or less exhausted the forensic scientist's knowledge until the mid-1970s. Due to the great progress in fingerprint techniques since then, a more sophisticated procedure, which provides much better results, is now practiced by advanced fingerprint laboratories. Figure 5.8 outlines the flowchart for fingerprint visualization on paper and cardboard, recommended in 1998 by the PSDB in England.[55] It distinguishes between wet and dry paper and it involves visual examination under white light, inherent fluorescence examination, and a sequence of three chemical steps: DFO, then ninhydrin, and finally physical developer (PD). According to their concept, which is also the standard system in many other advanced laboratories, ninhydrin treatment is considered a "primary route," while DFO and PD are "special routes." (PD *is* a primary route for *wet* paper). The Forensic Science Service (FSS) in London, whose Serious Crime Unit (SCU) applies perhaps the widest variety of fingerprint development methods,[56] uses a similar sequence: light examination, followed by DFO, ninhydrin and PD, and, finally scanning electron microscopy. The SCU still uses the NFN formulation for ninhydrin, but the introduction of HFE7100 has started.[57]

Ninhydrin can be applied by several methods: spraying a fine mist, dipping into a solution, or swabbing a solution onto the surface. Less conventional modes are exposure to ninhydrin fumes,[58] direct treatment with ninhydrin crystals without a solvent, or pressing a paper towel impregnated with ninhydrin solution against the item to be developed.[1] Only the first three methods (spraying, dipping, and swabbing) are used extensively. There is no general agreement on the method of choice, but dipping seems to be the most common technique for laboratory work.[42,49,55,59] Spraying is recommended for extremely fragile paper items such as tissue paper, which can fall apart if dipped into solution or tear if swabbed.[1] Swabbing is the least desirable mode of application because the swabbing action tends to smear ink on documents.[1]

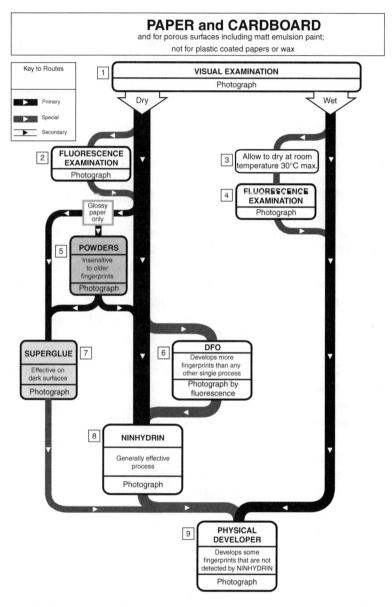

Figure 5.8 Flowchart for fingerprint visualization on paper and cardboard. (From *Manual of Fingerprint Development Techniques*, 2nd ed., T. Kent, Ed., PSDB, Home Office, (U.K.), 1998. With permission.)

In most cases, treatment after ninhydrin includes the application of heat. It is clear, however, that elevated temperatures also accelerate the formation of background discoloration. Thus, if the speed of development is not a crucial factor, for better contrast it is advisable to let the latent prints develop at room temperature in the dark, although the process may take days or even weeks.[42,46,49] Exposure times and temperatures vary considerably among the various groups. Oden and von Hofsten suggest heating to 80°C for a few minutes.[36] O'Hara recommends a much higher temperature (140°C).[60] Crown suggests processing at 100°C[43] for his petrol ether formulation, whereas Kent recommends 80°C and warns against heating certain items above 50°C.[49] It is clear, however, that if time permits, room-temperature development will always give the best "signal-to-noise" ratio, and this is the recommended technique.[46]

A number of groups have studied the influence of humidity on the quality of developed prints. In the mid-1960s, both Crown[61] and Mooney[62] reported that the presence of water vapors in the processing oven improves results. Moenssens found that best results are obtained during periods of high relative humidity and that "slow cure" at room temperature is preferable.[63] A study by Lesk established that optimum development is obtained by processing the ninhydrin-treated prints at 65 to 80% relative humidity.[64] In tests conducted by the U.S. Army Criminal Investigation Laboratory, the best results were obtained when ninhydrin-treated documents were maintained at 80% humidity and a temperature only slightly above room temperature.[1] The Royal Canadian Mounted Police (RCMP) laboratories in Ottawa recommend the use of a saturated sodium chloride solution in the development chamber to maintain the 75% relative humidity that is most desirable for the ninhydrin process.[65] A steam iron can be effectively used to accelerate the ninhydrin development of prints. The iron must not touch the paper surface, but be moved over the surface at a distance of 1 to 2 cm. Olsen, however, reports better contrast in humidity cabinet development. He also suggests not to use the iron method on cardboard or coated paper because steam condenses on such surfaces.[1] Development by placing the object over boiling water has been suggested by Rispling,[66] who also advises to watch the exhibit closely until coloration ceases. In 1976, Connor reported the results of a collaborative study that examined the effect of a steam iron on ninhydrin-treated prints on bond and newsprint papers. His study shows that latent prints are developed by this method within minutes after the ninhydrin treatment and that the mode of the ninhydrin application has very little effect on the results.[67] Consequently, the Association of Official Analytical Chemists (AOAC) adopted this method that same year.[68]

In their late 1970s studies, Morris[69] and then Jones and co-workers[70,71] reached the firm conclusion that steaming and heating after ninhydrin treatment of papers can lead to a significant increase in the quality and contrast of the marks revealed. Even when this improvement does not occur, there is no disadvantage in using this method; thus, they confidently recommend it for general use. The use of a microwave oven for steaming after ninhydrin treatment is recommended by Margot, Lennard, and co-workers.[72]

Specially designed cabinets for chemical development of fingerprints under controlled conditions of temperature and humidity have become a major tool in most advanced forensic laboratories.

Secondary Treatment with Metal Salts: Fingerprint Detection Aided by Lasers and Alternate Light Sources

Despite the fact that ninhydrin is regarded as "the latent fingerprint examiner's workhorse,"[73] it suffers from the following disadvantages and limitations:

1. The chemical process is slow.
2. Many paper samples contain ninhydrin-positive materials that give rise to the formation of intense background coloration and can obscure the developed prints.[42,46,74]*
3. Sensitivity is not always sufficiently high. Not all individuals excrete sufficient perspiration to leave identifiable prints using those methods known today.[43,46,74]
4. The contrast of ninhydrin-developed prints is often insufficient[46,48] on certain dark surfaces.
5. Prints developed with ninhydrin are not permanent. (There is debate among fingerprint practitioners as to whether or not this is a real problem.[43,59])

Hence, ninhydrin application to a document does not guarantee the development of latent fingerprints, although it may be known that the document was indeed touched by a certain person.[43] Considerable research efforts have been made toward the improvement of some of these drawbacks since the first application of ninhydrin to casework. In the beginning, most researchers focused on attempts to improve the formulations and working conditions. The crowning achievement of this approach was the development of the NFN formulation in 1974.[42] In 1977, the discovery of the potential of lasers for forensic science applications opened a new era in fingerprint technology. In that year, Dalrymple, Duff, and Menzel reported that latent fingerprints on various surfaces could be visualized by illumination with an argon-ion laser and observation through an appropriate filter.[75] Later studies showed that the percentage of latent prints detectable by their inherent luminescence under laser illumination was not very high, and researchers started to explore the possibility of combining lasers with fingerprint reagents.[12] This approach led to the next leap forward in the use of ninhydrin for fingerprint development.

---

* These background colors arise from the presence of natural organic constituents in the raw materials or from the various sizing or coating materials used to improve the surface properties (e.g., rag-based high-quality writing paper,[46] bank notes [where melamine has been used as a plasticizer], and some checks and postal money orders).[72]

In 1981, German reported that laser examination of ninhydrin-developed prints may reveal details unseen under conventional room lighting,[73] and a year later Herod and Menzel showed that weak ninhydrin-developed prints could be enhanced by examining them with a dye laser.[76] This observation was of limited practical value because it entailed the addition of a dye laser to the argon laser; the improvement in many cases was too small. It was the other discovery of this group, reported in the same year, that brought about substantial progress in the ninhydrin technique: the conversion of the purple ninhydrin-treated marks to fluorescent prints that can be detected under laser illumination.[77] Amino acid chemists have known for a long time that Ruhemann's purple spots on chromatographic plates change their color to red or orange after they have been treated with salts of certain metals such as nickel, cadmium, and zinc.[78-80] In fingerprint chemistry, this process was suggested as a means to overcome contrast problems on colored surfaces and also to improve the stability of the marks.[45,74] Herod and Menzel, who investigated this phenomenon, found that the marks not only changed color upon treatment with metal salts, but also became highly fluorescent under the argon laser. In their 1982 article, they wrote that "a pronounced improvement in detectability is observed when ninhydrin-treated latent fingerprints are sprayed with a solution of zinc chloride and subsequently subjected to argon laser examination."[77] This discovery quickly made an impact on many fingerprint laboratories. Many prints that could not be developed by conventional manner emerged after zinc chloride treatment and laser examination. The method also gave positive results on some nonporous surfaces that had been considered unsuitable for ninhydrin treatment.[77] Spectral data of the complex that is formed between Ruhemann's purple and zinc chloride were also reported in the same work. The 488-nm line of the argon laser was found ideal for excitation of the orange complex, which absorbs at about 485 nm and emits at 560 nm.

Since this discovery, luminescence procedures, in which nonfluorescent samples are converted into highly fluorescent products, have become an essential tool in most fingerprint laboratories. Analytical methods based on luminescence are much more sensitive — up to four orders of magnitude more sensitive than corresponding methods based on absorption.[81]* This perception has led to the development of "fingerprint-dedicated" argon lasers, and also alternative light sources that are cheaper, lighter, and easier to maintain. The potential use of the copper-vapor laser was discussed as early as 1982.[82,83] A year later, Warrener and co-workers reported the use of a xenon arc lamp equipped with a filter for fingerprint development by NBD-chloride,[13] and by ninhydrin followed by zinc chloride.[84] This group indicated

---

* Although the term "luminescence" includes both fluorescence and phosphorescence, most forensic applications involve only fluorescence, and this is what is predominantly implied throughout this chapter.

the importance of cooling the object (to the temperature of liquid nitrogen, −200°C) during the examination, which greatly enhances luminescence. Under such conditions, results are similar to those obtained with a 20-W argon laser. They recommend the use of xenon arc lamps by police forces that cannot afford argon lasers.[84] Since then, many more alternate light sources dedicated to fingerprint visualization after treatment with ninhydrin and zinc chloride have become commercially available. To name but a few: Luma-Lite in Canada,[85,86] Quaser in the U.K,[87,88] Omniprint in the U.S, the Australian Polilight (formerly Unilite),[89,90] and the Kawasaki FDW-200i in Japan.[91] Frequency-doubled Nd:YAG lasers were also considered for fingerprint use.[92] The efficiency of all these systems increases remarkably when the sample is cooled by liquid nitrogen during the fluorescence examination. The use of cadmium instead of zinc was suggested by Stoilovic, Warrener, and co-workers in 1986. In their studies, the cadmium complexes showed certain advantages over zinc complexes. They were less prone to development conditions and gave stable and reproducible results under extreme conditions of heat and humidity. Drawbacks of the cadmium reagents include toxicity and the need to cool the item to observe luminescence; results, however, were extremely rewarding.[42,93] The suggested procedure is to dip the ninhydrin-developed prints into a cadmium nitrate solution, let the solvent evaporate, cool it with liquid nitrogen, and then examine it with an appropriate light source. (The actual advantage of the use of cadmium vs. zinc salts is controversial. It was discussed in depth by Menzel and Warrener.[94])

X-ray diffraction studies by Lennard et al. on the cadmium complex of Ruhemann's purple show that each molecule of the complex contains one cadmium atom bound to one unit of Ruhemann's purple[95] (XIV, Figure 5.9), as opposed to the 1:2 ratio previously suggested.[92,96] Water was shown to be an essential component in the formation of the fluorescent complex, which explains the need for moisture in fingerprint enhancement by this technique.[95] Later crystallographic studies by Davies et al. also clarified the structure of the zinc complex.[97,98]

Ninhydrin Analogues

Structural Modifications: Benzo[f]ninhydrin and Related Compounds

Until the early 1980s, most attempts to improve the ninhydrin technique involved modification of formulations and working conditions. The chemical reagent remained unaltered. A totally different approach was demonstrated by Almog et al. in 1982. It was based on the perception that ninhydrin's special reactivity with amino acids had been discovered by Ruhemann by sheer

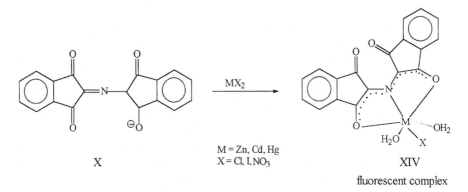

M = Zn, Cd, Hg
X = Cl, I, NO₃

X

XIV

fluorescent complex

Figure 5.9 Formation of Ruhemann's purple-metal complex. (From Lennard, C.J., Margot, P.A., Sterns, A., and Warrener, R.N., *J. Forensic Sci.*, 32, 597, 1987. With permission.)

coincidence, and that it was not the outcome of any theoretical design. They proposed a modification of the ninhydrin molecule in an attempt to enhance the color and fluorescence of the corresponding Ruhemann's purple complexes. It was assumed that compounds analogous to ninhydrin, containing the same active moiety — the cyclic vicinal triketone but with different groupings on the aromatic ring — might also react with amino acids to give colored products, and some of them could become new fingerprint reagents with improved properties. Expansion of the conjugated system and introduction of electron-donating or electron-withdrawing substituents can, in principal, modify the color by increasing the molar absorption coefficient (epsilon), or by shifting the absorption maximum towards longer or shorter wavelengths (red or blue shift). They named this group of compounds "ninhydrin analogues." Their initial experiments included the preparation of three ninhydrin analogues, all of which gave colored products with amino acids. One analogue in particular, benzo[f]ninhydrin (Figure 5.10), showed great promise. It developed latent fingerprints as dark green impressions, with a sensitivity similar to that of ninhydrin.[99]* The ability to develop a print of a specific color and then treat the developed print with zinc chloride to afford a complex that exhibits fluorescence or another color would aid in print visualization on a variety of backgrounds. In 1985, Menzel and Almog reported that the zinc complex of benzo[f]ninhydrin-developed prints showed luminescence properties that were superior to those obtained from the zinc complex of prints developed with ninhydrin.[92] This result stimulated interest in the preparation of ninhydrin analogues, which would serve as more sensitive fingerprint reagents. In 1986, Lennard et al. synthesized and

---

* Benzo[f]ninhydrin was prepared for the first time in 1957 by Meier and Lotter, who also reported the formation of a dark green color upon reaction with amino acids. They did not characterize the color spectroscopically and this reaction had no practical use.[100]

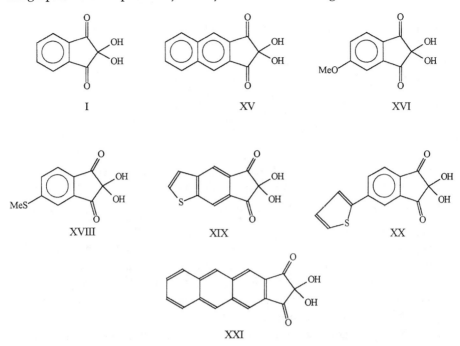

Figure 5.10 Ninhydrin (I) and some of its analogues that were prepared and evaluated as fingerprint reagents: I, ninhydrin; XV, benzo[f]ninhydrin; XVI, 5-methoxyninyhdrin; XVIII, 5-methylthioninhydrin; XIX, thieno[f]ninhydrin; XX, 5-(2-thienyl)ninhydrin; XXI, naphtho[f]ninhydrin.

tested nine ninhydrin analogues for their ability to develop fingerprints and to afford luminescent complexes upon treatment with metal salts.[101,102] The reagent 5-methoxyninhydrin (XVI, Figure 5.10) was found to yield prints that exhibited much more intensive fluorescence than with ninhydrin-developed prints. The advantages of 5-methoxyninhydrin were discussed in detail by Almog and Hirshfeld.[103] In 1987, it was adopted for operational use by Israeli Police and had an immediate and remarkable success in solving an extortion case.[103] A synthetic route to 5-methoxyninhydrin was also reported by this group.[104]* That same year, Joullié, Cantu, and co-workers reported a different synthetic pathway to benzo[f]ninhydrin that affords higher yield than obtained by the former group.[105]

Further studies in this series showed that the ninhydrin structure is not essential for fingerprint development, and that vicinal triketones of other types also react in the same manner. The most important prerequisite is a *cyclic* structure. Thus, compounds such as alloxan (V) and tetramethylcyclopentanetrione (XVII, Figure 5.11) also give a positive reaction with amino acids and with latent fingerprints.[106] Menzel, in 1989, demonstrated a time-resolved

* 5-Methoxyninhydrin has become commercially available under the name 2,2-dihydroxy-5-methoxy-1,3-indanedione (Aldrich Chemical Co., catalog no. 34 100-2).

Figure 5.11 Vicinal cyclic triketones other than ninhydrin that also give chromogenic reaction with amino acids: V, alloxan; XVII, 4,4,5,5-tetramethylcyclopentanetrione.

imaging system to suppress background luminescence of certain papers that may obscure fingerprint fluorescence. This was based on the observation that the lifetimes of natural paper luminescence are very short, whereas the lifetimes of the fingerprint fluorescence can be controlled by application of appropriate fluorogenic reagents. Thus, when europium trichloride is used as the metal salt in the secondary treatment stage, and benzo[f]ninhydrin as the primary reagent, the fluorescence of the complex has a much longer lifetime than the background. By using a pulsed laser such as a copper-vapor laser or specially arranged argon laser and appropriate electronic gating, it is possible to see only the fingerprint fluorescence after the background luminescence has long decayed.[107]

Although the laser-induced fluorescence of latent fingerprints developed with ninhydrin analogues greatly improved ninhydrin methodology, there were still considerable difficulties in applying them to practical work. Most of the analogues were not commercially available and the cost of those few that were available was extremely expensive. A number of research groups, particularly the joint effort of Joullié in Philadelphia and Cantu in Washington, D.C., have started to explore the possibility of developing efficient, cost-effective syntheses of ninhydrin analogues and to evaluate them. This group has not only devised very elegant synthetic routes to ninhydrin analogues, but it has also produced some very efficient analogues. The list of ninhydrin analogues that have been synthesized and evaluated since 1980 contains nearly 100 compounds. Most of these give a chromogenic reaction with amino acids and some are also fluorogenic. Particularly good results have been obtained with ninhydrin analogues containing divalent sulfur, such as 5-methylthioninhydrin,[109-111] (XVIII), thieno[f]ninhydrin,[111] (XIX), and 5-(2-thienyl)ninhydrin,[112] (XX, Figure 5.10). They exhibit good chromogenic as well as fluorogenic properties with amino acids and with latent fingerprints. Sulfur derivatives of ninhydrin and ninhydrin analogues have been reported by Menzel and Mekkaoui Alaoui to produce intensive luminescence after secondary treatment with europium and terbium salts.[113-115] Selenium-containing analogues have been prepared and evaluated as fingerprint reagents by Della, Kobus, and co-workers.[116,117] Other analogues that have been prepared and tested as fingerprint reagents are amino- and hydroxy-ninhydrins and a pyridine analogue (Almog et al.[118,119]), arylated ninhydrins (Joullié et al.[111,120-122] and Della et al.[116,117]), a thiophene analogue (Joullié, Cantu, and co-workers[123]), two "ninhydrin dimers" (Joullié et al.[124]), a pyrazine analogue (Frank et al.[125]), and a phenyldiazo-ninhydrin (Della and Taylor[116]). Alkyl ninhydrins were synthesized to obtain better solubility in nonpolar solvents (Hark and Joullié[122] and Pounds[126]). The effect of various alkoxy groups on the solubility and fluorogenicity of the analogues was recently reported by a joint team of the National Research Institute of Police Science and the Pharmaceutical Institute of Tohoku University in Japan.[127]

A list of ninhydrin analogues that have been prepared and evaluated can be found in Petrovskaia's Ph.D. thesis.[112] A comprehensive list of analogues, containing more than 80 compounds that have been published over the years, not only for fingerprint research, was recently composed by Hark.[128]

A joint team of the British PSDB and the Israel Police recently reported that the high hopes of benzo[f]ninhydrin had not been fulfilled. Despite the better contrast and fluorescence produced by this compound, the total number of latent prints that could be visualized by it was less than with ninhydrin.[129] Also, the longer homologue of ninhydrin, naphtho[f]ninhydrin (XXI, Figure 5.10), reported by Hallman and Bartsch gave disappointing results. It did not produce any visible reaction with amino acids.[130,131] Elber et al. have recently used computational methods to study Ruhemann's purple and analogous compounds. They suggest a theoretical explanation for the limited success in improving the color of the developed prints. Based on theoretical considerations, they have also designed new analogues that might afford more intense colors with latent fingerprints. Their best "candidates" are modified ninhydrin molecules, in which one or two of the side carbonyl oxygens are replaced by either divalent sulfur or by methylene groups.[132] These compounds have not yet been prepared.

Ninhydrin derivatives that are not exactly "analogues" but that are also used in fingerprint visualization are ninhydrin-hemiketals. Compounds of this type have been prepared by Takatsu et al. in Japan to substitute ninhydrin for fingerprint development on thermal paper which is contaminated by the conventional ninhydrin formulations. The rationale behind their study is that, like ninhydrin, its hemiketals might react with latent fingerprints, but they are much more soluble than ninhydrin in nonpolar solvents. Indeed, the hemiketal derived from ninhydrin and 3,5,5-trimethyl-1-hexanol (Figure 5.12) in hexane solution developed good prints on thermal paper without any contamination.[133] It is currently used by forensic science laboratories in Japan.[91]

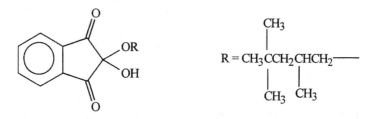

Figure 5.12 Alkoxyninhydrin (ninhydrin hemiketal) currently used in Japan for fingerprint visualization on thermal paper. (From Takatsu, M. et al., Development of a new method to detect latent fingerprints on thermal paper with *o*-alkyl derivative of ninhydrin, *Report of the National Institute of Police Science*, Japan, 44, 1, 1991.)

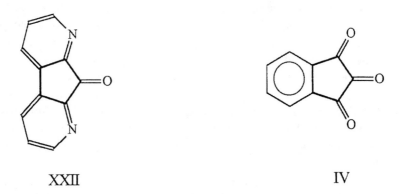

XXII   IV

Figure 5.13 1,8-Diazafluorene-9-one (DFO) (XXII) and the anhydrous form of ninhydrin (IV). Notice the resemblance of the active moiety in both molecules.

1,8-Diazafluorene-9-one (DFO)

In 1990, as a part of their search for new ninhydrin analogues, Grigg, Pounds, and co-workers modified the ninhydrin molecule even further. In addition to "regular" ninhydrin analogues, they also prepared and evaluated compounds that maintained only the essential functional group — the five-membered ring with one carbonyl in the center and two adjacent dipoles on both of its sides. One compound on their list, 1,8-diazafluorene-9-one [diazafluorenone or DFO, (XXII, Figure 5.13)], reacted with amino acids and with latent fingerprints on paper to afford both color and fluorescence. With amino acids it provided a red pigment whose structure closely resembled that of Ruhemann's purple[134] (Figure 5.14).

A thorough mechanistic study by Wilkinson in Canada supported Grigg's assumption[134] that the NH proton in the product is mobile between the nitrogen atoms. It also indicated the formation of a transient hemiketal as the active species in this reaction.[135]

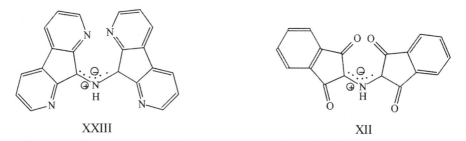

        XXIII   XII

Figure 5.14 The red pigment formed by the reaction of DFO with amino acids (XXIII). Notice the resemblance to Ruhemann's purple (XII). (From Grigg, R., Mongkolaussavaratana, T., Pounds, C.A., and Sivagnanam, S., 1,8-Diazafluorenone and related compounds. A new reagent for the detection of alpha amino acids and latent fingerprints, *Tetrahedron Lett.*, 31, 7215, 1990.)

Latent fingerprints that were treated with DFO displayed only a faint red color but they luminesced brightly under green light (absorption maximum at about 470 nm and emission maximum at about 570 nm[136]). There was no need for a secondary treatment with metal salt to induce luminescence, and the total number of identifiable prints developed by it was considerably higher than with ninhydrin. These properties very quickly made DFO the most important fluorogenic reagent for latent fingerprints. The best formulation still uses Fluorisol as the main carrier solvent, but a thorough study has been initiated to find an acceptable alternative.[137] The formulation proposed by the PSDB is a 0.025% solution of DFO in Fluorisol containing 3% methanol and 2% acetic acid. Optimal development conditions are 20 min at 100°C and no humidity.[55] Stoilovic's modification also included chloroform in the mixture, and the final concentration of DFO was 0.04%.[138] A non-CFC formulation based on petrol ether as the main carrier was suggested by Margot and Lennard.[139] Its main disadvantage is high flammability. Another non-CFC formulation, based on *tert*-butylmethyl ether, was suggested by Geide.[140] Conn, Lennard, and co-workers found that secondary treatment with metal salts had only a negligible effect on the luminescence although metal complexes had been formed.[141]

Several attempts to obtain an improved DFO reagent by modifying its molecule (DFO analogues) were unsuccessful.[134] There has been no follow-up to the observation of Frank and Handlin in 1993[142] that two compounds structurally related to DFO, one of them dipyridyl ketone, produce very strong fluorescence when reacted with amino acids. On the other hand, some ketals derived from DFO to increase its solubility in nonpolar solvents do react with latent fingerprints but not as well as DFO.[143]

At present, DFO is considered the best fluorogenic fingerprint reagent for paper and porous surfaces, and it is used as the first stage of the chemical sequence: DFO, ninhydrin, and PD.

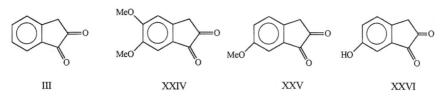

Figure 5.15 1,2-Indanedione (III) and some of its analogues that give fluorogenic reaction with amino acids and with latent fingerprints: III, 1,2-indanedione; XXIV, 5,6-dimethoxyindanedione; XXV, 6-methoxy-1,2-indanedione (and other isomers); XXVI, 6-hydroxy-1,2-indanedione (and other isomers). (From Hauze, D.B., Petrovskaia, O.G., Taylor, B., Joullié, M.M., Ramotowski, R., and Cantu, A.A., *J. Forensic Sci.*, 43, 744, 1998; Wiesner, S., Optimization of the Indanedione Process for Fingerprint Development, M.Sc. thesis, Casali Institute of Applied Chemistry, The Hebrew University of Jerusalem, Israel, 2001.)

1,2-Indanedione

The most recent, remarkable discovery in this field is 1,2-indanedione. To develop new routes to ninhydrin analogues, Joullié, Cantu, and co-workers synthesized and evaluated another class of compounds closely related to ninhydrin: 1,2-indanediones (Figure 5.15). These compounds were prepared and described in the chemical literature prior to Joullié, but never before had they been examined as potential amino acid or fingerprint reagents.

Methanolic solutions of various 1,2-indanediones were applied to amino acid spots on filter paper. They afforded light pink stains that fluoresce brightly upon illumination with green light.[144,145] Secondary treatment with zinc nitrate increased the fluorescence dramatically, particularly when 5,6-dimethoxy-1,2-indanedione (XXIV, Figure 5.15) was used as a reagent. The fluorescence is stronger than with DFO-treated stains. Heat and humidity also have an augmentative effect on the fluorescence, but cooling to liquid nitrogen temperature is unnecessary.

Initial experiments with latent fingerprints under similar conditions afforded brightly fluorescing fingerprint images.[145]

The effects of further structural modifications in the indanedione series were studied by Almog et al.; in their opinion, 1,2-indanedione itself, even without secondary treatment, is at least as sensitive as DFO.[146] They also devised a novel synthetic route to some indanediones[147] that could not be prepared by the original method developed by Cava et al.[148]

The first positive experiments with indanediones were carried out in methanolic solutions. Nevertheless, Petrovskaia and Joullié,[112] Wilkinson,[149] and Wiesner et al.[150] recommend the use of indanedione in alcohol-free carriers because alcohols (methanol, ethanol, isopropanol) reduce the effectiveness of the reagent due to the formation of hemiketals. Roux et al., however,

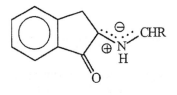

XXVII

Figure 5.16 The fluorescent product of the reaction between 1,2-indanedione and amino acid. (From Petrovskaia, O.G., Design and Synthesis of Chromogenic and Fluorogenic Reagents for Amino Acid Detection, Ph.D. thesis, University of Pennsylvania, Philadelphia, 1999.)

used methanol in their best formulation and did not notice any adverse effect. As opposed to Joullié,[144,145] they did notice a positive effect of cooling the exhibits to liquid nitrogen temperature.[151]

Acetic acid was found to have a blurring effect on the developed prints and, hence, is not recommended for use in indanedione solutions.[150] After checking the various parameters, Wiesner et al. suggested a working solution composed of 1,2-indanedione (0.2%) in HFE7100 solvent, containing about 7% ethyl acetate.[150] Preliminary observations indicate the following advantages of 1,2-indanedione over DFO:

1. Higher sensitivity (it detects more identifiable prints)
2. Higher solubility in nonpolar solvents
3. Good results in a non-CFC solvent (HFE7100)
4. Cost

The reaction mechanism of 1,2-indanedione with amino acids was explored by Petrovskaia and Joullié, who suggest the formation of a 1,3-dipole (XXVII, Figure 5.16) as the fluorescent species.[112]

Wiesner et al.[150] report that no new prints can be observed in a sequential treatment with ninhydrin after 1,2-indanedione. In the authors' opinion, this indicates a faster and more complete reaction of indanedione with amino acids than the DFO reaction with amino acids (after which ninhydrin does provide new prints). Thus, the use of indanedione may save one stage in the sequence: DFO, ninhydrin, PD, which can turn to indanedione and PD. Several groups in Germany, Switzerland, the United Kingdom, Canada, the United States, Australia, and Japan have initiated extensive studies to evaluate 1,2-indanedione for operational use. The Israel Police, Division of Identification and Forensic Science (DIFS), has already begun to use 1,2-indanedione in casework involving serious crimes.[152]

References

1. Olsen, R.D., *Scott's Fingerprint Mechanics*, Charles C Thomas, Springfield, IL, 1978.

2. Pounds, C.A., Developments in fingerprint visualization, in *Forensic Science Progress*, Vol. 3, Springer-Verlag, Berlin, 1988.

3. Caton, H.C., Physical and chemical aspects of latent print development, in *Proc. Conf. Sci. Fingerprints*, Police Scientific Development Branch, Home Office, London, 1974.

4. Chemical development of latent impressions, *FBI Law Enforcement Bull.*, 39, 8, 1970 (revised April 1976).

5. Udenfriend, S., Stein, S., Bohlen, P., Dairman, W., Leimgruber, W., and Weigele, M., A reagent for assay of amino acids, peptides, proteins and primary amines in the picomole range, *Science*, 178, 871, 1972.

6. Mayer, S.W., Meilleur, C.P., and Jones, P.F., The use of orthophthalaldehyde for superior visualization of latent fingerprints, *Identification News*, 9, 13, 1977.

7. Lee, H.C. and Attard, A.E., Comparison of fluorescamine, *o*-phthalaldehyde, and ninhydrin for the detection and visualization of latent fingerprints, *J. Police Sci. Admin.*, 7, 333, 1979.

8. Almog, J., Scope and limitations of the use of alloxan as a potential fingerprint reagent, Israel Police R&D Report DM/2037, Oct. 1982 (in Hebrew).

9. Almog, J., Rozen, S., and Scharf, G., Reaction of Naphthalene-2,3-Dicarboxaldehyde with Amino Acids and with Latent Fingerprints on Paper, Israel Police R&D Report DM/2037, Sept. 1981 (in Hebrew).

10. Carlson, R.G., Srinivasachar, K., Givens, R., and Matuszewski, B.K., New derivatizing agents for amino acids and peptides. 1. Facile synthesis of N-substituted 1-cyanobenz(*f*)isoindoles and their spectroscopic properties, *J. Org. Chem.*, 51, 3979, 1986.

11. Roach, M.C. and Harmony, M.D., Determination of amino acids in subfemtomole levels by high performance liquid chromatography with laser-induced fluorescence detection, *Anal. Chem.*, 59, 411, 1987.

12. Salares, V.R., Eves, C.R., and Carey, P.R., On the detection of fingerprints by laser excited luminescence, *Forensic Sci. Int.*, 14, 229, 1979.

13. Warrener, R.N., Kobus, H.J., and Stoilovic, M., An evaluation of the reagent NBD-chloride for the production of luminescent fingerprints on paper. I. Support for a xenon arc lamp being a cheaper and valuable alternative to an argon ion laser as an excitation source, *Forensic Sci. Int.*, 23, 179, 1983.

14. Almog, A., Zeichner, A., Shifrina, S., and Scharf, G., Nitro-benzofurazanyl ethers — a new series of fluorigenic fingerprint reagents, *J. Forensic Sci.*, 32, 585, 1987.

15. Pounds, C.A. and Jones, R.J., The application of chemical techniques in the development of latent fingerprints, unpublished, 1982.

16. Pounds, C.A. and Jones, R.J., Physicochemical techniques in the development of latent fingerprints, *Trends Anal. Chem.*, 2, 180, 1983.

17. Ruhemann, S., Cyclic di- and triketones, *J. Chem. Soc.*, 97, 1438, 1910.

18. Ruhemann, S., Triketohydrindene hydrate, *J. Chem. Soc.*, 97, 2025, 1910.

19. Kaufmann, V., Über ein Analogon des indigos in der indenereihe: Diphtalyläthen, *Ber. der D. Chem. Ges.*, 30, 382, 1897.

20. McCaldin, D.J., The chemistry of ninhydrin, *Chem. Rev.*, 60, 39, 1960 (and references therein).

21. Schönberg, A. and Moubacher, R., Studies on indene derivatives. II. Triketo-hydrindene, *J. Chem. Soc.* 98, 71, 1943.

22. Dutt, M.C. and Poe, T.T., Use of ninhydrin as a spray reagent for the detection of some basic drugs on thin-layer chromatography, *J. Chromatogr.*, 195, 133, 1980.

23. Schönberg, A. and Singer, E., Die Chemie des Ninhydrins und anderer cyclisher 1,2,3-Tricarbonylverbindungen, *Tetrahedron*, 34, 1285, 1978.

24. Joullié, M.M., Thompson, T.R., and Nemeroff, N.H., Ninhydrin and ninhy-drin analogues. Syntheses and applications, *Tetrahedron*, 47, 8791, 1991.

25. Rubin, M.B. and Gleiter, R., The chemistry of vicinal polycarbonyl compounds, *Chem. Rev.*, 100, 1121, 2000.

26. Ruhemann, S., Triketohydrindene hydrate. III. Its relation to alloxan, *J. Chem. Soc.*, 99, 792, 1911.

27. Ruhemann, S., Triketohydrindene hydrate. IV. Hydrindantin and its ana-logues, *J. Chem. Soc.*, 99, 1306, 1911.

28. Ruhemann, S., Triketohydrindene hydrate. V. The analogues of uramil and purpuric acid, *J. Chem. Soc.*, 99, 1486, 1911.

29. Schmidt, C.L.A., *The Chemistry of Amino Acids and Proteins*, Charles C Tho-mas, Springfield, IL, 1938.

30. Dent, C.E., A study of the behavior of sixty amino acids and other ninhydrin-reacting substances on phenol-"collidine" filter paper chromatograms with notes as to the occurrence of some of them in biological fluids, *Biochem. J.*, 43, 169, 1948.

31. Friedman, M. and Williams, L.D., Stoichiometry of formation of Ruhemann's purple in the ninhydrin reaction, *Bioorganic Chem.*, 3, 267, 1974.

32. Grigg, R., Malone, J.F., Mongkolaussavaratana, T., and Thianpatanagul, S., Cycloaddition reactions relevant to the mechanism of the ninhydrin reaction. X-ray crystal structure of the protonated Ruhemann's purple, a stable 1,3-dipole, *J. Chem. Soc., Chem. Commun.*, 421, 1986.

33. Bottom, C.B., Hanna, S.S., and Siehr, D.J., Mechanism of the ninhydrin reaction, *Biochemical Ed.*, 6, 4, 1978.

34. Grigg, R., Malone, J.F., Mongkolaussavaratana, T., and Thianpatanagul, S., X=Y-ZH Compounds as potential 1,3-dipoles. 23. Mechanisms of the reactions of ninhydrin and phenalene trione with alpha amino acids. X-ray crystal structure of protonated Ruhemann's purple, a stable azomethine ylide, Tetrahedron, 45, 3849, 1989.

35. Abderhalden, E. and Schmidt, H.S., Experiments with triketohydrindene hydrate, Hoppe Seyler's Zeit. Physiol. Chem., 85, 143, 1913.

36. Oden, S. and von Hofsten, B., Detection of fingerprints by the ninhydrin reaction, Nature, 173, 449, 1954.

37. Oden, S., Developing Fingerprints, U.S. Patent 2715–571, August 16, 1955 (Chem. Abstr., 49, 16276a, 1955).

38. Oden, S., Development of fingerprints, German Patent 934-850, November 3, 1955.

39. Schlacke, K.H. and Fuchs, T., Allergic contact eczema to ninhydrin, Derm-Beruf-Umwelt, 37, 179, 1989.

40. Hytonen, M., Martimo, K.P., Estlander, T., and Tupasela, O., Occupational IgE-mediated rhinitis caused by ninhydrin, Allergy, 51, 114, 1996.

41. Pirila, P., Estlander, T., Hytonen, M., Keskinen, H., Tupasela, O., and Tuppurainen, M., Rhinitis caused by ninhydrin develops into occupational asthma. Eur. Respir. J., 10, 1918, 1997.

42. Morris, J.R. and Goode, G.C., NFN — an improved ninhydrin reagent for detection of latent fingerprints, Police Res. Bull., 24, 45, 1974.

43. Crown, D.A., The development of latent fingerprints with ninhydrin, J. Crim. Law, Criminol. Police Sci., 60, 258, 1969.

44. Turbyfill, R.T., The development of latent fingerprints using non-flammable ninhydrin mixture (London method), Crime Laboratory Digest (FBI), 76, 6, 1976.

45. Morris, J.R., Extensions to the NFN (ninhydrin) reagent for the development of latent fingerprints, Unpublished, 1978.

46. Goode, G.C. and Morris, J.R., Latent Fingerprints: A Review of Their Origin, Composition and Methods for Detection, AWRE Report No. 022/83, United Kingdom (unclassified), Oct. 1983.

47. Tighe, D.J., Freon- plus two, Identification News, 34, 3, 1984.

48. Margot, P., Lennard, C., Stoilovic, M., Yong, S.J., and Warrener, R.N., Improved detection of latent fingerprints, Proc. of the Third Workshop in Advanced Fingerprint Techniques, Forensic Science Research Unit, Chemistry Department, Australian National University, Canberra, May 1986.

49. Kent, T., Ed., Manual of Fingerprint Development Techniques, Scientific Research and Development Branch (SRDB), Home Office (U.K.), 1986.

50. Watling, W.J. and Smith, K.O., Heptane, an alternative to the freon ninhydrin mixture, J. Forensic Identification, 43, 131, 1993.

51. Jungbluth, W.O., Replacement for CFC 113, *J. Forensic Identification*, 43, 226, 1993.

52. Hewlett, D.F. and Sears, V.G., Replacement for CFC 113 in the ninhydrin process. 1, *J. Forensic Identification*, 47, 287, 1997.

53. Hewlett, D.F., Winfield, P.G.R., and Clifford, A.A., The ninhydrin process in supercritical carbon dioxide, *J. Forensic Sci.*, 4, 487, 1996.

54. Hewlett, D.F., Sears, V.G., and Suzuki, S., Replacement for CFC 113 in the ninhydrin process. 2, *J. Forensic Identification*, 47, 300, 1997.

55. Kent, T., Ed., *Manual of Fingerprint Development Techniques*, 2nd ed., Police Scientific Development Branch (PSDB), Home Office, (U.K.), 1998.

56. Creer, K.E. and Brennan, J.S., The work of the serious crime unit, in *Proc. of the Int. Forensic Symp. on Latent Fingerprints, FBI*, FBI Academy, Quantico, VA, U.S. Government Printing Office, 1987.

57. Brennan, J.S., personal communication, Aug. 2000.

58. Taylor, S.C., Processing with ninhydrin fumes, *Identification News*, 29, 9, 1979.

59. Conway, J.P., Fingerprints and documents, in *Proc. of the Joint Meeting of the American Society of Questioned Document Examiners and the Crime Detection Laboratories, Royal Canadian Mounted Police*, Ottawa, Canada, 1965.

60. O'Hara, C.E., in *Fundamentals of Criminal Investigation*, Charles C Thomas, Springfield, IL, 1970.

61. Crown, D.A., Report on Conference on Latent Fingerprints, held at FBI Laboratory, Washington, D.C., April 1965.

62. Mooney, D.G., Development of latent fingerprints and latent palmprints by ninhydrin, *Identification News*, 16, 4, 1966.

63. Moenssens, A.A., in *Fingerprint Techniques*, Chilton, New York, 1971.

64. Lesk, J.A., Post-processing humidification in the development of latent fingerprints with ninhydrin, *Am. Acad. Forensic Sci. Newslett.*, January, 1971, p. 7.

65. Miles, C., Use of Salt Solution to Control Relative Humidity During Development of Ninhydrin Plates, FIRS technical Report No. 5, Royal Canadian Mounted Police (RCMP), Ottawa, Canada, 1987.

66. Rispling, O., Ninhydrin combats bank frauds, *Int. Criminal Police Rev.*, 245, 11, 1971.

67. Connor, C.M., Collaborative study of accelerated development of latent fingerprint images on paper by application of steam, *J. Assoc. Official Anal. Chemists* (AOAC), 59, 1003, 1976.

68. Brunelle, R.L., Report on forensic sciences, *J. Assoc. Official Anal. Chemists* (AOAC), 59, 354, 1976.

69. Morris, J.R., The application of a domestic steam iron for the development of latent fingerprints by the ninhydrin method, unpublished, 1978.

70. Jones, R.J., Pounds, C.A., and Reed, R.A., personal communication, 1980.

71. Jones, R.J. and Pounds, C.A., Use of steam and heat to enhance fingerprints on papers other than cheques following development with ninhydrin, unpublished, 1981.

72. Margot, P., Lennard, C., Stoilovic, M., Yong, S.J., and Warrener, R.N., New and improved fluorescent methods, in *Proc. of the 2nd Workshop in Advanced Fingerprint Techniques,* Forensic Science Research Unit, Chemistry Department, Australian National University, Canberra, Australia, July, 1984.

73. German, E.R., You are missing ninhydrin developed prints, *Identification News,* 31, 3, 1981.

74. Morris, J.R., Goode, G.C., and Godsell, J.W., Some new developments in the chemical detection of latent fingerprints, *Police Res. Bull.,* 21, 31, 1973.

75. Dalrymple, B.E., Duff, J.M., and Menzel, E.R., Inherent fingerprint luminescence — detection by laser, *J. Forensic Sci.,* 22, 106, 1977.

76. Herod, D.W. and Menzel, E.R., Laser detection of latent fingerprints: ninhydrin, *J. Forensic Sci.,* 27, 200, 1982.

77. Herod, D.W. and Menzel, E.R., Laser detection of latent fingerprints: ninhydrin followed by zinc chloride, *J. Forensic Sci.,* 27, 513, 1982.

78. Kawerau, E. and Wieland, T., Conservation of amino-acid chromatograms, *Nature,* 168, 77, 1951.

79. Krauss, A., Anfärbung von Aminosäuren mit Metallsaltz-Ninhydrin-Gemischen, *Z. Analyt. Chem.,* 229, 343, 1967.

80. Doi, E., Shibata, D., and Matoba, T., Modified colorimetric ninhydrin methods for peptidase assay, *Anal. Biochem.,* 118, 173, 1981.

81. Seitz, W.R., Fluorescence derivatization, in *CRC Crit. Rev. Anal. Chem.,* 8, 367, 1980.

82. Grove, E., Copper vapor lasers come of age, *Laser Focus Mag.,* July 6, 1982.

83. Almog, J., Research and development of new fluorescors for forensic purposes, presented at the *67th Annu. Conf. Int. Assoc. Identification,* Rochester, New York, July 1982.

84. Kobus, H.J., Stoilovic, M., and Warrener, R.N., A simple luminescent post-ninhydrin treatment for the improved visualization of fingerprints on documents in cases where ninhydrin alone gives poor results, *Forensic Sci. Int.,* 22, 161, 1983.

85. Watkin, J.E., An intense blue light lamp for exciting fingerprint fluorescence, in *Proc. Int. Fingerprint Conf.,* Scientific Research and Development Branch (SRDB), Home Office, London, November, 1984.

86. Watkin, J.E., Alternative lighting methods of detecting latent fingerprints, in *Proc. Int. Forensic Symp. Latent Fingerprints, FBI,* FBI Academy, Quantico, VA, U.S. Government Printing Office, 1987.

87. Kent, T., An operational guide to fingerprint techniques, in *Proc. Int. Fingerprint Conf.*, Scientific Research and Development Branch (SRDB), Home Office, London, November 1984.

88. Kent, T., Presentation on the methods used by the SRDB for fingerprint development, in *Proc. Int. Symp. on Latent Fingerprints, FBI*, FBI Academy, Quantico, VA, U.S. Government Printing Office, 1987.

89. Stoilovic, M., Kobus, H.J., Margot, P., and Warrener, R.N., Design of a versatile light source for fingerprint detection and enhancement, in *Proc. 9th Australian Int. Meeting of Forensic Sciences*, Melbourne, Australia, February 1986.

90. Stoilovic, M., Unilite 1: a versatile light system for fluorescence applications, especially those in forensic science, poster presented at the *Int. Forensic Symp. on Latent Fingerprints*, Forensic Science Research and Training Center, FBI Academy, Quantico, VA, July 1987.

91. Suzuki, S., National Institute of Police Science, Japan, personal communication, September 2000.

92. Menzel, E.R. and Almog, J., Latent fingerprint development by frequency-doubled neodymium:yttrium aluminium garnet (Nd:YAG) laser: Benzo[*f*]ninhydrin, *J. Forensic Sci.*, 30, 371, 1985.

93. Stoilovic, M., Kobus, H.J., Margot, P., and Warrener, R.N., Improved enhancement of ninhydrin developed fingerprints by cadmium complexation using low temperature photoluminescent technique, *J. Forensic Sci.*, 31, 432, 1986.

94. Menzel, E.R., Discussion of "Improved enhancement of ninhydrin developed fingerprints by cadmium complexation using low temperature photoluminescence techniques," and R.N. Warrener's response, *J. Forensic Sci.*, 32, 841, 1987.

95. Lennard, C.J., Margot, P.A., Sterns, A., and Warrener, R.N., Photoluminescent enhancement of ninhydrin developed fingerprints by metal complexation: structural studies of complexes formed between Ruhemann's purple and group IIb metal salts, *J. Forensic Sci.*, 32, 597, 1987.

96. Wieland, T., Die Trennung und Bestimmung der Naturlichen Aminosäuren, *Fortschritte Chem. Forsch.*, 1, 211, 1949.

97. Davies, P.J., Taylor, M.R., and Wainwright, K.P., Zinc(II) chloride-methanol complex of 2-[(1,3-diketo-1,3-dioxo-2H-inden-2-ylidene)amino]1H-indene-1,3-(2H) dionate(1-) sodium salt: a complex of Ruhemann's purple, *Acta Cryst.*, C51, 1802, 1995.

98. Davies, P.J., Kobus, H.J., Taylor, M.R., and Wainwright, K.P., Synthesis and structure of the zinc(II) and cadmium(II) complexes produced in the photoluminescent enhancement of ninhydrin developed fingerprints using group 12 metal salts, *J. Forensic Sci.*, 40, 565, 1995.

99. Almog, J., Hirshfeld, A., and Klug, J.T., Reagents for the chemical development of latent fingerprints: synthesis and properties of some ninhydrin analogues, *J. Forensic Sci.*, 27, 912, 1982.

100. Meier, R. and Lotter, H.G., Über Benz- und Naphthoindantrione, *Chem. Ber.*, 90, 220, 1957.

101. Lennard, C.J., Margot, P.A., Stoilovic, M., and Warrener, R.N., Synthesis of ninhydrin analogues and their application to fingerprint development: preliminary results, *J. Forensic Sci. Soc.*, 26, 323, 1986.

102. Lennard, C.J., Margot, P.A., Stoilovic, M., and Warrener, R.N., Synthesis and evaluation of ninhydrin analogues as reagents for the development of latent fingerprints on paper surfaces, *J. Forensic Sci. Soc.*, 28, 3, 1988.

103. Almog, J. and Hirshfeld, A., 5-Methoxyninhydrin: a fingerprint developer compatible with the copper-vapor laser, presented at the *Int. Forensic Symp. on Latent Fingerprints*, FBI Academy, Quantico, VA, July 1987.

104. Almog, J. and Hirshfeld, A., 5-Methoxyninhydrin: a reagent for the chemical development of latent fingerprints that is compatible with the copper-vapor laser, *J. Forensic Sci.*, 33, 1027, 1988.

105. Heffner, R., Safaryn, J.E., and Joullié, M.M., A new synthesis of benzo[*f*]ninhydrin, *Tetrahedron Lett.*, 28, 6539, 1987.

106. Almog, J., Reagents for chemical development of latent fingerprints: vicinal triketones — their reaction with amino acids and with latent fingerprints on paper, *J. Forensic Sci.*, 32, 1565, 1987.

107. Menzel, E.R., Detection of latent fingerprints by laser-excited luminescence, *Anal. Chem.*, 61, 557A, 1989.

108. Menzel, E.R., *Fingerprints Detection with Lasers*, 2nd ed., Marcel Dekker, New York, 1999.

109. Heffner, R. and Joullié, M.M., Synthetic routes to ninhydrins. Preparation of ninhydrin, 5-methoxyninhydrin and 5-(methylthio)ninhydrin, *Synth. Commun.*, 21, 2231, 1991.

110. Almog, J., Hirshfeld, A., Frank, A., Grant, H., Harel, Z., and Ittah, Y., 5-Methylthio ninhydrin and related compounds: a novel class of fluorogenic fingerprint reagents, *J. Forensic Sci.*, 37, 688, 1992.

111. Cantu, A.A., Leben, D.A., Joullié, M.M., Heffner, R.J., and Hark, R.R., A comparative evaluation of several amino acid reagents for visualizing amino acid (glycine) on paper, *J. Forensic Identification*, 43, 44, 1993.

112. Petrovskaia, O.G., Design and Synthesis of Chromogenic and Fluorogenic Reagents for Amino Acid Detection, Ph.D thesis (M.M. Joullié, supervisor), University of Pennsylvania, Philadelphia, 1999.

113. Mekkaoui Alaoui, I. and Menzel, E.R., Spectroscopy of rare earth-Ruhemann's purple complexes, *J. Forensic Sci.*, 38, 506, 1993.

114. Mekkaoui Alaoui, I. and Menzel, E.R., Emission enhancement in terbium-Ruhemann's purple complexes, *Forensic Sci. Int.*, 60, 203, 1994.

115. Mekkaoui Alaoui, I. and Menzel, E.R., Substituent effect on luminescence enhancement in europium and terbium Ruhemann's purple complexes, *Forensic Sci. Int.*, 77, 3, 1996.

116. Kobus, H.J., Pigou, P.E., Della, E.W., Taylor, B., and Davies, P.J., Fingerprint research in South Australia, in *Proc. Int. Symp. on Fingerprint Detection and Identification*, Ne'urim, Israel, Almog, J. and Springer, E., Eds., Hemed Press, 1995, 227.

117. Della, E.W., Janowski, W.K., Pigou, P.E., and Taylor, B.M., Synthesis of fingerprint reagents: aromatic nucleophilic substitution as a route to 5-substituted ninhydrins, *Synthesis*, 12, 2119, 1999.

118. Almog, J., Hirshfeld, A., Frank, A., Sterling, J., and Leonov, D., Aminoninhydrins: fingerprint reagents with direct fluorogenic activity — preliminary studies, *J. Forensic Sci.*, 36, 104, 1991.

119. Almog, J., unpublished results (see Ref. 111).

120. Hark, R.R., Hauze, D.B., Petrovskaia, O., Joullié, M.M., Jaouhari, R., and McKomiskey, P., Novel approaches toward ninhydrin analogs, *Tetrahedron Lett.*, 35, 7719, 1994.

121. Hark, R.R., Hauze, D.B., Petrovskaia, O., and Joullié, M.M., Chemical detection of fingerprints — synthesis of arylated ninhydrin analogs, in *Proc. Int. Symp. on Fingerprint Detection and Identification*, Ne'urim, Israel, Almog, J. and Springer, E., Eds., Hemed Press, 1995, 129.

122. Hark, R.R., Synthesis of Ninhydrin Analogs, Ph.D thesis (M.M. Joullié, supervisor), University of Pennsylvania, Philadelphia, 1996.

123. Hauze, D.B., Joullié, M.M., Ramotowski, R., and Cantu, A., Novel synthesis of thianinhydrin, *Tetrahedron*, 53, 4239, 1997.

124. Hauze, D.B., Petrovskaia, O., Joullié, M.M., and Hark, R.R., New reagents for the development of fingerprints, in *Proc. Int. Symp. on Fingerprint Detection and Identification*, Ne'urim, Israel, Almog, J. and Springer, E., Eds., Hemed Press, 1995, 119.

125. Frank, F.J., Borup, B., Brookman, J.A., Carr, A.J., Hurd, K.L., Renner, M., and Stowell, J.K., Preparation of ninhydrin analogs for fluorescent fingerprint development, poster presented at *"Spectrum 91,"* Int. Symp. Forensic Techniques, Detroit, Michigan, 1991.

126. Pounds, C.A., unpublished results (see Ref. 24).

127. Ohta, H., Suzuki, Y., Sugita, R., Suzuki, S., and Ogasawara, K., Examination of 5-alkoxyninhydrins as latent fingerprint visualization reagents, *Can. Soc. Forensic Sci. J.*, submitted for publication, 2000.

128. Hark, R.R., Table of ninhydrin analogs, personal communication, Sept. 2000.

129. Almog, J., Sears, V.J., Springer, E., Hewlett, D.F., Walker, S., Wiesner, S., Lidor, R., and Bahar, E., Reagents for the chemical development of latent fingerprints: scope and limitations of benzo[*f*]ninhydrin in comparison to ninhydrin, *J. Forensic Sci.*, 45, 538, 2000.

130. Hallman, J.L. and Bartsch, R.A., Synthesis of naphthoninhydrin, *J. Org. Chem.*, 56, 6423, 1991.

131. Almog, J. and Springer, E., unpublished results, 1993.

132. Elber, R., Frank, A., and Almog, J., Chemical development of latent fingerprints: computational design of ninhydrin analogues, *J. Forensic Sci.*, 45, 757, 2000.

133. Takatsu, M., Kageyama, H., Hirata, K., Akashi, T., Yoko Ta, T., Shiitani, M., and Kobayashi, A., Development of a new method to detect latent fingerprints on thermal paper with *o*-alkyl derivative of ninhydrin, *Report of the National Institute of Police Science*, Japan, 44, 1, 1991.

134. Grigg, R., Mongkolaussavaratana, T., Pounds, C.A., and Sivagnanam, S., 1,8-Diazafluorenone and related compounds. A new reagent for the detection of alpha amino acids and latent fingerprints, *Tetrahedron Lett.*, 31, 7215, 1990.

135. Wilkinson, D., Study of the reaction mechanism of 1,8-diazafluoren-9-one with the amino acid L-alanine, *Forensic Sci. Int.*, 109, 87, 2000.

136. Hardwick, S., Kent, T., Sears, V., and Winfield, P., Improvements to the formulation of DFO and the effects of heat on the reaction with latent fingerprints, *Fingerprint Whorld*, 19, 65, 1993.

137. Hewlett, D.F. and Sears, V.J., Formulation of amino acid reagents. Search for a safe effective replacement for CFCs, in *Proc. Int. Symp. on Fingerprint Detection and Identification*, Almog, J. and Springer, E., Eds., Ne'urim, Israel, 99, 1995.

138. Stoilovic, M., Improved method for DFO development of latent fingerprints, *Forensic Sci. Int.*, 60, 141, 1993.

139. Margot, P. and Lennard, C., *Fingerprint Detection Techniques*, 6th revised edition, Université de Lausanne, 1994.

140. Geide, B., Detection of latent fingerprints — DFO without CFC, in *Proc. Int. Symp. on Fingerprint Detection and Identification*, Almog, J. and Springer, E., Eds., Ne'urim, Israel, 1995, 95.

141. Lennard, C., The effect of metal salt treatment on the photoluminescence of DFO-treated fingerprints, personal communication, 1999.

142. Frank, F.J. and Handlin, N., Development of a latent fingerprint detection chemical: dibenzo-1,8-diazafluorenone, *M.A.F.S. Newslett.*, 22, July 1993.

143. Frank, A., Grant, H., and Almog, J., Preliminary Tests on the Use of Two New Ketals of DFO for the Development of Latent Fingerprints, presented in a closed meeting on advances in fingerprint detection, PSDB, Home Office, U.K., 1996.

144. Ramotowski, R., Cantu, A.A., Joullié, M.M., and Petrovskaia, O.G., 1,2-Indanedione: a preliminary evaluation of a new class of amino acid visualizing compounds, *Fingerprint Whorld*, 23, 131, 1997.

145. Hauze, D.B., Petrovskaia, O.G., Taylor, B., Joullié, M.M., Ramotowski, R., and Cantu, A.A., 1,2-Indanediones: new reagents for visualizing the amino acid components of latent prints, *J. Forensic Sci.*, 43, 744, 1998.

146. Almog, J., Springer, E., Wiesner, S., Frank, A., Khodzhaev, O., Lidor, R., Bahar, E., Varkony, H., Dayan, S., and Rozen, S., Latent fingerprint visualization by 1,2-indanedione and related compounds: preliminary results, *J. Forensic Sci.*, 44, 114, 1999.

147. Dayan, S., Almog, J., Khodzhaev, O., and Rozen, S., A novel synthesis of indanediones using the HOF.CH₃CN complex, *J. Org. Chem.*, 63, 2752, 1998.

148. Cava, M.P., Little, R.L., and Napier, D.R., Condensed cyclobutane aromatic systems. V. The synthesis of some alpha-diazoindanones: ring contraction in the indane series, *J. Am. Chem. Soc.*, 80, 2257, 1958.

149. Wilkinson, D., Spectroscopic study of 1,2-indanedione, *Forensic Sci. Int.*, 114, 123, 2000.

150. Wiesner, S., Optimization of the Indanedione Process for Fingerprint Development, M.Sc. thesis, (J.Almog and Y.Sasson, supervisors), Casali Institute of Applied Chemistry, The Hebrew University of Jerusalem, Israel, 2001.

151. Roux, C., Jones, N., Lennard, C., and Stoilovic, M., Evaluation of 1,2-indanedione for the detection of latent fingerprints on porous surfaces, *J. Forensic Sci.*, 45, 761, 2000.

152. Azoury, M. (Head, Latent Fingerprint Development Laboratory, Israel Police), personal communication, July 2000.

Fingerprint Detection with Photoluminescent Nanoparticles

6

E. ROLAND MENZEL

Contents

The exploitation of photoluminescence as a general approach to the detection of latent fingerprints began in 1976.[1] The rationale for the photoluminescence approach is the very high analytical sensitivity that photoluminescence techniques provide quite generally. One cannot do better than the detection of a single photon, a capability within reach in photoluminescence. Fingerprint luminescence excitation initially used lasers, but filtered lamps (these days referred to as alternate or alternative light sources) were employed as well, albeit at the expense of detection sensitivity in comparison with lasers. This sensitivity discrepancy still pertains today. The initial fingerprint photoluminescence investigation focused on fluorescence inherent to fingerprint residue. However, the utilization of fluorescent dusting powders and staining dyes, as well as reagents that would attack fingerprint constituents to yield a fluorescent product, was also anticipated from the outset. By the late 1970s,

211

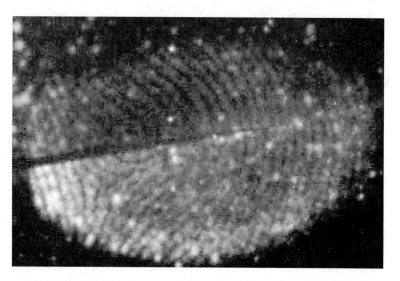

Figure 6.1 Ninhydrin/ZnCl$_2$ vs. ninhydrin/InCl$_3$ fingerprint photoluminescence development.

various fluorescent dusting powders had been developed.[2] Dye staining, first demonstrated in 1976,[1] came into its own in the early 1980s in concert with cyanoacrylate ester fuming.[3] This staining is today one of the most successful photoluminescence procedures for detection of fingerprints on smooth surfaces, regardless of the age of the fingerprint. Numerous staining dyes can be employed. The post-treatment of ninhydrin-developed latent fingerprints by zinc chloride, first reported in 1982,[4] made fingerprints on porous items (mostly paper) tractable as well, and is today quite routine. Sensitivity improvements to this procedure, involving ninhydrin analogs, notably benzo(f)ninhydrin[5] and 5-methoxyninhydrin[6] followed. The zinc chloride post-treatment of ninhydrin-processed fingerprints was until very recently unsurpassed in terms of the intensity of the obtained photoluminescence. However, recent work carried out in Japan has identified indium chloride as being superior.[7] The InCl$_3$ is used in the same way as ZnCl$_2$. Figure 6.1 depicts an example of the comparison of ZnCl$_2$ vs. InCl$_3$ treatment of a ninhydrin-processed fingerprint. More intense luminescence can be obtained with GaCl$_3$ because Ga has a lower atomic number than In. However, GaCl$_3$ reacts fairly violently with water (which occurs in methanol that has been exposed to ambient air). Thus, GaCl$_3$ is not as practical as InCl$_3$. Diazafluore-9-one is a relatively recent reagent that can be used instead of ninhydrin/zinc chloride.[8] It is now routinely employed in a number of crime laboratories. With the above procedures, and a number of others for special situations,[9] photoluminescence detection of fingerprints has assumed a prominent place worldwide as a major routine methodology. Photoluminescence detection of latent fingerprints has been instrumental in the solution of many major cases (e.g., Polly Klaas, Nightstalker). To the best of this author's knowledge, laser detection holds the record for the oldest fingerprint developed and identified in a criminal case over 40 years old.[10] In the author's laboratory, ridge detail of fingerprints dating back to the American Civil War has been developed by laser. The photoluminescence approach has found use also in other criminalistic applications,[9] such as document examination, fiber analysis, locating seminal fluid, and various instances of trace evidence detection.[11] The current state of the methodology has been dealt with extensively in journals as well as books, including the first edition of *Advances in Fingerprint Technology*.[12] Thus, the focus in this second edition is on upcoming methodologies designed to permit detection of latent fingerprints on articles that display very intense background luminescence which masks the fingerprint luminescence obtained with the current procedures. This is a pervasive major problem that still plagues the photoluminescence detection of fingerprints and, indeed, all photoluminescence-based analytical techniques.

The Essence of Time-Resolved Imaging

Whether in analytical chemistry, biotechnology, or criminalistics, the detection of a weak photoluminescence in the presence of a strong background fluorescence is carried out following the same basic principles. They make use of the difference between the luminescence lifetimes of the background and analyte emissions. We begin by inquiring into the origin of this lifetime difference.

Luminescence Lifetimes[9]

The emission of light by substances can have a number of causes, among them heat (incandescence) and chemical reaction (chemiluminescence), as in the luminol reaction with blood. For our purposes, the most important origin of luminescence, however, is the prior absorption of light (excitation) to give rise to photoluminescence. On the basis of luminescence lifetime (i.e., the decay time of the luminescence intensity once the excitation is cut off) two categories of photoluminescence were distinguished long before the quantum-mechanical underpinnings were understood; namely fluorescence of short lifetime and phosphorescence of long lifetime. The slowness concept distinguishing the two light emissions has evolved over time (toward shorter lifetimes of phosphorescence). The distinction between fluorescence and phosphorescence is placed on a less arbitrary footing when one examines the quantum-mechanical origin of the photoluminescence of typical organic molecules — which we are mostly concerned with in fingerprint work. For purposes of understanding their photoluminescence, these molecules can be thought of to good approximation as being two-electron systems. When the molecule is in the ground (unexcited) state, the two optically active electrons occupy the same molecular orbital, namely, the highest occupied molecular orbital (HOMO). Their spins must be antiparallel to satisfy the exclusion principle. The total spin (S) of the two electrons, namely the sum of the two spins (1/2 each), is thus zero and the spin multiplicity (2S + 1) is 1. The state is, accordingly, a singlet state. On optical excitation, one of the electrons is promoted to a molecular orbital of higher energy via the absorption of the excitation illumination, namely, to the lowest unoccupied molecular orbital (LUMO). The molecule is now in the excited state that gives rise to photo-luminescence. If no electron spin flip has taken place during the excitation process, the excited state is still a singlet state and the decay to the singlet ground state (i.e., electron jump back to HOMO), accompanied by emission of light, is termed *fluorescence*. If a spin flip has taken place, however, which is legal in terms of the exclusion principle because the two electrons no longer occupy the same orbital, the excited state becomes a triplet state (S = 1, 2S + 1 = 3) and the decay to the singlet ground state is termed *phosphorescence*. The distinction between fluorescence and phosphorescence on the basis of electron spins is traced back to the nature of the electric dipole operator that describes the emission of light. It does not operate on spin. Thus, an allowed transition, namely one that can occur quickly, one that comes with a short lifetime, involves ground and excited states of the same spin multiplicity (2S + 1). When the spin multiplicities of the two states differ, the transition is forbidden and thus does not occur quickly; hence, a long lifetime. This definition of fluorescence and phosphorescence is not universally followed. For example, the luminescences of lanthanides are often (sloppily) referred to as fluorescences although the spin multiplicities of the involved states differ by even more than discussed above, and the lifetimes of lanthanide luminescences are very long compared to typical fluorescence lifetimes. Recombination and trap luminescences, as found in semiconductor materials, are a different matter still. In this chapter we reserve the term "fluorescence" to the transition between molecular singlet states. Other transitions are referred to by the catch-all terms "luminescence" and "emission," or are called "phosphorescence" when appropriate according to the above-described criterion.

Basics of Time-Gated Fingerprint Detection

Suppose a latent fingerprint has been treated such that it phosphoresces and assume that it is located on a fluorescent article. Now illuminate the article with an appropriate laser (filtered lamps are generally not useful for time-resolved fingerprint detection) that is periodically turned on and off and assume there is on hand an imaging device that can be turned on and off

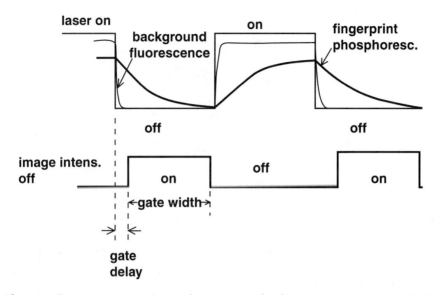

Figure 6.2 Time-gating scheme for time-resolved imaging to suppress background fluorescence.

synchronously with the laser. One then has the scheme depicted in Figure 6.2, in which the gate width denotes the time the imaging device is on and the gate delay represents the time interval between laser cut-off and imaging device turn-on. The delay is needed to ensure that the background fluorescence has decayed by the time the imaging device becomes active. The imaging device turns off before onset of the next laser illumination cycle. The imaging device is typically a gateable CCD camera, namely a CCD camera equipped with a proximity-focused microchannel plate image intensifier.[9,13] Figure 6.3 shows a typical block diagram of the pertinent imaging apparatus. The system depicted in the figure utilizes a mechanical light chopper, namely a rotating wheel with holes in it. This is appropriate when the fingerprint luminescence has a lifetime of millisecond order. The system in Figure 6.3 calls for a laser of relatively high power, such as the Ar-laser typically employed in current routine fingerprint work. One can operate with much smaller lasers in systems in which fingerprints are scanned by a focused laser beam that is deflected by a pair of rotating mirrors,[14] in much the same way as the electron beam rastering in the acquisition of television images. Such systems tend to be slow, but have the virtue, apart from the small laser, of requiring only a cheap detector, such as a photomultiplier tube, instead of the expensive gateable CCD camera. For shorter lifetimes, which are beyond the capability of mechanical devices, an electro-optic light modulator or similar device would replace the light chopper. Now, however, optical alignment and electrical biasing of the modulator make for difficulties as well as

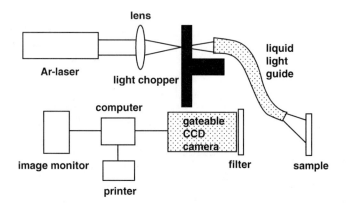

Figure 6.3 Block diagram of time-gated imaging apparatus.

increased expense. For time-resolved imaging in such situations, a different approach is often taken. Time-gated imaging typically pertains to the domain of lifetimes longer than roughly 1 μs.

Basics of Phase-Resolved Imaging

Note that a fingerprint detection system based on the phase-resolved concept has yet to be developed. However, this is just a matter of time, given that phase-resolved imaging systems have been in operation for some time in applications such as cell microscopy. If one modulates the intensity of the illuminating laser light sinusoidally instead of on-off as in Figure 6.2, the thus excited luminescence is then also sinusoidal in intensity but is delayed with respect to the excitation by a phase that is related to the luminescence lifetime. There is also a related luminescence demodulation. The situation is shown in Figure 6.4, with normalized excitation and emission. ϕ is the phase and m the demodulation. The effect of the angular modulation frequency ω, namely $2\pi f$ (where f is the modulation frequency), on the phase and demodulation is depicted in Figure 6.5. Multiple luminescence lifetimes in phase-resolved spectroscopy and imaging can be distinguished by varying the modulation frequency. Modulation frequencies of hundreds of megaHertz are readily obtainable. Thus, lifetimes of nanosecond order become accessible. It is only necessary that the analyte luminescence have a lifetime significantly different from that of the background for phase-resolved imaging to suppress the background. However, the fingerprint luminescence lifetime will generally be longer in practise than that of the background because shortening of luminescence lifetime is generally attended by decrease in luminescence quantum yield (i.e., decrease in luminescence intensity). The desired fingerprint luminescence lifetimes typically range from about 10 ns to about 1 μs (as compared to background fluorescence lifetimes of roughly 1 ns). A basic

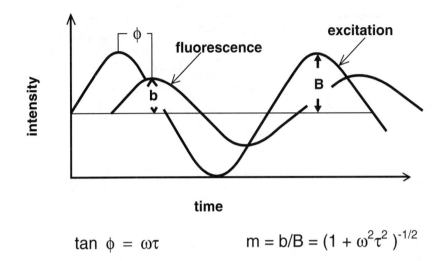

$$\tan \phi = \omega\tau \qquad\qquad m = b/B = (1 + \omega^2\tau^2)^{-1/2}$$

Figure 6.4 Phase shift and demodulation of luminescence vs. excitation (Φ = phase shift, ω = modulation angular frequency, τ = luminescence lifetime, m = demodulation).

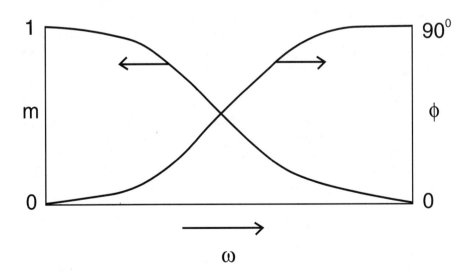

Figure 6.5 Phase and demodulation vs. modulation angular frequency.

block diagram of the pertinent imaging apparatus is shown in Figure 6.6. More sophisticated versions are described elsewhere.[9] Here, one is primarily concerned with fingerprint treatments that yield luminescence lifetimes appropriate to the time-gated and phase-resolved domains, rather than the details of instrumentation.

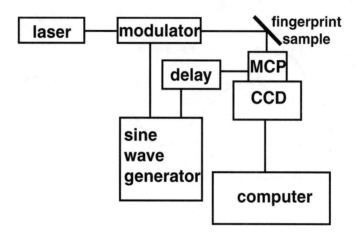

Figure 6.6 Block diagram of phase-shift/demodulation apparatus for time-resolved imaging.

Fingerprint Treatments

Fingerprint treatments suitable for time-resolved imaging began to be explored in the late 1980s. At first, transition metal complexes that yield charge-transfer phosphorescences were successfully examined and applied to fingerprint development by dusting or staining.[15] However, such complexes could not be utilized for chemical fingerprint development, thus limiting the approach primarily to smooth surfaces. Next, lanthanide-based procedures were explored. These have the potential of forming a universal photoluminescence approach to fingerprint detection, being applicable, in principle, to all types of surface and to fingerprints of any age. They have by now reached a reasonable level of maturity. However, problems persist with the lanthanide (rare earth) approaches, thus prompting more recent investigation of photoluminescent semiconductor nanocomposites.

Lanthanide-Based Procedures

The concept of time-resolved fingerprint detection for purposes of background fluorescence suppression actually dates back to 1979.[16] Its feasibility then was explored using a rotating cylinder with slots cut into it to turn the laser illumination on and off. The photographic camera was placed such that the sample would come into its view at a time after laser cut-off, as shown in Figure 6.7. The arrangement resembles a phosphoroscope, a device that dates back to the 19th century. The sample was a fingerprint dusted with a powder that contained a Tb^{3+} complex, yielding a green luminescence of millisecond-order lifetime. The fingerprint was located on yellow notepad

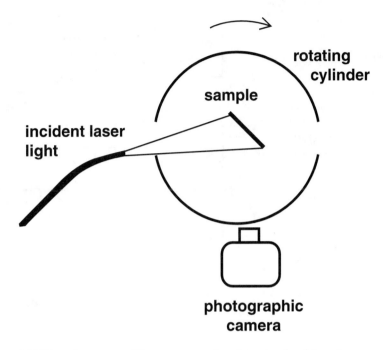

Figure 6.7 Phosphoroscope-like apparatus for time-resolved imaging.

paper, which yields a very intense greenish yellow fluorescence. The feasibility of background elimination was demonstrated with the apparatus and sample. However, practicality was lacking, in the sense that the size of the rotating cylinder limits the size of the article to be examined, given that the article must fit inside the cylinder. The apparatus cannot be sufficiently scaled up in size for general purposes because of limitations in rotation speed of the cylinder, as well as decreased camera image resolution with increasing cylinder size. The practicality issue was resolved in the early 1990s with a time-gated system as depicted in Figure 6.3. The corresponding fingerprint treatments at first involved lanthanide chemistries in which the zinc chloride post-ninhydrin step was replaced by a lanthanide halide (typically $EuCl_3$ or $TbCl_3$).[17] Subsequently, lipid-specific chemistries were explored.[18] Dusting and staining procedures involving lanthanide complexes were developed in the early to mid-1990s. The various lanthanide procedures are detailed in *Fingerprint Detection with Lasers, 2nd ed., revised and expanded.*[9] The basic underpinnings of the lanthanide general strategy will thus only be briefly outlined. For chemical fingerprint processing, the general features of the involved lanthanide complexes are shown in Figure 6.8. The conjugating ligand serves to selectively bind to the fingerprint, and the complex of step 1 in the figure is nonluminescent. The sensitizing ligand, attached subsequently, produces the lanthanide luminescence by absorbing the excitation

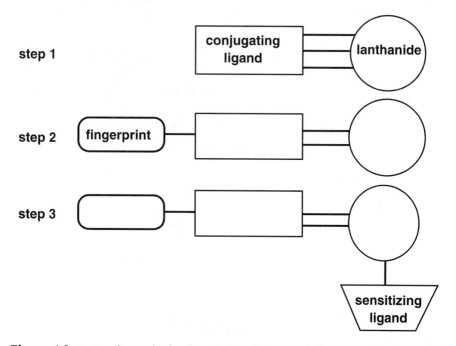

Figure 6.8 Basic scheme for lanthanide-based chemical fingerprint development.

light and transferring the excitation energy to the lanthanide ion by an energy transfer process akin to Forster intermolecular energy transfer.[9] For dusting and staining, the conjugating ligand is not needed. Figure 6.9 shows the energy-transfer scheme for europium complexes.[9] At the time of this writing, problems associated with chemical processing of fingerprints older than about 1 week still persist. Furthermore, the excitation of lanthanide complexes demands ultraviolet (UV) light and thus is not compatible with many laser systems currently in use in fingerprint laboratories. An ultraviolet-capable argon-ion laser is a suitable excitation source. When time-resolved imaging is not mandatory — namely, when background fluorescence is not a problem — the fingerprint work can utilize an ordinary UV lamp. Exploration of fingerprint processing with photoluminescent semiconductor nanoparticles as well as dendrimer application to fingerprint development were initiated about a year ago to remedy the above problems. These nanoparticle approaches are promising, especially in the time-resolved context, and are taken up in the remainder of this chapter. It is anticipated that they will form the next milestone in fingerprint detection methodology.

Photoluminescent Semiconductor Nanocomposites

Semiconductor materials such as CdS, CdSe, CdTe, InP, and InAs, which normally are not luminescent, can become intensely luminescent when particles,

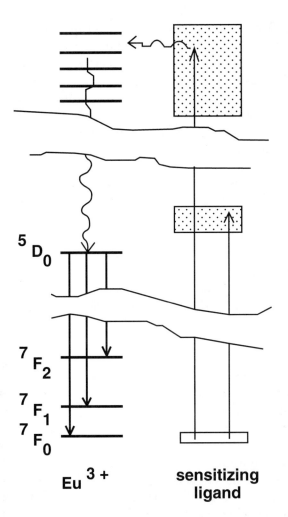

Figure 6.9 Ligand-to-europium energy transfer and europium luminescence energy-level diagram (waved arrows denote radiationless transitions and straight arrows radiative ones).

typically in crystalline form, become very small (i.e., of nanometer order in size). Such nanoparticles can be quite robust. They are typically encapsulated with ZnS, silica, or organic material. This capping is sometimes referred to also as derivatization or functionalization, especially when an organic compound is involved, which is sometimes also referred to as a surfactant. The encapsulation amounts to covering the nanocrystal with a layer of material that may serve a variety of functions, for example, passivation to optimize luminescence efficiency, serving as a site for attachment of conjugating ligands designed for specificity of chemical binding, serving this labeling function itself, serving to solubilize the nanocrystal, and preventing aggregation of nanocrystals. Photoluminescent semiconductor nanoparticles have recently become the subject of intense investigation in the biotechnology arena, mostly for labeling purposes.[19,20] DNA sequencing is an example. The salient virtues that distinguish the nanoparticles (referred to also as quantum dots, nanocrystals, and nanocomposites, depending on morphology) from ordinary fluorescent labels are that their absorption and luminescence wavelengths (colors) can be tuned by varying the particle size and that the luminescence lifetimes are long, ranging from roughly 10^{-8} to 10^{-6} s, thus making the nanoparticles suitable for time-resolved spectroscopy and time-resolved imaging, with flexibility in terms of useful laser light sources. These features are valuable from a biotechnology perspective and are, in principle, equally pertinent to the fingerprint context, thus prompting a study of their potential utility in fingerprint detection that commenced in 1999.[9] Because of financial and manpower constraints, this investigation has to date only aimed at reduction to practice[21] (i.e., demonstration of feasibility rather than work-up of routine recipes). Nonetheless, a variety of nanoparticle systems and fingerprint chemistries have been examined. Practical recipes will presumably follow once the best general approaches have been delineated.

CdS Nanocrystals[22]

Photoluminescent semiconductor nanocrystals may be expected to be used for fingerprint detection in various ways, namely by incorporation into dusting powder in a manner akin to fluorescent dye blending with magnetic powder[9] by staining, especially once fingerprints have been exposed to cyanoacrylate ester; or by chemical bonding to constituents of fingerprint residue. In photoluminescence detection of fingerprints, the staining approach generally tends to be more effective when applicable to the article under examination, than dusting. Thus, the focus in this chapter section is on staining with CdS nanocrystals. As a preface to this mode of fingerprint detection, the photophysical properties of CdS quantum dots are examined, primarily to assess suitability for phase-resolved imaging to suppress background fluorescence, but also to determine suitable excitation wavelengths.

     The employed CdS nanocrystal samples, prepared in inverse micelles[23,24] and capped with dioctyl sulfosuccinate (sodium salt), were obtained from Professor John T. McDevitt (Chemistry Department, University of Texas, Austin). Solubilization of the nanocrystals utilized heptane or a mixture of hexanes ($CH_3C_4H_8CH_3$). Solutions had quantum dot concentrations of milligram/milliliter order. Absorption spectra in these solvents exhibited band edges at about 440 nm and very broad absorbance (with some structure, but not absorption peaks as in typical atomic or molecular spectra) that increased with decreasing wavelength to 300 nm, the lowest wavelength in our absorption measurements. The spectra, fairly typical of semiconductor absorption

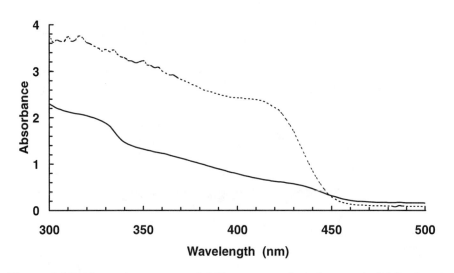

Figure 6.10 Absorption spectra of CdS nanocrystals in hexane (solid line) and heptane (dashed line).

spectra, are shown in Figure 6.10. They serve to determine the sizes of the nanocrystals,[23] which were deduced to have radii of 3 to 4 nm. The nanocrystal luminescence (band width about 100 nm) peaked at about 580 nm, with a second, weaker luminescence band in the 400 to 450-nm range. In terms of intensities as a function of excitation power, excitation wavelength, solvent system, etc., the luminescence spectroscopy of nanocrystals tends to be more complex than that of typical fluorescent molecules because in nanocrystals one likely has a number of different, and quite variable, trap states that contribute to the luminescence, including surface traps, as well as the intrinsic semiconductor recombination process. Thus, the spectroscopic features generally need to be examined for the samples at hand, with literature results serving as approximate guides only. Lifetime measurements for heptane solution used phase-shift/demodulation techniques, as described earlier, and employed a HeCd laser (operating at 325 nm). The lifetime measurement corresponded to the total luminescence (transmitted to the detector through a long-wavelength-pass filter). Laser modulation frequencies ranged from 0.1 to 100 MHz. The fit to the obtained phase shift and demodulation curves, analogs to the curves shown in Figure 6.5, yielded three lifetime components. Approximately 70% of the luminescence intensity corresponded to emission with lifetime of about 1000 ns, about 25% to emission with lifetime of about 70 ns, and about 5% to emission with lifetime of 0.54 ns. This latter is excitonic emission and the obtained lifetime is in good agreement with the literature.[25] Total luminescence lifetime measurement was made, rather than lifetime measurement at a particular wavelength or a set of particular wavelengths, because fingerprint luminescence imaging usually involves the total luminescence.

Figure 6.11 Photoluminescence of fingerprint on soft drink can fumed with cyano-acrylate ester and subsequently stained with CdS nanocrystal heptane solution.

Because staining with fluorescent dye after cyanoacrylate ester fuming is a very successful fingerprint detection methodology, we employed the above dioctyl sulfosuccinate-capped CdS nanocrystals, dissolved in heptane or hexane, in this manner. Sample fingerprints were placed on a soft drink can (Coca Cola®) and on aluminum foil, and were fumed with cyanoacrylate ester. The samples were then immersed in the nanocrystal solutions for times ranging from a few seconds to a few minutes. Immersion times were not critical. The samples were then left to dry. Luminescence examination under an Ar-laser operating in the near-UV (a good excitation regime) revealed amply intense luminescence. Because there was a generally heavy coverage of the immersed sample portion masking fingerprint detail, samples were subjected to gentle rinsing with hexane to remove excess nanocrystal deposition, leaving behind fingerprint detail. An example is shown in Figure 6.11. This photograph and all others below were taken with a digital camera (Kodak DC 120) equipped with a close-up lens. Because background fluorescence was not an issue with the utilized samples, it was not necessary to perform time-gated or phase-resolved imaging.

Any preferential adherence of the organically capped CdS nanocrystals to unfumed fingerprints would involve nonpolar fingerprint constituents, such as lipids, and these readily dissolve in hexane or heptane (particularly the former, which is more aggressive than the latter because of lower viscosity). Thus, unfumed fingerprints on metal, plastic, glass, etc. could not be developed by the above staining. However, on black electrical tape (sticky side), unfumed fingerprints could be stained successfully with heptane nanocrystal solution and with heptane rinsing. General optimization work in terms of solvent delivery systems is called for.

CdS/Dendrimer Nanocomposites[26,27]

Dendrimers — polymers of tree-like structure — have lately begun to command intense attention[28] in many areas of science, especially in connection with their incorporation with nanoparticles of various kinds for purposes of applications that include cancer drug delivery, catalysis, waste clean-up, optical devices, etc. Of particular interest here is a photoluminescent nanocomposite of CdS with Starburst® (PAMAM) dendrimer that was first (outside the forensic science arena) described by Sooklal, Hanus, Ploehn, and Murphy.[29] The nanocomposite contains nanoparticle-size clusters of CdS that are incorporated into aggregates of dendrimer molecules. The Starburst® dendrimers are of particular interest from our perspective because they are commercially available (Aldrich), a must for any practical utilization in fingerprint laboratories. These dendrimers come with either amino or carboxylate terminal functional groups, which are useful for chemical fingerprint processing. Depending on size, amino-functionalized Starburst® (PAMAM) dendrimers are referred to as generation 0, 1, 2, 3, 4, ... They have, respectively, 4, 8, 16, 32, 64, ... terminal amino groups. Similarly, generation –0.5, 0.5, 1.5, 2.5, 3.5, ... have, respectively, 4, 8, 16, 32, 64, ... terminal carboxylate (sodium salt) groups. The first three generations of each type are shown in Figures 6.12 and 6.13.

The initial CdS/dendrimer nanocomposite study involved generation 0, 1, and 4 dendrimer (4, 8, 64 amino terminal groups, respectively). As purchased, the dendrimers come in methanol solution. The preparation in methanol of the CdS/dendrimer nanocomposite simply involves diluting the dendrimer solution and adding to it small quantities (aliquots) of equimolar methanol solutions, in equal volumes, of cadmium nitrate and of sodium sulfide. In the absence of dendrimer, the reaction of the cadmium nitrate and sodium sulfide would produce the cadmium sulfide as a precipitate in large clumps. In the presence of dendrimer, however, an aggregate of CdS of nanoparticle size with the dendrimer is formed, as is depicted in Figure 6.14. The aliquots of cadmium nitrate and sodium sulfide may be added to the dendrimer solution simultaneously or sequentially in either order. In our experiments, either five or ten aliquots of each reagent were used to produce the desired nanocomposite, with concentrations as described shortly. In addition to the methanol formulation of the CdS/dendrimer nanocomposite, a 10% methanol: 90% water formulation was also investigated. The nanocomposite preparation utilized 1:9 methanol:water solutions of the dendrimer, cadmium nitrate, and sodium sulfide instead of pure methanol solutions, but was otherwise conducted the same way. The rationale for the 1:9 methanol:water solvent system was simply the general desirability of water-based chemistry. The methanol served for initial dissolution of reagents and was then added to the water.

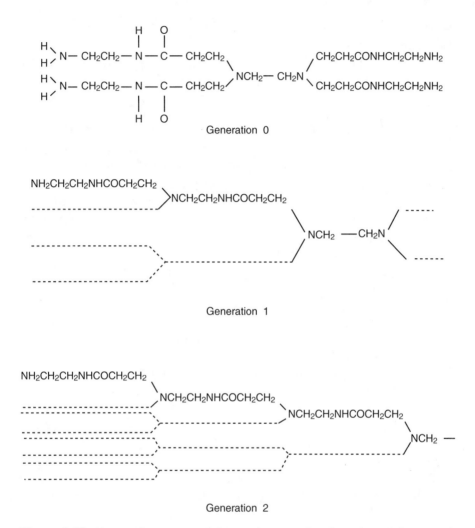

Figure 6.12 Chemical structures of NH_2 functionalized Starburst® (PAMAM) dendrimers.

For physical fingerprint treatments akin to dye staining, fingerprints (fresh to 1-day-old) were placed on aluminum foil and Ziploc® (polyethylene) sandwich bags. Some of the samples were fumed with cyanoacrylate ester before staining with the nanocomposite, while other fingerprints were stained without the pre-fuming. With nanocomposites in methanol, the best results were invariably obtained, regardless of concentrations, when the nanocomposites involved the generation 4 dendrimer rather than generation 0 or 1. Thus, this dendrimer is the focus of the discussion that follows. With dendrimer concentration greater than about 10^{-4} M, solutions were quite tacky and produced too much background via indiscriminate adherence to the

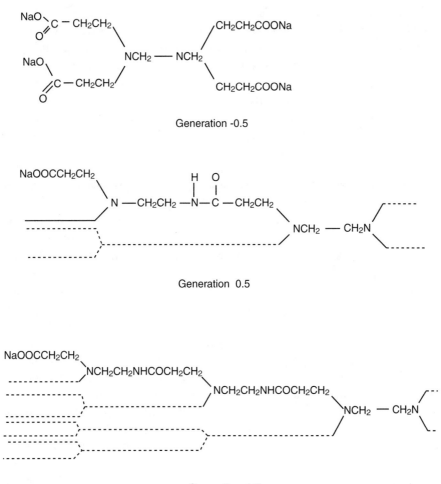

Figure 6.13 Chemical structures of COO⁻ functionalized Starburst® (PAMAM) dendrimers.

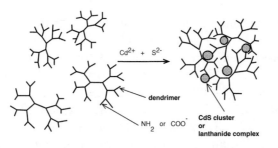

Figure 6.14 CdS/dendrimer nanocomposite formation.

sample, rather than preferential adherence to the fingerprint on the sample. Thus, the dendrimer concentrations employed ranged from 2 to $8 \times 10^{-5}\ M$ in methanol as well as 1:9 methanol:water preparations. In methanol solution, the observed luminescence was blue-green regardless of CdS concentration in the nanocomposite and increased with the CdS concentration. For $2 \times 10^{-5}\ M$ dendrimer concentration, the nanocomposite precipitated out essentially immediately when the CdS concentration exceeded about $2 \times 10^{-3}\ M$. An optimal CdS/dendrimer (generation 4) concentration of $8 \times 10^{-4}/2 \times 10^{-5}\ M$ produced solutions stable for several days at least, at room temperature. The situation was rather different for the 1:9 methanol:water case. Here, the luminescence color was generally yellow-orange and optimal CdS/dendrimer (generation 4) concentration was $2 \times 10^{-4}/8 \times 10^{-5}\ M$. Unlike in methanol, no nanocomposites could be formed with generation 0 and 1 dendrimer in 1:9 methanol:water because of immediate precipitation. That luminescence colors were invariant with concentrations, in methanol and also in 1:9 methanol:water, indicates that the CdS nanocluster sizes are invariant, with nanocluster concentrations in the aggregates with generation 4 dendrimer varying. The optimizations cited above were assessed on the basis of luminescence intensity in solution as well as in fingerprint development, with solution stability demanded as well.

Absorption spectra of CdS/generation 4 dendrimer solutions in methanol and 1:9 methanol:water were shape-wise similar to the CdS nanocrystal spectra shown in Figure 6.10. A comparison with literature spectra[23] indicated CdS nanocluster sizes of about 2.5 and 3 nm, respectively. Luminescence excitation spectra yielded intensity drop-off at wavelengths longer than about 360 and 390 nm, respectively, in agreement with the absorption band edges. That the luminescence color in the methanol:water case is nonetheless orange, that is, unusually far red-shifted (in comparison with the blue-green luminescence in the methanol case), suggests the presence of Forster-type energy transfer[9] in the methanol:water system. As in the CdS nanocrystal case, luminescence lifetime measurements by phase-shift/demodulation techniques were best interpreted by three component fits. In the methanol case, the main component, with intensity fraction of about 0.6, had a 120-ns lifetime. The next component, with about 0.3 intensity fraction, had a 30-ns lifetime. The third component had a 3.5-ns lifetime. In the methanol:water case, the longest-lived component had a 300-ns lifetime and an intensity fraction of about 0.35. The next component, with 60-ns lifetime, had an intensity fraction of about 0.45. The shortest-lived component had a luminescence lifetime of about 4.5 ns. The lifetime data were reproducible over a range of CdS/dendrimer concentrations in both the methanol and methanol:water solution systems. Solution emission spectra showed broad luminescences of 100 nm

Figure 6.15 Photoluminescence of fingerprint on polyethylene fumed with cyanoacrylate ester and subsequently stained with CdS/generation 4 dendrimer methanol solution.

full-width at half-maximum peaked at about 480 nm in methanol and 130 nm fwhm peaked at about 550 nm in 1:9 methanol:water.

Fingerprint staining with the methanol and methanol:water formulations simply involved dipping the aluminum foil and polyethylene samples and then letting them dry completely. In the customary staining with fluorescent dyes such as rhodamine 6G, the article is immersed for no more than a few seconds or is sprayed with the dye solution. In the CdS/dendrimer nanocomposite case, however, the immersion involved not seconds, but hours. Methanol solution dipping was not successful with unfumed fingerprints because the agressive methanol tended to dissolve away the fingerprint. Cyanoacrylate ester pre-fumed fingerprints, on the other hand, developed readily on both aluminum foil and polyethylene. An example is shown in Figure 6.15. The luminescence excitation was at 50 mW, near-UV, from an Ar-laser. The methanol:water CdS/dendrimer solutions lent themselves to fumed as well as unfumed fingerprints on the aluminum foil and polyethylene samples. Dipped articles were typically left overnight in the solution before luminescence examination. Development of unfumed fingerprints on paper was attempted but was not successful because of excessive adherence of the nanocomposites everywhere on the paper. The long immersion times required for fingerprint processing suggest that a chemical reaction of the amino functionality of the dendrimer with carboxylic acid (or ester) of the fingerprint, or, for that matter, perhaps with the cyanoacrylate ester functionality, is involved, rather than physical preferential deposition, as in the staining with dye such as rhodamine 6G. The chemistry would be an amidation, as shown in Figure 6.16. This corresponds to a chemical labeling strategy widely used in biotechnology.

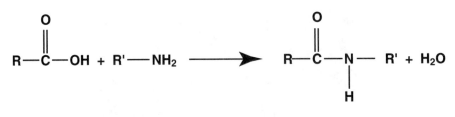

Figure 6.16 General scheme of amidation reaction.

Diimide Mediation of Fingerprint Development with CdS/Dendrimer Nanocomposites[27]

The amidation of Figure 6.16 could, in principle, involve the reaction of generation 4 dendrimer (amino-terminal functional groups) with fatty acids of fingerprint residue or the reaction of generation 3.5 dendrimer (carboxylate-terminal functional groups) with amino acids or proteins of fingerprint material. Both prospects were investigated. In either case, the direct reaction as depicted in Figure 6.16 is likely not very efficient because the involved OH group of the carboxylic acid is a poor leaving group (i.e., one difficult to displace). A remedy that has been reported in the biochemistry literature[20] and that is fairly commonly used in that field involves the mediation of the amidation by a carbodiimide, as is shown in the reaction scheme of Figure 6.17. For this purpose, the most widely used carbodiimide is dicyclohexylcarbodiimide. However, it dissolves in nonpolar solvents, which are not very well-suited for fingerprint work. Indeed, dissolving the diimide in dichloromethane caused (lipid components of) fingerprints to be dissolved. However, the problem can be remedied by employing a carbodiimide soluble in water, namely 1-(3-dimethylaminopropyl)-3-ethylcarbodiimide hydrochloride, whose structure is shown in Figure 6.18. Initially, the 1:9 methanol:water solvent system was chosen for the diimide, with fingerprints on aluminum foil (no background due to indiscriminate adherence of CdS/dendrimer, as with paper) immersed in the diimide solution prior to exposure to the nanocomposite. However, prolonged immersion in this diimide solution resulted in chemical attack on the aluminum foil itself, producing a tarnished appearance of the foil. Thus, the methanol was deleted. A standard solution of 2.5% (by weight) diimide in water served for fingerprint pretreatment. Fingerprints immersed in pure water for the same time served as controls. Subsequent fingerprint processing by CdS/generation 4 dendrimer used $2 \times 10^{-4}/8 \times 10^{-5}$ M nanocomposite formulation in 1:9 methanol:water. Diimide pretreatment for times of about 1 hr or less produced no enhancement in fingerprint development compared to the water controls. However, with time spans between about 5 and 24 hr, significant enhancement was observed, with the enhancement leveling off by 24 hr. These observations are indicative

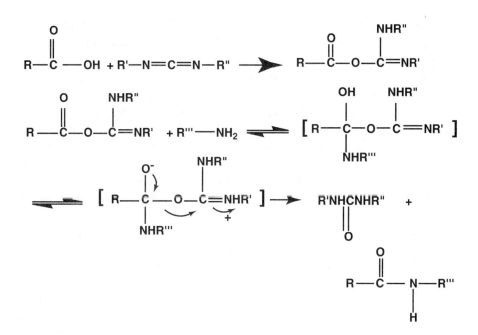

Figure 6.17 Carbodiimide-mediated amidation reaction.

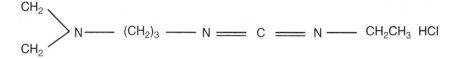

Figure 6.18 Structure of 1-(3-dimethylaminopropyl)-3-ethylcarbodiimide hydrochloride.

of chemical fingerprint labeling. Results with polyethylene, paper, and cyanoacrylate ester-fumed fingerprints suggest an additional contribution by preferential physical adherence of the nanocomposite to fingerprint material. In general, chemical reaction rates increase with increasing temperature. Accordingly, the diimide pretreatment was examined at 60°C in comparison with room temperature. At the elevated temperature, severe chemical attack on the aluminum foil substrate of samples occurred for heating times longer than about 1 hr. For shorter heating times, no fingerprint development enhancement was observed. If there is chemical binding of the generation 4 nanocomposite to fingerprint constituents in the absence of diimide, one might expect an enhancement of fingerprint development with temperature upon direct application of the CdS/dendrimer solution. Such enhancement was indeed observed.

The amidation reaction depicted in Figure 6.16 should, in principle, occur when carboxylate-functionalized dendrimer reacts with amino acid or protein of fingerprint residue. Thus, we examined CdS/generation 3.5 dendrimer utility for fingerprint development. The choice of generation 3.5 dendrimer was made to permit direct comparison with generation 4 dendrimer, both generations having 64 terminal functional groups. The preparation of the nanocomposite was as described earlier, with methanol as well as 1:9 methanol:water ($2 \times 10^{-4}/8 \times 10^{-5}$ M concentration) solvent systems. As before, methanol solutions were ineffective on unfumed prints, which tended to be dissolved away. Staining of cyanoacrylate ester fumed prints yielded results very similar to those encountered with nanocomposites based on generation 4 dendrimer, with no advantage derived from the use of the generation 3.5 dendrimer. In contrast with what was observed with generation 4 dendrimer use, the 1:9 methanol:water formulation of the generation 3.5 nanocomposite produced no fingerprint development whatsoever for unfumed fingerprints on aluminum foil or polyethylene at room temperature and in the absence of carbodiimide. This might not be entirely surprising in that different constituents of the fingerprint are probed in the two cases and because the amino acid of the fingerprint might be buried beneath lipids in lipid-rich fingerprints, which pertained to our study (fingerprints rubbed on the forehead prior to deposition). This would be aggravated by the inherent incompatibility of the polar solvent system with lipids. However, one should realize that a certain level of incompatibility between fingerprint and reagent solvent system is mandatory to ensure that the fingerprint not be dissolved. The situation is reminiscent of what is encountered in lipid fingerprint development with lanthanide chelates.[18] There, the addition of a small amount of acetone to the solvent system served to solubilize fingerprint lipids just enough for reaction. This was not successful with the generation 3.5 nanocomposite, but crisp luminescent fingerprint detail was obtained with the generation 4 nanocomposite. This suggests that solubility issues are not responsible for the failure of fingerprint development with the generation 3.5 nanocomposite formulation. Accordingly, we next examined the prospect of pretreatment of the generation 3.5 dendrimer with diimide prior to exposure of fingerprints to the dendrimer. The successful sequence involved first mixing in stoichiometric amounts the diimide with the generation 3.5 dendrimer, keeping in mind that the latter has 64 functional terminal groups, in 1:9 methanol:water. The mixture was then heated overnight at 60°C. CdS was subsequently incorporated by aliquot addition, as described earlier, and fingerprint samples were finally immersed in the solution. Figure 6.19 shows a fingerprint developed via this treatment sequence. The fingerprint luminescence was orange. The stoichiometric addition of diimide (about 1.5 ×

Figure 6.19 Photoluminescence of fingerprint (on aluminum foil) developed by diimide-mediated CdS/generation 3.5 dendrimer treatment (see text).

10^{-2} M diimide to 2.4×10^{-4} M dendrimer) was intended to minimize the formation of ester in the fingerprint residue itself upon subsequent sample immersion. The ester formed would tie up the amino acid of the fingerprint that otherwise would react with dendrimer. The heating step was essential. Without it, fingerprint development was only faint. The diimide reacts with aluminum foil to give it a tarnished appearance, much like tarnished silver. Without the heating step, this tarnishing resulted upon immersion of aluminum foil samples. One can thus presume that the counterproductive reaction with fatty acid of the fingerprint residue also occurs. With heating, on the other hand, no foil tarnishing was seen, indicating that the diimide had been tied up by the dendrimer, as desired. Formation of the CdS/dendrimer nanocomposite followed by diimide addition (prior to fingerprint sample immersion) was not successful, perhaps because of excessive aggregation prior to the addition of the diimide. Although the above-described fingerprint labeling by dendrimer, as mediated by carbodiimide, has only been explored for feasibility to date, rather than having reached the practical recipe stage, a reasonable grasp of the underlying chemistry has hopefully emerged.

Incorporation of Lanthanide Complexes into Dendrimers[21]

Because dendrimers have many voids (of varying sizes), one can envision intercalation of molecules in the dendrimer (i.e., their placement into voids

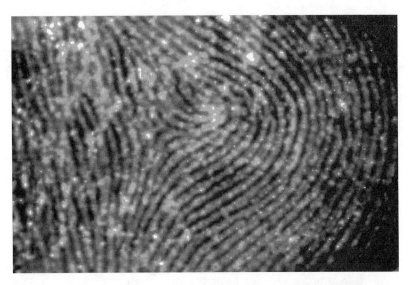

Figure 6.20 Photoluminescence of fingerprint on aluminum foil developed by diimide-mediated treatment with europium complex/generation 3.5 dendrimer.

of the dendrimer) in much the same way in which catalysts and cancer drugs are envisioned to be incorporated into dendrimers, as depicted in Figure 6.14. Preliminary work indicates that this is feasible, as shown in Figure 6.20. The europium complex with thenoyltrifluoroacetone,[9] generation 3.5 Starburst® (PAMAM) dendrimer, 1:9 methanol:water solvent system, carbodiimide, and sample (fingerprint on aluminum foil) immersion for 24 hr were involved. A control sample processed similarly, but in the absence of the dendrimer, failed to produce comparable fingerprint development (red luminescence under near-UV excitation).

Cadmium Selenide Nanocrystals[30]

The fabrication of cadmium selenide nanocrystals involves high-temperature chemistry that must be performed under an inert (Ar) atmosphere — which comes with considerable difficulty and hazard. At present, these nanocrystals are not commercially available, except perhaps in research (milligram) sample quantity (at high price). However, companies are forming at this time, such that one can anticipate that a range of CdSe nanocrystals will become commercially available in the near future. CdSe quantum dots are typically encapsulated with zinc sulfide. The encapsulant, quite apart from its protective function, serves as substrate for the attachment of conjugating ligands that are designed to selectively label substances of interest. The structure of encapsulated and functionalized nanocrystals is depicted in Figure 6.21. The work done to date on thus functionalized quantum dots has primarily targeted the

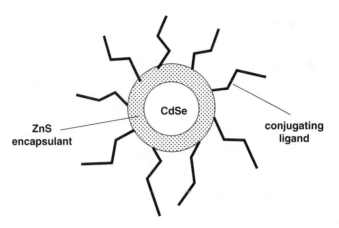

Figure 6.21 Structure of encapsulated and functionalized CdSe nanocrystal.

biotechnology arena, and the functionalization has tended to involve carboxylate and amino groups. Given the above-described dendrimer investigation, we have in place a chemistry that should lend itself to the fingerprint context. Because of the high cost and low availability of CdSe nanocrystals, we have to date only addressed fingerprint development with carboxylate-functionalized ones (obtained from Quantum Dot Corp., Palo Alto, CA). Diimide mediation of the chemical fingerprint labeling was essential (fingerprints 1-month-old on aluminum foil). Heating was not useful, destroying the nanocrystals. Nanocrystals are generally stored at low temperature (about 4°C) to prevent flocculation. No fingerprint development was obtained at that temperature, even with sample immersion for up to 5 days. At room temperature, 24-hr fingerprint immersion in a water solution containing in 1 μM concentration the water-soluble CdSe/ZnS/carboxylate functionalized nanocrystals and in 8 μM concentration the water-soluble 1-(3-dimethylaminopropyl)-3-ethylcarbodiimide hydrochloride produced development of luminescent fingerprints. An example is shown in Figure 6.22. The carbodiimide relative concentration was kept low (one would normally use higher concentration) to prevent flocculation of nanocrystals. The low nanocrystal concentration itself was dictated by the limited nanocrystal supply.

In keeping with semiconductor characteristics (i.e., broad band-structure characteristics in absorption), the utilized nanocrystals luminesced under excitation that could range from the ultraviolet to the red. This makes for greater flexibility in terms of the excitation light source. The comparatively rather sharp red luminescence peaked at 635 nm and had full-width at half-maximum of 35 nm (comparable to molecular fluorescence); the absorption/luminescence spectra are shown in Figure 6.23. Luminescence lifetime measurements were best interpreted by two-component fits. These yielded

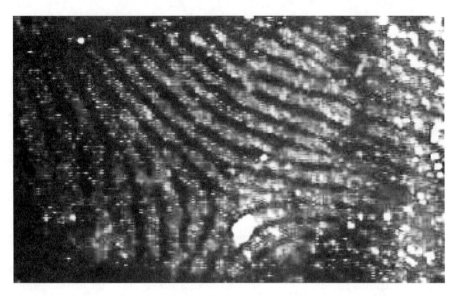

Figure 6.22 Photoluminescence of fingerprint on aluminum foil developed by diimide-mediated treatment with ZnS-encapsulated and carboxylate-functionalized CdSe nanocrystal water solution.

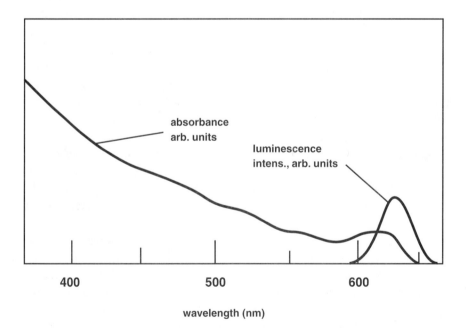

Figure 6.23 CdSe nanocrystal absorption and luminescence spectra.

components of about equal intensity fractions and lifetimes of 3 and 9.5 ns for carboxylate functionalized nanocrystals and of 6 and 24 ns for amino-functionalized ones. Note that nanocrystal sizes can be tailored to produce luminescence ranging from blue to red. Typically, luminescence lifetimes would increase as the emission blue-shifts. We chose red-emitting nanocrystals for study to maximize excitation flexibility.

Ongoing Investigations

From the work on nanocrystals and naocomposites done to date, as described above and including the utilization of dendrimers and the functionalizations with carboxylate and amino groups, it would appear that a fair understanding of the involved chemistry is at hand and that this is a chemistry that potentially offers much flexibility in fingerprint processing. Thus, current work is beginning to tackle the formulation of recipes of practicality. In particular, our aim is to devise procedures for porous surfaces, especially papers, which thus far remain elusive. Furthermore, work is in progress to optimize staining-type approaches in concert with cyanoacrylate ester-fumed fingerprints. In addition to the utilization of nanocrystals and nanocomposites, we are expanding the exploration of the incorporation of lanthanide complexes into dendrimers. The driving force behind this direction is the fact that the very long lanthanide luminescence lifetimes permit time-resolved imaging by time-gated techniques, which are simpler than the phase-resolved counterparts. The diimide-mediated amidation reaction that forms the core of the chemical fingerprint development described in this chapter involves an intermediate O-acylurea derivative of the carbodiimide that is reported to be unstable. Instead of nucleophilic attack by the primary nitrogen of the amino compound to form the amide, it may undergo hydrolysis, regenerating the starting carboxylic acid and producing a urea derivative of the carbodiimide. To assist the amidation reaction, N-hydroxysuccinimide has been reported in biochemical application.[31] The compound produces a stable active ester that then reacts with the amino compound to yield the amide. We are currently exploring the application of this approach, as shown in the reaction scheme of Figure 6.24, to fingerprint development. While the biochemistry literature may at times be a good guide to chemistries applicable to the fingerprint context, it is worthwhile to reiterate that there is a major difference between the two fields in that in chemistry one generally wants reagent and analyte to be soluble in the same solvent, whereas in the fingerprint situation one must have incompatibility of the fingerprint and the reagent. Otherwise, fingerprint detail will bleed, at best — or be obliterated altogether.

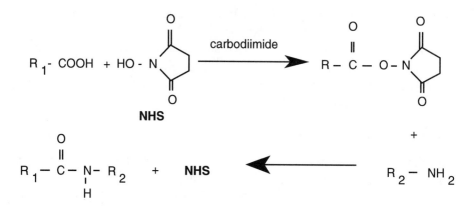

Figure 6.24 Carbodiimide- and N-hydroxysuccinimide-assisted amidation.

References

1. Dalrymple, B.E., Duff, J.M., and Menzel, E.R., Inherent fingerprint luminescence — detection by laser, *J. Forensic Sci.*, 22, 106-115, 1977.

2. Menzel, E.R., *Fingerprint Detection with Lasers*, New York: Marcel Dekker, 1980.

3. Menzel, E.R., Burt, J.A., Sinor, T.W., Tubach-Ley, W.B., and Jordan, K.J., Laser detection of latent fingerprints: treatment with glue containing cyanoacrylate ester, *J. Forensic Sci.*, 28, 307-317, 1983.

4. Herod, D.W. and Menzel, E.R., Laser detection of latent fingerprints: ninhydrin followed by zinc chloride, *J. Forensic Sci.*, 27, 513-518, 1982.

5. Menzel, E.R. and Almog, J., Latent fingerprint development by frequency-doubled neodymium:yttrium aluminum garnet (Nd:YAG) laser: benzo(f)ninhydrin. *J. Forensic Sci.*, 30, 371-382, 1985.

6. Almog, J. and Hirshfeld, A., 5-Methoxyninhydrin: a reagent for the chemical development of latent fingerprints that is compatible with the copper-vapor laser. *J. Forensic Sci.*, 33, 1027-1030, 1988.

7. Takatsu, M., (National Police Agency, Japan), personal communication, 1999.

8. Pounds, C.A., Grigg, R., and Monkolaussavaratana, T., The Use of 1,8-Diazafluoren-9-one (DFO) for the Fluorescent Detection of Latent Fingerprints on Paper, Report No. 669, Central Research and Support Establishment, Home Office Forensic Science Service, Aldermaston, U.K., 1989.

9. Menzel, E.R., *Fingerprint Detection with Lasers*, 2nd ed., revised and expanded, New York: Marcel Dekker, 1999.

10. Stames, N.S., Interesting case, *Identification News*, 34(10), 13, 1984.

11. Creer, K.E., The detection and photography of fluorescent marks, in *Fluorescence Detection*, Menzel, E.R., Ed., *Proc. SPIE*, 743, 175-179, 1987.

12. Lee, H.C. and Gaensslen, R.E., Eds. *Advances in fingerprint technology*, New York: Elsevier, 1991.

13. Murdock, R.H. and Menzel, E.R., A computer interfaced time-resolved imaging system, *J. Forensic Sci.,* 38, 521-529, 1993.

14. Roorda, R.D., Ribes, A.C., Damaskinos, S., Dixon, A.E., and Menzel, E.R., A scanning beam time-resolved imaging system for fingerprint detection, *J. Forensic Sci.,* 45, 563-567, 2000.

15. For example: Menzel, E.R., Laser detection of latent fingerprints: tris(2,2'-bipyridyl)ruthenium(II) chloride hexahydrate as a staining dye for time-resolved imaging, in *Fluorescence Detection II,* Menzel, E.R., Ed., *Proc. SPIE,* 910, 45-51, 1988.

16. Menzel, E.R., Laser detection of latent fingerprints — treatment with phosphorescers. *J. Forensic Sci.,* 24, 582-585, 1979.

17. For example: Menzel, E.R., Detection of latent fingerprints by laser-excited luminescence, *Anal. Chem.,* 61, 557A-561A, 1989.

18. For example: Allred, C.E. and Menzel, E.R., A novel europium-bioconjugate method for latent fingerprint detection, *Forensic Sci. Int.,* 85, 83-94, 1997.

19. Bruchez, Jr., M., Moronne, M., Gin, P., Weiss, S., and Alivisatos, A.P., Semiconductor nanocrystals as fluorescent biological labels, *Science,* 281, 2013–2016, 1998.

20. Chan, W.C.W. and Nie, S., Quantum dot bioconjugates for ultrasensitive nonisotopic detection, *Science,* 281, 2016–2018, 1998.

21. Menzel, E.R., Fingerprint Development Methods, U.S. Patent application No. 09/487,702 (2000).

22. Menzel, E.R., Savoy, S.M., Ulvick, S.J., Cheng, K.H., Murdock, R.H., and Sudduth, M.R., Photoluminescent semiconductor nanocrystals for fingerprint detection, *J. Forensic Sci.,* 45, 545-551, 2000.

23. Ogawa, S., Fan, F.F., and Bard, A.J., Scanning tunneling microscopy, tunneling spectroscopy, and photoelectrochemistry of a film of Q-CdS particles incorporated in a self-assembled monolayer on a gold surface, *J. Phys. Chem.,* 99, 11182–11189, 1995.

24. Steigerwald, M.L., Alivisatos, A.P., Gibson, J.M., Harris, T.D., Kortan, R., and Muller, A.J., Surface derivatization of semiconductor cluster molecules, *J. Am. Chem. Soc.,* 110, 3046-3050, 1998.

25. O'Neil, M., Mahron, J., and McLendon, G., Dynamics of electron-hole pair recombination in semiconductor clusters, *J. Phys. Chem.,* 94, 4356–4363, 1990.

26. Menzel, E.R., Takatsu, M., Murdock, R.H., Bouldin, K.K., and Cheng, K.H., Photoluminescent CdS/dendrimer nanocomposites for fingerprint detection, *J. Forensic Sci.,* 45, 758-761, 2000.

27. Bouldin, K.K., Menzel, E.R., Takatsu, M., and Murdock, R.H., Diimide-enhanced fingerprint detection with photoluminescent CdS/dendrimer nanocomposites, *J. Forensic Sci.,* 45, 1239-1242, 2000.

28. Dagani, R., Jewel-studded molecular trees, *C&EN,* Feb 8, 33-36, 1999.

29. Sooklal, K., Hanus, L.H., Ploehn, H.J., and Murphy, C.J., A blue-emitting CdS/dendrimer nanocomposite, *Adv. Mater.*, 10, 1083–1087, 1998.

30. Menzel, E.R., Photoluminescence detection of latent fingerprints with quantum dots for time-resolved imaging, *Fingerprint Whorld*, 26, 119-123, 2000.

31. Sehgal, D. and Vijay, I.K., A method for the high efficiency of water-soluble carbodiimide-mediated amidation, *Anal. Biochem.*, 218, 87-91, 1994.

Silver Physical Development of Latent Prints

7

ANTONIO A. CANTU
JAMES L. JOHNSON

Contents

0-8493-0923-9/01/$0.00+$1.50
© 2001 by CRC Press LLC

Introduction

Background

Since its introduction to latent print examiners in the mid-1970s, the silver physical developer (Ag-PD) has become the standard reagent in many forensic laboratories to follow ninhydrin for visualizing latent prints on porous evidence such as paper.[1-4] The normal process for visualizing latent prints on porous surfaces is to first visualize the amine-containing compounds (such as amino acids and proteins) using DFO, ninhydrin, 1,2-indanedione, or their analogues and then to visualize what remains with the Ag-PD. Most of the amine-containing compounds are water soluble and thus their visualizing reagents are in a nonaqueous carrier. The Ag-PD is water based and thus it visualizes the water-insoluble portion of the latent print residue. These components not only include fats and oils (both of which are lipids) but also water-resistant proteins, lipoproteins, and even water-soluble components (amino acids, proteins, urea, salts, etc.) that get trapped in the lipids as they "dry" and harden (through oxidation). Not all latent print residue contains both water-soluble and water-insoluble components together. Some contain mostly the former, while some contain mostly the latter. Thus, for porous surfaces, both the amine visualizing reagents (DFO, ninhydrin, etc.) and the Ag-PD are needed to obtain as many latent prints as possible. At present, no reagent has been as successful as the Ag-PD for visualizing the water-insoluble components of latent print residue on paper. Thirty-year-old prints on paper have been developed on test materials using this reagent.

Carrier Solvents

As indicated above, the Ag-PD treatment is normally preceded by an amino acid visualization treatment. The carrier solvent for the amino acid visualizing reagents must be nonaqueous because the amine-containing compounds they visualize are water soluble; an aqueous carrier would wash them away. Furthermore, the organic solvent used must not be so strong that it dissolves the water-insoluble components that remain. There have been numerous formulations over the years for making such reagents. All of these contain one major solvent such as acetone, methanol, hexane, heptane, petroleum ether, or Freon 113 (1,1,2-trichlorotrifluoroethane). Of these, acetone is the most likely to remove lipids, particularly if they are fresh. For several years, Freon was the most favored; however, the current ban on chlorofloro-carbons (CFCs) has forced the forensic community to search for other solvents such as HFC-4310mee (Vertrel XF or 2,3-dihydrodecafluoropentane) and HFE-7100 (methylnonafluorobutane).[5] The carrier solvent for Ag-PDs is distilled water rather than tap water, which contains chlorides that cause silver to precipitate as silver chloride. Tap water also contains organic species, which can reduce silver ions to silver. Water removes ninhydrin-developed prints and water-soluble inks (most jet printing inks and certain non-ball-point writing inks) from documents. Consequently, the Ag-PD process can be detrimental to evidence in other forensic examinations (e.g., handwriting and ink analysis).

The Silver Physical Development Process

Silver Physical Development in Photographic Chemistry

The silver physical development process now used to visualize latent prints is borrowed from photographic chemistry.[6-10] The emulsion of photographic film or paper is a thin coat consisting of photosensitive silver halide crystals densely distributed in a gelatin matrix. The photosensitivity of these crystals is increased by the presence of a trace amount of silver sulfide specks on their surface; these specks are formed when certain sulfur compounds are present in the gelatin in trace amounts. A "speck" as used here means a small aggregate or assembly of atoms or molecules. To develop a silver halide-based latent photographic image, early photographic chemists employed the now-traditional chemical developer, but they also used the now-photographically abandoned silver physical developer. In both cases, the developer distinguishes between photo-exposed and unexposed silver halide embedded in a gelatin matrix. Silver physical development is much slower than chemical development but it gives a finer grain development. After development, both require fixation (e.g., with sodium thiosulfate) to obtain the final developed image.

The Photographic Developers

As indicated, there are two types of developers for developing latent photographic images. A *chemical developer* contains a reducing agent (a developer such as hydroquinone in a basic solution) that selectively reduces only the photo-exposed silver halide to metallic silver. A *silver physical developer* contains silver ions *and* a reducing agent that selectively reduces the silver ions to metallic silver only *on the surface* of photo-exposed silver halide. To be this selective, the reducing agent is in a state controlled by concentration, pH, and sometimes complexing agents. A typical reducing agent used in some of the original or classical Ag-PDs consisted of Metol (monoethyl-*p*-aminophenol sulfate), which is most active in a slightly basic solution, with some citric acid to suppress its activity. Other names for Metol include Elon (Kodak), Photol, Pictol, Rhodol, and Veritol.[7,8] The stability of the classical Ag-PDs is very low because silver colloids are spontaneously formed in solution and these grow uncontrollably until precipitation occurs. Their stability was found to increase by adding "protective colloids" such as gum Arabic to the formulation.[11] However, it was not until surfactants were better known that photographic scientists discovered that cationic surfactants suppressed the growth of the spontaneously formed silver colloids, which in most cases are negatively charged. This, along with the use of a "controllable" (reversible) reducing agent (specifically, the ferrous/ferric redox couple), gave a more stable Ag-PD.[12]

Development Centers

Both the chemical and physical developers selectively act on the photo-exposed silver halide crystals rather than on the unexposed. This selectivity is caused by the specks of silver (and the sensitizing silver sulfide specks) found together only on the surface of the photo-exposed silver halide crystals. These specks are referred to as "development sites." The silver specks are formed by the light-induced photochemical reduction of silver halide, and the silver sulfide specks result from silver reacting with the traces of "sensitizing" sulfur introduced into the gelatin. For *chemical development,* the Gurney-Mott theory shows the role of these (Ag and Ag_2S) specks in the chemical reduction of the photo-exposed silver halide crystals on which they reside. The reduction of a photo-exposed silver halide crystal to silver metal begins on the specks and as reduction occurs, the silver grows from the specks as intertwined filaments. For an aggregate of crystals being reduced, the filaments intertwine together to form what Walls and Attridge[6] refer to as looking like "steel wool." These aggregates of filaments are black due to light getting "trapped" in their configuration (i.e., they bounce the light), and because this light is partially absorbed, each reflection attenuates the light. For *silver physical development,* these specks are the nucleation or catalytic sites for the reduction of silver ions by the reducing agent, both of which are present in the developer. The silver deposits around the specks and forms silver particles that begin as colloids ranging in size from 1 nm to 200 nm; however, these can grow beyond colloidal size (>200 nm) to form conductive layers. The configuration and shape of these particles dictates their color appearance. Their color can range from gold, brown, gray, to black. In general, however, these silver colloids are black because in most cases their configuration is that of silver strands wrapped into a sphere and such configurations have light-trapping capabilities. These silver particles grow thicker in size rather than in length (like the filaments do), making this process suitable for fine grain development.

Fixation

As indicated above, placing a photographic film or paper developed by either developer in a sodium thiosulfate (hypo) fixing bath gives the final developed image. For film or paper chemically developed, the hypo treatment dissolves away the unexposed silver halide. The dissolved silver is in the form of a silver-thiosulfate complex, $Ag(S_2O_3)_2^{3-}$. For film or paper physically developed (with the Ag-PD), the hypo treatment removes the unexposed silver halide and also the photo-exposed silver halide, leaving intact the deposited silver that formed around it. If a photographically exposed film or paper is first fixed (e.g., with hypo) rather than developed chemically, the fixing process removes *both* unexposed and photo-exposed silver halide, but leaves behind (in the emulsion) the silver and silver sulfide nucleating specks that resided on the surface of the photo-exposed silver halide crystals. Thus, an Ag-PD will develop an image from such post-fixed films/paper. This is referred to as *post-fixation development.*

Comments

As can be deduced, silver physical development involves a solution containing silver ions and a reducing agent in such combination that the reducing agent only reduces the silver ions on the surface of a catalyst (the development sites). It is not truly physical, but chemical. However, early photographic chemists wished to distinguish such developers from chemical developers by noting that the physical developers deposit silver as particles on the latent photographic image. For visualizing latent prints, ordinary physical methods that visualize by deposition include dry powders, aqueous solutions of colloidal gold, and aqueous solutions of small particles such as molybdenum disulfide (MoS_2) particles.

The Silver Physical Development Process of Latent Prints on Porous Surfaces

The discovery that silver physical developers visualize latent prints on porous surfaces occurred in the United Kingdom (U.K.). Goode and Morris[13] give an excellent history of the development of the Ag-PD in the U.K. The following is a partial chronology of the development of the current Ag-PD used in latent print visualization.

Jonker, Molenaar, and Dipple[12] (The Netherlands, 1969). These researchers from the Philips Research Laboratory in Einhoven, The Netherlands, developed an Ag-PD system for photofabricating printed circuit boards. Morris (see below) later discovered that this Ag-PD also visualized latent prints on paper. In fact, the Ag-PD currently used on latent prints is the Philips formulation with minor modifications made by Morris. The Philips Ag-PD differs from other Ag-PDs used in photographic science in that it is highly stabilized. To stabilize it, Jonker et al. used a cationic surfactant *and* a ferrous/ferric (reversible) redox couple, along with citric acid, to reduce the silver ions. The cationic surfactant stabilizes the system by suppressing the growth of spontaneously formed (and negatively charged) silver colloids in solution. The reversibility of the redox couple, which consists of ferrous and ferric ions complexed with citric acid, adds to the stability of the system in the following way: it facilitates the control of the system's potential to deposit silver (this potential is given by E_{cell}) and thus allows one to easily keep this potential close to zero (to suppress the formation of spontaneously formed silver colloids in solution), but still positive (to allow the reduction of silver ions).

Collin and Thomas (U.K., 1972). According to Goode and Morris,[13] Collin and Thomas investigated the use of one of the classical silver physical developers to enhance prints developed by the vacuum metal deposition process. The idea was sound. These authors knew that silver physical developers detect very low levels of silver metal and other metals. It is, for example, one of the most sensitive methods that Feigl[11] cites for detecting silver (his book was first published in English in 1937). Thus, they reasoned that because the vacuum metal deposition process, after the initial deposition of gold, deposits zinc or cadmium all over the surface and in the fingerprint furrows, but not on the fingerprint ridges, then an Ag-PD should enhance the furrow regions. They noted the potential of its use but were limited by the instability of the classical Ag-PD they used.

Fuller and Thomas[14] (U.K., 1974). These authors also investigated a classical Ag-PD for visualizing latent prints on fabrics and paper. They used the Metol/citric acid reducing agent in their Ag-PD. The interesting part of their work lies in their Appendix 1 (process modifications). It is surprising that many of the ideas they had are now being further investigated. For example, regarding their suggestion to use metals other than silver, Dr. Kevin Kyle of the Special Technologies Laboratory (a Department of Energy [DOE] Laboratory located in Santa Barbara, CA) has investigated a copper-based physical developer. The DOE funded this project during 1998–1999 and the U.S. Secret Service managed the research. Other ideas of Fuller and Thomas include sequential treatment with Ag-PD components and film-transfer methods.

Morris[15] (U.K., 1975). Morris was the first to document the use of the "Philips Physical Developer" (a name given by Morris to the "FC-1" silver physical developer formulated by Jonker, Molenaar, and Dipple in The Netherlands) for visualizing latent prints on paper. It uses the reversible ferrous/ferric redox couple with citric acid for the reducing agent. The FC in the Philips formulation FC-1 stands for ferrous/ferric citric. In our opinion, this is Morris' Ag-PD pioneering work. It introduced the currently used Ag-PD. Morris clearly saw the potential of the Ag-PD for visualizing latent prints on water-soaked paper (he obtained prints even after 12 days of immersion). He saw it as a post-ninhydrin reagent. He also provided a hypothesis for how the developer works, proposing that "trigger" materials exist on the latent print residue that act as catalytic nuclei and initiate the physical development process (similar to the silver and silver sulfide specks on the photo-exposed silver halide crystals in photography). These "trigger" materials include: (1) wax esters (lipids) because these can strip away the surfactant shell from (spontaneously formed) silver nuclei formed in solution, and (2) chloride ions (found only on paper that has not been exposed to water) because this promotes the formation of silver chloride, which photoreduces to silver metal. In both cases, silver nuclei are created on the latent print residue. In the first case they are from the silver micelles in solution and in the second case they come from the silver ions in solution. Morris only worked with the surfactant-stabilized Ag-PD he called the "Philips Physical Developer," but we will see later that removing the surfactant and reducing the silver content gives a semi-stable Ag-PD that works as well. Thus, the "surfactant stripping" mechanism stated above needs to be modified. We will see later an extension of Morris' hypothesis that states that for Ag-PD to work, the Ag-PD must contain negatively charged colloidal silver (or silver sols) in solution. When these are sufficiently small, they are attracted to the lipid residue before becoming surrounded by the surfactant molecules, if they are in an Ag-PD containing a surfactant.

Knowles et al.[16] (U.K., 1976, 1977, 1978).   Knowles and several co-workers worked on a series of projects all under the heading "Development of Latent Fingerprints on Patterned Papers and on Papers Subjected to Wetting." In addressing prints on patterned paper (paper with high background printing), they focused on the radioactive toning enhancement method. Knowles, Jones, and Clark (1976) evaluated a radioactive sulfur (^{35}S) toning method; Knowles, Lee, and Wilson (1977) performed some operational trials with the Sussex Police and, to a lesser extent, with the Metropolitan Police; and Knowles, Lee, and Wilson (1978) performed other operational trials. Overall, the three series of projects showed that the radioactive toning method was feasible and the authors strongly recommended its use.

Mughal[17] (U.K., 1977).   Working as a student at the Police Scientific Development Branch (PSDB), Mughal did an extensive study of cationic surfactants (all alkylammonium acetates from C_8 to C_{18}). He prepared these and tested their micelle forming ability and investigated how micelle age affects the rate of silver deposition from an Ag-PD. His research suggested using n-dodecylammonium acetate because it was found to give the best stability over time (69 hrs).

Melton and Myers[18] (U.S., 1977).   Independent of the work being done in the U.K., Melton and Myers of the Battelle Columbus Laboratories (Columbus, OH) studied several novel latent print visualization methods under contract with the Federal Bureau of Investigation (FBI). They also proposed silver physical development. Their hypothesis of why it should work had some similarities to that of Morris. They said that because the silver nitrate method works by the silver ions (1) reacting with halide salts in latent print residue and then photochemically reducing to silver and/or (2) getting reduced to silver by some reducing agents in the latent print residue, then silver physical development should do two things: create the necessary silver nuclei for physical development and carry out the physical development. Like Fuller and Thomas, they experimented with one of the classical chemical developers. Melton and Myers, however, went further and made several Ag-PDs using silver nitrate, several chemical developers, and several complexing agents. Among the chemical developers used were hydroquinone, ascorbic acid, and Elon; among the complexing agents used were di- and tetra-sodium EDTA, potassium tartrate and bitartrate, sodium sulfite, citric acid, and sodium citrate. The complexing agents where chosen to target either the silver ions or the developing agent, or both. (*Note:* Citric acid also changes the pH and, consequently, the reducing ability of the reducing agent used.) They made a series of observations and recognized that silver physical development had great potential for visualizing latent prints on paper. Although they would have recognized this had they been aware of Morris' pioneering work, it is remarkable to note that these two groups were independently studying the potential of this reagent.

Millington[19] (U.K., 1978).   Millington studied the effect of light illumination on the silver physical development process and found that it influences the performance of such developers. It affects the stability of the reagent, the rate of development, and generates more background development.

Hardwick[20] (U.K., 1981).   Sheila Hardwick from PSDB was the first (*ca.* 1984) to put the currently used Ag-PD in the police laboratory as a practical reagent to use in casework. She distilled the work of others into one operating manual or user's guide. She is also among the first (*ca.* 1984) to suggest an acidic wash pretreatment (using nonchlorinated acids such as maleic acid) to reduce background development on basic paper.

Goode and Morris[13] (U.K., 1983).   This report, in our opinion, should have been published as a book. It has a wealth of information and, to this day, remains one of the most authoritative sources for latent print visualization methods. It has laid the foundation for other work. In their section on physical development, Goode and Morris discuss the development, proposed mechanisms, and use of the surfactant-stabilized silver physical developer. Their procedure calls for prewashing with a solution containing an anionic surfactant (Terigitol) because they claim that this improves latent print visualization on surface-coated or plastic materials (such as pressure-sensitive plastic tapes), both of which are nonporous. The reasoning, we hypothesize, is that the surface area of print residue on nonporous surfaces is not as great as that of print residue on porous surfaces and thus an anionic surfactant is needed to give the residue a negative ionic character. Basically, the surfactant molecule's neutral, long side chain penetrates the lipid portion of print residue, leaving the negative end exposed. The residue thus acquires a negative charge. It attracts positively charged micelles to it and provides better "surfactant stripping." Apparently, its effectiveness in improving visualization was not that significant because the current procedure does not call for this step; it only calls for two prewashes: the distilled water wash and the acidic wash (with a nonchlorinated acid) for basic paper. Furthermore, paper washed with a solution containing an anionic surfactant would probably not yield any visible prints when treated with a surfactant-free Ag-PD (see later discussion).

Mechanism of Silver Physical Development

Hereafter, we refer to the currently used silver physical developer as the UK-PD. Again, this is the one based on what Morris[15] called the Philips Physical Developer.

Electrochemical Considerations[1]

The key chemical reaction in silver physical developer is the catalytic reduction of silver ions by the reducing agent. For this case, where we use the UK-PD, the key reactions are

$$Ag^+ + Fe^{2+} \rightleftharpoons Ag + Fe^{3+} \tag{7.1}$$

$$Fe^{3+} + H_3Cit \rightleftharpoons FeCit + 3H^+ \tag{7.2}$$

$$Ag^+ + Fe^{2+} + H_3Cit \rightleftharpoons Ag + FeCit + 3H^+ \tag{7.3}$$

where H_3Cit is the (triprotic) citric acid and Cit^{3-} is the (trinegative) citrate ion. Equation (7.1) is the reduction of the silver ions, Equation (7.2) is the formation of the ferric citrate complex. The reaction quotient Q obtained from Equation (7.3) is

$$Q = [FeCit][H^+]^3/[Ag^+][Fe^{2+}][H_3Cit] \tag{7.4}$$

This shows the strong dependence of Q on $[H^+]$ and thus on pH. It shows that the silver physical development process is highly pH dependent.

Having chosen the reversible ferrous/ferric redox couple for the reducing agent gives the advantage that the process [Equation (7.3)] is reversible and therefore treatable as an equilibrium system. Because the process is electrochemical (silver gets reduced to silver metal as ferrous ions get oxidized to ferric ions), it can be thought of as an electrochemical cell consisting of two vessels connected by a salt bridge. One vessel contains the silver solution and the other vessel contains the redox solution. In this case, the driving force of the cell is the cell potential, E_{cell}. It is also the driving force of the reaction. This driving force is obtained from the Nernst equation. At room temperature (25°C), this is given by:

$$E_{cell} = E°_{cell} - 59 \log Q \text{ (millivolts, mV)} \tag{7.5}$$

where

$$E°_{cell} = E°_{red} + E°_{ox} \tag{7.6}$$

$E°_{red}$ is the standard reduction potential for $e^- + Ag^+ \rightleftharpoons Ag$,

$$E°_{red} = 799.6 \text{mV} \tag{7.7}$$

$E°_{ox}$ is the standard oxidation potential for $Fe^{2+} + H_3Cit \rightleftharpoons FeCit + 3H^+ + e^-$.

$$E°_{ox} = -794.6 \text{mV} \tag{7.8}$$

Therefore,

$$E°_{cell} = E°_{red} + E°_{ox} = 5.0 \text{ mV} \tag{7.9}$$

$E°_{ox}$ is derived from the oxidation potential of $Fe^{2+} \rightleftharpoons Fe^{3+} + e^-$ (−771 mV) *and* the formation constant of $Fe^{3+} + H_3Cit \rightleftharpoons FeCit + 3H^+$ ($K_{formation} = 0.398$).

The driving force, E_{cell}, of the process and the thermodynamic Gibb's free energy, ΔG, are related by

$$\Delta G = - nFE_{cell} \tag{7.10}$$

where n is the number of electrons involved in the electrochemical reaction (n = 1 in our case), F is Faraday's constant (96,487 coulombs/equivalent), E_{cell} is in volts (i.e., joules/coulomb), and ΔG is in joules. Consequently, a positive E_{cell} means a negative free energy and this means the process is thermodynamically feasible and can proceed. For the Philips physical developer, the cell potential is $E_{cell} = 90$ mV. Using Equations 7.5 and 7.9, this corresponds to Q = 0.03625. The reaction proceeds until equilibrium is reached because at equilibrium, $\Delta G = 0$ and thus $E_{cell} = 0$ and $Q = K_{eq}$. At

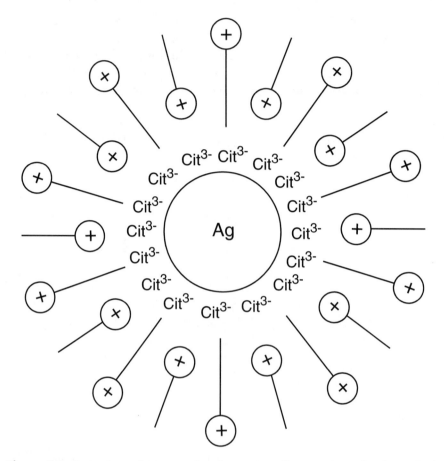

Figure 7.1 Cationic surfactant molecules surrounding a negatively charged silver colloidal particle in a staggered manner, forming a positively charged micelle. The silver colloidal particle is negatively charged due to adsorbed citrate ions (Cit³⁻).

equilibrium, the potential to deposit silver completely ceases. Because E^o_{cell} = 59 log K_{eq}, then $K_{eq} = 1.21$.

Stability of a Silver Physical Developer

By carefully choosing the concentrations of the components, one can obtain a reaction quotient Q such that E_{cell} is small but still positive. This is what one wants in designing a stabilized silver physical developer because it suppresses the spontaneous formation of silver particles in solution.[12] The other component necessary for stabilizing the developer is the addition of a cationic surfactant to keep any spontaneously formed silver particles from growing. The spontaneously formed silver particles acquire a negative charge from the surrounding citrate ions by adsorption (see Figure 7.1). The cationic surfactant surrounds these negatively charged particles, forming micelles. The surfactant molecules are long-chain alkyl compounds with a positive end (an R–NH$_3^+$ group). They arrange themselves on the negatively charged silver particle in a staggered way: one with the positive end pointing toward the particle and an adjacent one with the positive end pointing outward (see Figure 7.1).[12] These micelles have two properties: they are positively charged (because the molecules arrange themselves in a staggered way) and they form a thick cover. Both of these prevent positive silver ions from approaching them and thus prevent their growth. Saunders[21] formulated a simplified physical developer (SPD) that contains no surfactant. For it to have any stability, he had to significantly reduce the amount of AgNO$_3$ (by 72%) and the ferrous/ferric redox couple (by 25%). It performs well during its stable period (about 1 hr) and thus helps to understand the role of the colloidal silver with or without using surfactants.

Silver Image Formation

The reduction of the silver ions to silver metal by the oxidizing agent occurs on nucleation or catalytic sites. In photographic chemistry, where silver physical developers were first applied, the catalytic nucleation sites are on the photo-exposed silver bromide crystals of the photographic emulsion. The silver specks and silver sulfide specks are the actual sites. For *visualizing latent prints*, there is one explanation for the silver physical development of latent prints that have not been wetted and several hypotheses for those that have been wetted.[1]

- For the non-wetted (dry) residue, Morris[15] contends that the sodium chloride in the latent print residue triggers the physical development. The silver ions form an insoluble salt with the chloride ions and the resulting silver chloride gets photoreduced to silver with ambient light, thus creating the silver nucleation sites.
- For the wetted residues, a hypothesis being proposed here is that the silver physical developer actually provides the nucleation sites as spontaneously formed silver particles attach themselves electrostatically on the latent print residue.

A Hypothesis for the Silver Physical Development of Latent Prints Residue

This chapter section expands on the hypothesis mentioned above that requires the Ag-PD to contain spontaneously formed silver particles. Cantu[1] has discussed several proposed explanations for the silver physical development of latent prints as well as the reasons why such development occurs better on porous than on nonporous surfaces. The most likely of the reasons for physical development is based on the work by Morris[15] and the ideas of

Saunders.[22] Both workers recognized the importance of having negatively charged silver colloid particles *and* a low pH in the Ag-PD solution. Both of these are present in the UK-PD. The colloidal particles are selectively adsorbed on the print residue (which is positively charged), become neutralized, and function as catalytic nucleation sites for silver physical development.

Charge of Latent Print Residue

The reason the print residue is positively charged is that in an acidic environment, residue components containing amine groups ($R–NH_2$) and carbon-carbon double bonds ($-C=C-$) get protonated.[23] Among the compounds with carbon-carbon double bonds in the print residue are the unsaturated lipid components and among the amines are insoluble proteins, lipoproteins, and even water-soluble proteins and amino acids that get trapped in the lipid matrix as the print dries and hardens by oxidation. The protonation reactions are

$$R–NH_2 + H^+ \rightarrow R–NH_3^+ \tag{7.11}$$

$$-C=C- + H^+ \rightarrow -\overset{\overset{\displaystyle H^+}{\frown}}{C}-C- \tag{7.12}$$

Note that another way of providing a positive charge to the residue is by the complexation of silver ions with the double bonds in alkenes:[24]

$$-C=C- + Ag^+ \rightarrow -\overset{\overset{\displaystyle Ag^+}{\frown}}{C}-C- \tag{7.13}$$

Formation of Nucleating Sites on Latent Print Residue

As stated, the role of the cationic surfactant in the stabilized UK-PD is to suppress the growth of the spontaneously formed and negatively charged silver particles. Without the surfactant, these particles grow uncontrollably; however, when the surfactant is used, they begin as negatively charged particles and gradually grow and reverse their charge until they are fully encased with surfactant molecules (micelle formation). At this point they cease to grow and are positively charged. These negatively charged particles have an electrostatic attraction toward the cationic surfactant molecules; however, in the vicinity of the positively charged print residue, they are also attracted to the residue. In the proximity of the residue, the attractive forces are competitive. For particles formed in the bulk solution, micelle formation is dominant and this leads to stability; but for particles formed near the residue, particle attachment is preferred. The attachment or binding process is not immediate and probably requires that the silver particle not grow significantly during the process (more on this below). The attachment process neutralizes the particles and makes them catalytic nucleation sites for silver physical development. Another way of depositing negatively charged silver particles on the positively charged residue is by the "surfactant stripping" process suggested by Morris. This involves already-formed silver micelles in the vicinity of the print residue and the process is probably slower because both the micelle and the residue are positively charged.

Formation of Silver Physical Developer Particles on Latent Print Residue: Silver Image Formation

Once the print residue acquires the catalytic nucleation sites, silver physical development occurs on these sites. The final particles that grow on these sites are spherical, about 5 to 40 µm in diameter, and are made up of strands of silver (see Figure 7.2). The gray to black color of these particles is attributed to their size and configuration. The print image is made up of a dense accumulation of these particles.

Substrates

Porous vs. Nonporous Surfaces

Silver physical developers visualize latent prints better if they are on porous or semiporous surfaces rather than on nonporous surfaces. On porous surfaces, latent print residue enters into and spreads throughout the porous structure. It thus has a greater surface area and is more exposed than on a nonporous surface. Because of this, more nucleating sites are formed on such residue and silver physical development (silver particle deposition and growth) occurs sooner and to a greater extent. Another reason why Ag-PDs, whether (cationic) surfactant stabilized or not, do not visualize latent prints on nonporous surfaces well is because newly formed, negatively charged silver particles grow. With a cationic surfactant, they also grow but after a certain point their growth is reduced and their charge is reversed. That is, these developers cannot retain particles of a fixed size and concentration long enough for a sufficient number of them to adhere to the latent print residue. Although the use of colloidal gold to create nucleation sites for subsequent silver physical development is discussed later, it is sufficient to say that treatment with negatively charged, fixed-size colloidal gold particles (at sufficiently low pH to create a positive residue) does bring about sufficient particle

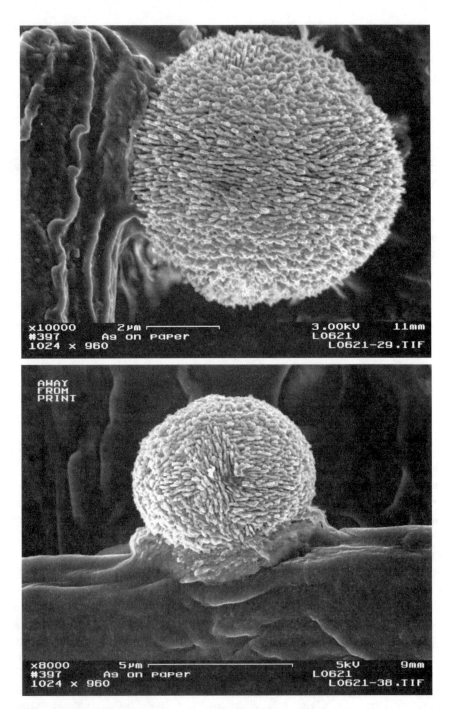

Figure 7.2 Scanning electron microscope (SEM) images of silver particles adhered to paper fibers with print residue. (Images taken by Jim Young and Gary Mong, Pacific Northwest National Laboratory, Richland, WA.)

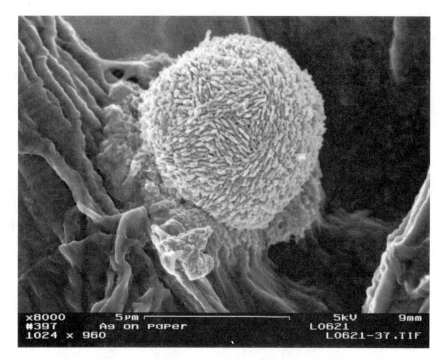

x8000   5μm   5kV   9mm
#397   Ag on Paper   L0621
1024 x 960   L0621-37.TIF

Figure 7.2 (continued)

adherence on residue that is on porous or nonporous surfaces. However, on nonporous surfaces, the colloidal gold treatment can take up to 120 min to have a sufficient amount of particles adhere to latent print residue.

Alkaline Paper

Alkaline paper has a pH > 7, as opposed to acid paper which has a pH < 7. Paper with calcium carbonate filler is alkaline. The alkalinity results from calcium carbonate being a salt of a weak acid (carbonic acid) and a strong base (calcium hydroxide). Although it is practically insoluble in water, it dissolves, then hydrolyzes and produces a basic solution. If alkaline paper is treated with an Ag-PD, it turns black, which upon drying sometimes turns brownish-black; the most likely reason for this is that the silver physical developer becomes destabilized by the paper — and only in the vicinity of the paper — causing the developer to deposit silver, silver oxide, and/or ferric oxide on the paper. To elaborate on this, the alkalinity of the paper causes a local change in pH, which causes destabilization. The destabilization causes a premature reduction of silver on the paper. The hydroxide ions locally formed in the paper react with the developer's ferric ions and silver ions to produce insoluble ferric hydroxide and silver hydroxide, respectively, on the paper and these convert to ferric oxide (Fe_2O_3 or rust) and silver oxide (brown-black Ag_2O), respectively, upon drying. To avoid this, alkaline paper is neutralized by treating it with acid. The acid, however, must not be a chlorinated acid (such as hydrochloric acid) because this introduces chloride ions, which react with silver to produce photosensitive silver chloride. Hardwick[20] introduced the use of maleic acid. The concentration currently used is 2.5% (w/v). The Forensic Science Services (FSS) in London, U.K. uses a dilute solution (1%) of nitric acid.[25,26] Others have used a 2.5% (w/v) malic acid solution, which is less costly than maleic acid. Household vinegar (5% acetic acid) works as well.[27] The paper is treated until all bubbling ceases. The net reaction that takes place is:

$$CaCO_3 + 2H^+ \rightarrow Ca^{2+} + H_2O + CO_2 \text{ (gas)} \qquad (7.14)$$

Preparation and Use of the Silver Physical Developer

Preparation

During preparation of the reagents associated with the silver physical development process, protective attire such as gloves, labcoat, protective eyewear, and mask should be worn. All containers used during the process should be rinsed with distilled water prior to use.

The Acid Pretreatment Reagent

Acids containing chlorine (e.g., hydrochloric acid) should not be used. A maleic acid solution is recommended, although as indicated above, dilute nitric or acetic acid also work. The maleic acid solution is made by thoroughly mixing 25 g maleic acid into 1 l distilled water. This solution has an indefinite lifetime.

The Silver Physical Developer Reagent

The following formulation is for the UK-PD.[1-4,13,15] It involves preparing three stock solutions and a working solution from these. The three stock solutions are made as follows and in the order given:

1. Ferrous/ferric redox solution (with citric acid) stock solution:
   a. Measure 900 ml distilled water into a clean container.
   b. Thoroughly dissolve 30 g ferric nitrate (nonadyrate) into the distilled water.
   c. Thoroughly dissolve 80 g ferrous ammonium sulfate (hexahydrate) into the above solution.

    d. Thoroughly dissolve 20 g citric acid (anhydrous) into the above solution.

    e. The final solution should contain no undissolved crystals.

2. Detergent solution

    a. Measure 1 l distilled water into a clean container.

    b. Thoroughly dissolve 4 g n-dodecylamine acetate into the distilled water.

    c. Thoroughly dissolve 4 g Synperonic-N into the above solution.

3. Silver nitrate solution

    a. Measure 100 ml distilled water into a clean container.

    b. Thoroughly dissolve 20 g silver nitrate into the distilled water.

    c. Once the silver nitrate has totally dissolved, store the solution in an amber glass bottle.

These stock solutions have an indefinite lifetime. The detergent solution may have a slightly cloudy appearance while the other two solutions should be clear. The working solution is made as follows and in the order given:

- Measure 900 ml redox solution into a clean container.
- Add 40 ml detergent solution to the above solution and thoroughly mix for approximately 5 min.
- Add 50 ml silver nitrate solution to the above solution and thoroughly mix for about 5 min.

The lifetime of the working solution is between 1 and 2 weeks. If a white precipitate begins to form at the bottom of the container, a new solution should be made.

The Hypochlorite Post-Treatment Reagent

This reagent consists of a 1:1 (v/v) dilution of a household "chlorine" bleach with water (50% dilution). These bleaches contain between 5 and 6% sodium hypochlorite. Some use a 3:1 (v/v) water:bleach solution (25% dilution). This solution is stable indefinitely.

Procedure

In the procedure used by the U.S. Secret Service, one clean glass tray is used for all the treatments: water pre-wash, acid pre-wash, Ag-PD treatment, and hypochlorite post-wash. The solutions are disposed of properly (check local regulators) after each step. In some cases, the Ag-PD and maleic acid can be reused; however, this depends on the number of items processed and the nature of the contaminants on the items (e.g., reagents are not reused if they processed items with biohazardous contaminants).

Water and Acid Pretreatments

The water pretreatment involves distilled water and is used to remove any dirt or debris that may be present on the evidence. It will also remove ninhydrin-developed prints and stains as well as water-soluble inks. The acid pretreatment is absolutely necessary for basic papers because these usually contain (alkaline) calcium carbonate.

Silver Physical Development

This part of the process produces the visible prints, with their color ranging from gray to black. It should be performed in subdued light because silver nitrate can photo-reduce to silver and increase background development; it also reduces the activity of the developer. Prints begin to appear within 5 to 10 min and processing should stop once sufficient contrast is achieved. Processing time ranges from 10 to 30 min.

Water and Hypochlorite Post-Treatments

Once the development is complete, the evidence is washed in running tap water. Some recommend distilled water because tap water produces colloidal size silver chloride particles that can become lodged in the paper and darken with time. We have found that using running water for about 5 min gets rid of these particles and chemicals from the Ag-PD (e.g., ferric, ferrous, and silver ions). To enhance the darkness of the print and lighten the background (assuming the background is not high in silver physical development), Phillips et al.[2] found that treating the evidence with a 50% solution of household bleach (hypochlorite) for approximately 2 to 3 min gave this result. If the background is high in silver physical development, then it too will darken. The reaction occurring is the conversion of silver to silver oxide. After this, the evidence is washed again in running tap water and dried; drying can be done with a photodryer. The evidence is photographed using film. The resulting photograph can be digitally scanned for digital enhancement.

Examples

This chapter section provides casework examples of additional prints developed by the Ag-PD process, ninhydrin prints enhanced by the Ag-PD, Ag-PD prints enhanced by hypochlorite, and Ag-PD prints enhanced by digital processing.

Figure 7.3 compares a ninhydrin palm print on a letter and the same letter after Ag-PD treatment. The Ag-PD process brought out an additional fingerprint in the middle of the palm print. Figure 7.4 shows how the Ag-PD process enhanced a ninhydrin print on a forged United States Treasury check. Figure 7.5 shows two things: the enhancement of a ninhydrin print on a counterfeit $20 note and the removal by the Ag-PD treatment of the jet ink that printed the counterfeit. Figure 7.6 shows an Ag-PD print before and after enhancement with

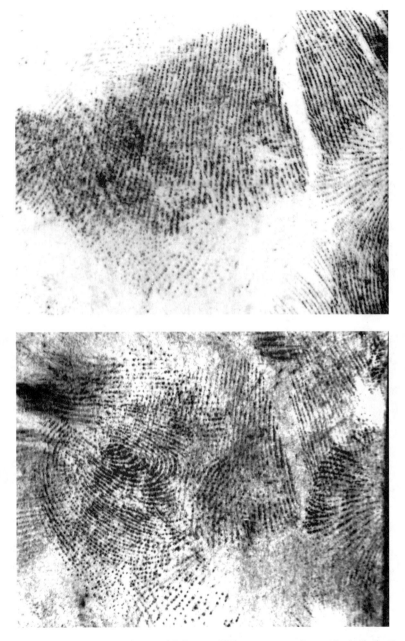

Figure 7.3 Comparison of a ninhydrin palm print on a letter before (top) and after Ag-PD treatment (bottom). Additional fingerprint is revealed.

hypochlorite bleach; and Figure 7.7 compares an Ag-PD print on a forged check with a patterned background and the same print after removing the background digitally using the Fast Fourier Transform (FFT) technique.

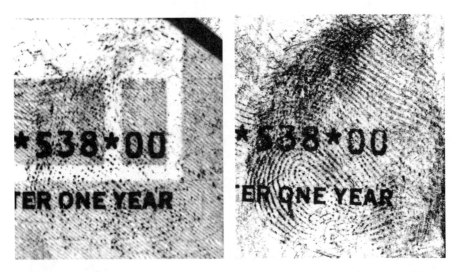

Figure 7.4 Comparison of a ninhydrin print on a forged United States Treasury check before (left) and after Ag-PD treatment (right). Ninhydrin print is enhanced.

Figure 7.5 Comparison of a ninhydrin print on a counterfeit $20 note before (left) and after Ag-PD treatment (right). Ninhydrin print is enhanced and ink (from inkjet printer) is removed.

The Multi-Metal Deposition Process

Background

Saunders[28,29] introduced the multi-metal deposition (MMD) method for visualizing latent prints on porous and nonporous surfaces. It is a modification of a biochemical technique used for staining proteins.[30] The method

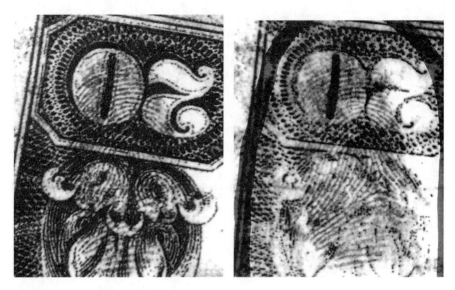

Figure 7.6 Comparison of an Ag-PD print on a counterfeit $20 note before (left) and after hypochlorite bleach treatment (right). Ag-PD print darkens and background lightens.

involves treating the test species (proteins in the biochemical case and latent prints in our case) with a colloidal gold solution (having a pH ~ 2.7) and then with a weak solution of silver physical developer. The colloidal gold particles are highly negatively charged and thus bind strongly with the target species to form catalytic nucleating sites for silver physical development. In this technique, one speaks of silver *amplifying* the gold image.

Porous vs. Nonporous Surfaces

As indicated above, compared to the silver physical development method, which visualizes latent prints on porous rather than nonporous surfaces, the MMD method is able to visualize prints on both surfaces. Silver physical developers form and supply the colloidal particles that bind to the latent print residue and these become the critical catalytic nucleating sites. Once these particles bind, they then grow in the development process. The MMD method, on the other hand, supplies already-formed colloidal particles that do not grow and can thus build up if given sufficient time. They grow only during the silver physical development stage as silver builds up on them. Recall that for binding to occur, the silver or gold particles must reside on the latent print residue for a sufficient amount of time without growing significantly. Thus, for nonporous surfaces (where the surface area of the latent print residue is less expansive than on a porous surface), the MMD method must be given enough time to form a sufficient number of gold

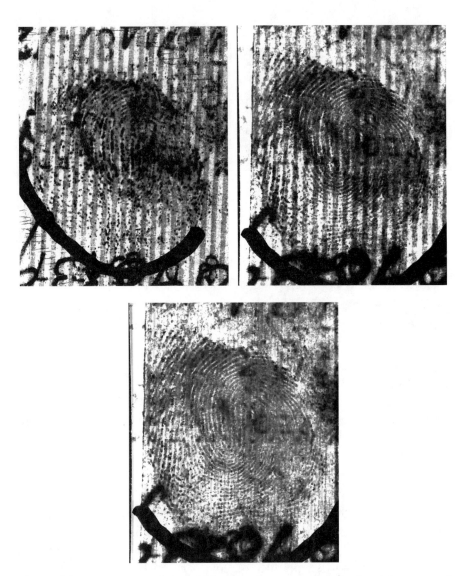

Figure 7.7 Comparison of a ninhydrin print on a forged check with patterned background before (top left) and after Ag-PD treatment (top right) and after subtracting the patterned background using digital FFT methods (bottom).

nucleating sites so that good contrast is obtained with silver amplification. For porous surfaces, some investigators have found the MMD method results in excessive background development. This will occur if the unbound gold (i.e., gold particles that get occluded in the paper fibers) is not properly removed. This is why the washing procedure after the gold treatment is very important.

Formulation and Procedure[29]

Colloidal Gold Solution (Gold Sol)

To prepare this solution, one needs a 10% (w/v) tetrachloroauric acid stock solution, a 1% (w/v) trisodium citrate stock solution, a 0.5 *M* (9.6% w/v) citric acid stock solution, and Tween 20 (a non-ionic surfactant/detergent). The stock solutions must be made with distilled or deionized water (i.e., it must be free of divalent ions, chlorine, and organic substances). These stock solutions are stable indefinitely. To prepare 1 l of the colloidal gold working solution, add 1 ml of the 10% tetrachloroauric acid stock solution to 1 l distilled water and bring to a boil. Rapidly add 10 ml of the 1% trisodium citrate stock solution and continue boiling gently for 10 min. The resulting colloidal gold solution should be "port wine" in color. Turn off the heat and add 5 ml Tween 20. Mix well and let cool to room temperature. When cool, add 10 ml of a 1% polyethylene glycol (molecular weight 10–15,000) and adjust the pH to 2.7 with 0.5 *M* citric acid (about 1 ml). Restore the volume to 1 l with distilled water. Store in clean glass or plastic container in a refrigerator. The gold sol is stable for at least 3 months. The gold colloidal particles prepared in this way have an average size of about 30 nm. Margot and Lennard[3] use 15 ml trisodium citrate instead of 10 ml and exclude the polyethylene glycol.

Modified Silver Physical Developer

Two stock solutions are needed: a ferrous/ferric redox couple stock solution and a 20% (w/v) silver nitrate solution. These stock solutions have an indefinite shelf life when stored in clean glass bottles (dark glass for the silver nitrate solution). The redox stock solution is prepared by sequentially dissolving into 1 l distilled water, 33 g ferric nitrate nonahyrate, 89 g ferrous ammonium sulfate hexahydrate, 22 g citric acid, and 1 ml Tween 20. The working solution (the modified silver physical developer) is prepared by adding one part 20% silver nitrate solution to 99 parts of redox solution. The working solution should be prepared just prior to using because it is only stable for about 15 min. Saunders later revised the formulation of the redox stock solution to be about half as concentrated (16 g ferric salt, 43 g ferrous salt, 11 g citric acid, and 0.25 ml Tween 20). This provides the same results but less quickly.

There are two points to be noted. First, a non-ionic surfactant is used instead of a more stabilizing cationic surfactant. Cationic surfactants prevent the silver from depositing around the bound gold particles. One reason for this may be that the bound gold particles are not fully neutralized and the cationic surfactant surrounds them, forming a protective shield that keeps out silver ions. Second, the amount of silver in the final developer is sufficiently low

(0.2%) to not form silver oxide when used in alkaline paper; therefore, there is no need to neutralize alkaline paper. This, in fact, is fortuitous because neutralization produces unwanted calcium ions (see below).

Procedure

Porous items should be prewashed several times with distilled water for 20 to 30 min. A maleic acid pretreatment should be avoided for alkaline paper as this creates divalent calcium ions which destabilize the colloidal gold solution. Nonporous items only need a single distilled water prewash of about 10 min unless they are quite dirty (then several washes are necessary). Soak the items in the colloidal gold solution for 30 to 120 min, but avoid over-development. Rinse the items in distilled water. For paper, rinse in several changes of distilled water for 15 min or more. Any gold colloids that are trapped/occluded in the paper fibers must be removed to reduce background interference. Place the items in freshly prepared modified silver physical developer for 5 to 15 min. Silver amplification takes place almost immediately; therefore, the items should be removed once good contrast between the print and background is obtained. Finally, rinse in tap water to remove excess developer, air dry, and photograph.

More Recent Formulations

Since Saunders' work, most of the research performed on the MMD method has been by Dr. Bertrand Schnetz, who obtained his Ph.D. doing this work at the Institut de Police Scientifique et de Criminologie, University of Lausanne (Switzerland). In 1993,[31] Schnetz experimented with replacing colloidal gold with protein-bound colloidal gold. This would bind to the latent print residue and then this would be amplified with enzymes or stains forming colored or fluorescent products. In 1997, he introduced the MMD II method. It recommends using siliconized glassware and colloidal gold particles with a particle size diameter of 14 nm (compared to 30 nm for the Saunders MMD). Recently, Schnetz published his most recent optimization of the method.[32]

Enhancement Techniques

For silver physically developed prints that are *weak* or have a *strong interfering background*, one can use several enhancement techniques to improve the contrast between the print and its background. The latter includes prints on dark or highly patterned surfaces. The enhancement techniques can be grouped into at least three classes: optical, physical, and chemical. Because a detailed description of these is already available,[1] they are only summarized here. The optical or photoreproductive methods include simple photocopying methods, standard film photographic methods, and digital image capture methods.

Optical Methods

Photocopying Methods

Photocopying methods are usually used to intensify a weak print. The effect is caused in part by the high contrast their images are meant to have, but also by the fact that the spectral sensitivity of their "cameras" is different from that of the human eye. In the latter case, if the spectral sensitivity reaches out into the near-infrared region, the contrast of certain background colors weakens while that of the Ag-PD print does not. ("Ag-PD" is also used as an *adjective* to mean silver physically developed.)

Film Photographic Methods

The versatility available to both film and digital photographic methods includes the choice of illuminating and viewing filters. In fact, use of laser illumination or illumination from an alternate light source is often used in photographing evidence. With film photography, one also has a choice of films of different sensitivities and of chemical development methods. Thus, photographic enhancement techniques involve a judicious choice of illuminating filters, viewing filters, film sensitivities, and processing methods to obtain the optimum contrast from a latent print image.

Digital Imaging Methods

As with film photography, digital photography also uses diverse illuminating and viewing filters. Similar to the human eye, photographic films, CCD cameras, optical scanners, and digital cameras have their own spectral sensitivities and this plays a critical role in the enhancement scheme. However, the greatest advantage of capturing a digital image is what can be done with the image afterward. Image processing software that is designed to enhance image contrast includes Image-Pro (from Media Cybernetics) and Photoshop (from Adobe). Combining this enhancement capability with the choices of filtered illuminating/viewing conditions provides a powerful approach to optimize contrast. For example, the image of an Ag-PD print on a colored background viewed at two separate wavelengths can be manipulated to remove the background. This follows because the silver image has the same level of gray over a large spectral range but not the colored background. Also, well-defined patterned backgrounds can be removed by Fourier transform methods. Images can be taken before and after development and compared to remove background completely.

X-Ray and Scanning Electron Microscopy Methods

Because silver is X-ray opaque, an Ag-PD print, which consists of a dense collection of silver particles (see Figure 7.2), should attenuate X-rays. Images of such prints can be obtained using transmission soft X-ray methods but the print resolution is not as high as that of prints on images obtained using other X-ray methods. One is scanning electron microscopy (SEM) equipped with an X-ray fluorescence detector capable of doing elemental mapping, and the other is SEM capable of generating a backscatter electron image. The latter has been used in the U.K. to eliminate background printing from Ag-PD prints on dark printed surfaces. For this to work, the background (which is normally printing) must not contain materials that cause silver physical development! Certain inks contain lipids, colloidal metallic salts, and metallic-based dryers that can potentially promote silver physical development.

Chemical Methods

Because an extensive review of the chemical methods that have been developed and used mostly in the U.K. to enhance Ag-PD prints is already available,[1] only a few are briefly discussed here. In any of these methods, a *prewash step* must be performed to remove as much as possible the following substances that may be on or in the paper: ferrous, ferric, silver and calcium ions, ferric citrate, silver chloride particles (formed by washing with tap water), and silver particles (either from the solution or formed on/in the paper background). Some of these may be difficult to remove, particularly the particles that are well attached to or occluded in the paper and ions that strongly adhere to cellulose fibers. Saunders[33,34] recommends washing with distilled water that contains 1% (v/v) Tween 20, with at least three changes of water.

Bleaching

These methods replace silver, which is gray to black in color due to its configuration (see Figure 7.2), with a substance of lighter color. They are used to lighten Ag-PD prints that appear on dark surfaces. The methods developed by Morris and Wells[35] are mostly borrowed from photographic chemistry and those of Saunders[33,34] are based on silver chemistry. In both cases, the conversion of silver is to a silver halide: silver bromide, silver chloride, or silver iodide. The conversion is usually performed under subdued light because these substances are photosensitive and can revert back to silver (though in a different configuration). Morris and Wells[35] cite two methods for forming the bromide: via oxidation with Br_2/KBr and via oxidation with $K_3Fe(CN)_6$/KBr. Saunders prepares the silver chloride using a dilution of the ferrous/ferric (citric acid) redox system and table salt. He forms the silver iodide using ferrous/ferric (citric acid) redox system and KI.

Intensification

These methods are used to enhance weak Ag-PD prints. There are at least four methods. The simplest of these is redipping in Ag-PD. This causes further development on existing silver particles contributing to their growth. It does not always add new particles to give a greater density of particles and also it could increase the build-up of silver in the background. Goode and Morris[13] proposed an intensification method that involves conversion of the silver to silver sulfide (Ag_2S), followed by silver physical development using a nitrate/nitrite redox couple. Saunders suggests a rather novel intensification method that uses the ferrous/ferric (citric acid) redox couple and a dilute sodium chloride (NaCl) solution. Its mechanism is not fully understood. The fourth method involves sodium hypochlorite (NaOCl). A 25 to 50% solution of household bleach, which is 5 to 6% NaOCl, lightens the background and intensifies the print. The most likely mechanism is that silver oxide (Ag_2O) is formed. Except for the redipping method, all of these methods change the composition and surface characteristics of the original silver particle and both changes contribute to its change and intensification in color.

Radioactive Sulfur Toning and Autoradiography

This method was developed in the U.K.[36] for removing interfering background from Ag-PD prints. It involves converting the silver to radioactive silver sulfide ($Ag_2{}^{35}S$), where ^{35}S is the β-emitting radioactive isotope of sulfur used, followed by autoradiography for imaging. As mentioned for the X-ray methods, if the background contains printing, the ink must not contain materials that cause silver physical development to occur. If it does, any silver particles on the printing will also be converted to silver sulfide and be radio-imaged.

Current Research

Non-Silver Physical Development

There are at least two problems of economics with Ag-PDs: the silver is expensive and about 20 to 50% of it is not used during the useful lifetime of the developer.[26] The latter fact indicates that the developer is rather inefficient and that a good portion of silver is thrown away when the exhausted Ag-PD solution is disposed. At present, there is no way to replenish used Ag-PD. In 1969, Jonker et al.[12] mentioned ways of making non-noble metal physical developers and later, in 1976,[37] Molenaar et al. worked on optimizing the copper physical developer. Dr. Kevin Kyle from the Special Technologies Laboratory, Santa Barbara, CA, assisted the United States Secret Service (USSS) in adapting the copper physical developer of Molenaar et al.[37] for visualizing latent prints on paper. Preliminary results show promise, but there is much to be done to optimize the system. This work was supported by the Special Technologies Program of the U.S. Department of Energy.

Diffusion Transfer

The USSS is investigating a method of transferring Ag-PD prints onto photographic paper or film. The method is based on ideas of Dr. Edwin Land during his development of the Polaroid transfer method.[38] The actual process is referred to as diffusion transfer.[39] To perform the transfer, one needs two items: receiver paper/film and an activator solution. The receiver paper/film is a gelatin-coated material in which the gelatin contains activation sites for silver physical development and the activator is a photographic developer (e.g., hydroquinone) plus hypo (sodium thiosulfate). The transfer materials currently being tested by the USSS are Kodak PMT matt receiver paper and Kodak PMT activator. For transferring an Ag-PD print onto the paper/film, the silver image is first converted to a silver bromide image using any of the bromination methods. The brominated print is then placed on the receiver paper/film and after this some activator solution is placed on the back of the paper with the print. This is pressed with a rubber roller and then the paper with the print is carefully lifted from the receiver paper/film. The receiver paper/film, which now contains the print image without background, is allowed to dry. As mentioned, if the background is printing with ink that causes silver physical development, then this will also transfer. At present, this project is still under development.

Fluorescent Ag-PD

The idea of converting the silver image of an Ag-PD into a fluorescent image has enormous advantages; it strengthens the contrast of weak prints and it removes background interference (i.e, if the background is not printed with ink that promotes silver physical development). Thus far, there has been no simple conversion of silver to a silver fluorescent compound. What has been done is borrowed from photographic "toning" chemistry. In the mid-to-late 1920s, motion picture photographic scientists created ways to change a silver image into colored images.[40] One that formed a red image involved a rhodamine dye. At the time, the interest was in the red color product and not its fluorescent properties. Under USSS guidance and with support from the Special Technologies Program of the U.S. Department of Energy, Dr. Kevin Kyle of the Special Technologies Laboratory, Santa Barbara, CA, modified the photographic chemistry to apply it to an Ag-PD print. The resulting print fluoresces in the furrow areas rather than on the ridges and there is no background fluorescence. The mechanism is rather detailed[1] and is not discussed here.

Test of Effectiveness

Currently in our laboratory the effectiveness of an Ag-PD is crudely tested using a test paper strip with a spot of gold chloride on it. The density of the gold chloride spot (gold chloride/area) is high because it is made with a relatively concentrated (20 mg/l) gold chloride solution. The Ag-PD reduces the gold chloride to elemental gold and this catalyzes the deposition of silver. It only tests if the Ag-PD deposits silver on nucleation sites — not how well or how fast. Barford et al.[26] observed that the ferrous ion and silver ion concentrations were the most critical factors affecting the effectiveness of an Ag-PD. They found that the UK-PD performed best (with development time ≤20 min) when the silver ion concentration does not fall below 50% of its original concentration and the ferrous ion concentration does not fall below 60% of its original concentration. Seeing the importance of obtaining these concentrations, they determined the ferrous ion concentration using potentiometric titration and the silver ion concentration using a silver/sulfide solid-state electrode. Currently, Dr. Kyle is working on an alternate way of obtaining the ferrous ion concentration.[41] Also, Cantu is currently working with the Institut de Police Scientifique et de Criminologie (University of Lausanne, Lausanne, Switzerland) in developing a test strip containing gold chloride spots of equal size but of decreasing density. The test strip is placed into the Ag-PD at two different times to estimate the rate and sensitivity of development.

Conclusion

Silver physical developer is a powerful reagent for recovering latent prints on porous surfaces that the amino acid visualizing reagents failed to develop. It works on the water-insoluble components of latent print residue and, consequently, works on water-soaked evidence. When it is used after a colloidal gold pretreatment, its working ability is extended to nonporous surfaces. A mechanism by which it works has been proposed. It is built on several observations and offers avenues one can take to improve the current or create new physical developers. At present, the U.S. Secret Service uses about 1600 liters (423 gallons) of Ag-PD annually. It has increased the number of prints found on evidence and brought about more convictions than when ninhydrin was used alone.

References

1. Cantu, A.A., On the composition of silver physical developers used to visualize latent prints on paper, *Forensic Sci. Rev.*, 13, 29, 2001.
2. Phillips, C.E., Cole, D.O., and Jones, G.W., Physical developer: a practical and productive latent print developer, *J. Forensic Ident.*, 40, 135, 1990.

3. Margot, P. and Lennard, C., *Fingerprint Detection Techniques,* 6th revised edition, Institut de Police Scientifique et de Criminologie, Universite de Lausanne, Lausanne, Switzerland, 1994.

4. *Manual of Fingerprint Detection Techniques,* Home Office, Police Scientific and Development Branch, London, 1992.

5. Kent, T., Hewlett, D.F., and Sears, V.G., A "Green" formulation for ninhydrin, *81st Annu. Int. Assoc. for Identification Educational Conference and Training Seminar,* Greensboro, NC, July 1997.

6. Walls, H.J. and Attridge, G.G., *Basic Photo Science,* Focal Press, London, 1977.

7. Larmoure, L., *Introduction to Photographic Principles,* Dover, New York, 1965.

8. Zakia, R. and Stroebel, L., Eds., *The Focal Encyclopedia of Photography,* 3rd ed., Focal Press, Boston, 1993.

9. James, T.H., Ed., *The Theory of the Photographic Process,* 4th ed., Macmillan, New York, 1977.

10. Bunting, R.K., *The Chemistry of Photography,* Photoglass Press, Normal, IL, 1982.

11. Feigl, F. and Anger, V., *Spot Tests in Inorganic Analysis,* Elsevier, Amsterdam, 1972, 424.

12. Jonker, H., Molenaar, A., and Dippel, C.J., Physical development recording system. III. Physical development, *Photo. Sci. Eng.,* 13, 38, 1969.

13. Goode, G.C. and Morris, J.R., Latent Fingerprints: A Review of Their Origin, Composition, and Methods of Detection, Report 022/83, Atomic Weapons Research Establishment, Aldermaston, U.K., 1983.

14. Fuller, A.A. and Thomas, G.L., The Physical Development of Fingerprint Images, Technical Memorandum 26/74, Home Office Scientific Research and Development Branch, London, U.K., 1974.

15. Morris, J.R., The Detection of Latent Fingerprints on Wet Paper Samples, Memo No. 36, Atomic Weapons Research Establishment, Chemistry Division, Aldermaston, U.K., 1975.

16. Knowles, A.M., Jones, R.J., and Clark, L.S., Development of Latent Fingerprints on Patterned Papers and on Papers Subjected to Wetting, Tech. Memos Nos. 6/76, 12/77, and 5/78; Home Office Police Scientific Development Branch, London, U.K., 1976–78.

17. Mughal, M.A., The Influence of Micelle Age on the Rate of Deposition of Silver from a Physical Developer Solution, Technical Memorandum 21/77 (reprinted as publication 60/80), Home Office Police Scientific Development Branch, London, U.K., 1977.

18. Melton, C.W. and Myers, W.C., Development of Improved and New Methods for the Detection and Recovery of Latent Fingerprints, Final Report to the Federal Bureau of Investigation (1977 Sept. 28), Battelle Columbus Laboratories, Columbus, OH, 1977. Permission to cite this reference was provided by the Federal Bureau of Investigation.

19. Millington, S., The Influence of Light on the Performance of a Physical Developer System, Technical Memorandum 13/78, Home Office Police Scientific Development Branch, London, U.K., 1978.

20. Hardwick, S.A., User Guide to Physical Developer — A Reagent for Detecting Latent Fingerprints; User Guide No. 14/81; Home Office Police Scientific Development Branch, London, U.K., 1981.

21. Saunders, G., The Simplified Physical Developer, report presented at the *Third Int. Conf. of Fingerprint Development Chemistry*, U.S. Secret Service: Washington, D.C., May, 19–21, 1993.

22. Saunders, G., personal communication, 1996.

23. Morrison, R.T. and Boyd, R.N., *Organic Chemistry*, Allyn and Bacon, Boston, 1961, 114.

24. Cotton, F.A., Wilkinson, G., Murillo, C.A., and Bohmann, M., *Advanced Inorganic Chemistry*, 6th ed., John Wiley, New York, 1999, 1093.

25. Brennan, J., personal communication, 1999.

26. Barford, A.D., Brennan, J.S., Hooker, R.H., Price, C.J., Operational experiences in the use of physical developers for detecting latent marks (work in progress).

27. Ramotowski, R., A comparison of different physical developer systems and acid pre-treatments and their effects on developing latent prints, *J. Forensic Ident.*, 50, 363, 2000.

28. Saunders, G., Multimetal Deposition Method for Latent Fingerprint Development, Progress Report to the USSS, February 27, 1989. Also in the *Proceedings — 74th Annu. Educational Conf. Int. Assoc. Identification*, Pensacola, FL, July 1989.

29. Saunders, G.C., Cantu A.A., Burns, C.D., Seifert, D.C., and Johnson, J.J., Multimetal deposition technique for latent fingerprint visualization, unpublished manuscript, ca. 1990.

30. DeMey, J., Colloidal Gold Probes in Immunocytochemistry, in *Immunohistochemistry, Practical Application in Pathology and Biology*, Polak, J.M. and Van Noorden, S., Eds., John Wright and Sons, London, 1983, 82.

31. Schnetz, B., Latent fingerprint and colloidal gold: new reinforcement procedures, Abstract, International Association of Forensic Science, Dussoldorf, Germany, 1993.

32. Schnetz, B. and Margot, P., Latent fingermarks, colloidal gold and multimetal deposition (MMD). Optimisation of the method, *Forensic Sci. Int.*, in press.

33. Saunders, G., Fingerprint Chemistry I, Final Report to the U.S. Secret Service, Washington, D.C., Aug. 14, 1996.

34. Saunders, G., Fingerprint Chemistry II, Final Report to the U.S. Secret Service, Washington, D.C., Oct. 4, 1997.

35. Morris, J.R. and Wells, J.M., An Examination of Intensification Procedures for Enhancing Silver Images produced by Fingerprint Reagents and Autoradiography; Memo No. 394, Atomic Weapons Research Establishment, Chemistry Division, Aldermaston, U.K., July 1976.

36. Knowles, A.M., Lee, D., and Wilson, D., Development of Latent Fingerprints on Patterned Papers and Papers Subjected to Wetting. An Operational Trial of a New Reagent System — 35SPD, Technical Memorandum 12/77, Home Office Police Scientific Development Branch, London, U.K., 1977.

37. Molenaar, A., Heynen, G.H.C., and van den Meerakker, E.A.M., Physical development by copper complexes using ferrous-ferric ions as a redox system, *Photo. Sci. Eng.*, 20, 135, 1976.

38. Land, E.W., A new one-step photographic process, *J. Opt. Soc. Am.*, 37, 61, 1947.

39. Levenson, G.I.P., Diffusion transfer and monobaths, in *The Theory of the Photographic Process*, 4th ed., James, T.H., Ed., Macmillan, New York, 1977, chap. 16.

40. Crabtree, J.I. and Ives, C.E., Dye toning with single solutions, *Soc. Mot. Pict. Eng.*, 12, 967, 1928.

41. Kyle, K., personal communication, 1999.

Automated Fingerprint Identification and Imaging Systems

8

ANIL JAIN
SHARATH PANKANTI

Contents

Introduction

More than a century has passed since Alphonse Bertillon first conceived and then industriously practiced the idea of using body measurements for solving crimes.[1] Just as his idea was gaining popularity, it faded into relative obscurity because of the far more significant and practical discovery of the uniqueness of the human fingerprint.* Soon after this discovery, many major law enforcement departments embraced the idea of first "booking" the fingerprints of criminals so that their records are readily available and later using leftover fingerprint smudges (latents), so that the identity of criminals can be determined. These agencies sponsored a rigorous study of fingerprints, developed scientific methods for visual matching of fingerprints and strong programs/cultures for training fingerprint experts, and applied the art of fingerprint identification for nailing down the perpetrators.

Despite the ingenious methods improvised to increase the efficiency of the manual method of fingerprint indexing and search, the ever-growing demands on manual fingerprint identification quickly became overwhelming. The manual method of fingerprint indexing resulted in a highly skewed distribution of fingerprints into bins (types): most fingerprints fell into a few bins and this resulted in search inefficiencies. Fingerprint training procedures were time-intensive and slow. Further, demands imposed by painstaking attention needed to visually match the fingerprints of varied qualities, the tedium of monotonic nature of the work, and increasing workloads due to a higher demand on fingerprint identification services all prompted the law enforcement agencies to initiate research into acquiring fingerprints through electronic media and automatic fingerprint identification based on the digital representation of the fingerprints. These efforts have led to the development of automatic/semi-automatic fingerprint identification systems over the past few decades. This chapter attempts to present the current state-of-the-art in fingerprint sensing and identification technology.

The objective is to present a high-level overview of fingerprint sensing and matching technology so as to provide the reader with some insights into the strengths and limitations of the automation in matching fingerprints. Because of space limitation, the focus is only on the core technology rather than the details of the commercial systems. The existing elaborate manual protocols (e.g., What is a core? How are fingerprints indexed/filed in a manual system?) are not described for similar reasons. Readers are referred to Reference 2 for an excellent exposition on these subject matters.

The remainder of this chapter is organized as follows: introduction of emerging applications of automatic fingerprint matching and its implications;

---

* In 1983, the Home Ministry Office, U.K., accepted that no two individuals have the same fingerprints.

Table 8.1 Biometric Applications

Forensic	Civilian	Commercial
Corpse identification	National ID	ATM
Criminal investigation	Driver's license	Access control
Parenthood determination	Welfare disbursement	Cellular phone
	Border crossing	Credit card

From Jain, A.K., Hong, L., and Pankanti, S., Biometric identification, *Commun. ACM*, 91–98, Feb. 2000.

description of functional components of a typical fingerprint identification system, summary of some of the challenges involved in automatic fingerprint-based identification; discussion of topics related to fingerprint sensing technology; description of the issues related to representing the useful information contained in a fingerprint image; presentation of automatic extraction of the most commonly used fingerprint representation (i.e., minutiae); an overview of fingerprint classification and matching algorithms; a summary of a fingerprint image enhancement algorithm; issues peculiar to large-scale identification systems; and fingerprint identification system performance evaluation issues.

Emerging Applications

As mentioned, law enforcement agencies were the earliest adopters of fingerprint identification technology. More recently, increasing identity fraud has created a growing need for biometric technology* for positive person identification in a number of non-forensic applications. Is this person authorized to enter this facility? Is this individual entitled to access the privileged information? Is the given service being administered exclusively to the enrolled users? Answers to questions such as these are valuable to business and government organizations. Because biometric identifiers cannot be easily misplaced, forged, or shared, they are considered more reliable for personal identification than traditional token- or knowledge-based methods. Table 8.1 summarizes typical applications of biometrics for positive person identification. The objectives of these applications are user convenience (e.g., money withdrawal without ATM card and PIN), better security (e.g., difficult to forge access), and more efficiency (e.g., lower overhead for computer password maintenance).

A significant limitation of the existing biometrics-based personal identification systems is that their accuracy performance is not perfect. These systems sometimes falsely accept an impostor (false accept error) and falsely reject a genuine user (false reject error). Typically, the two error rates depend

* Biometrics refers to use of distinctive physiological (e.g., fingerprints, face, retina, iris) and behavioral (e.g., gait, signature) characteristics for automatically identifying individuals.[3]

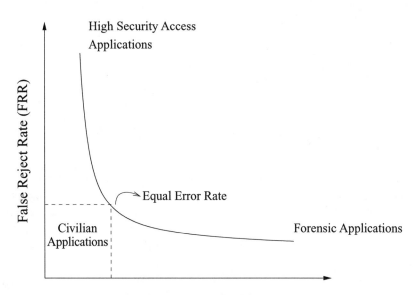

Figure 8.1 Receiver operating characteristics (ROC) curve of a system illustrates false reject rate (FRR) and false accept rate (FAR) of a matcher at all operating points (threshold, T). Each point on an ROC defines FRR and FAR for a given matcher operating at a particular threshold. High security access applications are concerned about break-ins, and hence operate the matcher at a point on ROC with a small FAR. Forensic applications desire to catch a criminal even at the expense of examining a large number of false accepts, and hence operate their matcher at a high FAR. Civilian applications attempt to operate their matchers at the operating points, with both low FRR and low FAR. (From Jain, A., Bolle, R., and Pankanti, S., *Biometrics: Personal Identification in Networked Society*, Kluwer, Massachusetts, December, 1999.)

on the system operating point (called decision threshold) and their relationship is characterized by a receiver operating characteristic (ROC). Figure 8.1 illustrates a hypothetical ROC and typical operating points for different biometric applications.

Tremendous success of fingerprint-based identification technology in law enforcement applications, decreasing cost of the fingerprint sensing devices, increasing availability of inexpensive computing power, and growing identity fraud/theft have all ushered in an era of fingerprint-based person identification applications in commercial, civilian, and financial domains.

A typical law enforcement identification system serves a different purpose than those of the emerging biometric applications. Most of the financial and commercial applications require identity verification (also known as authentication), which involves confirming/denying a claimed identity based on fingerprint information, given a claim to a specific identity (e.g., Joe Smith).

That is, given a fingerprint known to have originated from, for example, Joe Smith's left index finger and another print from a left index finger, the system will determine whether the second print, indeed, belongs to Joe Smith. The law enforcement systems, on the other hand, primarily deal with recognition (also popularly referred to as *identification*, as in automatic fingerprint identification system), which involves establishing the identity of the person based on the fingerprint information. Given a fingerprint(s), possibly without any knowledge of the finger position (i.e., left index), the system, by *searching* through the database of available fingerprints associated with the known identities, will determine whether the print is associated with an identity.* The task of identity verification is much easier than that of identity recognition: the former involving just one comparison while the latter involves multiple comparisons with fingerprints in the database. Although some civilian applications involve identity recognition, the underlying design considerations are different (see Figure 8.1). Despite these differences in the functionalities among different fingerprint identification application domains, all the fingerprint based systems rely on the distinctive individual information in fingerprints — the fingerprint expertise which has primarily resided within law enforcement agencies for more than a century. Further, the authors believe that law enforcement agencies will eventually also be closely involved in studying the civilian/commercial/financial fingerprint (and more generally biometric) applications as well.

For any biometric measurement to be incorporated into a positive person identification system, it is necessary that such measurements be acceptable to society. Despite the *criminal* stigma associated with fingerprints, a recent CNN poll found that fingerprints rate high in social acceptability.[4] While acceptability is a complex (and mutable) phenomenon depending on confounding factors including individual/institutional trust, religious and personal beliefs/values, and culture, two system issues influence acceptability: system security[5] and individual privacy.[6,7] The security issues ensure that the intruders will neither be able to access the individual information/measurements (e.g., obtain fingerprint information) nor be able to pose as other individuals by electronically interjecting stale and fraudulently obtained biometrics measurements (e.g., surreptitiously lifted fingerprints from surfaces touched by the individuals) into the system. It is desirable that a personal identification system uses the biometric measurements exclusively for the purposes for which they were acquired. For example, it may be possible to glean information about the medical conditions of individuals from their

---

* The term "identification" is used in this chapter either to refer to the general problem of identifying individuals (identification/recognition and authentication/verification) or to refer to the specific problem of identifying (recognizing) an individual from a database which involves one to many searches. We rely on the context to disambiguate the reference.

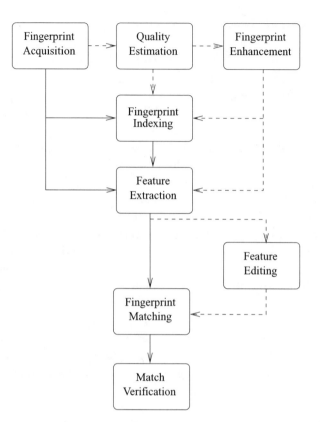

Figure 8.2 Functional block diagram of an "automatic" fingerprint identification system. The dotted lines illustrate alternative paths. Some of the functional
blocks (e.g., indexing) can be performed either by an expert or a computer. The
feature editing and match verification tasks are performed by an expert. Typically,
a fingerprint matcher passes a ranked list of 10 to 100 fingerprints for the match
verification stage; a fingerprint expert browses the *original* fingerprint images (as
opposed to their representations) to confirm/reject a candidate match.

biometric measurements. Second, people are concerned about *linkages*:
unauthorized usage of biometric measurements across different identification systems (e.g., criminal and civilian fingerprint identification systems) to
link the identities of people and to gather/track individual information that
may otherwise be unavailable. It is necessary to enforce systemwide mechanisms to ensure the usage of the biometric measurement for its proscribed
intent. As novel applications of fingerprints (and other biometric identifiers)
become more widespread, law enforcement agencies will be increasingly
involved in resolving the frauds involving repudiation (e.g., users denying having
accessed the system), coercion (e.g., users claiming to have been forced into the
system), contamination (e.g., erroneous acquisition of biometrics identifier not
associated with the intended user), and circumvention (e.g., unauthorized user

illegitimately gaining access to the system). Consequently, agencies may not only be required to pass judgments about the identities related to biometric identifiers but also about the integrity of the systems and the validity of the biometric measurements.

System Architecture

A fingerprint identification system is an automatic pattern recognition system that consists of three fundamental stages: (1) data acquisition: the fingerprint to be recognized is sensed; (2) feature extraction: a machine representation (pattern) is extracted from the sensed image; and (3) decision-making: the representations derived from the sensed image are compared with a representation stored in the system. The comparison typically yields a matching score quantifying the similarity between the two representations. If the score is higher than a threshold (determined by the system operating point [see Figure 8.1]), the representations are determined to have originated from the same finger(s). In an identification system, multiple comparisons may be needed. Often, the stored representations in the database are partitioned into bins, based either on information extrinsic to the sensed input measurements (e.g., sex and age of the individual) or on information intrinsic to the sensed image (e.g., fingerprint class or type [see "Fingerprint Classification" section]). As a result, the input fingerprint need not be searched in the entire database, but only in the particular bin(s) of interest.

Different systems may use different numbers of available fingerprints (multiple impressions of a single finger or single impressions of multiple fingers) for person identification. The feature extraction stage may involve manual override and editing by experts. Image enhancement may be used for poor-quality images (see "Fingerprint Enhancement" section).

Challenges

While significant progress has been made in automatic fingerprint identification, there are still a number of research issues that need to be addressed to improve system accuracy. Most of the shortcomings in the accuracy of an automatic fingerprint identification system can be attributed to the acquisition process:

Inconsistent Contact

The act of sensing distorts the fingerprint. Determined by the pressure and contact of the finger on the glass platen, the three-dimensional shape of the finger gets mapped onto the two-dimensional surface of the glass platen. Because the finger is not a rigid object and because the process of projecting the finger surface onto the image acquisition surface is not precisely controlled, different impressions of a finger are related to each other by various transformations. The most problematic of these projections appears to be *elastic* distortions of the friction skin of the finger that displaces different portions of the finger (ever so slightly) by different magnitudes and in different directions (see Figure 8.14).

Non-uniform Contact

The ridge structure of a finger would be completely captured if ridges belonging to the part of the finger being imaged are in complete physical/optical contact with the image acquisition surface and the valleys do not make any contact with the image acquisition surface (see Figure 8.6). However, the dryness of the skin, shallow/worn-out ridges (due to aging/genetics), skin disease, sweat, dirt, and humidity in the air all confound the situation, resulting in a non-ideal contact situation. In the case of inked fingerprints, an additional factor may include inappropriate inking of the finger; this results in "noisy," low-contrast images, which leads to either spurious or missing minutiae.

Irreproducible Contact

Manual work, accidents, etc. inflict injuries to the finger, thereby changing the ridge structure of the finger either permanently or semi-permanently. Further, each impression of a finger may possibly depict a different portion of its surface. This may introduce additional spurious fingerprint features.

Feature Extraction Artifacts

The feature extraction algorithm (see, for example, "Minutiae Feature Extraction" section) is imperfect and introduces measurement errors. Various image processing operations might introduce inconsistent biases to perturb the location and orientation estimates of the reported fingerprint structures from their gray-scale counterparts.

Sensing

The act of sensing itself adds noise to the image. For example, in the live-scan fingerprint acquisition method, residues from the previous fingerprint capture may be left behind. A typical imaging system geometrically distorts the image of the object being sensed due to imperfect imaging conditions. In the Frustrated Total Internal Reflection sensing scheme (see "Fingerprint Sensing" section), for example, there may be a geometric distortion because the image plane is not parallel to the glass platen.

Apart from the fingerprint acquisition and feature extraction issues, there are three major additional challenges.[10] Although a number of automatic fingerprint classification methods (see "Fingerprint Classification" section) have been proposed and some of them are used in operational systems, fingerprint classification still remains one of the most difficult problems for both humans and machines. Currently, the fingerprint classification framework is mainly intended for human experts; this may not be optimal for an automatic system.

In designing any automatic pattern recognition system, an important issue is the performance assessment of the system: how to evaluate the performance of a given system or how to verify that a deployed system satisfies certain performance specifications. Unfortunately, the performance evaluation problem is far from well established.

In the absence of a good fingerprint compression scheme, storing hundreds of millions of fingerprints is too expensive. The wavelet-based method, Wavelet/Scalar Quantization (WSQ), which has been proposed as the standard for fingerprint compression, can compress a fingerprint image by a factor of 10 to 25 (see Figure 8.3).[11,12] An algorithm that can reach an even higher compression ratio is an important research topic.

Fingerprint Sensing

Depending on whether the acquisition process is offline or online, a fingerprint may be either (1) an inked fingerprint, (2) a latent fingerprint, or (3) a live-scan fingerprint.

The term inked fingerprint is used to indicate that the fingerprint image is obtained from an impression of the finger on an intermediate medium such as paper. An example of a rolled inked fingerprint is shown in Figure 8.4a. Typically, the first step in capturing a rolled impression of a fingerprint is to place a few dabs of ink on a slab and roll it out smoothly with a roller until the slab is covered with a thin, even layer of ink. The finger is then rolled from one side of the nail to the other side over the inked slab, which inks the ridge patterns on top of the finer completely. After that, the finger is rolled on a piece of white paper so that the inked impression of the ridge pattern of the finger appears on the white paper. Rolled inked fingerprints impressed on paper can be electronically scanned into digital rolled fingerprints using optical scanners or video cameras. The rolled acquisition method has remained a standard technique for fingerprint acquisition for more than a 100 years.[2,16] Rolled inked fingerprints tend to have a large area of valid ridges and furrows, but have large deformations due to the inherent nature of the rolled acquisition process. Acquisition of rolled fingerprints is cumbersome, slow, and requires practice and skill. In the context of an automatic personal

(a)

(b)

(c)

Figure 8.3 Fingerprint compression: (a) an uncompressed fingerprint image; (b) portion of image in (a) compressed using a generic image compression algorithm, JPEG[13]; and (c) portion of image in (a) compressed using Wavelet/Scalar Quantization (WSQ), a compression algorithm specifically developed for compressing images. Both JPEG and WSQ use a compression ratio of 12.9; JPEG typically introduces blocky artifacts and obliterates detailed information. See Reference 14 for more detailed imagery.

identification system, it is both infeasible and socially unacceptable to use the rolled inked method to acquire fingerprints in the operational phase, although it may be feasible to use the rolled inked method in the enrollment phase.*

Another method of acquiring an inked impression is called a dab (see Figure 8.4b). In this method, the inked finger is simply impressed on the paper without rolling it from nail to nail. Obviously, the fingerprint dab images cover a smaller fingerprint pattern area, but there is a smaller distortion in the print.

---

* For example, Master Card relies on inked impressions for enrollment.

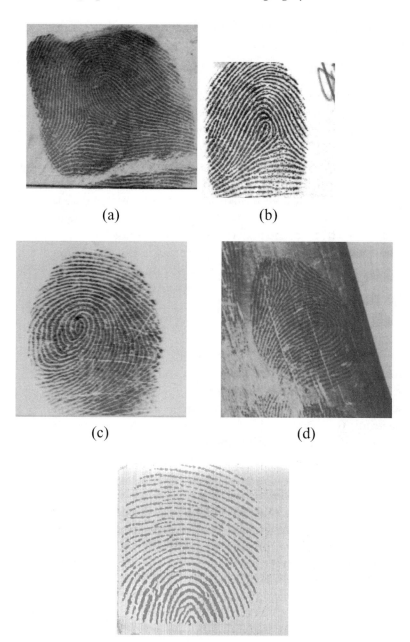

(a)   (b)

(c)   (d)

(e)

Figure 8.4 Comparison of different fingerprint impressions: (a) a rolled inked fingerprint (from NIST 4 database); (b) an inked dab fingerprint (from NIST 4 database); (c) live-scan (dab) fingerprint (captured with a scanner manufactured by Digital Biometrics); (d) a latent fingerprint; (e) fingerprint captured using a solid-state sensor. (From Jain, A.K. and Pankanti, S., *Handbook for Image and Video Processing*, Bovik, A., Ed., ©Academic Press, April 2000.)

In forensics, a special kind of inked fingerprints, called latent fingerprints, is of great interest. Constant perspiration exudation of sweat pores on fingerprint ridges and intermittent contact of fingers with other parts of the human body and various objects leave a film of moisture and/or grease on the surface of fingers. In touching an object (e.g., a glass), the film of moisture and/or grease may be transferred to the object and leave an impression of the ridges thereon. This type of fingerprint is called a latent fingerprint. Latent fingerprints are very important in forensics. Actually, a major task in forensic fingerprinting application is searching and reliably recording latent fingerprints, which is dealt with elsewhere in this book. An example of a latent fingerprint is shown in Figure 8.4d.

The live-scan fingerprint is a collective term for a fingerprint image obtained directly from the finger without the intermediate step of getting an impression on paper. A live-scan fingerprint is usually obtained using the dab-method, in which a finger is impressed on the acquisition surface of a device without rolling.* A number of sensing mechanisms can be used to sense the ridge and furrows of the finger impressions, including (1) optical frustrated total internal reflection (FTIR),[17-19] (2) ultrasonic reflection,[20-22] (3) optical total internal reflection of holograms,[23-25] (4) thermal sensing of the temperature differential (across the ridges and valleys),[26,27] (5) sensing of differential capacitance (across the ridges and valleys),[28-31] and (6) non-contact 2-D or non-contact 3-D scanning.[32,33] Scanners based on these physical processes can be used to acquire the fingerprint impressions directly and these acquisition methods eliminate the intermediate digitization process of inked impressions and enable the design of online verification systems. Depending on the clarity of ridge structures of scanned fingers and acquisition conditions, live-scan fingerprints vary in quality. Because of the online nature of this acquisition method, it is possible to directly observe the print being acquired; such a visual feedback turns out to be the single most important factor in controlling the quality of acquired fingerprints.

The most popular technology to obtain a live-scan fingerprint image is based on the optical frustrated total internal reflection (FTIR) concept.[17] When a finger is placed on one side of a glass platen (prism), ridges of the finger are in contact with the platen, while the valleys of the finger are not in contact with the platen. The remainder of the imaging system essentially consists of an assembly of an LED light source and a CCD camera placed on the other side of the glass platen. The laser light source illuminates the glass at a certain angle and the camera is placed such that it can capture the laser light reflected from the glass. The light that is incident on the plate at the

---

* It is also possible to capture a rolled live-scan fingerprint. Some vendors use elaborate software and/or scanner arrangements to capture rolled fingerprint live-scan images from one or more live-scan dabs.

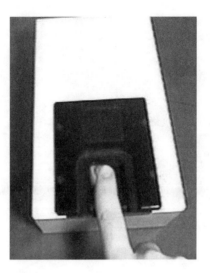

Figure 8.5 FTIR fingerprint scanner manufactured by Digital Biometrics. (From Digital Biometrics, Digital Biometrics Homepage, http://www.digitalbiometrics.com/. With permission.)

glass surface touched by the ridges is randomly scattered, while the light incident at the glass surface corresponding to valleys suffers total internal reflection, resulting in a corresponding fingerprint image on the imaging plane of the CCD. An example of a live-scan fingerprint is shown in Figure 8.4c. Figure 8.5 shows an FTIR fingerprint scanner and Figure 8.6 depicts the sensing mechanism. Typically, an optical live-scan fingerprint scanner images span an area that is approximately 0.75 in.[2]. There are vendors that supply optical scanners which are also capable of imaging very large areas of friction skin and facilitate ten-print or palmprint/soleprint scanning (see, for example, References 32 and 35).

The other live-scan modalities of fingerprint acquisition strive to (1) reduce the size/price of the optical scanning system, (2) improve the quality/resolution of the prints, and/or (3) improve the geometric/photometric/elastic distortion characteristics involved in the image capture. For example, by scanning the internal layers of friction skin (as opposed to scanning the superficial surface layers of the friction skin), an ultrasound method of fingerprint imaging is believed to be capable of acquiring a very clear fingerprint image even if the impressed finger does not apparently have clear ridge structures. Imaging in a typical FTIR optical scanner suffers from geometric distortion because the fingerprint surface (platen) is not parallel to the imaging surface. Hologram-based live scans avoid this problem and hence the resulting fingerprint images are believed to have better spatial fidelity. Further, the edge-lit holograms[23] avoid bulky illumination optics and are thus compact. Some hologram-based scanners have demonstrated

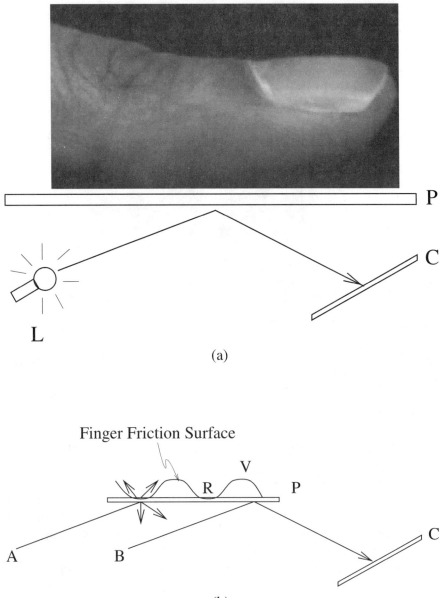

Figure 8.6 Optical fingerprint sensing. (a) Imaging geometry consists of a laser source (L) illuminating a finger resting on a glass platen/prism (P) and an imaging surface (C). (b) Frustrated total internal reflection: the ray A incident at the ridge/glass interface scatters while the ray B falling at the valley/glass interface suffers total internal reflection and the reflected rays are collected at the imaging surface.

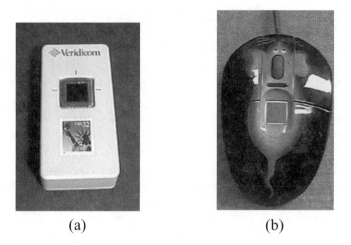

(a)   (b)

Figure 8.7 Solid-state fingerprint chips. (a) Differential capacitance fingerprint chip manufactured by Veridicom. (From Veridicom. Veridicom Homepage. http://www.veridicom.com/.) (b) A capacitance-based fingerprint imaging mouse made by Siemens. (Siemens. The ID Mouse from Siemens. http://www.fingertip.de/.)

1000 dpi resolution[36] in laboratory settings. Thomson CSF manufactures a "sweep"-based fingerprint scanner based on thermal sensing; this scheme claims to have significantly better reliability in harsh environmental conditions and a large imaging area. The contact-less scanners permit imaging without contact and hence eliminate the problems related to elastic distortion in the fingerprints caused by contact with the presentation surface. Optical scanners are too large to be readily integrated in a number of applications such as laptop security, cellular phone security, and notebook security. Recently, a number of different types of compact solid-state fingerprint chips have become available. These solid-state chips can be manufactured at very low cost if made in large quantities. Figure 8.7 shows two commercially available solid-state fingerprint chips.

Live-scan fingerprinting is an emerging technology and it is too early to assess its strengths based on the existing commercial products. At this moment, with respect to imaging area, gray-scale resolution, and spatial resolution, (rolled) inked fingerprints appear to be superior to the optical live-scans; optical FTIR live-scans are superior to solid-state fingerprints sensors. The forensic community has extensively evaluated the quality of live-scan fingerprints and expressed concerns about quality of fingerprints acquired using live-scan fingerprint sensors. In its quest to establish minimum requirements for fingerprint acquisition for criminal applications, various U.S. Government agencies have compiled compliance specifications for the optical live-scan fingerprints (see, for example, image quality specifications (IQS).[38,39]

Fingerprint Representation

A fingerprint is a smoothly flowing pattern of alternating valleys and ridges, the ridges and valleys being parallel in most regions. Several permanent and semi-permanent features such as scars, cuts, bruises, cracks, and calluses are also present in a fingerprint.

What information is available in fingerprints to enable sound judgment about whether two prints have originated from the same finger or from two distinct fingers? To reliably establish whether two prints came from the same finger or different fingers, it is necessary to capture some *invariant* representation (features) of the fingerprints: the features which over a lifetime will continue to remain relatively unaltered irrespective of the cuts and bruises, the orientation of the finger placement with respect to the medium of the capture, occlusion of a small part of the finger, the imaging technology used to acquire the fingerprint from the finger, or the elastic distortion of the finger during the acquisition of the print.

Several representations have been used to assess fingerprint similarity. Fingerprint representations can be broadly categorized into two types: global and local. A global representation is an overall attribute of the finger and a single representation is valid for the entire fingerprint and is typically determined by an examination of the entire finger. A local representation consists of several components, each component typically derived from a spatially restricted region of the fingerprint. Typically, global representations are used for fingerprint indexing and local representations are used for fingerprint matching.

One of the significant global features used for fingerprints is its class or type. The overall fingerprint pattern is typically categorized into a small number of classes. Several fingerprint classification schema exist and, as mentioned earlier, we will avoid delving into the details of the classifications schema adopted by different automatic identification systems. A typical fingerprint classification scheme categorizes the prints into the following six major classes: whorl, right loop, left loop, arch, twin loop, and tented arch (see Figure 8.8).* Sometimes, a synthetic category called *scars* is included to classify fingerprints mutilated with scars, thus obscuring the possibility of accurately determining its true class.

Fingers can also be distinguished based on features such as ridge thickness, ridge separation, or ridge depths. Some examples of global representation include information about locations of critical points (e.g., core and delta) in a fingerprint. Core-delta ridge count feature, sometimes simply referred to as the ridge count, measures the number of ridges between core

---

* A typical AFIS may use the following eight classes: (1) whorl, (2) radial loop, (3) ulnar loop, (4) double loop, (5) arch, (6) tented arch, (7) accidental, and (8) central pocket loop.

and delta points (see Figure 8.8) on a finger.* All these features measure an overall property of a finger and these similarities are referred to as global or generic features.

Major representations of the local information in fingerprints are based on finger ridges, pores on the ridges, or salient features derived from the ridges. Sometimes, the entire fingerprint itself (or some condensed form of it) is used as the fingerprint representation.[40,41] The most widely used local features are based on minute details (minutiae) of the ridges (Figures 8.9 and 8.10). The pattern of the minute details of a fingerprint forms a valid representation of the fingerprint. This representation is compact and captures a significant component of individual information in fingerprints; compared to other representations, minutiae extraction is relatively more robust to various sources of fingerprint degradation. Most types of minute details in fingerprint images are not stable and cannot be reliably identified by automatic image processing methods. Therefore, in automatic fingerprint matching, only the two most prominent types of minute details are used for their stability and robustness: (1) ridge ending and (2) ridge bifurcation. In addition, because various data acquisition conditions such as impression pressure can easily change one type of minutiae into the other, typical minutiae-based representations do not make any distinction between these two types of features and are collectively referred to as minutiae. The simplest of the minutiae-based representations constitute a list of points defined by their spatial coordinates with respect to a fixed image-centric coordinate system. Typically, however, these minimal minutiae-based representations are further enhanced by tagging each minutiae (or each combination of minutiae subset, e.g., pairs, triplets) with additional features. For example, each minutiae could be associated with the orientation of the ridge at that minutiae; or each pair of the minutiae could be associated with the ridge count, which is the number of ridges visited during the linear traversal between the two minutiae. The ANSI-NIST standard representation of a fingerprint is predominantly based on minutiae and includes one or more global attributes such as orientation of the finger, locations or core or delta,** and fingerprint class. Typically, in a live-scan fingerprint image of good quality, there are approximately 40 to 60 minutiae (in a typical 512×512 image).

Another local fingerprint feature is sweat pore information. The location and densities of the minute sweat pores have been found to contain information helpful in distinguishing individuals.[36]

---

* Some categories of fingerprints do not intrinsically have any core or delta. In such cases, an automatic system may in some consistent way define other landmark features of fingerprints in lieu of core-delta ridge count, core, and/or delta.

** Core and delta are the two distinctive global structures in a fingerprint.[2] See Figure 8.8c.

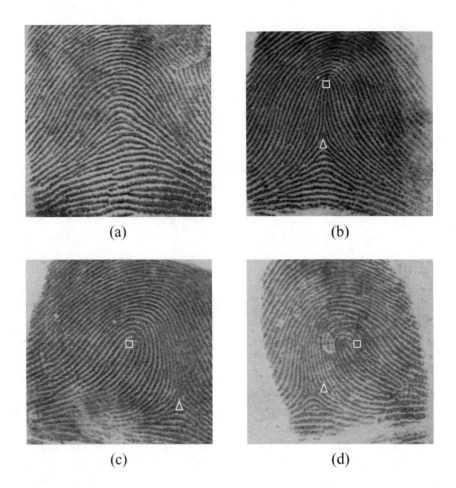

(a)   (b)

(c)   (d)

Figure 8.8 A fingerprint classification schema involving six categories: (a) arch, (b) tented arch, (c) right loop, (d) left loop, (e) whorl, and (f) twin loop. Critical points in a fingerprint, called core and delta, are marked as squares and triangles, respectively. An arch does not have a delta or a core. One of the two deltas in (e) and both deltas in (f) are not imaged. A sample minutiae ridge ending (o) and ridge bifurcation (×) are illustrated in (e). Each image is 512 × 512 with 256 gray levels and is scanned at 512 dpi resolution. (From Jain, A., Hong, L., Pankanti, S., and Bolle, R., On-line identity-authentication system using fingerprints. *Proc. IEEE (Special Issue on Automated Biometrics)*, 85(9), 1365–1388, ©IEEE, September 1997.)

The guidelines for (visual) matching of fingerprints are quite elaborate. A fingerprint expert often relies on subtle and complex reasoning to argue whether two prints originated from a single finger or two distinct fingers. For example, an expert can visually localize several rich features of a fingerprint with remarkable accuracy. These features include the locations of core, delta, islands, dots, short ridges, ridge endings, ridge bifurcations, and numerical

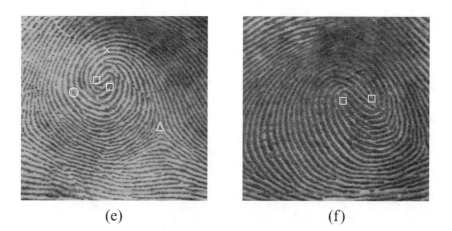

(e)   (f)

Figure 8.8 (continued)

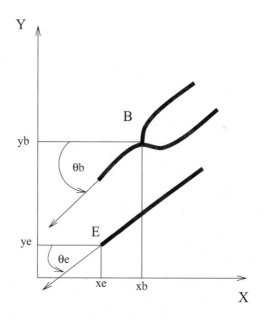

Figure 8.9 Schematic representation of a ridge ending (E) and a ridge bifurcation/branching (B). A minutiae is typically quantified by its (x, y) coordinates and the orientation of the abutting ridge. Different representation conventions are used by different automatic fingerprint identification systems.

values of orientation of the ridges, and number of ridges between two features (ridge counts). An expert can reliably use judgments about scars, complex visual textures, sweat pores, and ridge thickness to rule out false matches. It is not an exaggeration to state that research in automatic fingerprint identification has been mostly an exercise in imitating the performance of a human fingerprint

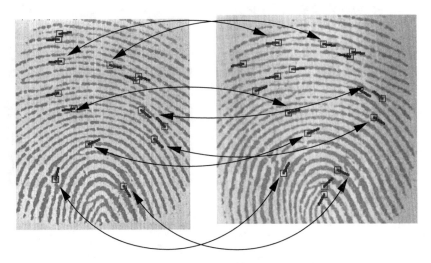

Figure 8.10 Relative configuration of ridge endings and branchings between two impressions of the same finger. The minutiae were extracted using the algorithm in Reference 9 and the correspondences were manually determined for illustration.

expert without access to the many underlying information-rich features an expert is able to glean from visual examination. The lack of such a rich set of informative features in automatic systems is primarily due to the unavailability of complex modeling techniques and image processing techniques that can reliably and consistently extract detailed features in the presence of noise.

It should be noted that, at least in the context of law enforcement/forensic applications of fingerprint-based identification, the machine representations alone are not considered a sufficient basis for assessing the matching outcome and other visual features of the original fingerprint can sway the final decision. Although there are FBI recommendations about the minimum number of corresponding minutiae for declaring a "fingerprint match," a fingerprint expert can overrule such recommendations based on his/her visual judgment. For an illustration of the danger in exclusively relying on parsimonious representations such as minutiae, see Reference 43.

Considering the relative simplicity of the automatically extracted fingerprint representations and the brittleness of the processing algorithms, especially in the context of poor quality fingerprints, an expert is actively involved in the processing/classification/matching stages of a typical fingerprint identification system, especially in forensic applications.

Minutiae Feature Extraction

This chapter section summarizes a typical automatic feature extraction algorithm for minutiae representation. An outline of feature extraction related

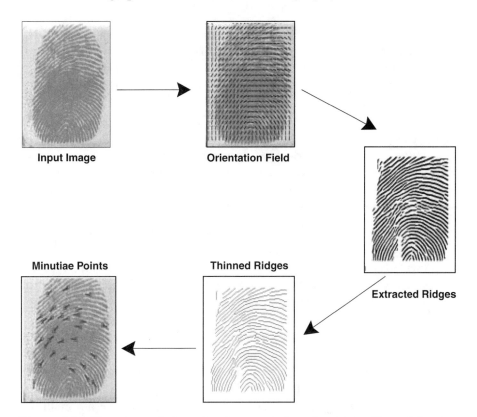

Input Image   **Orientation Field**

Minutiae Points   **Thinned Ridges**

Extracted Ridges

Figure 8.11 Flowchart of the minutiae extraction algorithm. (From Jain, A., Hong, L., Pankanti, S., and Bolle, R., On-line identity-authentication system using fingerprints, *Proc. IEEE (Special Issue on Automated Biometrics)*, 85(9), 1365–1388, September 1997.)

to fingerprint classification is presented in the next chapter section, while detailed exposition of these algorithms is presented in References 9 and 10. Computation of fingerprint quality estimation and fingerprint ridge count is not presented here due to space limitation and readers are referred to typical algorithms presented elsewhere in the literature.[44,45]

The overall flowchart of a typical minutiae extraction algorithm is depicted in Figure 8.11. This particular method of minutiae extraction consists mainly of three stages: (1) orientation field estimation, (2) ridge extraction, and (3) minutiae extraction and post-processing. First, for an input image, the local ridge orientation is estimated and the region of interest is located. Then, ridges are extracted from the input image, refined to get rid of the small speckles and holes, and thinned to obtain eight connected single-pixel-wide ridges. Finally, minutiae are extracted from the thinned ridges and refined using some heuristics. We assume that the resolution of input fingerprint images is 500 dpi, which is the recommended resolution for automatic fingerprint identification by the FBI.

A minutiae feature extractor finds the ridge endings and ridge bifurcations from the input fingerprint images. If ridges can be perfectly located in an input fingerprint image, then minutiae extraction is a relatively simple task of extracting singular points in a thinned ridge map. However, in practice, it is not always possible to obtain a perfect ridge map. The performance of currently available minutiae extraction algorithms depends heavily on the quality of the input fingerprint images. Due to a number of factors (aberrant formations of epidermal ridges of fingerprints, postnatal marks, occupational marks, problems with acquisition devices, etc.), fingerprint images may not always have well-defined ridge structures.

Orientation Estimation

A gray-level fingerprint image, I, is defined as an $N \times N$ matrix, where $I(i, j)$ represents the intensity of the pixel at the ith row and j^{th} column. Typically, fingerprints are 8-bit gray-level images and a pixel grey level in a fingerprint can nominally range from 0 to 255. The actual gray levels in a fingerprint may span significantly smaller range either due to (1) poor finger contact with the sensor, (2) poor imaging, or (3) shallow ridges/valleys. Many systems first preprocess the fingerprint images before subjecting them to the processing steps described below. This preprocessing might typically consist of either gray-level smoothing, contrast stretching, and/or spatial/frequency domain filtering. In extreme cases, a very poor fingerprint can be automatically enhanced (see "Fingerprint Enhancement" section).

An *orientation field/image* is defined as an $N \times N$ image, where $O(i, j)$ represents the local ridge orientation at pixel (i, j). The local ridge orientation cannot be meaningfully determined from the gray value at pixel (i, j) alone; it is typically computed from pixels of the surrounding (rectangular block) region. An image is divided into a set of $w \times w$ nonoverlapping blocks and a single local ridge orientation is defined for each block. Typically, w is determined by the image resolution and magnitude of w is comparable to one to two inter-ridge distances (e.g., 32×32 pixels in a 512-dpi fingerprint image).

One approach to ridge orientation estimation relies on local image gradient. A gray-scale gradient is a vector whose orientation indicates the direction of the steepest change in the gray values and whose magnitude depends on the amount of change of the gray values in the direction of the gradient. The local orientation in a block can be determined from the constituent pixel gradient orientations of the block in several ways. For example, one could determine the block gradient orientation by averaging the pixel gradient orientations.[46] An alternative method of determining block gradient orientation relies on a voting scheme involving pixel gradient orientations.[47] Another method[48] uses a least-square optimization scheme involving the pixel gradient orientations.

The rationale for determining a single orientation for each block of $w \times w$ pixels (rather than for each pixel) is computational efficiency. Consequently, in regions of a fingerprint with smoothly flowing parallel ridges, representing a single ridge orientation for an entire block is not unreasonable, but in the regions where the ridges are sharply changing their directions (e.g., regions surrounding core or delta) or the regions with cuts/scars, the choice of local ridge direction per block is ambiguous. Note that in a fingerprint image, the ridges oriented at 0° and the ridges at 180° in a local neighborhood cannot be differentiated from each other.

Segmentation

The objective of this stage is to locate the actual region in the fingerprint image depicting the finger (region of interest) and discard the regions of the image containing irrelevant information (e.g., dirt, smudges leftover from previous acquisitions, and spurious [pencil] markings in inked impressions). This stage is also sometimes referred to as foreground/background detection. Note that this stage is *not* responsible for discriminating the ridges against valleys. A typical approach to segmentation might involve smearing (spatial gray-scale smoothing) the fingerprint image and using fixed/adaptive thresholding to discard background region. This approach can produce reasonable results for a good-quality print but may not easily remove the extraneous artifacts in a poor-quality fingerprint image. A method of segmentation based on the concept of *certainty level* of orientation field estimation is described here.

After the orientation field of an input fingerprint image is estimated, a region of interest localization algorithm, which is based on the local *certainty level* of the orientation field, is used to locate the region of interest within the input image. The certainty level of the orientation field in a block quantifies the extent to which the pixel gradient orientations agree with the block gradient orientation. For each block, if the certainty level of the orientation field is below a threshold, then all the pixels in this block are marked as background pixels. Because the computation of certainty level is a by-product of the local ridge orientation estimation, it is a computationally efficient approach. The authors have found that this method of segmentation performs reasonably well in detecting the region of interest.

Ridge Detection

As alluded earlier, the objective of the ridge detection algorithm is to separate ridges from valleys in a given fingerprint image. Previous approaches to ridge detection have used either global or adaptive thresholding, that is, pixels darker/brighter than a constant/variable threshold are determined to be pixels depicting a ridge in the fingerprint. These straightforward approaches generally do not work well for noisy and low-contrast portions of the image.

A more reliable property of the ridges in a fingerprint image is that the gray-level values on ridges attain their local minima[*] along a direction normal to the local ridge orientation.[9,48] Pixels can be identified to be ridge pixels based on this property. Given the local ridge orientation at a pixel (i, j) in the foreground portion of the image, a simple test can be devised to determine whether the gray-level values in the fingerprint image attain a local minima at (i, j) along a direction normal to the ridge orientation. The resultant image is a binary image; for example, the loci of the minima are marked 1 and all other pixels are marked 0. The ridges thus detected are typically thick (e.g., 3 pixels wide) and standard thinning algorithms[49] can be used to obtain 1-pixel thin ridges. Thinned ridges facilitate the detection of minutiae. Before applying a thinning algorithm, spurious structures (e.g., dirt) detected as ridges must be discarded based on their (small) area.

Minutiae Detection

Once the thinned ridge map is available, the ridge pixels with three-ridge pixel neighbors are identified as ridge bifurcations and those with one-ridge pixel neighbor are identified as ridge endings. However, all the minutiae thus detected are not genuine due to image processing artifacts and the noise present in the fingerprint image.

Post-processing

In this stage, typically, genuine minutiae are gleaned from the extracted minutiae using a number of heuristics. For example, too many minutiae in a small neighborhood may indicate the presence of noise and they could be discarded. Very close ridge endings that are oriented anti-parallel to each other may indicate spurious minutiae generated by a break in the ridge due either to poor contrast or a cut in the finger. Two very closely located bifurcations sharing a common short ridge often suggest extraneous minutiae generated by bridging of adjacent ridges as a result of dirt or image processing artifacts.

Fingerprint Classification

Fingerprints have been traditionally classified into categories based on the information contained in the global patterns of ridges. In large-scale fingerprint identification systems, elaborate methods of manual fingerprint classification

---

[*] In a fingerprint image where ridges are darker than valleys.

systems were developed to index individuals into bins based on classification of their fingerprints. These methods of binning eliminate the need to match an input fingerprint to the entire fingerprint database in identification applications, thereby significantly reducing the computing requirements.[50-52]

Efforts in automatic fingerprint classification have been exclusively directed at replicating the manual fingerprint classification system. Figure 8.8 shows one prevalent manual fingerprint classification scheme that has been the focus of many automatic fingerprint classification efforts. It is important to note that the distribution of fingers into the six classes (shown in Figure 8.8) is highly skewed (32.5% left loop, 32.5% right loop, 30% whorl, 5% other). A fingerprint classification system should be invariant to rotation, translation, and elastic distortion of the frictional skin. In addition, often a significant part of the finger may not be imaged (e.g., dabs frequently miss deltas) and the classification methods requiring information from the entire fingerprint may be too restrictive for many applications.

A number of approaches to fingerprint classification have been developed. Some of the earliest approaches did not make use of the rich information in the ridge structures and exclusively depended on orientation field information. Although fingerprint landmarks provide very effective fingerprint class clues, methods relying on the fingerprint landmarks alone may not be very successful due to lack of availability of such information in many fingerprint images and to the difficulty in extracting the landmark information from the noisy fingerprint images. As a result, a successful approach needs to (1) supplement the orientation field information with ridge information; (2) use fingerprint landmark information when available, but devise alternative schemes when such information cannot be extracted from the input fingerprint images; and (3) use structural/syntactic pattern recognition methods in addition to statistical methods. We summarize a method of classification[10] that takes into consideration the above-mentioned design criteria that has been tested on a large database of realistic fingerprints to classify fingers into five major categories: right loop, left loop, arch, tented arch, and whorl*.

The orientation field determined from the input image may not be very accurate and the extracted ridges may contain many artifacts and, therefore, cannot be directly used for fingerprint classification. A ridge verification stage assesses the reliability of the extracted ridges based on the length of each connected ridge segment and its alignment with other adjacent ridges. Parallel adjacent subsegments typically indicate a good-quality fingerprint region; the ridge/orientation estimates in these regions are used to refine the estimates in the orientation field/ridge map.

---

* Other types of prints (e.g., twin-loop) are not considered here but, in principle, could be lumped into "other" or "reject" category.

1. *Singular points.* The Poincare index[46] computed from the orientation field is used to determine the number of delta (N_d) and core (N_c) points in the fingerprint. A digital closed curve, ψ, about 25 pixels long, around each pixel is used to compute the Poincare index as defined below.

   Given a fingerprint orientation field, the Poincare index at a pixel (i, j) is the integration (summation) of all differences in orientations of successive pixels along a square shaped curve centered around pixel (i, j). The Poincare index at most of the pixels in a fingerprint image is equal to zero and these points are called non-singular points. The pixels with non-zero Poincare index always take a value of $1/2$ or $-1/2$ and are called singular points. The Poincare index of a core-shaped singular point has a value of $1/2$, and the Poincare index of a delta-shaped singular point has a value of $-1/2$.

   The size of the square used for computing the Poincare index is crucial for the performance of a singular point detection algorithm. If it is too small, then a small perturbation of orientations may result in spurious singular points being detected. On the other hand, if it is too large, then a true pair of core and delta which are close to one another can be ignored because the Poincare index of a digital curve that includes an equal number of cores and deltas is 0. For a 512-dpi fingerprint image, for example, a square curve with a length of 25 pixels can be used for computation of the Poincare index. The results of the Poincare index cannot be directly used to obtain core/delta point locations and may need some post-processing.[10]

2. *Symmetry.* The feature extraction stage also estimates an axis that is locally symmetric to the ridge structures at the core and computes (1) α, the angle between the symmetry axis and the line segment joining core and delta, (2) β, the average angle difference between the ridge orientation and the orientation of the line segment joining the core and delta, and (3) γ, the number of ridges crossing the line segment joining core and delta. The relative position, R, of delta with respect to the symmetry axis is determined as follows: R = 1 if the delta is on the right side of symmetry axis, R = 0 otherwise.

3. *Ridge structure.* The classifier not only uses the orientation information but also utilizes the structural information in the extracted ridges. This feature summarizes the overall nature of the ridge flow in the fingerprint. In particular, it classifies each ridge of the fingerprint into three categories:
   - Non-recurring ridges: the ridges that do not curve very much
   - Type-1 recurring ridges: ridges that curve approximately π
   - Type-2 fully recurring ridges: ridges that curve by more than π

The classification algorithm summarized here (see Figure 8.12) essentially devises a sequence of tests for determining the class of a fingerprint

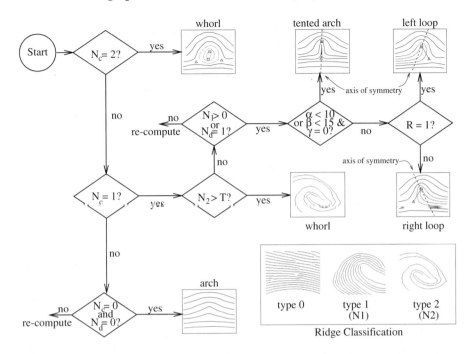

Figure 8.12 Flowchart of fingerprint classification algorithm. Inset also illustrates ridge classification. The "re-compute" option involves starting the classification algorithm with a different preprocessing (e.g., smoothing) of the image. (From Hong, L., Automatic Personal Identification Using Fingerprints, Ph.D. thesis, Michigan State University, 1998. With permission. Jain, A.K. and Pankanti, S. Fingerprint classification and matching, in A. Bovik, Ed., *Handbook for Image and Video Processing*, ©Academic Press, April 2000. With permission.)

and conducts simpler tests near the root of the decision tree. For example, two core points are typically detected for a whorl (see Figure 8.12, which is an easier condition to verify than detecting the number of Type-2 recurring ridges.) Another highlight of the algorithm is that if it cannot detect the salient characteristics of any category from the features extracted in a fingerprint, it re-computes the features with a different pre-processing method. For example, in the current implementation, the differential pre-processing consists of a different method/scale of smoothing the image. As can be observed from the flowchart, the algorithm detects (1) whorls based upon detection of either two core points or a sufficient number of Type 2-recurring ridges; (2) arch based upon the inability to detect either delta or core points; (3) left (right) loops based on the characteristic tilt of the symmetric axis, detection of a core point, and detection of either a delta point or a sufficient number of Type-1 recurring ridges; and (4) tented arch based on the presence of a relatively upright symmetric axis, detection of a core point, and detection of either a delta point or a sufficient number of Type-1 recurring ridges.

Table 8.2   Five-Class Classification Results on the NIST-4 Database; A = Arch, T = Tented Arch, L = Left Loop, R = Right Loop, W = Whorl

True Class	Assigned Class				
	A	T	L	R	W
A	**885**	13	10	11	0
T	179	**384**	54	14	5
L	31	27	**755**	3	20
R	30	47	3	**717**	16
W	6	1	15	15	**759**

From Jain, A.K. and Pankanti, S. Fingerprint classification and matching, in A. Bovik, Ed., *Handbook for Image and Video Processing,* ©Academic Press, April 2000. With permission.

Table 8.2 shows the results of the fingerprint classification algorithm on the NIST-4 database which contains 4000 images (image size is 512 × 480) taken from 2000 different fingers, 2 images per finger. Five fingerprint classes are defined: (1) arch, (2) tented arch, (3) left loop, (4) right loop, and (5) whorl. Fingerprints in this database are uniformly distributed among these five classes (800 per class). The five-class error rate in classifying these 4000 fingerprints is 12.5%. The confusion matrix is given in Table 8.2; numbers shown in bold font are correct classifications. Because a number of fingerprints in the NIST-4 database are labeled as belonging to possibly more than one class, each row of the confusion matrix in Table 8.2 does not sum up to 800. For the five-class problem, most of the classification errors are due to misclassifying a tented arch as an arch. By combining these two categories into a single class, the four-class error rate drops from 12.5% to 7.7%. In addition to the tented arch-arch errors, the errors primarily result from misclassifications between arch/tented arch and loops and from poor image quality.

Fingerprint Matching

Given two (test and template) representations, the matching module determines whether the prints are impressions of the same finger. The matching phase typically defines a metric of the similarity between two fingerprint representations. It also defines a threshold to decide whether or not a given pair of representations belongs to the same finger (mated pair).

Only in the highly constrained systems (see, for example, Reference 41) and situations could one assume that the test and template fingerprints depict the same portion of the finger and that both are aligned (in terms of displacement from the origin of the imaging coordinate system and of their orientations) with each other. Thus, in typical situations, one needs to (either, implicitly or explicitly) align (or register) the fingerprints (or their representations) before deciding whether the prints are mated pairs. Further, there are two additional challenges involved in determining the correspondence between two aligned fingerprint representations (see Figure 8.13): (1) dirt/leftover smudges on the sensing device and the presence of scratches/cuts on the finger either introduce spurious minutiae or obliterate the genuine minutiae; and (2) variations in the area of finger being imaged and its pressure on the sensing device affect the number of genuine minutiae captured and introduce displacement of the minutiae from their "true" locations due to *elastic* distortion of the fingerprint skin. Such elastic distortions and feature extraction artifacts account for minutiae matching errors even after the prints are in the best possible alignment.

A typical strategy for fingerprint matching is to first align the fingerprint representations and then examine the prints for *corresponding* structures in the aligned representations. Because solutions to both the problems (alignment and correspondence) are interrelated, they are (implicitly) solved simultaneously.

A number of strategies have been employed in the literature to solve the alignment problem. Typically, it is assumed that the alignment of the test and template fingerprints involves an overall displacement (translation) and rotation. The scale variations, shear transformations, and local elastic deformations are often overlooked in the alignment stage. In image-based representations, the alignment of the prints can be obtained by optimizing their image correlation. In ridge representations of the fingerprints, portions of ridges can be used to align the prints.[9] In minutiae-based representations, the alignment process typically uses predominantly minutiae positions; minutiae angles are not significantly involved because they are vulnerable to image noise/distortion. Other supplementary information (e.g., connectivity, nearest neighboring minutiae, ridge count) can often participate in the alignment process. In minutiae-based alignment, a single minutia, pairs of minutiae, or triplets of minutiae have been used to hypothesize an alignment. In Reference 48, for example, all possible test and template minutiae pair correspondence possibilities are exhaustively considered; each hypothesized pairing votes for all feasible translations and rotations. In Reference 51, an input minutia triplet votes for a feasible transformation to congruent template triplet. The transformation receiving the maximum number of votes is deemed to be the best transformation.

Once the prints are aligned, the corresponding structures in the aligned representations provide the basis for computing the matching *score*. In image-based representation, the correlation coefficient generated during the alignment can serve as a matching score. The elastic deformation, shear transformation, and scale variations may impose severe limitations on the utility of image correlation and image-based representations. In an *elastic* minutia-based

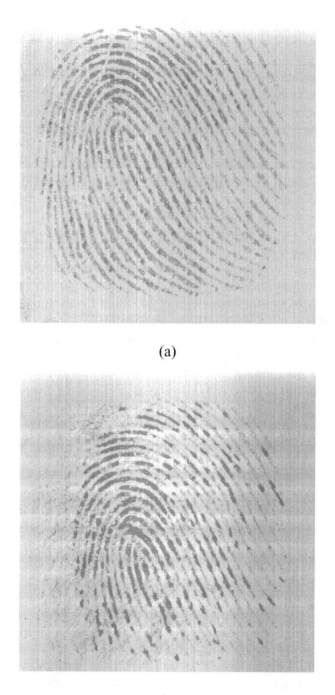

(a)

(b)

Figure 8.13 Two different impressions of the same finger. To know the correspondence between the minutiae of these two fingerprint images, all minutiae must be precisely localized and the deformations must be recovered.

Figure 8.14 Aligned ridge structures of mated pairs. Note that the best alignment in one part (center) of the image results in large displacements between the corresponding minutiae in the other regions (bottom right). (From Jain, A., Hong, L., Pankanti, S., and Bolle, R., On-line identity-authentication system using fingerprints, *Proc. IEEE (Special Issue on Automated Biometrics)*, 85(9), 1365–1388, September 1997.)

matching, the test minutiae are searched in a square region centered (bounding box) around each template minutia in the aligned representation. The elastic matchers account for small local elastic deformations.

Figure 8.14 illustrates a typical situation of aligned ridge structures of mated pairs. Note that the best alignment in one part (center) of the image can result in a large amount of displacement between the corresponding minutiae in the other regions (bottom right). In addition, observe that the distortion is nonlinear: given distortions at two arbitrary locations on the finger, it is not possible to predict the distortion at all the intervening points on the line joining the two points. Accommodating such large nonlinear distortions was the motivation underlying the design of the adaptive elastic string matching algorithm.[9]

The operation of the adaptive elastic string matching algorithm (string matcher, for short) is similar to an elastic matcher. As in an elastic matcher, the test minutiae are searched in the bounding box neighborhood of each template minutia. In the string matcher, however, the size of the bounding box around each template minutia, unlike in elastic matcher, is not constant. The bounding box size is adjusted based on the estimate of the local deformation; the estimate of the local deformation is derived from the bounding boxes of the already matched minutia in the neighborhood of the current template minutiae.

The string matcher first selects a pair of corresponding minutiae in test and template representations based on information associated with an adjoining portion of ridge; the minutiae sets in this pair of minutiae are called the reference test and reference template minutiae. The string matcher uses three attributes of the aligned minutiae for matching: its distance from the reference minutiae (radius), angle subtended to the reference minutiae (radial angle), and local direction of the associated ridge (minutiae direction). The algorithm initiates the matching by first representing the aligned input (template) minutiae as an input (template) minutiae string. The string representation is obtained by imposing a linear ordering on the minutiae using radial angles and radii. The resulting input and template minutiae strings are matched using an inexact string matching algorithm to establish the correspondence.

The inexact string matching algorithm essentially transforms (edits) the input string to template string and the number of edit operations is used to define the (dis)similarity between the strings. While permitted edit operators model the fingerprint impression variations (deletion of the genuine minutiae, insertion of spurious minutiae, and perturbation of the minutiae), the penalty associated with each edit operator reflects the likelihood of that edit operation. The sum of penalties of all the edits (edit distance) defines the similarity between the input and template minutiae strings. Among several possible sets of edits that permit the transformation of the input minutiae string into the reference minutiae string, the string matching algorithm chooses the transform associated with the minimum cost using dynamic programming.

The algorithm tentatively considers a candidate (aligned) input and a candidate template minutiae to be a mismatch if their attributes are not within a tolerance window (see Figure 8.15) and penalizes them for the deletion/insertion edit operation. If the attributes are within the tolerance window, the amount of penalty associated with the tentative match is proportional to the disparity in the values of the attributes in the minutiae. The algorithm accommodates for the elastic distortion by adaptively adjusting the parameters of the tolerance window based on the most recent successful tentative match. The tentative matches (and correspondences) are accepted if the edit distance for those correspondences is smaller than any other correspondences.

There are several approaches to converting minutia correspondence information to a matching *score*. One straightforward approach for computing the score S is

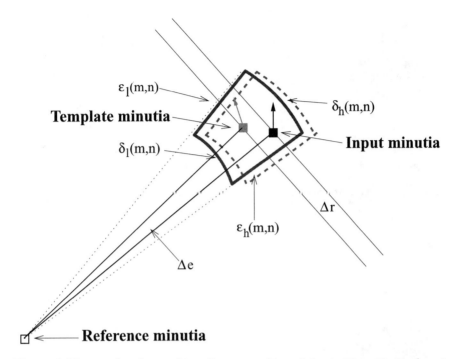

Figure 8.15 Bounding box and its adjustment. (From Jain, A., Hong, L., Pankanti, S., and Bolle, R., *Proc. IEEE (Special Issue on Automated Biometrics)*, 85(9), 1365–1388, ©IEEE, September 1997.)

$$S = \frac{100 M_{PQ} M_{PQ}}{M_P M_Q} \tag{8.1}$$

where M_{PQ} is the number of corresponding minutiae, and M_P and M_Q are the total number of minutiae in template and test fingerprints, respectively. In some matchers, the total number of minutiae [M_P and M_Q in Equation (8.1)] is not used. After the correspondence is determined, an *overall* bounding box only for corresponding test and template minutiae is computed. The matching score S_B is then computed as:

$$S_B = \frac{100 M_{PQ} M_{PQ}}{M_{Pb} M_{Qb}} \tag{8.2}$$

where M_{PQ} is the number of corresponding minutiae, and M_{Pb} and M_{Qb} are the number of minutiae in the overall bounding boxes computed for template and test fingerprints, respectively. Often, different normalizations are used

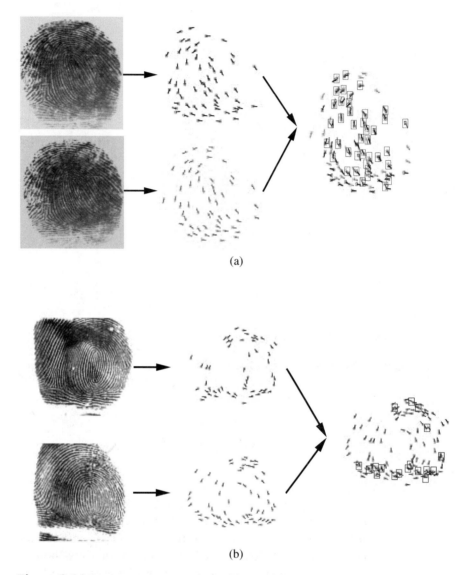

Figure 8.16 Fingerprinting matching: (a) Matching two impressions of the same finger, matching score = 49; (b) matching fingerprints from two different fingers, matching score = 4.

for different counts of the total number of minutiae. The matching score when matching two impressions of the same finger is expected to be higher than when matching two fingerprints from different fingers (Figure 8.16).

Due to space limitations, other important classes of fingerprint matchers based on topological (ridge connectivity) information are not included here; however, readers are referred to the literature[53,54] for related information.

Fingerprint Enhancement

The performance of a fingerprint feature extraction and image matching algorithm relies critically on the quality of the input fingerprint images. The ridge structures in poor-quality fingerprint images are not always well defined, and hence cannot be correctly detected. This leads to the following problems: (1) a significant number of spurious minutiae may be created, (2) a large percentage of genuine minutiae may be ignored, and (3) large errors in minutiae localization (position and orientation) may be introduced. To ensure that the performance of the minutiae extraction algorithm will be robust with respect to the quality of fingerprint images, an enhancement algorithm that can improve the clarity of the ridge structures is necessary. Traditionally, forensic applications have been the biggest end users of fingerprint enhancement algorithms because the important ridge details are frequently obliterated in the latent fingerprints lifted from a crime scene. Over-inking, under-inking, imperfect friction skin contact, fingerprint smudges left from previous live-scan acquisitions, adverse imaging conditions, and improper imaging geometry/optics are some of the systematic reasons for poor-quality fingerprint images. It is widely acknowledged that at least 2 to 5% of the target population have poor-quality fingerprints: fingerprints that cannot be reliably processed using automatic image processing methods. We suspect this fraction is even higher in reality when the target population consists of (1) older people, (2) people who suffer routine finger injuries in their occupation, (3) people living in dry weather conditions or having skin problems, and (4) people who have poor fingerprints due to genetic attributes. With the increasing demand for cheaper and more compact fingerprint scanners, fingerprint verification software cannot afford the luxury of assuming good-quality fingerprints obtained from the optical scanner. The cheaper and more compact semiconductor sensors not only offer smaller scan area but also typically poor-quality fingerprints.

Fingerprint enhancement approaches[55-58] often employ frequency domain techniques[56,58,59] and are computationally demanding. In a small local neighborhood, the ridges and furrows approximately form a two-dimensional sinusoidal wave along the direction orthogonal to local ridge orientation. Thus, the ridges and furrows in a small local neighborhood have well-defined local frequency and orientation properties. The common approaches employ bandpass filters that model the frequency domain characteristics of a good-quality fingerprint image. The poor-quality fingerprint image is processed using the filter to block the extraneous noise and pass the fingerprint signal. Some methods can estimate the orientation and/or frequency of ridges in each block in the fingerprint image and adaptively tune the filter characteristics to match the ridge characteristics.

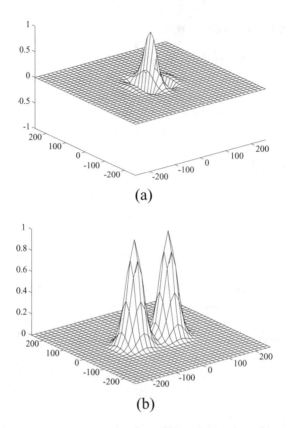

Figure 8.17 An even-symmetric Gabor filter: (a) Gabor filter tuned to 60 cycles/width and 0° orientation; (b) corresponding modulation transfer function (MTF). (From Hong, L., Automatic Personal Identification Using Fingerprints, Ph.D. thesis, 1998.)

One typical variation of this theme segments the image into non-overlapping square blocks of width larger than the average inter-ridge distance. Using a bank of directional bandpass filters, each filter generating a strong response indicates the dominant direction of the ridge flow in the finger in the given block. The resulting orientation information is more accurate, leading to more reliable features. A single block direction can never truly represent the directions of all the ridges in the block and may consequently introduce filter artifacts. One common directional filter used for fingerprint enhancement is the Gabor filter.[60] Gabor filters (see Figure 8.17) have both frequency-selective and orientation-selective properties. For example, a properly tuned Gabor filter will pass only fingerprint ridges of certain spatial frequency flowing in a certain specific direction. Typically, in a 500 dpi, 512 × 512 fingerprint image, a Gabor filter with $u_0 = 60$ cycles per image width (height), the radial bandwidth of 2.5 octaves, and orientation θ models the fingerprint ridges flowing in the direction $\theta + \pi/2$.

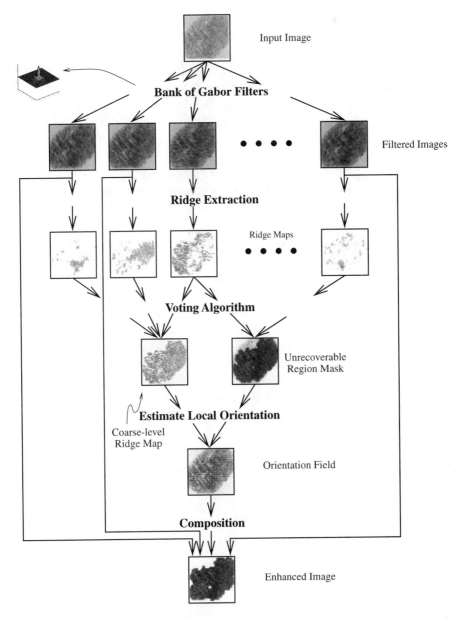

Figure 8.18 Fingerprint enhancement algorithm. (From Hong, L., Automatic Personal Identification Using Fingerprints, Ph.D. thesis, 1998. With permission. Jain, A.K. and Pankanti, S., *Handbook for Image and Video Processing*, Bovik, A., Ed., ©Academic Press, April 2000.)

A novel approach to fingerprint enhancement proposed by Hong et al.[10] (see Figure 8.18) is summarized here. It decomposes the given fingerprint image into several component images using a bank of directional Gabor bandpass filters and extracts ridges from each of the filtered bandpass images.[9] By integrating information from the sets of ridges extracted from filtered images, the enhancement algorithm infers the region of fingerprint where there is sufficient information available for enhancement (recoverable region) and estimates a coarse-level ridge map for the recoverable region. The information integration is based on the observation that genuine ridges in a region evoke a strong response in the feature images extracted from the filters oriented in the direction parallel to the ridge direction in that region and at most a weak response from the filters oriented in the direction orthogonal to the ridge direction in that region. The resulting coarse ridge map consists of the ridges extracted from each filtered image which are mutually consistent; portions of the image where the ridge information is consistent across the filtered images constitute *recoverable* regions. The orientation field estimated from the coarse ridge map is more reliable than the orientation estimation from the input fingerprint image. After the orientation field is obtained, the fingerprint image can then be adaptively enhanced using the local orientation information. Typically, given the local orientation θ at a pixel (x, y), the enhanced image pixel is chosen to be pixel (x, y) of the Gabor filter that has orientation θ. When Gabor filter with orientation θ is not available, the enhanced pixel (x, y) can be linearly interpolated from the two Gabor filters with orientations closest to θ. The interpolation is computationally efficient because the filtered images are already available during the previous stages of enhancement and it produces good results.

Examples of fingerprint image enhancement are shown in Figure 8.19. An example illustrating the results of the minutiae extraction algorithm on a noisy input image and its enhanced counterpart are shown in Figure 8.20. The improvement in matching performance by incorporating image enhancement module was evaluated using the fingerprint matcher described in the previous chapter section. Figure 8.21 shows the ROC curves for the matcher that were obtained with and without image enhancement module on a database consisting of 700 fingerprint images of 70 individuals (10 fingerprints per finger per individual). It is clear that the image enhancement has improved the performance of the matcher over this database.

Large-Scale Systems Issues

Typically, in a large-scale identification problem, given a fingerprint and a large database of fingerprints (e.g., millions), one would like to find out whether any one of the prints in the database matches the given fingerprint. A straightforward solution to this problem involves matching the given fingerprint with each fingerprint in the database. However, in this approach, the expected number of matches required to solve the identification problem increases linearly with the database size. It is therefore desirable to find more efficient solutions to the identification problem.

There have been two primary approaches to make the identification searches more efficient. In the first approach, the database is organized so that certain matches can be ruled out based on the information extrinsic/intrinsic to the fingerprints. When the number of necessary matches is reduced based on the information extrinsic to the fingerprints, the solution is commonly referred to as *filtering*. For example, the database can be presegmented based on information about sex, race, age, and other bio-/geographical information related to the individual. In *binning*, a fingerprint's intrinsic information (e.g., fingerprint class) is used to reduce the number of matches.[61]

The percentage of the total database to be scanned, on average, for each search is called the "penetration coefficient," P, which can be defined as the ratio of the expected number of comparisons required for a single input image to the total number of prints in the entire database. Based on published results, we believe that binning can achieve a penetration coefficient of about 50%. The second approach for making the search more efficient is to reduce the *effective* time given for each match. Given a matching algorithm, the effective time per match can be reduced by directly implementing the entire algorithm or components of it in special hardware. The other method of reducing the effective time per match is by parallelizing the matches, that is, using multiple processors and assigning a fraction of the matches to each processor. Some vendors have resorted to optical computing[41] to achieve a very high matching throughput.

Scalability of accuracy performance of a large-scale identification system is a more formidable challenge than its speed performance. If the accuracy performance associated with matching each pair of fingerprints (e.g., verification accuracy) is characterized by false accept (FAR_v) and false reject (FRR_v) rates, the identification accuracy performance of the system with n records in the database (one per identity) can then be expressed as:

$$FRR_i = FRR_v \times FCR \qquad (8.3)$$

$$FAR_i = 1 - \left(1 - FAR_v\right)^{n \times P} \qquad (8.4)$$

under the underlying assumptions that (1) the outcome of each match is an independent event, (2) all the records in the database are correctly classified, (3) FCR is the probability of falsely classifying (binning) the given fingerprint into a wrong bin, and (4) the misclassification and mismatching events are independent.

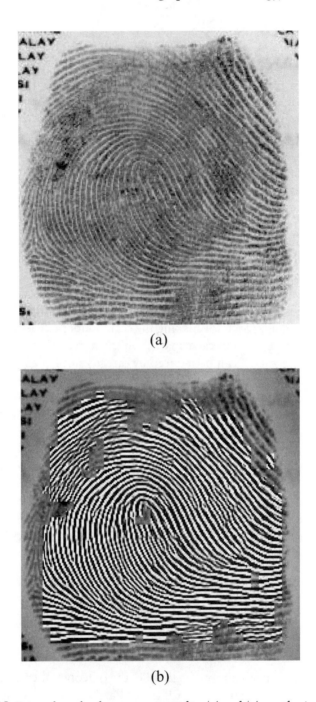

(a)

(b)

Figure 8.19 Examples of enhancement results: (a) and (c) are the input images; (b) and (d) show enhanced recoverable regions superimposed on the corresponding input images.

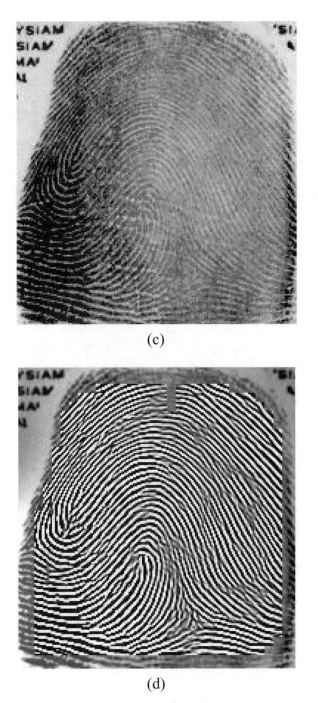

(c)

(d)

Figure 8.19 (continued)

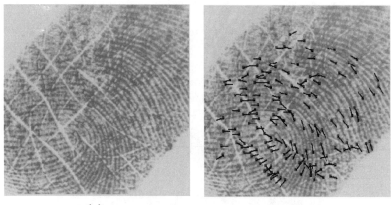

(a)   (b)

(c)

Figure 8.20 Fingerprint enhancement results: (a) a poor-quality fingerprint; (b) minutia extracted without image enhancement; and (c) minutiae extracted after image enhancement. (From Hong, L., Automatic Personal Identification Using Fingerprints, Ph.D. thesis, 1998).

A significant implication of the above accuracy equations is that the false accept rates of the identification deteriorate as a function of the size of the database (see Figure 8.22). Consequently, an effective identification system requires a very accurate matcher.

System Evaluation

Given a fingerprint matcher, one would like to assess its accuracy and speed performance in a realistic setting. This chapter section primarily deals with accuracy performance evaluation issues.

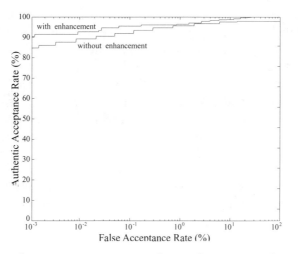

Figure 8.21 Performance improvement due to fingerprint enhancement algorithm. (From Hong, L., Automatic Personal Identification Using Fingerprints, Ph.D. thesis, 1998.)

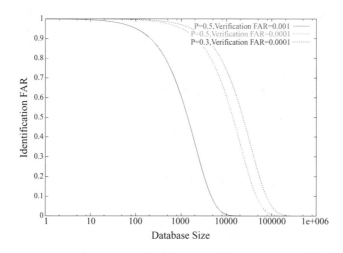

Figure 8.22 False acceptance error rates of verification (matcher) and identification systems. For example, a matcher that can match with a false acceptance error rate (FAR) of 10^{-4} and a classifier with a penetration ratio (P) of 0.5 could *typically* result in an *identification* system (database population of 14,000 distinct fingers, 1 finger per individual) with a false acceptance error rate of approximately 0.5. That is, the likelihood of the system determining a match from an arbitrary input fingerprint matching one of the 14,000 (actually, only half of them because of the classifier penetration ratio) fingerprints is 0.5.

Given two fingerprints, a decision made by a fingerprint identification system is either a "match" or a "no-match." For each type of decision, there are two possibilities: either the decision reflects the true state of the nature or otherwise. Therefore, there are a total of four possible outcomes: (1) a genuine (mated) fingerprint pair is accepted as a "match," (2) a genuine fingerprint mated pair is rejected as "non-match," (3) a non-mated fingerprint pair (also called an impostor) is rejected as a "non-match," and (4) an impostor is accepted as a "match" by the system. Outcomes (1) and (3) are correct, whereas (2) and (4) are incorrect. Thus, probabilities of a matcher committing false accept (or false match) and false reject (false non-match) errors are two necessary components to characterize the accuracy performance of a system. Note that false accept and false reject error rates are related to each other through the score threshold parameter determined by the system operating point. Further, it is widely acknowledged[62] that false accept/reject error rates at a single operating point do not provide sufficient information for system accuracy performance characterization; it is recommended that a curve, called ROC, describing the false accept/reject error rates at all possible score thresholds be plotted for a comprehensive perspective of the system accuracy, and this information provides a useful basis for system evaluation and comparison.

To generate an ROC, a set of mated fingerprint pairs (e.g., a sample of genuine distribution) and a set of non-matching fingerprint pairs (e.g., a sample of impostor distribution) is necessary. The matcher scores resulting from mated fingerprint pairs are used to generate the genuine score probability distribution, and the scores from non-mated fingerprint pairs are used to generate the impostor score probability distribution. Given a threshold score T, impostor scores larger than T contribute to the false accept error and the corresponding area under the impostor distribution curve quantifies the false accept error at that threshold (see Figure 8.23). Similarly, genuine scores smaller than T contribute to the false reject error and the corresponding area under the genuine distribution quantifies the false reject error at that threshold.

For any performance metric to be able to precisely generalize to the entire population of interest, the test data should (1) be representative of the population and (2) contain enough samples from each category of the population. The samples are collected so that the method of sensing and the method of presentation of the finger closely correspond to those in the real situations. Fingerprint images collected in a very controlled and non-realistic environment provide overly optimistic results that do not generalize well in practice. Typically, the collected database has a significant number of non-mated pairs but lacks a sufficient number of mated paired samples. Further, the collection of two fingerprint impressions comprising a sample mated pair should be separated by a sufficient time period. Different applications, depending on whether the subjects are cooperative, and habituated, whether the target population is benevolent or subversive, may require a completely different

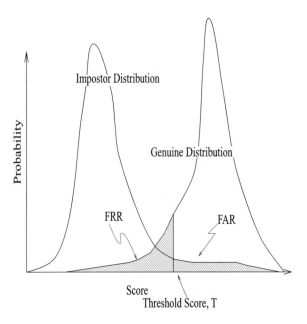

Figure 8.23 Probability distributions of matcher scores from genuine mated and impostor fingerprint pairs. FRR and FAR denote the false reject and false accept error rates, respectively.

sample set. Finally, the system may have to be tuned to peculiarities of the sample data (without overtuning it to arrive at optimistic error rate estimates). Techniques such as data sequestering[63] may be necessary to avoid overtuning the system.

In principle, one can use the false (impostor) acceptance rate (FAR), the false (genuine individual) reject rate (FRR) at a single operating point, and the equal error rate (EER)* to indicate the identification accuracy of a biometric system.[64,65] In practice, these performance metrics can only be estimated from empirical data and the estimates of the performance are dependent on the fingerprint database used in the experiments. Therefore, they are meaningful only for a specific database in a specific test environment. For example, the performance of a biometric system as claimed by its manufacturer had an FRR of 0.3% and an FAR of 0.1%. An independent test by the Sandia National Laboratory found that the same system had an FRR of 25% with an unknown FAR.[66] To provide a more reliable assessment of a biometric system, some more descriptive measures of performance are necessary. Receiver operating characteristic curve (ROC) is one such descriptive measure of performance (see Figure 8.21).

---

* Equal error rate is defined as the error rate value where FAR and FRR are equal.

Conclusions and Future Prospects

Fingerprint-based personal identification is an important biometric technique with many current and emerging applications. This chapter has provided an overveiw of fingerprint-based personal identification, including an outline of some of the important issues involved in the design of fingerprint-based identification systems and algorithms for fingerprint feature extraction, enhancement, matching, and classification. A brief summary of the performance of these algorithms was also provided, in addition to a discussion of issues related to fingerprint representation, fingerprint identification system architecture, and performance evaluation.

Fingerprint-based identification has come a long way since its inception more than 100 years ago. The first primitive scanners designed by Cornell Aeronautical Lab/North American Aviation Inc. were unweildy beasts with many problems as compared to sleek, inexpensive, and relatively miniscule semiconductor sensors. Over the past few decades, research and active use of fingerprint matching and indexing have also advanced our understanding of individuality information in fingerprints and efficient ways of processing this information. Increasingly inexpensive computing power, cheap fingerprint sensors, and the demand for security/efficiency/convenience have led to the viability of fingerprint matching information for everyday positive person identification in recent years.

There is a popular misconception that automatic fingerprint matching is a fully solved problem because it was one of the first applications of automatic pattern recognition. Despite notions to the contrary, there are a number of challenges that remain to be overcome in designing a completely automatic and reliable fingerprint matcher, especially when images are of poor quality as in the case of latent prints. Although automatic systems are successful, the level of sophistication of automatic systems in matching fingerprints today cannot rival that of a dedicated, well-trained fingerprint expert. Still, automatic fingerprint matching systems offer a reliable, rapid, consistent, and cost-effective solution in a number of traditional and newly emerging applications. The performance of various stages of an identification system, including feature extraction, classification, and minutiae matching, do not degrade gracefully with a deterioration in the quality of the fingerprints. Most of these deficiencies in the existing automatic identification systems are overcome by having an expert interact with the system to compensate for the intermediate errors. As mentioned, significant research appears to be necessary to enable us to develop feature extraction systems that can reliably and consistently extract a diverse set of features that provide rich information comparable to those commonly used by the fingerprint experts.

In most pattern recognition applications (e.g., OCR), the best-performing commercial systems use a combination of matchers, matching strategies, and representations. There is limited work being done in combining multiple fingerprint matchers;[67,68] more research/evaluation of such techniques is needed. The proprietary set of features used by the system vendors and a lack of a meaningful information exchange standard makes it difficult — if not impossible — for law enforcement agencies to leverage the complementary strengths of different commercial systems. Multi-modal (e.g., multiple biometrics) systems provably deliver better performance than any single constituent biometric.[69] The lack of standardization also poses challenges in integrating different biometrics (e.g., face and finger,[70] finger and speech[71]) in the context of forensic identification systems.

On a more speculative note, perhaps, using human intuition-based manual fingerprint identification systems may not be the most appropriate basis for the design of automatic fingerprint identification systems; there may be a need for exploring radically different features[40,52] rich in discriminatory information, radically different methods of fingerprint matching,[51] and more ingenious methods for combining fingerprint matching and classification that are amenable to automation.

Only a few years ago it seemed as if the interest in fingerprint matching research was waning. As mentioned, due to increasing identity fraud in our society, there is a growing need for positive person identification. Cheap fingerprint sensors, the easy availability of inexpensive computing power, and our (relatively better) understanding of individuality information in fingerprints (compared to other biometrics) have attracted significant commercial interest in fingerprint-based personal identification. Consequently, dozens of fingerprint identification vendors have mushroomed in the past few years. Pervasive embedded applications of fingerprint-based identification (e.g., in a smart card or in a cell phone) may not be far behind. The authors strongly believe that higher visibility of (and liability from) performance limitations of commercial fingerprint identification applications will fuel a much stronger research interest in some of the most difficult research problems in fingerprint based identification. Some of these difficult problems will entail solving not only the hard core pattern recognition challenges, but also confronting the very challenging system engineering issues related to security and privacy.

Acknowledgments

We are grateful to Prof. Jay Siegel, Department of Criminal Justice, Michigan State University, for his detailed comments and editorial suggestions. Thanks also to Chris Brislawn, Los Alamos National Laboratory, for sharing

WSQ-related illustrations (Figure 8.3). We appreciate the help of Lin Hong, Salil Prabhakar, Arun Ross, and Dan Gutchess in preparing this manuscript.

References

1. H.T.F. Rhodes. *Alphonse Bertillon: Father of Scientific Detection.* Abelard-Schuman, New York, 1956.

2. Federal Bureau of Investigation. *The Science of Fingerprints: Classification and Uses.* U.S. Government Printing Office, Washington, D.C., 1984.

3. A. Jain, R. Bolle, and S. Pankanti. *Biometrics: Personal Identification in Networked Society.* Kluwer, Massachusettes, December 1999.

4. S. Collins. *CNN Quick Poll, Trading PINS for Body Parts, August 18.* http://www.cnn.com/2000/TECH/computing/08/18/biometrics/index.html, 2000.

5. B. Schneier. Inside risks: the uses and abuses of biometrics. *Commun. ACM,* 42(8):136, Aug 1999.

6. J.D. Woodward. Biometrics: Privacy's foe or privacy's friend? *Proc. IEEE (Special Issue on Automated Biometrics),* 85(9), 1480–1492, September 1997.

7. J.L. Wayman. Federal biometric technology legislation. *Special Issue on Biometrics, IEEE Computer Magazine,* 33(2), 76–80, Feb. 2000.

8. A.K. Jain, L. Hong, and S. Pankanti. Biometric identification. *Commun. ACM,* 91–98, Feb. 2000.

9. A. Jain, L. Hong, S. Pankanti, and R. Bolle. On-line identity-authentication system using fingerprints. *Proc. IEEE (Special Issue on Automated Biometrics),* 85(9), 1365–1388, September 1997.

10. L. Hong. Automatic Personal Identification Using Fingerprints. Ph.D. thesis, Michigan State University, 1998.

11. C.M. Brislawn. WSQ/FAQ homepage. ftp://www.c3.lanl.gov/pub/misc/WSQ/FBI_WSQ_FAQ.

12. M.M.S. Chong, R.K.L. Gray, H.N. Tan, and J. Liu. Automatic representation of fingerprints for data compression by B-spline functions. *Pattern Recognition,* 25(10), 1199–1210, October 1992.

13. JPEG Committee. JPEG Homepage. http://www.jpeg.org/public/jpeghomepage.htm.

14. C.M. Brislawn. The FBI Fingerprint Image Compression Standard. http://www.c3.lanl.gov/brislawn/FBI/FBI.html.

15. A.K. Jain and S. Pankanti. Fingerprint classification and matching. In A. Bovik, Ed., *Handbook for Image and Video Processing.* Academic Press, April 2000.

16. A. Moenssens. *Fingerprint Techniques.* Chilton Book Company, London, 1971.

17. M. Hartman. Compact fingerprint scanner techniques. In *Proc. Biometric Consortium, Ninth Meeting.* June 11–12, San Jose, CA, 1996.

18. M. Hase and A. Shimisu. Entry method of fingerprint image using a prism. *Trans. Inst. Electron. Commun. Eng. Japan*, J67-D, 627–628, 1984.

19. F. Karen. Encryption, smart cards, and fingerprint readers. *IEEE Spectrum*, 26(8), 22, 1989.

20. J. Schneider. Improved image quality of live scan fingerprint scanners using acoustic backscatter measurements. In *Proc. Biometric Consortium, Ninth Meeting*, June 11–12, San Jose, CA, 1996.

21. Ultra-Scan. Ultra-Scan Homepage. http://www.ultra-scan.com/, 2000.

22. W. Bicz, D. Banasiak, P. Bruciak, Z. Gumienny, S. Gumulinski, D. Kosz, A. Krysiak, W. Kuczynski, M. Pluta, and G. Rabiej. Fingerprint Structure Imaging Based on an Ultra-Sound Camera. http://www.optel.com.pl/article.htm, 2000.

23. *Edge Lit Hologram for Live-scan Fingerprinting*. http://www.ImEdge.com/, 1997.

24. Y. Fumio, I. Seigo, and E. Shin. Real-time fingerprint sensor using a hologram. *Appl. Optics*, 31(11), 1794, 1992.

25. I. Seigo, E. Shin, and S. Takashi. Holographic fingerprint sensor. *Fujitsu Scientific & Technical J.*, 25(4), 287, 1989.

26. J. Klett. Thermal imaging fingerprint technology. In *Proc. Biometric Consortium, Ninth Meeting*, April 8–9, Crystal City, VA, 1997.

27. C.S.F. Thomson. Thomson CSF Homepage. http://www.tcs.thomson-csf.com/Us/standard/finger.htm, 1998.

28. N.D. Young, G. Harkin, R.M. Bunn, D.J. McCulloch, R.W. Wilks, and A.G. Knapp. Novel fingerprint scanning arrays using polysilicon TFT's on glass and polymer substrates. *IEEE Electron Device Lett.*, 18(1), 19–20, Jan. 1997.

29. K. McCalley, D. Setlak, S. Wilson, and J. Schmitt. A direct fingerprint reader. In *Proc. CardTech SecurTech, Vol. I. Technology*, May 13–16, Atlanta, GA, 1996, 271–279.

30. Harris Semiconductor. Harris Semiconductor Homepage. http://www.semi.harris.com/fngrloc/index.htm, 1998.

31. Veridicom. Veridicom Homepage. http://www.veridicom.com/.

32. Biometrics Partners. Biometric Partners Homepage. http://www.biometric-partners.com/, 2000.

33. F.R. Livingstone, L. King, J.-A. Beraldin, and M. Rioux. Development of a real-time laser scanning system for object recognition, inspection, and robust control. In *Proc. SPIE on Telemanipulator Technology and Space Telerobotics*, Volume 2057, 7–9 September, Boston, MA, 1993, 454–461.

34. Digital Biometrics. Digital Biometrics Homepage. http://www.digitalbiometrics.com/.

35. Sagem Morpho. Sagem Morpho Homepage. http://www.morpho.com.

36. A. Roddy and J. Stosz. Fingerprint features — statistical analysis and system performance estimates. *Proc. IEEE*, 85(9), 1390–1421, 1997.

37. Siemens. The ID Mouse from Siemens. http://www.fingertip.de/.

38. American National Standard for Information Systems. Data Format for the Interchange of Fingerprint Information, Doc#ANSI/NIST-CSL 1-1993, Appendices F and G. ftp://ard.fbi.gov/pub/IQS/spec/. America National Standards Institute, New York, 1993.

39. Criminal Justice Information Services. Interim IAFIS Image Quality Specifications for Scanners. www.engr.sjsu.edu/biometrics/publications_appendixg.html.

40. A.K. Jain, S. Prabhakar, L. Hong, and S. Pankanti. Filterbank-based fingerprint matching. *IEEE Trans. Image Processing*, 9(5), 846–859, May 2000.

41. Access Control Applications Using Optical Computing. http://www.mytec.com/, 1997.

42. American National Standard for Information Systems. Data Format for the Interchange of Fingerprint Information, doc#ansi/nist-csl itl 2000, NIST special report 500, 245, 2000.

43. E. German. Problem Idents. Facial and scar mark and tattoo (SMT) http://onin.com/fp/problemidents.html.

44. R.M. Bolle, S. Pankanti, and Y.-S. Yao. System and Method for Determining the Quality of Fingerprint Images, U.S. Patent No. 5,963,656, 1999.

45. R.M. Bolle, S.E. Colville, and S. Pankanti. System and Method for Determining Ridge Counts in Fingerprint Image Processing. U.S. Patent No. 6,111,978, 2000.

46. M. Kawagoe and A. Tojo. Fingerprint pattern classification. *Pattern Recognition*, 17(3), 295–303, 1984.

47. B.M. Mehtre and B. Chatterjee. Segmentation of fingerprint images — a composite method. *Pattern Recognition*, 22(4), 381–385, 1989.

48. S. Chen, N. Ratha, K. Karu, and A.K. Jain. A real-time matching system for large fingerprint database. *IEEE Trans. Pattern Anal. and Machine Intell.*, 18(8), 799–813, 1996.

49. T. Pavlidis. *Algorithms for Graphics and Image Processing*. Computer Science Press. 1982.

50. G.T. Candela, P.J. Grother, C.I. Watson, R.A. Wilkinson, and C.L. Wilson. PCASYS: A Pattern-Level Classification Automation System for Fingerprints. NIST-Tech. Report NISTIR 5647, August 1995.

51. R. Germain, A. Califano, and S. Colville. Fingerprint matching using transformation parameter clustering. *IEEE Computational Science and Engineering*, 4(4), 42–49, 1997.

52. A.K. Jain, S. Prabhakar, and L. Hong. A multichannel approach to fingerprint classification. *IEEE Trans. Pattern Anal. and Machine Intell.*, 21(4), 348–359, April 1999.

53. M. Sparrow and P. Sparrow. *A Topological Approach to the Matching of Single Fingerprints: Development of Algorithms for Use on Latent Fingermarks,* U.S. Government Publication. Gaithersburg, MD: U.S. Dept. of Commerce, National Bureau of Standards, Washington, D.C., 1985.

54. J.H. Wegstein. An Automated Fingerprint Identification System. Technical Report 500-89, National Bureau of Standards, 1982.

55. L. O'Gorman and J.V. Nickerson. An approach to fingerprint filter design. *Pattern Recognition,* 22(1), 29–38, 1989.

56. T. Kamei and M. Mizoguchi. Image filter design for fingerprint enhancement. In *Proc. ISCV '95,* Coral Gables, FL, 1995, 109–114.

57. D.C. Huang. Enhancement and feature purification of fingerprint images. *Pattern Recognition,* 26(11), 1661–1671, 1993.

58. L. Coetzee and E. Botha. Fingerprint recognition in low quality images. *Pattern Recognition,* 26(10), 1441–1460, 1993.

59. L. Hong, A.K. Jain, S. Pankanti, and R. Bolle. Fingerprint enhancement. In *Proc. 1st IEEE WACV,* Sarasota, FL, 1996, 202–207.

60. A.K. Jain and F. Farrokhnia. Unsupervised texture segmentation using Gabor filters. *Pattern Recognition,* 24, 1167–1186, 1991.

61. J.L. Wayman. Fundamentals of Biometric Technology. http://www.engr.sjsu.edu/biometrics/publications.html.

62. UK Govt. Biometrics Working Group. Best Practices in Testing and Reporting Biometric Device Performance, version 1.0. http://www.afb.org.uk/bwg/bestprac10.pdf, March 2000.

63. P.J. Phillips, H. Moon, S.A. Rizvi, and P.J. Rauss. The FERET evaluation methodology for face recognition algorithms. *IEEE Trans. on Pattern Anal. Mach. Intell.,* 22(10), 1090–1104, 2000.

64. J.G. Daugman. High confidence visual recognition of persons by a test of statistical independence. *IEEE Trans. on Pattern Anal. Mach. Intell.,* 15(11), 1148–1161, 1993.

65. J.G. Daugman and G.O. Williams. A proposed standard for biometric decidability. In *Proc. CardTech/SecureTech Conf.,* Atlanta, GA, 1996, 223–234.

66. J. Campbell Jr., L. Alyea, and J. Dunn. Biometric Security: Government Applications and Operations. http://www.biometrics.org/REPORTS/CTSTG96/index.html, 1996.

67. A.K. Jain, S. Prabhakar, and S. Chen. Combining multiple matchers for a high security fingerprint verification system. *Pattern Recognition Lett.,* 20(11–13), 1371–1379, 1999.

68. S. Prabhakar and A.K. Jain. Devision-level fusion in biometric verification. To appear in *Pattern Recognition,* 2001.

69. L. Hong, A. Jain, and S. Pankanti. Can multibiometrics improve performance? In *Proc. AutoID'99*, Summit, NJ, October 1999, 59–64.

70. L. Hong and A. Jain. Integrating faces and fingerprints. *IEEE Trans. Pattern Anal. Mach. Intell.*, 20(12), 1295–1307, December 1998.

71. A.K. Jain, L. Hong, and Y. Kulkarni. A multimodal biometric system using fingerprints, face and speech. In *Proc. of 2nd Int. Conf. on Audio- and Video-based Biometric Person Authentication*, Washington, D.C., March 22–24, 1999, 182–187.

Measurement of Fingerprint Individuality

9

DAVID A. STONEY

Contents

0-8493-0923-9/01/$0.00+$1.50
© 2001 by CRC Press LLC

Introduction

This chapter examines the underlying statistical basis for fingerprint comparisons and reviews the efforts that have been made to measure friction ridge variability as it relates to forensic comparison and identification of fingerprints.

This chapter does not consider the foundational information that supports the practice of fingerprint identification. That is, the chapter does not review the embryology, comparative anatomy, and genetics of friction ridge skin. These well-developed areas of study do contribute essential information that establishes the feasibility and utility of fingerprint identifications, but they do not provide criteria for concluding that two fingerprints were made by the same finger. Neither does the long-standing practice and effectiveness of fingerprint evidence provide such criteria.

This chapter is specifically concerned with the question: How much correspondence between two fingerprints is sufficient to conclude that they were both made by the same finger? The amount of correspondence has two dimensions: *quantity* and *quality*. Quantity itself includes two aspects. The first is how much of the skin surface is represented in the comparison; and the second is how many (and what kind of) details make up the correspondence. The dimension of *quality* in a fingerprint correspondence is determined by how clearly and accurately the skin surface is represented in the two prints.

An adequate answer to the question posed in the preceding paragraph is not currently available. The best answer at present to the question, "How much is enough?" is that this is up to the individual expert fingerprint examiner to determine, based on that examiner's training, skill, and experience.[1] Thus, we have an ill-defined, flexible, and explicitly subjective criterion for establishing a fingerprint identification. The need for a standard, objective criterion has itself been controversial because subjective methods have been so universally effective and accepted for so long. Even admitting the need, there is considerable difficulty in defining meaningful measurements for quality and quantity in fingerprint comparisons. This difficulty will become apparent in this review of the efforts that have been made.

The chapter begins by looking at the foundational aspects and standards that are in place regarding the making of a fingerprint identification; that is, the criteria for establishing that two fingerprints were made by the same finger.

Standards in Fingerprint Identification

Any unbiased, intelligent assessment of fingerprint identification practices today reveals that there are, in reality, no standards. That is, the amount of correspondence in friction ridge detail that is necessary for a conclusion of identity has not been established. There is an even more basic deficiency, however. There is no methodology in place that is capable of measuring the amount of correspondence in a fingerprint comparison. And there is a third, corollary deficiency: there is no methodology in place that is capable of measuring the amount of detail that is available in a fingerprint for comparison to another. In summary, one cannot:

1. Measure the amount of detail in a (single) fingerprint that is available to compare
2. Measure the amount of detail in correspondence between two fingerprints
3. Objectively interpret the meaning of a given correspondence between two fingerprints

AFIS technology, while holding promise in these areas, has been and remains restricted to the task of screening millions of prints and efficiently selecting candidates for fingerprint comparison. Although this is an important, effective and, indeed, revolutionary task, the comparison itself is reserved for the individual fingerprint examiner. The examiner applies personal, subjective criteria that, despite all its historical precedent, legal acceptance, and public confidence, are both vague and flexible.

Although not directly the subject of this chapter, the above deficiencies are compounded by the fact that neither the education of fingerprint examiners, nor the process of fingerprint comparison is standardized. Furthermore, there have been no objective studies providing validation of the subjective processes that are in place.

Recognition of the above deficiencies does not mean that the fingerprint practices are discredited, that they have no foundational basis, or that the process is necessarily unreliable. Given the Daubert criteria,[2] however, the question of reliability is a reasonable one to ask. Legal scrutiny of fingerprints is, after more than 80 years of uncritical public and judicial acceptance, entirely appropriate.

Without objective standards, however, what foundational aspects for fingerprint identification do we have?

The Laws or Premises Underlying Fingerprint Identifications

For many years, two "laws of fingerprints" have been asserted as the foundation for fingerprint identifications:[3]

1. Fingerprints never change (apart from temporary abrasion and permanent scarring).
2. No two fingerprints (made from different fingers) are alike.

The first of these assertions is a necessary foundation for fingerprint comparison and it is readily proved by both empirical observations and by the well-established anatomy and morphogenesis of friction ridge skin. It is not in dispute, but neither is it relevant to our question: How much correspondence between two fingerprints is sufficient to conclude that they were both made by the same finger? The second law asserts the individuality of complete fingerprints, but it is nearly meaningless to the process of fingerprint comparison. Left out is the reality that fingerprint comparisons involve prints with widely varying quality and quantity of ridge detail, ranging from near-perfect reproductions of a finger's friction ridge skin to blurred smudges that may show no ridge detail at all.

More recently, the two laws of fingerprints have been presented somewhat more formally as three premises:[4]

1. Friction ridges develop on the fetus in their definitive form before birth.
2. Friction ridges are persistent throughout life except for permanent scarring.
3. Friction ridge patterns and the details in small areas of friction ridges are unique and never repeated.

A fourth premise added in response to recent legal scrutiny[5] is

4. Individualization can result from comparison of prints containing sufficient quantity and quality of friction ridge detail.

The first two premises (permanence) are, as with the first law, demonstrably true and irrelevant to the issue at hand. The third premise asserts uniqueness of the patterns and details on the skin surface. This is undoubtedly true in an absolute sense, but is also irrelevant. We are concerned with comparison of two printed reproductions of this skin surface. What amount of detail is reliably retained in a print? Can we recognize it? Can we accurately determine correspondence in this detail? How reliably can we form conclusions from the correspondence?

The fourth premise is more to the point, but it merely asserts that comparison *can* be performed and that opinions of individualization *can* result. It brings us no closer to defining the amount of agreement that is necessary.

The Basis for Absolute Identification

What, then, is the foundational basis for fingerprint comparison practice? The argument for absolute identification begins with the observation of the extreme variability of friction ridge patterns, ridge characteristics, intrinsic ridge shapes, and pore locations. Traditionally, fingerprint individuality has been discussed with reference to the ridge characteristics, or fingerprint minutiae. These characteristics are now classified as a portion of Second Level Detail, which encompasses the paths and the ridges (along with any scars, incipient ridges, or flexion creases).[6] The relative position, orientation, and type of fingerprint minutiae within the ridge pattern are extremely variable, even among identical twins. This is known to be because, in addition to overall genetic influences,[7] the positions of minutiae within the friction ridge pattern are determined by the highly variable dynamics of fetal hand development. The extreme variability in minutiae among fingerprints is readily appreciated if one takes prints from different individuals and an attempt is made to successively find a correspondence in a group of three, then four, then five minutiae. A correspondence in four minutiae might well be found upon diligent, extended effort when comparing the full set of prints of one individual with those of another person. (In doing this, one might well ignore other, finer detail that distinguishes the two prints, but then again, such detail might well be absent in prints of less clarity.) For a legitimate correspondence of five points between different individuals, it might mean searching for weeks among many different individuals. A correspondence of six points might be a lifetime's search. Unfortunately, although there is extensive collective experience among casework examiners,[8] there has been no systematic study such as that described above.

Nonetheless, the fingerprint examiner's opinion of absolute identification is a logical extension of this process, including as its final step a "leap of faith" where, in the critical, experienced (but subjective) judgment of the examiner, it is inconceivable that the fingerprint could have come from another person's finger.

Important factors that enter into the professional judgment of an absolute identification are

1. The extent of the prints (area and number of ridge characteristics)
2. The clarity of the prints
3. The presence or absence of dissimilarities
4. The examiner's training, experience, skill, and ethics

Limitations of Traditional Points of Comparison

The number of corresponding minutiae, or "points," is a convenient, somewhat objective feature to use when discussing fingerprint comparisons. Because of their nearly universal use when describing fingerprint comparisons, and because of the historical acceptance of 12 "points" as a conclusive basis for a determination of identity, fingerprint minutiae have been the central focus when considering fingerprint individuality.

For many years, the use of the number of points has been discussed and debated among the profession, with the key focus being: should there be a formally established minimum number of "points" that is needed for an absolute identification? And, if so, what is this number?[9-11] After much consideration and debate, there is (explicitly) no minimum number of minutiae deemed necessary for an identification, although some countries maintain legal or administrative requirements. Nonetheless, there is a least historical agreement that 12 corresponding simple ridge characteristics are sufficient to prove identity.[9] In the United States, it is generally regarded that six minutiae are too few for absolute identification. Seven or eight are generally accepted as enough, *if they satisfy an experienced examiner.*[12]

Although the number of points is a convenient summary of a comparison, it is insufficient and incomplete. Lacking are the consideration of (1) the clarity of the ridge detail that is being compared, (2) the finer details that are present in the friction ridge prints, and (3) allowance for differences in "value" that would account for unusual or special features in the ridge characteristics. In the United States, these features are subjectively evaluated by fingerprint examiners.

Many other countries, however, do have a minimum point requirement for legal admissibility. Even so, there is formal international agreement that no scientific basis exists for requiring that a predetermined minimum number of friction ridge features must be present in two impressions to establish a positive identification.[10,13] Left unanswered, and usually unasked, is: What scientific basis does exist is for establishing the positive identification? This leads us to examine the statistical basis for fingerprint identifications, which is the principal focus of this chapter.

Fingerprint Individuality Models

Soon after the recognition of the value of fingerprints for personal identification, the degree of individuality present in a fingerprint pattern became of interest. Attempts to provide a probabilistic estimate of fingerprint individuality began with Galton's investigations in 1892,[14] and continue to the present day. There have been ten distinct approaches, including those of:

1. Galton[14]
2. Henry-Balthazard[15,16]
3. Roxburgh[17]
4. Amy[18]

5. Trauring[19]
6. Kingston[20]
7. Osterburg et al.[21]
8. Stoney and Thornton[22,23]
9. Champod[11,24]
10. Meagher, Budowle, and Ziesig[25]

Each of these models focuses on fingerprint minutiae. Alternative approaches based on the fingerprint pore structure are of corollary interest but are outside the scope of this chapter.

Galton Model (1892)

Description of the Galton Model

Galton[14] made the first attempt to quantify fingerprint individuality. His approach was to divide a fingerprint into small regions, such that the ridge detail within each region could be treated as an independent variable. Galton worked with photographic enlargements of fingerprints. The enlargements were placed on the floor and paper squares of various sizes were allowed to fall haphazardly on the enlarged fingerprint. Galton then attempted to reconstruct the ridge detail that was masked by the paper squares, given the surrounding ridges. He sought the size of square region where he could successfully predict the actual ridge detail with a frequency of 1/2. Galton found that for a square region "six ridge intervals" on a side, he was able to correctly predict the hidden detail with a frequency of 1/3, and consequently concluded that a square region with five ridge intervals on a side was very nearly the size he was seeking.

To ensure that any errors would overestimate the chance of fingerprint duplication, Galton used a six ridge interval square region and then assumed a probability of 1/2 for finding the existing minutiae configuration, given the surrounding ridges. The total area of a complete fingerprint was estimated to consist of 24 such square regions. Assuming independence among these regions, Galton calculated the probability of a specific fingerprint configuration, given the surrounding ridges, $P(C/R)$, using Equation (9.1):

$$P(C/R) = (1/2)^{24} = 5.96 \times 10^{-8} \qquad (9.1)$$

Galton next estimated the chance that a particular configuration of surrounding ridges would occur. Two factors were considered: (1) the occurrence of general fingerprint pattern type, and (2) the occurrence of the correct number of ridges entering and exiting each of the 24 regions. Galton estimated the probability for coincidence of pattern type (termed Factor B by Galton) as 1/16, and the probability that the correct number of ridges would enter and exit each region (termed Factor C by Galton) as 1/256. The latter estimate was largely arbitrary, and both were presented by Galton as grossly overestimating the "true" probabilities.

Combining the frequencies of finding the necessary ridge pattern outside the six ridge interval regions with the frequencies of finding all necessary ridge detail within the regions, Galton then predicted the probability of finding any given fingerprint, $P(FP)$, using Equation (9.2):

$$P(FP) = (1/16)(1/256)(1/2)^{24} = 1.45 \times 10^{-11} \qquad (9.2)$$

Assuming a world population of approximately 16 billion human fingers, Galton concluded that, given any particular finger, the odds of finding another finger that showed the same ridge detail would be approximately one in four (1/4).

Discussion of the Galton Model

Galton's model has been criticized by Roxburgh,[26] by Pearson,[27] and Kingston.[9,28] Most of this criticism has focused on Galton's basic assumption that, given the surrounding ridges, there is a probability of 1/2 for the occurrence of any particular ridge configuration in one of the six ridge interval regions.

Pearson considered this assumption "drastic" and suggested an alternative approach for determining the probability of a particular configuration. Assuming that the position of a minutia can be resolved to within one square ridge interval, there would be 36 possible minutia locations within one of Galton's regions. Assuming one minutia in each of 24 independent regions, Pearson calculated the probability of any given configuration using Equation (9.3):

$$P(C/R) = (1/16)(1/256)(1/36)^{24} = 1.09 \times 10^{-41} \qquad (9.3)$$

Pearson noted that the actual probability would be smaller for two reasons: (1) because minutiae are not uniformly restricted to a single minutia in each Galton region, (2) because of variability in minutia type.

Roxburgh's criticism of Galton's model[26] is more fundamental. He noted that Galton investigated only variation within single fingerprints, whereas his conclusions concerned variation among different fingerprints. This is a basic confusion by Galton of "within-group" and "between-group" variation. Roxburgh presented a series of illustrations showing that these two levels of variation need have no relationship with one another. Roxburgh conceded that Galton calculated the probability that Galton could reconstruct any particular print wholly in square regions, six ridge intervals on a side. Roxburgh argued, however, that the probability of 1/2 for a correct guess is influenced by the size of the region relative to the ridge characteristics, rather than by the variation or distribution of the characteristics themselves. If a one ridge interval square region were used, an observer could always guess correctly. Under these circumstances, it would be possible to reconstruct any particular print, given the ridges surrounding the squares, and yet not be able to say anything about variation between fingerprints. Roxburgh pointed out that Galton's analysis proceeds as if he had surveyed a number of fingerprints, comparing square regions in corresponding positions within the prints. Had Galton done this, Roxburgh would have agreed with the analysis. The actual experiments, however, were quite different; and as a result, Roxburgh rejected Galton's model.

Kingston[9,28] made somewhat the same point, noting that Galton's ability to guess the content of a square region is not an indication of the variation in actual fingerprint patterns. If Galton had shown that his region could contain only two configurations, given the surrounding patterns, Kingston would have accepted the basis for Galton's calculations. Seeing no evidence to support this contention, however, Kingston also rejected Galton's model.

These criticisms by Kingston and Roxburgh are only partially valid. Galton intended his Factors B and C to summarize much of the variation among fingerprints. His Factor B accounted for variation in general pattern type and his Factor C accounted for variation in the number of ridges entering and leaving each square region. Clearly, the values of Factor C would change radically if the size of the region were to vary. In particular, for the limiting cases where the ability to guess the content of the region approached certainty, the value of Factor C would become very small. Unfortunately, Galton did not consider his two "Factors" in any detail, and instead chose arbitrary and excessively large estimates for both factors.

If one accepts the concept of Galton's Factors B and C, the question becomes whether or not Galton's experiments reasonably approximate a survey of corresponding regions in different fingerprints. It is clear that Galton had this in mind when he wrote:[28]

> When the reconstructed squares were wrong, they had nonetheless a natural appearance.... Being so familiar with the run of these ridges in fingerprints, I can speak with confidence on this. My assumption is that any one of these reconstructions represents lineations that might have occurred in nature, in association with the conditions outside the square, just as well as the lineations of the actual prints.

Galton continued, making a further assumption:

> ... when the surrounding conditions alone are taken into account, the ridges within their limits may either run in the observed way or in a different way, the chance of these two contrasted events being taken (for safety's sake) as approximately equal.

The weakness of Galton's model lies in the magnitude of the above approximation and in the arbitrary value chosen for Factor C. One can justly criticize his final figure as a gross underestimate of fingerprint variability. Pearson's calculations of the variability in one of Galton's regions may be closer to reality, but both his hypothesis and Galton's remain untested.

The Henry-Balthazard Models (1900–1943)

Description of the Henry-Balthazard Models

The Henry-Balthazard approach is used in six closely related, fairly simplistic models for fingerprint individuality. Each employs a fixed probability **P** for the occurrence of one minutia. Assuming independence of these occurrences, the models calculate the probability of a particular configuration of N minutiae using Equation (9.4):

$$P(C) = (\mathbf{P})^N \tag{9.4}$$

Henry[15] was the first to use this approach in 1900, and Balthazard[16] in 1911 made the most extensive analysis. Minor variations are encountered in the works of Bose,[30] Wentworth and Wilder,[31] Cummins and Midlo,[32] and Gupta.[33]

Henry Model (1900)

Henry[15] chose an arbitrary probability of one fourth for the occurrence of each minutia, as well as for the general pattern type, and the core-to-delta ridge count. To use his method, one counts the number of minutiae; if the pattern type is discernable, one adds two minutia equivalents. This value is used as N, with 1/4 as *P*.

Balthazard Model (1911)

Balthazard's method[16] is particularly important because it is the historical basis for widely accepted rules regarding fingerprint individuality. Balthazard assumed that for each minutia, there were four possible events:

1. Fork directed to the right
2. Fork directed to the left
3. Ending ridge directed to the right
4. Ending ridge directed to the left

Assigning an equal probability for each of these events, Balthazard took P as 1/4 and N as the number of minutiae. He concluded that to observe N coincidentally corresponding minutiae, it would be necessary to examine 4^N fingerprints.

Balthazard went on to calculate the number of minutiae needed for conclusive identification. His criterion was that there should be an expectation of 1 or less for the occurrence of the minutia configuration in the suspect population. Assuming a world population of 15 billion human fingers, 17 corresponding minutiae would be needed. (Under his model, 17 corresponding minutiae would be found with a frequency of only about 1 in 17 billion.) Balthazard considered a lesser number of corresponding minutiae (for example, 11 or 12) to be sufficient for an unequivocal identification if one could be certain that the fingerprint donor was restricted to a particular geographical area (e.g., North America, California).

Bose Model (1917)
Bose[30] also assumed a value of one fourth for P, but arrived at this value using a different rationale. He reasoned that there were at least four possibilities at each square ridge interval location in a fingerprint. These were

1. Dot
2. Fork
3. Ending ridge
4. Continuous ridge

Wentworth and Wilder Model (1918)
Wentworth and Wilder[31] felt that Balthazard's value of one fourth for P was absurdly high, and proposed a value of 1/50 for P. This was an intuitive estimate of the value, with no further justification or explanation.

Cummins and Midlo Model (1943)
Cummins and Midlo[32] adopted the value of 1/50 that was suggested by Wentworth and Wilder, but they also introduced a "pattern factor" to account for variation in the overall fingerprint pattern. Cummins and Midlo estimated that the most common fingerprint pattern occurred with a probability of 1/31. (The estimate was for an ulnar loop, and included the core-to-delta

ridge count.) Equation (9.5) gives Cummins and Midlo's calculation for N corresponding minutiae and a corresponding pattern.

$$P(C) = (1/31)(1/50)^N \qquad (9.5)$$

Gupta Model (1968)

Gupta[33] conducted a survey of minutiae to estimate his values for P. He first selected a particular minutia type and position. He then searched 1000 fingerprints with ulnar loop patterns for a corresponding minutia in the chosen position. This resulted in a prediction of the frequency of encountering the particular minutia type in the particular minutia position. Gupta found that forks and ending ridges were encountered with a frequency of about 8/100, and that the remaining variety of minutia types were encountered with an average frequency of about 1/100. He therefore chose a value of $P = (1/10)$ for forks and ending ridges, and assigned a value of $P = (1/100)$ for the less-common minutia types (e.g., dots, hooks, and enclosures). A pattern factor of (1/10) and a factor for correspondence in ridge count (1/10) were also applied.

Discussion of the Henry-Balthazard Models

The Henry-Balthazard models share a rather casual assumption of independence, and most of them are arbitrary oversimplifications. Henry's method is purely arbitrary, as is Wentworth and Wilder's. Balthazard's choice of P was based on the number of possible minutia events. He has been criticized for allowing only four possible events[9,31] and for failing to include a "pattern factor."[34] The work of Amy[18] has shown that Balthazard's events are not equally probable.

Bose's model does not consider the possible events for each minutia, but rather possible events at each ridge interval location. Thus, one of the allowed events is "a continuous ridge," that is, no minutia at all. Bose's assumption of equal probability for his four events is grossly in error, as pointed out by Roxburgh.[35] A continuous ridge is by far the most common event, and dots are much less common than either forks or ending ridges.

Gupta has an experimental basis for his minutia type frequencies, and he requires a correspondence in position as well as type. His work is weakened by his failure to precisely define the various minutia types, and by the apparently arbitrary choice of the minutia types and positions that he surveyed.

Despite the simplicity of the Henry-Balthazard models, they may be useful as a measure of fingerprint individuality. The value of 1/4 for P may indeed grossly underestimate the individuality of fingerprints. Wentworth and Wilder's value of 1/50, or Gupta's split values of 1/10 and 1/100, could be closer to reality. In any case, there may be some empirically derived value of P for which the model is adequate. This possibility remains unexplored.

The emphasis in the Henry-Balthazard models is on variation in minutia type; variation due to minutia location is not explicitly considered. Most of the remaining models partition fingerprint individuality into three categories: variation in overall ridge pattern, variation in minutia location, and variation in minutia type. We see Balthazard's two possible minutia types, with two possible orientations, incorporated into the models of Roxburgh, Amy, and Trauring. Bose's concept of minutia locations is seen in the model of Osterburg et al. Note that Bose ignores minutia orientation, allows a wider variety of minutia types, and includes "continuous ridges" as one of the possible types.

Roxburgh Model (1933)

Description of the Roxburgh Model

The Roxburgh model[17] had, until 1985,[23] been totally ignored by the forensic science community. Roxburgh based his model on a polar coordinate system. A configuration of concentric circles spaced one ridge interval apart is taken to represent the ridge flow of the fingerprint. An axis is drawn extending upward from the origin and is rotated clockwise. As the angle from the initial position increases, minutiae are encountered. For each minutia, the ridge count from the origin is noted, along with the type of minutia. The types of minutiae allowed by Roxburgh are identical to Balthazard's: a minutia may be either a fork or an ending ridge and may be oriented in one of two (opposite) directions. Rotation of Roxburgh's axis results in an ordered list of minutia types and ridge counts from the origin.

Roxburgh decided simply to order the minutiae, rather than use an angular measure, because by doing so he could avoid determination of how precisely minutia position could be resolved along each of the ridges.

After defining this system for minutia coding, Roxburgh calculated the total variability which could occur under the model. He initially assumed that the ridge count and minutia types were independent and that the possibilities for each were equally likely. Assuming N minutiae, R concentric ridges, and T minutia types, the number of possible combinations for ordered data is given by Equation (9.6):

$$\text{Number of combinations} = (RT)^N \qquad (9.6)$$

An additional pattern factor P was introduced as an estimate for the probability of encountering the particular fingerprint pattern and core type.

The total variability was calculated using Equation (9.7) with the following values for the parameters: $P = 1000$, $N = 35$, $R = 10$, and $T = 4$.

$$\text{Number of combinations} = (P)(RT)^N$$

$$= 10^3(10 \times 4)^N$$

$$= 1.18 \times 10^{59} \tag{9.7}$$

The value of 35 for N was used because it had been Galton's estimate for the number of minutiae in a fingerprint, and the value of 4 for T was used because of the four options for minutia type. Roxburgh estimated P using Galton's finger print classification system where there are 1024 different classification types. R was taken as a conservative value; there are many more than 10 semicircular ridges in a complete fingerprint pattern. The result of Equation (9.7) was therefore presented as a conservative upper bound for the total number of possible fingerprint types under the model.

Roxburgh next considered the question of correlation of successive ridge counts and successive minutia types. Using 271 fingerprints, he recorded the first four minutiae in each print. The data were classified by the sequence of ridge numbers and the minutia types. Without statistical analysis, Roxburgh noted that there appeared to be a roughly even distribution with respect to ridge number sequences, and also with respect to the numbers of forks and ending ridges with each ridge count. He did observe, however, an excess of those minutiae that cause production of ridges compared to those that cause loss of ridges. Roxburgh attributed this to the clockwise rotation of his axis and a general tendency for ridges to diverge as one proceeds from the vertical.

The largest group of fingerprints showing the same sequence of minutia types had eight members. Roxburgh therefore used the value of (271/8) as a conservative estimate of the variability of four minutiae with respect to type. For one minutia, the value would be the fourth root of this (or 2.412). Roxburgh proposed this corrected value of T to adjust for the observed correlation.

Up to this point, only ideal fingerprints had been considered. Roxburgh further modified his model to allow for poorly defined or poorly recorded prints. Poor recording of fingerprints may cause a true fork to appear as an ending ridge, either above or below the ridge bearing the fork. Similarly, a true ending ridge may appear as a fork, joining either the ridge above or the ridge below. (It should also be recognized that quite apart from recording difficulties, the nature of some minutiae may be uncertain on the skin surface itself.)

The term "connective ambiguity" is used here to describe the general phenomenon in which one is uncertain of the minutia type. In the extreme, connective ambiguity allows two additional configurations for each minutia.

There is not only opportunity for change in minutia type, but for a change in ridge count as well. Roxburgh suggested the use of a factor Q (for quality) to assess the impact of connective ambiguity. The value of Q varies, depending on the quality of the fingerprint. It ranges from 1 in an ideal print to 3 in a print where complete connective ambiguity must be acknowledged. (3 is used as the limit because there are three possibilities for minutia type and ridge count when complete connective ambiguity is acknowledged.) Roxburgh estimated Q as 1.5 for a "good average" print, 2.0 for a "poor average" print, and 3 for a "poor" print. The factor Q decreases the number of distinguishable minutia configurations, contributing a factor of $(1/Q)$ for each minutia. Equation (9.6) thus becomes Equation (9.8):

$$\text{Number of configurations} = (P) \, [(RT)/Q]^N \qquad (9.8)$$

Roxburgh made one additional correction to account for circumstances where the fingerprint pattern is insufficiently clear to allow proper determination of the ridge count from the core. The relative positions of the minutiae are not affected, but there is some uncertainty regarding the position of the whole configuration relative to the core. A factor C was introduced, defined as the number of possible positionings for the configuration. The pattern factor P was divided by C to correct for this uncertainty. In the extreme where the pattern is not at all apparent, the factor P must be dropped altogether.

Roxburgh's final equation for the number of possible minutia configurations is Equation (9.9):

$$\text{Number of configurations} = (P/C) \, [(RT)/Q]^N \qquad (9.9)$$

For a good average fingerprint, showing the pattern type and 35 minutiae, Roxburgh defines his variables as $T = 2.412$, $R = 10$, $N = 35$, $P = 1000$, $Q = 1.5$, and $C = 1$. Assuming each configuration is equally likely, Equation (9.10) gives the chance of duplication of a particular configuration of 35 minutiae.

$$P(\text{duplication}, N = 35) = 1/(1.67 \times 10^{45})$$

$$= 5.98 \times 10^{-46} \qquad (9.10)$$

For any particular case, Roxburgh recommends estimating the number of individuals who could have had access to the location where the fingerprint was found (be it the entire population of a country, city, or whatever). The chance of duplication of a particular configuration of minutiae in this population may then be considered, and the number of minutiae necessary for any desired confidence level may be determined. Roxburgh suggested that a chance of duplication of 1 in 50,000 would be an appropriate confidence level for an identification, and presented a table with the number of corresponding minutiae needed for various populations and fingerprint qualities.

Discussion of the Roxburgh Model

Roxburgh's model is both novel and conceptually advanced. There are a number of noteworthy aspects that warrant discussion, including:

1. The use of a polar coordinate system
2. Treatment of correlation among neighboring minutiae
3. Adjustments for fingerprint quality and for connective ambiguity
4. Consideration of variation in the position of the minutia configuration relative to the pattern core

Roxburgh introduced most of these concepts for the first time and repeatedly drew upon actual experimental observations. His work must be considered revolutionary in these respects. It is remarkable and lamentable that Roxburgh's model escaped the attention of most subsequent investigators. No review or even a citation of Roxburgh's work appeared in the forensic science literature for more than 50 years.

Roxburgh's polar coordinates are a natural choice for whorl patterns with radial symmetry, and for fingertips where ridges are semicircular and nearly concentric. The model is not directly applicable where ridges form loops, triradii, or patternless, parallel ridges. Broader application results if the origin is allowed to move along a reference ridge. An axis could thus sweep up one side of a loop and down the other, or across a series of parallel ridges.

Roxburgh briefly considered a second model, similar to Pearson's, that used rectangular coordinates to define minutia position. Each minutia was assumed to occupy 2.5 square ridge units, and minutia density was estimated as 1 per 25 units. Assuming minutiae to be evenly distributed, this allows for 10 possible positions per minutia. If each position is equally likely, then the probability for occupancy for a given minutia position is estimated at 1/10. For more accuracy, Roxburgh suggested that resolution of minutia positions be treated differently along ridges than across them. Across ridges we can easily distinguish a one ridge unit interval, whereas along ridges Roxburgh suggested an average resolution of 3.5 ridge intervals. At this point in his presentation, Roxburgh pointed out the convenience of his polar coordinate model, in which the question of resolution need not be considered.

Although Roxburgh's model is simplified by avoiding minutia resolution, resolution is clearly a fundamental aspect of fingerprint individuality and its omission will be a major defect in any fingerprint model. Roxburgh argues that, in practice, it is relative distances between minutiae that one compares, and that the criteria for correspondence among minutia positions varies with the distance between them. Stated differently, minutiae on neighboring ridges will show comparatively less variation in relative position than will minutiae separated by several ridges. These observations help characterize the complexity of the problem but they do not diminish its fundamental importance. By sidestepping the issue of resolution, Roxburgh weakened his model.

This weakness, however, is overshadowed by the ingenuity that Roxburgh showed when he refined his model. He first considered correlation of minutiae. Although he "eyeballed" the lack of correlation among successive ridge counts and among minutia types, his observations had an experimental basis and are distinguished as the first (and nearly only) consideration of correlation among minutiae. Roxburgh did find a correlation among minutia orientations, a correlation he attributed to the generally observed divergence of ridges at the fingertips. A somewhat crude over-correction was made for this correlation: Roxburgh simply assumed that the correlation for all types and orientations of minutiae was equal to the maximum that he had observed among all the various combinations.

Roxburgh next considered the effect of print quality on connective ambiguity. Galton[36] discussed connective ambiguity and undoubtedly made allowances for it when he judged his ability to guess ridge structures. Roxburgh, however, was the first to make specific allowance for connective ambiguity and to link the allowance to print quality. Print quality has a direct influence on how much connective ambiguity is allowable. Even in excellent prints, an occasional minutia will exhibit variability in recording. The presence of more than a few would warrant suspicion of nonidentity. In poorly recorded prints, however, one must allow this variation in virtually all minutiae. In this extreme, we know only that a new ridge appears in a given location. The three possible minutiae that could produce the ridge account for Roxburgh's correction factor $Q = 3$.

Roxburgh's last refinement of his model was an assessment of the uncertainty of the position of an entire minutia configuration within the overall pattern. Roxburgh observed that when one does not have a clearly defined reference point, such as a pattern core, one can make several positionings in an attempt to find a corresponding minutia configuration. The absence of a reference point thus increases the possibility of chance correspondence by a factor equal to the number of possible positionings. In hindsight, this point is obvious and simply amounts to an observation that there are several opportunities for a particular event to occur. Of the remaining fingerprint models, only those of Amy and Osterburg incorporate this important feature (although it is considered by Stoney and by Champod).

Amy Model (1946–1948)

Description of the Amy Model

Amy[18] defined two general contributions to fingerprint individuality: variability in minutia type (his *facteur d'alternance*) and variability in number and position of minutiae (his *facteur topologique*).

Variability in Minutia Type

Amy assumed the same possible minutia types as did both Balthazard and Roxburgh: minutiae could be either forks or ending ridges and could have one of two opposite orientations. Using a database of 100 fingerprints, Amy determined that the relative frequencies of forks and ending ridges were 0.40 and 0.60, respectively. He also noted that divergence or convergence of ridges was very common; and that when this occurs, there is an excess of minutiae with one orientation. Amy estimated a frequency of 0.75 for minutiae with one orientation and a frequency of 0.25 for minutiae with the opposite orientation.

With F1 forks and E1 ending ridges in one direction, and F2 forks and E2 ending ridges in the other, Amy calculated the probability of a particular ordering (A1) using Equation (9.11), which reduces to Equation (9.12):

$$P(A1) = [(0.75)\ 0.4]^{F1}\ [(0.25)\ 0.4]^{F2}\ [(0.75)\ 0.6]^{E1}\ [(0.25)\ 0.6]^{E2} \quad (9.11)$$

$$P(A1) = (0.3)^{F1}(0.1)^{F2}(0.45)^{E1}(0.15)^{E2} \quad (9.12)$$

Amy pointed out that in the general case, one does not know the absolute orientation of the minutia configuration. Accordingly, a probability with the reversed orientations must also be considered and made part of the calculation. Thus, $P(A2)$ is given by Equation (9.13):

$$P(A2) = (0.3)^{F2}(0.1)^{F1}(0.45)^{E2}(0.15)^{E1} \quad (9.13)$$

The total probability of the ordering of the minutia configuration (Amy's *facteur d'alternance*) is given by $P(A1) + P(A2)$, which reduces to Equation (9.14):

$$P(A) = (0.1)^{F1+F2}(0.15)^{F1+E2}[3^{(F1+E1)} + 3^{(F2+E2)}] \quad (9.14)$$

Variation in Number and Position of Minutiae

Amy next considered the variation in number and position of minutiae. Consider a square patch of ridges, n ridge interval units on a side. Let $P(L)$

be the probability that there will be p minutiae in the patch. Let N be the total number of arrangements of the p minutiae, and let $(N\{t\})$ be the number of these arrangements that are indistinguishable from the particular arrangement of minutiae at issue. The probability of having p minutiae forming a configuration of type t in a square patch n ridge intervals on a side is defined as $P(T)$ (Amy's *facteur topologique*) in Equation (9.15):

$$P(T) = P(L\{n,p\})(N\{t\})/(N) \qquad (9.15)$$

The patch size is actually variable because the borders of the patch are not precisely defined. Amy therefore summed the possible values of n, giving Equation (9.16):

$$P(T) = \Sigma[(L\{n,p\})(N\{t\})/N]/\Sigma[P(L\{n,p\})] \qquad (9.16)$$

Assuming a minimum distance between two minutiae of one ridge interval, there are n^2 positions in which to have p minutiae. Using an estimate of average minutia density of 1 per 22.5 square ridge intervals, the binomial theorem gives the values for $P(L)$ and N in Equation (9.17) and (9.18). Substituting the results of Equation (9.17) and (9.18) into (9.16) gives Equation (9.19) for $P(T)$.

$$P(L) = \binom{n}{k}(0.0444)^P (0.9556)^{n^2-p} \qquad (9.17)$$

$$N = \binom{n}{k} \qquad (9.18)$$

$$P(T) = \frac{(0.9556)^{n^2(N\{t\})}}{\binom{n}{k}(0.9556)^{n^2}} \qquad (9.19)$$

It remains to calculate $N\{t\}$, the total number of possible minutia arrangements that are of the particular type t (i.e., indistinguishable from one given minutia configuration).

Amy noted that relative — rather than absolute — positioning is of concern and proposed that the event necessary for positional identity between two fingerprints is only that the same number of minutiae appear on corresponding ridges of the fingerprints. This means that variation from absolute positioning of minutiae along a ridge is disregarded; instead, there is merely an ordering of the minutiae. Under these assumptions $N(t)$ would include all the possible permutations of minutiae occurring on the same ridge and each of these permutations would be equivalent under the model. For one minutia on a ridge, there are n possible positions; for two minutiae, there are $[n(n-1)/2]$ positions; for three minutiae, there are $[n(n-1)(n-2)/3]$; etc. Each ridge contributes a factor of this type to $N\{t\}$, depending on the number of minutiae that appear on the ridge.

A second contribution to $N(t)$ arises from ridges without minutiae that occur at the print border. Amy argued that if there are q such minutia-free ridges at the upper border, then arrangements with $(q-1)$ minutia-free ridges at the upper border and one minutia-free ridge at the bottom border would be indistinguishable. In general, for q minutia-free ridges at the borders, there would be $(q+1)$ possible arrangements of these ridges, each resulting in an indistinguishable fingerprint pattern.

Based on the above two contributions, Amy calculated $N\{t\}$, given n, p, and the number of ridges with 0, 1, 2, etc. minutiae. If there is only one minutia per ridge and no interior ridges without minutiae, then $q = n - p$ and $N\{t\}$ is given by Equation (9.20). If there are z internal ridges without minutiae, Equation (9.21) results.

$$N\{t\} = n^p(n - p + 1) \tag{9.20}$$

$$N\{t\} = n^p(n - p + 1 - z) \tag{9.21}$$

Two minutiae on one ridge and one on each of the others results in Equation (9.22). Two minutiae on each of two ridges and one on each of the others results in Equation (9.23), and the formula generalizes easily.

$$N\{t\} = \frac{(n)(n-1)}{2} n^{(p-2)}(n - p + 2 - z) \tag{9.22}$$

$$N\{t\} = \frac{(n)^2(n-1)^2}{4} n^{(p-4)}(n - p + 3 - z) \tag{9.23}$$

Amy noted that the foregoing analysis failed when clusters of minutiae appeared on one ridge. A problem of definition results: when does one ridge become two ridges? To address this issue, Amy defined "groups." A group is an interconnected cluster of minutiae that is treated as if it were a single ridge. Amy noted that within these groups, not all relative types and positions of minutiae are possible, and some new types of positioning are created.

Correction factors (G) were introduced to account for this difference between the predicted and actual possibilities. Amy calculated G for clusters of 2 to 6 minutiae.

Probability for a Particular Minutiae Configuration

Amy's estimate for the frequency of a particular minutia configuration $P(C)$ is given in Equation (9.24). This incorporates the correction factor G, along with $P(A)$ and $P(T)$ from Equations (9.15) and (9.20).

$$P(C) = P(A) * P(T) * (G) \tag{9.24}$$

Chance of False Association

Amy noted that the chance of false association depends on the number of comparisons one makes. Thus, if a frequency of a particular configuration is $P(C)$, the chance that a given area is not of this configuration is $[1 - P(C)]$; and for R comparisons, the probability of association by random $P(AR)$ is given by Equation (9.25).

$$P(AR) = 1 - [1 - P(C)]^r \tag{9.25}$$

Taylor expansion yields Equation (9.26), which reduces to Equation (9.27) when $P(C)$ and $[r \times P(C)]$ are small.

$$P(AR) = 1 - [1 - (r)P(C) + \frac{(r)(r+1)}{2} P(C)^2 ...] \tag{9.26}$$

$$P(AR) = (r)P(C) \tag{9.27}$$

Amy calculated the number of comparisons r as follows. Consider a fingerprint of unknown origin that fills a square region, n ridge intervals on a side. This print is to be compared to a larger, known fingerprint, represented by a square region with N ridge intervals on a side. The number of horizontal positions that the smaller unknown print can occupy in the larger print is given by $(N - n + 1)$. There are an equal number of vertical positions, one for each ridge. Therefore, the total number of positions for comparison is given by Equation (9.28):

$$\text{Number of positions} = r = (N - n + 1)^2 \tag{9.28}$$

The value of N (in ridge intervals) is estimated by taking the square root of the area of the known prints. Amy estimated a value of 9.49 for thumbs, 8.37

for the other fingers, and 31.62 for palms. The total number of positions for one person is calculated in Equation (9.29). When palms are not examined, the appropriate equation is Equation (9.30).

$$r = 2(9.49 - n + 1)^2 + 8(8.37 - n + 1)^2 + 2(31.62 - n + 1)^2 \qquad (9.29)$$

$$= 12n^2 - 256n + 1986$$

$$r \text{ (no palms)} = 10n^2 - 192n + 923 \qquad (9.30)$$

Up to this point, only patternless fingerprints had been considered. Amy reasoned that where loops, whorls, and triradii exist, the number of positions for comparison is less, regardless of whether or not the unknown fingerprint contains such patterns. Assuming the worst case, with a patternless unknown print, then for each pattern present on an individual, n positions are excluded from comparison in each dimension. Letting s equal the number of pattern singularities on a person's hands, the number of comparisons can be recalculated using Equation (9.31):

$$\text{Number of comparisons} = r - n^2 s \qquad (9.31)$$

Final Equation for the Chance of Random Association

Amy's final equation for the chance of a random association is Equation (9.32), which combines Equation (9.24), (9.25), and (9.31).

$$P(AR) = 1 - [1 - P(A)P(T)(G)]^{r - n^2 s} \qquad (9.32)$$

Amy concluded by calculating the chances of random association for a series of examples with different numbers of minutiae and different group arrangements. In a subsequent paper,[37] Amy presented tables that considerably simplify the calculation of an upper bound for the chance of random association; and in a final paper,[38] Amy calculated the number of minutiae needed to limit the chance of random association to one in a billion. He also noted that when fingerprint files are searched as a means of developing a candidate for comparison, the factor r increases and the criteria for identification become more stringent.

Discussion of the Amy Model

Amy's model is comparable to Roxburgh's in complexity, innovation, and general approach. These two investigators recognized many of the same issues and their responses were closely related. Both models begin by dividing fingerprint individuality into two parts: variability of minutia type and variability of minutia position.

Amy's consideration of minutia type was more sophisticated than Roxburgh's in two respects. First, Amy experimentally determined the relative frequencies of forks and ending ridges instead of assuming that the two types were equally likely. Second, Amy made an estimate of the tendency of minutiae to have the same orientation, based on his observations in 100 fingerprints. This tendency occurs because ridges tend to converge or diverge as they flow around pattern areas. Roxburgh had observed this and corrected for it by introducing a factor based on the greatest degree of correlation he had observed. Amy's approach was more realistic because he incorporated probabilities for the alternative orientations directly into his calculation.

Amy's treatment of minutia positional variation was also more sophisticated than Roxburgh's. Amy treated both the number of minutiae and the area of the fingerprint as variables. He used the binomial theorem and an estimate of minutia density to calculate both the probability of a given number of minutiae and the probability of any particular positional arrangement. These calculations require definition of the possible minutia positions within a fingerprint. Amy assumed that the minimum distance between two minutiae was one ridge interval. The number of possible minutia positions was thus equal to the area in square ridge intervals. The issue here is not the ability to resolve minutia positions, but rather to determine the number of possible minutia positions. Amy considered the problem of minutia resolution by another, more questionable process.

When comparing fingerprints, we are unable to distinguish among all the possible minutia configurations. Roxburgh recognized this and was content to use a resolution of one ridge interval across ridges and merely to order the minutiae along ridges; this, in essence, avoids the issue. Amy's treatment was more complex but he made a functionally equivalent approximation. Amy assumed that any positional arrangement that has the same number of minutiae on each ridge will be indistinguishable. This means that, in fact, only minutia ordering along the ridges is considered. This assumption is a serious flaw in Amy's model, even more so than in Roxburgh's. In both models, the assumption is unrealistic because one's ability to distinguish minutia configurations is far greater than one's ability merely to note their sequence along a ridge. In Amy's model, the approximation is also particularly difficult to apply. Roxburgh only required a ridge count as a radial measure; the continuity along a particular ridge was of no concern. The Amy model strives to preserve the concept of individual ridges, while still allowing multiple minutiae on a ridge. The concept of "groups" must therefore be introduced, and interconnected ridge systems must be defined as a single compound ridge. The complexity introduced by Amy's group correction factor is awkward enough; but more importantly, Amy's model can in no way account for the connective ambiguities of minutiae. Connective ambiguities prevent the definition of discrete, interconnected ridge systems. Amy totally ignored this issue and provided no consideration of, or correction for, connective ambiguities. Inasmuch as connective ambiguities are an unavoidable feature of fingerprint comparison,[39,40] Amy's model is consequently not a realistic assessment of fingerprint individuality.

Amy next introduced a correction factor for featureless border ridges, stating that it does not matter whether such ridges appear above or below the central, minutia-bearing ridges: the central ridges alone contain the features that determine distinguishability among minutia configurations. This feature of Amy's model is incorrect. When a fingerprint of unknown origin is being compared to known fingerprints, any minutia-free ridges in the known print are very much a part of the comparison. Should the known prints have minutiae on these ridges, there is a discrepancy and nonidentity will ensue. It is true that for the patch of ridges that Amy uses for his unknown prints, one cannot distinguish among the permutations of the featureless border ridges. But when comparing these unknown prints to the larger known prints, the permutations are by no means equivalent.

Amy concluded his work with a calculation of the chances of false association. Given the size of the ridge configuration, Amy estimated the number of possible positionings for these ridges on a person's hands. The number of positionings varies, depending on the size of the ridge configuration, whether both palms and fingers are to be considered, and the presence of pattern elements in either the fingerprint trace or the person's hands. The purpose of calculating the possible positionings is to estimate the number of trials one has in which to find an indistinguishable ridge configuration. At each possible positioning, one makes a comparison and there is a chance of false association.

Obviously, the more possible positionings for a fingerprint trace on an individual, the greater the chance of false association. This idea was scarcely novel; both Galton and Balthazard recognized one positioning for each of a person's ten fingers. Roxburgh introduced his Factor C, the number of possible positionings that a configuration could have relative to pattern core. Amy, however, extended this concept to include all the fingers and the palms. Furthermore, Amy made the critical observation that the more people to whom one compares a fingerprint, the less is the significance of any resulting association. Each person in a suspect population represents a set of trials, and each trial carries with it the chance of false association. Of all the proposed models, only Amy treats this issue properly. Others either ignore the multiple comparisons because of positionings, assume comparison with a geographically defined population, or imply that there is only one comparison. Amy alone appreciated that the number of trials defined by the suspect population is the relevant quantity.

Trauring Model (1963)

Description of the Trauring Model

Trauring[19] estimated the chances of coincidental fingerprint association in connection with a proposed automatic identification system. The system is based on prior selection of reference minutiae on a finger and the recording of a number of test minutiae. Relative coordinates derived from the reference minutiae are used to describe the positions of the test minutiae. As proposed, the test minutiae appear within the triangular region described by the reference minutiae, and the approximate positions of the reference minutiae on the finger are known.

Trauring made the following assumptions:

- Minutiae are distributed randomly.
- There are two minutia types: forks and ending ridges.
- The two minutia types are equally likely to occur.
- The two possible orientations of minutiae are equally likely to occur.
- Minutia type, orientation, and position are independent variables.
- For repeated registration of one individual's finger, the uncertainty in the position of the test minutiae relative to the reference minutiae does not exceed 1.5 ridge intervals.

Under these assumptions, the correspondence of a test minutia requires its presence within a circular region of radius 1.5 ridge intervals (area = 7.07 square ridge intervals). The chance of a minutia appearing in this region is equal to the minutia density (s) multiplied by the area. The minutia may be one of two equally likely types, and has one of two equally likely orientations. The probability of a corresponding test minutia, given acceptable reference minutiae, $P(TM/RM)$, is therefore given by Equation (9.33).

$$P(TM/RM) = (0.707)/(4s) = 0.07(s) \tag{9.33}$$

If the chance of encountering an acceptable set of reference minutiae on one finger is r, then each person has a $(10 \times r)$ probability that the reference minutiae will be present on one of their ten fingers. If the number of test minutiae is N, then the chance of random correspondence of any one of an individual's fingers with a previously defined fingerprint is given by Equation (9.34).

$$P(\text{corresponding individual}) = (10r)(0.177s)^N \qquad (9.34)$$

Based on his observations of 20 fingerprints, Trauring found a maximum value of 0.11 for minutia density. He also estimated that the probability of correspondence of three randomly corresponding reference minutiae could be conservatively taken as 1/100. Substituting these values for s and r gives Equation (9.35).

$$P(\text{corresponding individual}) = \frac{(0.1944)^N}{10} \qquad (9.35)$$

Discussion of the Trauring Model

Trauring's perspective differs somewhat from the other investigators; he developed his model not to study fingerprint individuality, but rather to estimate the ability of computerized optics to identify a particular finger. Our purpose here is to evaluate Trauring's model as it applies to fingerprint individuality, a function for which it was not actually proposed. Automatic comparisons by computer favor the introduction of continuous rectangular coordinates. When fingerprints are compared manually, however, actual distances between minutiae are not compared; instead, ridge counts are made across ridges and relative distances are compared along ridges. It is understandable that for computerized recording and comparison of fingerprints, the ridge count might be dispensed with; in doing so, however, one departs from reality. Ridge count is an essential part of the actual identification criteria and its omission weakens Trauring's model.

Trauring's model is similar to the Henry-Balthazard models, although better thought out. Trauring's first five assumptions are identical to Balthazard's and the result fits the Henry-Balthazard format ($p = 0.4641$ for the three reference minutiae and thereafter $p = 0.1944$). Trauring, however, laid a better foundation for his model. His derivation was based on consideration of minutia density, estimates of error in minutia positioning, and the concept of reference and test minutiae. Trauring shares some of the faults of the simple models; he assumed minutia types and orientations to be equally probable, and considered neither connective ambiguity nor correlation among minutiae.

The most important feature of Trauring's model is his concept of reference minutiae. Trauring used the locations of three reference minutiae to bring a finger into register. Positions of the remaining "test" minutiae were determined relative to these reference minutiae. In actual fingerprint comparison, a similar process is followed. A characteristic group of minutiae or a ridge pattern such as a loop or delta is used as a reference point, and a comparison with other prints begins by searching for this reference point. If a corresponding reference point is found, the remaining minutiae are used to test the comparison. Ridge count from the reference point, relative lateral position, orientation, and minutia type are factored into the comparison. Each minutia sought is a test of the hypothesis that the prints are from the same individual.

Although no other fingerprint model explicitly distinguishes between reference and test minutiae, the issue has arisen in different forms. Galton, Henry, Cummins and Midlo, and Roxburgh used "pattern factors" to estimate the chances of encountering a particular fingerprint pattern type. Pattern cores and delta regions, and even diverging ridges in arch patterns, provide good reference points. Roxburgh also allowed for uncertainty in position of minutiae with his Factor C, the number of possible positionings of the minutia configuration relative to the pattern core. Amy considered the number of possible positionings of a partial print on the whole of the palmar surface. The "reference points" of loops, triradii, and whorls eliminate some of the possible positionings, increasing his factor n. Apart from these indirect treatments, however, the concept of test and reference minutiae remains undeveloped in its application to conventional fingerprint comparison.

Kingston Model (1964)

Description of the Kingston Model

Kingston[20] divided his model for fingerprint individuality into three probability calculations, in much the same fashion as Amy. He first calculated the probability of finding the observed number of minutiae in a fingerprint of the observed size. Next, he calculated the probability that the particular minutiae positions would be observed. And finally, he calculated the probability that minutiae of the observed type would occupy the positions.

Probability of the Observed Number of Minutiae

Kingston estimated the probability of a particular number of minutiae from the minutia density, assuming a Poisson distribution. This assumption was justified by his experimental observations for the core area of ulnar loops. Minutia density was measured for the specific type of fingerprint pattern and the specific location within this pattern. Graphs were constructed of expected minutia number vs. the size of the sample region. For a region of given size, the expected minutia number y was read, and the probability of the observed number was calculated from Equation (9.36):

$$P(N \text{ minutiae}) = (e^{-y})(y^N / N!) \tag{9.36}$$

Probability of the Observed Positioning of Minutiae

Kingston next calculated a probability for the observed positioning of minutiae. He assumed that each minutia occupied a square region 0.286 mm on a side. This size region was chosen from experimental observations of minutia clustering. Within this square region, other minutiae are excluded, and thus the center positions of other minutiae are excluded from a square region 0.571 mm on a side.

An uncertainty of 0.286 mm in measurement of a minutia position was also assumed, a value based on repeated coordinate readings from a single fingerprint.

Under these assumptions, Kingston proceeded as follows. Consider N minutiae occurring in a region that is S square millimeters in area. The number of distinguishable minutia positions within this region is given by Equation (9.37):

$$(\text{Number of positions}) = (S) / (0.571)^2 = (S) / (0.082) \qquad (9.37)$$

One minutia position is used for reference and located at any position with a probability of unity. Subsequent minutiae are located with equal probability over the remaining unoccupied area. The excluded, occupied area for minutia i is given by Equation (9.38). The probability of the particular set of positionings is therefore calculated using Equation (9.39).

$$\text{Occupied area} = (i-1)(0.571)^2 = (i-1)/(0.082) \qquad (9.38)$$

$$P(\text{positionings}) \prod_{i=2}^{N} \frac{(0.082)}{[S-(i-1)(0.082)]} \qquad (9.39)$$

The value given by Equation (9.39) is used except where the minutiae are sufficiently close so that the excluded regions about the minutiae overlap. Where there is overlap, the total area excluded to the next minutia is less than the given value. Presence of the overlap also causes the order in which the minutiae are taken to affect the calculation. Kingston cautioned against ignoring this overlap, but did not consider the magnitude of the error this would cause. Should significant error occur, Kingston recommended taking an average over all possible orderings of the minutiae.

Probability of the Observed Minutiae Types

To estimate the probability of correspondence in minutia type, Kingston determined the relative frequencies of minutia types in a survey of 2464

Table 9.1 Kingston's Relative Frequencies of Minutiae (N = 2464)

Ending ridge	0.459
Fork	0.341
Dot	0.083
Enclosure	0.032
Bridge	0.019
Triradii	0.017
Other	0.031
Total	0.982 (sic)

minutiae in 100 ulnar loops. The results are given in Table 9.1. The probability for a correspondence in minutia types was calculated as the product of the relative frequencies for each of the n minutiae.

Overall Probability of a Given Configuration

Combining the probability of the observed minutia types P with Equation (9.39) gives Equation (9.40), which calculates a value for filling the observed minutia positions with the observed minutia types. Combining Equations (9.36) and (9.40) gives Equation (9.41), Kingston's final probability for a given minutia configuration P(C).

$$P(\text{positions, types}) = (P_1)\prod_{i=2}^{N}(P_i)\frac{(0.082)}{[S-(i-1)(0.082)]} \qquad (9.40)$$

$$P(C) = (e^{-y})(y^N/N!)(P_1)\prod_{i=2}^{N}(P_i)\frac{(0.082)}{[S-(i-1)(0.082)]} \qquad (9.41)$$

Kingston included no additional factor for a correspondence in pattern type. Instead, he considered the pattern singularities to be special types of minutiae. Triradii were explicitly considered as described in Table 9.1, and an arbitrary frequency of 0.25 was assigned to recurring ridges.

Chances of False Association

Kingston calculated the probability of false association using the Poisson distribution. Suppose there exist K persons with the given minutia configuration as seen in a fingerprint. If we select one of these persons at random, then the probability that we have the actual person who made the print is $(1/K)$. For small probabilities of occurrence, K takes on a Poisson distribution with parameter $y = np$, where n is the size of the relevant population and p is the probability of the event. The expectation of $(1/K)$ is thus given by

Equation (9.42). The denominator is the Taylor expansion for the exponential function, less one. Making this substitution results in Equation (9.43).

$$E(1/K) = \frac{\sum_{i=1} (1/K)(y^K/K!)}{\sum_{i=1} (y^K/K!)} \tag{9.42}$$

$$E(1/K) = 1/(e^y - 1)\sum_{i=1} (y^K)/(K)(K!) \tag{9.43}$$

Whereas $(1/K)$ is the probability that the correct person is found, $1 - (1/K)$ gives the probability that an error has occurred. This value turns out to be very close to $(y/4)$ for y in the range of 1 to 1 in 1 billion.

Discussion of the Kingston Model

The general similarity between the Kingston model and the Amy model was mentioned earlier. Both models initially determine the probability of a particular number of minutiae in a region of given size. Second, they compute the possible permutations of minutia positions; and third, they consider variation in minutia type. The principle difference between the two models is that Amy attempts to describe minutia position within the ridge structure, whereas Kingston ignores this structure and uses the coordinates of minutia positions.

For calculating the probability of a particular number of minutiae, Kingston used the Poisson distribution; Amy had used the binomial distribution. These two probability distributions are closely related; the Poisson is merely a special case of the binomial. Both describe the distribution of the number of successes, given a number of statistically independent trials. In our specific example, *events* are the occurrence of minutiae and the *probability* is that a particular number of minutiae will occur in a region of a given size. Two parameters are necessary to describe the binomial distribution: (1) the probability of the event and (2) the number of trials. Thus, Amy used a probability of 0.0444 for a minutia to occur within a unit area and took the number of trials as total area of the region. When the number of trials is high and the probability of the event is low, the binomial probabilities are accurately given by the Poisson distribution. The Poisson distribution is described using only a single parameter: the expected number of events. Although this expectation is dependent on the number of trials and the probability of the event, these two parameters need not be individually determined. Kingston used average minutia counts in different-sized regions to obtain an empirically derived Poisson parameter.

Kingston used an empirical approach because he had observed variations in minutia density among different-sized regions and among different locations within the fingerprint. Amy had simply assumed a uniform minutia density. Kingston's data established that increased minutia densities occur near deltas and near loop cores. As one proceeds outward from these regions, the density falls off, creating a lower overall density as the size of the region increases. Kingston adjusted for these phenomena by restricting his consideration to circular regions about the core of loops and empirically determining the expected number of minutiae for regions of different size. Such an assumption is inherent in the use of the Poisson (or binomial) distribution, and thus there is an inconsistency in the model. We can infer that for small regions, Kingston assumed that the density may be taken as constant. This assumption might well be valid in some areas of the fingerprint. Unfortunately, Kingston chose an area where the density varies dramatically. His data show that the density falls off nearly 50% as the radius of a circular region about the fingerprint core changes from three ridge intervals to six.[41]

Kingston made this same inconsistent assumption when he considered variation in minutia position. His method was to sequentially add minutiae to a region. The probability that each successive minutia will occupy any particular position is determined by the ratio of minutia size to the remaining unoccupied space. No provision is made for the proximity of the minutia to the core, or for any variations in minutia density.

Further difficulty with Kingston's modeling of minutia position is encountered with his definitions of minutia size and resolution. Kingston assumed that each minutia occupied a square region 0.286 mm on a side. This is equivalent to 0.333 square ridge intervals. Amy had used a full square ridge interval region; thus, Kingston allowed three times more minutia positions than Amy. This difference obviously has a profound effect on number of possible minutia arrangements.

Kingston's choice of minutia size is unrealistic when evaluated within the actual ridge structure. Minutiae on adjacent ridges can be no closer than one ridge interval. Along a ridge, the question becomes one of definition. When do two minutiae which are very close become one event? Kingston did not describe his criteria for determining minutia type, but did classify "spurs" and "double bifurcations" as simple bifurcations (forks). "Dots," "enclosures," and "bridges" were given separate categories. By allowing this variety in minutia type, Kingston in effect redefined any two minutiae that appeared close to one another. Two opposing forks would be redefined as an enclosure, a fork with a quickly terminating branch would be redefined as a spur and included as a simple fork, and a very short segment of a ridge would be redefined as a dot. This redefinition of events prevents minutiae from getting closer than one or two ridge intervals from one another. The effective number of minutia positions is thus considerably less than Kingston had assumed.

Kingston also used an inappropriately small value for minutia resolution. He accepted correspondence only if a minutia was found in an area of 0.082 mm² about the expected position. Trauring had used an area of 1.73 mm², even after correcting for fingerprint distortion using reference minutiae. Kingston's value was determined by noting the error in repeated measurements on a single fingerprint, in contrast to measurements of different prints from the same finger. This is a fundamental error. We are not interested in how many distinguishable patterns we can measure, but in how we can distinguish among prints from different fingers. Kingston made no allowance for the minor printing variations that are present even under ideal conditions.

Kingston's modeling of minutia positional variation therefore has three serious flaws: (1) the inconsistent assumption of uniform density, (2) excessively small minutia size, and (3) excessively high minutia resolution. A relatively minor omission is the failure to consider positioning of the minutia configuration as a whole. Inasmuch as the Kingston model is restricted to the core areas of loops, this omission is not serious; the loop pattern allows positioning of the configuration on the finger. Furthermore, the model allows arbitrary positioning of one minutia as a starting point.

Kingston's approach to variation in minutia type differed fundamentally from the previous models. Kingston allowed a much greater variety of minutiae and assigned probabilities based on their relative frequencies. Orientation of minutiae, however, was not incorporated within the model. (It would be difficult to use orientation in a meaningful way without reference to the ridge structure.)

When minutia types other than forks and ending ridges are defined, three issues are highlighted. First, one notes that the new minutia types are compound forms of forks, ending ridges, or both. This is necessarily so because there are only two fundamental operations that can occur to produce a new ridge. Second, one notes that there is a continuum between the compound forms and distinct fundamental forms. That is, for example, if two opposing forks are close to one another, they are defined as an "enclosure." As the distance between the forks is increased, one finds a continuum between what is defined as an enclosure and what is defined as two distinct forks. Definition of the compound forms must therefore include a (somewhat arbitrary) judgment of where the compound character is lost. The third issue is that the frequencies of the compound forms are much lower and much more variable than those of the fundamental forms.

If one is to use the compound forms, it is appropriate to assign weights based on their frequency of occurrence. This principle has been applied subjectively for some time in fingerprint comparison,[42] but Osterburg's survey[43] demonstrated that there was no consensus among fingerprint examiners regarding these frequencies. Amy[18] assigned variable weights to minutiae but only considered the fundamental types. Santamaria[44] was the first to propose specific weighting of compound minutiae. His method was simply to assign a weight equal to the number of fundamental minutiae which were required to produce the compound one. Kingston was the first to include frequencies of compound minutiae in a model for fingerprint individuality. Gupta[33] based his model on the frequencies of compound minutia types found in specific locations within the fingerprint.

Two problems arise from Kingston's use of compound minutiae. The first, as alluded to above, is a problem of definition. When are two fundamental minutiae sufficiently close to form a compound minutia? Kingston does not state his own criteria but does observe that differences in minutia classification account for variation between his own frequencies and those determined by other investigators.[35] The second problem is that no provision is made for connective ambiguity. This affects not only the comparison of minutiae, but also the frequencies that are assigned. For example, a connective ambiguity at one end of an enclosure (frequency 0.032) would result in classification as either a spur, which Kingston includes with forks (0.341), or as a combination of a fork and an ending ridge ($0.459 \times 0.341 = 0.157$). The latter reclassification to two minutiae would also markedly affect the probability calculations for both the number and position of minutiae.

Kingston concluded his model with a calculation of the chances of false association, assuming a partial fingerprint with a given incidence. We have seen a variety of approaches to this problem. Galton[14] and Balthazard[16] compared the incidence of the fingerprint to the world population and considered an identification to be absolute when the expectation within the population was less than 1. Roxburgh[17] accepted an identification when the incidence was below 1/50,000. Amy[18,34] took the actual number of comparisons into account, his chance of false association was the probability of occurrence multiplied by the number of comparisons. Kingston's method is analogous to Galton's and Balthazard's, although his techniques are much more refined.

Using the Poisson distribution, Kingston calculated the probability that among the world population there would be N individuals with a fingerprint identical to the given one. N must be greater than or equal to 1 because the existence of the print is known. The Poisson probabilities are multiplied by $1/N$, which is the chance of randomly selecting any particular one of these individuals. If there is only one individual in the world with identical fingerprints, then the identification is valid. If there are two individuals, the chance is 1/2 that the identification is valid; and if three individuals, the chance is 1/3; etc. Kingston's calculation answers the following question:

> Given a fingerprint from an unknown source, and assuming an individual is selected randomly from among all persons who actually have the finger-print pattern on their fingers, what is the probability that this one individual made the fingerprint?

The situation is analogous to having all N persons who can make the print present in a closed room. One of the persons inside is randomly selected, and we ask for the probability that this person is the actual source of the print. We can but note that the person is one of the possible sources and that the probability is $1/N$ that we have the correct person. The frequency of the fingerprint determines the magnitude of N, the number of persons in the room.

Contrast this situation with one in which the individuals within the room are selected randomly with respect to fingerprint type, and where we test the individuals to determine if they could have actually made the evidence print. The number of persons in the room (N) now represents a population of suspects to be tested using the evidence print. If fingerprints of an individual in this suspect group match the evidence print, what is the significance of this finding? This question parallels the practice of fingerprint comparison, whereas Kingston's does not. Kingston had assumed that his suspect has been selected solely on the basis of correspondence with the fingerprint. Rarely would this be the case; most often, identification by a partial fingerprint would be a nearly independent event. The comparison would be used to test a few possible suspects rather than to define the suspect group. When many suspects are screened by means of the fingerprint, the chances of false association rise, as pointed out by Amy. Only in the hypothetically absurd extreme, in which the entire population of the world is screened, is Kingston's calculation valid.

To answer the appropriate question posed above, one must compare the chance of the evidence occurring under two hypotheses:

H_1: that the individual in fact made the print
H_2: that another (random) individual made the print

Under H_1, it is certain that the print would match the individual. Under H_2, the probability is the frequency of incidence multiplied by the number of attempts made to compare the print. A likelihood ratio of these two probabilities gives the relative support of the evidence for the two competing hypotheses.[45]

Osterburg Model (1977–1980)

Description of the Osterburg Model

Osterburg et al.[21] used a 1-millimeter grid to divide fingerprints into discrete cells. Within each cell, 1 of 13 minutia events was allowed. These events are given in Table 9.2 with their observed frequencies of occurrence in 39 fingerprints (8S91 cells). Under an assumption of cell independence, the probability of a given set of cell types was taken as the product of the probabilities for each cell, as given in Equation (9.44):

$$P \text{ (set of cells)} = \prod_{i=1}^{n} (p_i) \tag{9.44}$$

Osterburg noted that, according to general practice, the weakest identification which is considered absolute is an identification based on 12 ending ridges. Equation (9.45) gives the probability under the model for this configuration, given an average fingerprint area of 72 mm².

$$P \text{ (12 endings)} = (0.766)^{60}(0.0832)^{12} = 1.25 \times 10^{-21} \tag{9.45}$$

Osterburg proposed that any configuration of cells that exceeded this value be accepted as proof of identity, regardless of the actual number and type of minutiae.

Osterburg corrected for the number of possible positionings of a fingerprint in a way analogous to Amy's model. Suppose the unknown partial fingerprint occupies a rectangular region that measures W millimeters wide and L millimeters high. For a fully recorded print, these values are about 15 and 20 mm, respectively. The number of positionings of the unknown partial fingerprint on ten full fingerprints is calculated in Equation (9.46):

$$\text{Number of positionings} = 10(15 - W + 1)(20 - L + 1) \tag{9.46}$$

The result of Equation (9.44) must be multiplied by the result of Equation (9.46) to obtain the probability of random association for an individual.

The chance of false association for an individual was given using an analysis identical to that of Kingston. The essential feature is to estimate the number of possible sources K in a population of size N and weigh each probability of K by $(1/K)$.

Sclove[46,47] made substantial modifications to the Osterburg model to account for the experimentally observed non-independence of cells and for multiple occurrences within one cell. Sclove found that occupied cells tended

Table 9.2 Osterburg's and Sclove's Relative Frequencies of Minutiae in 1 mm Cells (N = 8591 cells)

Event	Osterburg Frequency	Sclove Frequency
Empty cell	0.766	...
Ending ridge	0.0832	0.497
Fork	0.0382	0.159
Island	0.0177	0.103
Dot	0.0151	0.102
Broken ridge	0.0139	...
Bridge	0.0122	0.0558
Spur	0.00745	0.035
Enclosure	0.00640	0.0263
Delta	0.00198	0.0135
Double fork	0.00140	0.00637
Trifurcation	0.00058	0.00279
Multiple events	0.0355	
Total	1.00	1.00

to cluster. The probability that any one cell is occupied increases regularly with the number of occupied neighboring cells. To model this dependency, Sclove assumed a one-sided Markov-type process. That is, the assumption was made that the probability of a cell being occupied depends only on the outcomes of four of the neighboring cells. Under this model, estimates were made of the conditional probability of occupancy of the cell, given the number of adjacent occupied cells. For border cells, where information regarding the adjacent cells is incomplete, estimates of occupancy were possible by considering the minimum and maximum number for adjacent cell occupancies.

Sclove also proposed a different treatment for multiple occurrences within one cell. Osterburg's method included a cell category of "multiple events." Based on a within-cell data analysis, Sclove justified an assumption of a Poisson distribution for the number of occurrences per cell. The mean number of occurrences in this distribution is, in turn, affected by the number of preceding occupied cells. Sclove noted that his method avoids the need to define minutia density variations across the pattern. Local differences in density are accounted for by the dependent probabilities of cell occupancy.

Calculation of the probability for a given cell configuration proceeds by noting the number of occurrences in each cell, along with the number of preceding occupied adjacent cells. The appropriate conditional mean is then selected from a table based on the number of occupied cells. The Poisson probability for the observed number of occurrences within each cell can then be calculated. This probability is then multiplied by the relative frequencies of any occurrences that appear in the cell. The latter were determined from Osterburg's data and are presented here in the final column of Table 9.2.

Discussion of the Osterburg Model

The Osterburg model is appealing because it is simple to apply and is statistically sophisticated. It is particularly useful for the comparison of individuality among different fingerprints. If some standard configuration of minutiae is defined, the model provides a means to compare other minutia configurations to the standard. The feature that allows this comparison is simply the weighting of compound minutiae by their frequencies of occurrence. Both Santamaria[44] and Kingston[20] had used this concept, but Osterburg's treatment is far more rigorous and perceptive. He has been the only investigator to consider the errors in minutia frequencies. Santamaria's method amounted to a mere suggestion that compound minutiae be weighted according to the number of fundamental minutiae composing them. Kingston used actual frequencies of occurrence of the compound minutiae, but did not consider errors in these frequencies and did not give his criteria for classification of compound minutiae types. As a result, one does not know when two closely spaced minutiae should be considered as a compound form. Osterburg defined his compound minutiae precisely, and Sclove provided definite treatment for other closely spaced minutiae.

Positioning of minutiae is also well treated for comparing the individuality of different fingerprints. Osterburg defined position using a millimeter grid that divided the fingerprint into discrete cells. Discrete cells allowed extensive treatment of correlation by Sclove, making the model robust to local variations in density. (Recall that these variations had been a major problem in Kingston's model.) Osterburg ignored positioning within the cells, but the cells were small, equivalent to about two ridges on a side. Furthermore, Sclove's treatment of multiple events provided flexibility within the cell structure.

Cells that are empty contribute to individuality within the Osterburg model. This is an important feature that has not been included in many of the fingerprint models. Bose[30] was the only other investigator to directly consider the value of featureless ridges. Bose's rudimentary model allowed four equally likely events at each square ridge interval, one of which was a continuous ridge. His model grossly exaggerates the value of a continuous ridge: a single ridge extending for five ridge intervals would be assigned a frequency of less than 1 in a 1000. It is clear, however, that a patch of ridges without minutiae does possess some individuality. Cummins and Midlo[48] pointed out that this contribution makes their estimate of fingerprint individuality more conservative. The other Henry-Balthazard models,[15,16,31,33] along with Roxburgh[17] and Trauring,[19] deny this contribution. Kingston[20] and Amy[18] have indirectly addressed the issue. Each includes a separate calculation of the probability of finding the observed number of minutiae, given the area of the fingerprint. Amy, however, has denied the value of minutia-free border ridges when making his final calculation of $N\{t\}$. Galton[14] allowed a factor of 0.5 for a six ridge interval square region, regardless of content. A featureless region of this size would be assigned a frequency of 0.0908 by Osterburg.

Thus far, we have been discussing the use of Osterburg's model for comparing the individuality in different prints, rather than for determining the significance of a fingerprint comparison. This distinction is important. Comparison of individuality among prints amounts to determining the information content of a fingerprint pattern. In this determination, we are not particularly concerned with the different ways in which the pattern can be expressed or with the details of the pattern. Precise ridge counts would not be expected to significantly affect the information content and it is reasonable that two prints differing only in the placement of one or two minutiae would have nearly the same identification value. Connective ambiguities and deformation of the fingerprint might affect the calculation of information content to some degree, but the problem is not serious. For example, a typical connective ambiguity would create uncertainty about whether a minutia was a fork or an ending ridge. We might assume the minutia to be one or the other, or perhaps take an average of the two frequencies of occurrence. Deformation would affect the relationship of the fingerprint pattern to Osterburg's grid; but without gross distortion, these changes would have little effect on the overall calculation. The number of cells containing the various features would remain practically the same. Where events are grouped differently by the deformation, the effect is also small, as demonstrated by Sclove.[46]

When Osterburg's model is used to evaluate a fingerprint comparison, however, these minor irritations become major weaknesses. The most serious weakness is the omission of the fingerprint ridge structure. Sclove[47] recognized this deficiency in the model, but noted that the calculations would become much more complex with a ridge-dependent metric.

Departure from the ridge structure has been discussed in connection with the Trauring and Kingston models. A model that does not recognize ridges cannot incorporate the basic features of fingerprint comparison. Relative positions of minutiae are not established by absolute distances; only in a topological sense are these positions constant. It is the ridges that serve as landmarks in fingerprint comparison by establishing relative positions through ridge count, establishing orientation of minutiae and correcting for distortions that may be present. Trauring[19] at least recognized the two minutia orientations and offered a means to correct for distortions using reference minutiae. Both the Kingston and Osterburg models ignore these fundamental issues. Osterburg's identification criterion is the occurrence of the same events in corresponding cells as defined by the grid. If a print happens to be slightly compressed or stretched, there could be no such correspondence. If deformation of the grid is allowed, then we admit that not all of the possible configurations of cells are distinguishable, and the foundation of the model is seriously threatened.

Uncertainty in positioning of the grid has a similar effect. Osterburg proposed that the grid first be placed on the fingerprint of unknown origin, and that the comparison proceed by attempting positionings on known fingerprints. Cell-by-cell positionings are accounted for in the model as a feature of the comparison process, although minor positionings and rotations are not. On a single print, these minor operations will create multiple descriptions under the Osterburg model. Again, this means that not all of the possible descriptions will represent distinguishable fingerprints.

The presence of a variety of descriptions within the model for a single fingerprint is suggestive of Amy's $N\{t\}$, that is, the number of minutia arrangements indistinguishable from the one at issue. A correction of this type might be introduced if the number of possible descriptions for one fingerprint were calculated. The calculation would need to incorporate minor horizontal and vertical positionings, rotational positionings, and allowable deformations of the print. Some of the difficulties could be avoided if the grid were positioned in a definite manner relative to some landmark within the print. This is conceptually equivalent to using reference minutiae. The print core, delta regions, or characteristic groups of minutiae might be used. If widely spaced minutiae were used, deformation could be corrected for using Trauring's technique. If any of these modifications were made, however, the simplicity of the Osterburg model would be lost, and although improved, the fundamental importance of ridge count would remain unrecognized.

Connective ambiguity also poses a serious problem to the use of the Osterburg model for evaluation fingerprint comparisons. For any one fingerprint, there will be a variety of minutia configurations that would be identifiable. Variation in minutia type must be allowed during the comparison process. Osterburg joins the Kingston, Amy, Trauring, and Henry-Balthazard models in failing to provide for this essential feature of fingerprint comparison.

Osterburg completed his model with a discussion of the probabilities of false association. Included was a correction for possible positionings, analogous to Amy's. In this respect, there is a recognition that the chance of false association increases with the number of possible comparison positions. The bulk of Osterburg's argument, however, was identical to Kingston's and suffers the same flaws. Most importantly, it assumed that an individual is selected at random from the set of persons who actually have a compatible fingerprint, rather than selected at random from a suspect population.

Stoney and Thornton Model (1985–1989)

Based on the work in Stoney's thesis,[23] Stoney and Thornton[49] critically reviewed earlier fingerprint models and detailed a set of features that should be included in a fingerprint identification model, many of which are echoed in a short criticism by the Federal Bureau of Investigation.[50] Stoney and Thornton followed their review with a survey and description of fingerprint minutia variation that incorporated some of the desired model features.[22,51] Additional data analysis and modifications were later presented by Stoney.[52-54]

Model Features Proposed by Stoney and Thornton

Ridge Structure and Description of Minutia Location

To bear any relation to actual fingerprint comparison, a model must be founded on the ridge structure — this is a fundamental necessity. The ridge system provides topological order to the fingerprint, correcting for minor distortions and providing the basis for comparing the relative positions of minutiae. Locally, the ridge system defines two directions: across the ridge flow and along it. Relative positions of minutiae should be described differently along these two directions. When measuring across ridges, a discrete variable is available: the ridge count. Along the ridges, a continuous linear measure should be used and acceptable error in the continuous measure should be defined.

Description of Minutia Distribution

A description of minutia distribution is needed, one that incorporates these same two measures. None of the models reviewed has such a description. Those models that do utilize ridge counting between minutiae require only that minutiae be ordered correctly on any given ridge.

A comprehensive description of minutia distribution must accommodate local variations in minutia density as well as variation as a result of different patterns of ridge flow. Kingston has demonstrated that rather substantial local variations in minutia density occur. These depend in part on the presence of pattern elements: recurving ridges and triradii. Sclove's modification of Osterburg's model is self-correcting for variations in density, and perhaps this model can be adapted to include discrete ridge counts. However, a more fundamental relationship exists between minutiae and the ridge flow. If an equal number of ridges flow in and out of a region, then for each minutia that produces a ridge, there must be a minutia that consumes a ridge. Imbalance in minutia orientation results in regions with converging or diverging ridges. Thus, if the overall pattern of ridge flow is known, information is also available concerning the orientations and distribution of minutiae. This aspect of minutia distribution has not been included in any of the fingerprint models, but it is obviously an essential element of any comprehensive treatment.

Orientation of Minutiae

Along the ridge flow, two fundamentally distinct orientations of minutiae should be recognized. With the exception of the simple dot, minutiae are formed when ridges are either added to or lost from the system. Minutia orientations, similar to ridge counts, are robust to fingerprint distortions and provide objective criteria for comparison.

Variation in Minutia Type

The difficulties encountered when using compound minutiae have been discussed. Minutiae are best considered as one of three fundamental types: the fork, the ending ridge, or dot. Compound varieties arise when the fundamental types are positioned close to one another. Relative frequencies of the fundamental types should be used, but correlations with the pattern of ridge flow, neighboring minutia types, and minutia density need to be considered.

Variation among Prints from the Same Source

Treatment of variation among fingerprints from one finger is a crucial element of a fingerprint comparison model. We have noted that ridge counts and minutia orientations are robust to fingerprint distortions. Ridge spacing, curvature, and distance between minutiae are variable. Some criteria must be given for acceptable variation in these parameters. The relevant issue is for a particular fingerprint of unknown origin, what is the set of known fingerprint configurations that we would judge to be in agreement? We must characterize this set to calculate the chances of encountering one of its members. The problem is not simple. If the unknown fingerprint appears distorted, we would naturally tolerate more variation. We would also accept more variation as the distance between minutiae increases. A fingerprint model must incorporate these features into the comparison criteria.

Connective ambiguities must also be allowed. As noted by Roxburgh, the quality of the unknown print determines the magnitude of the allowance. In the extreme, each minutia can be considered as one of three possibilities and the ridge count can be affected. It is unrealistic to allow connective ambiguity for all minutiae in the general case, but it is unremarkable to encounter a few ambiguities — even in excellent prints. The amount of ambiguity to be tolerated must be established, based on the quality of the unknown fingerprint, so that the set of acceptable known configurations can be established.

Number of Positionings and Comparisons

The value of any fingerprint for identification is inversely proportional to the chance of false association. This chance depends on the number of comparisons that are attempted. Each attempt carries a potential for chance correspondence; and the greater the number of attempts, the greater the overall chance of false association. "Attempt" means both the number of possible positionings on one individual and the number of different individuals with which the print is compared. A fingerprint model should address this issue and provide a means to determine the number of attempted comparisons.

Description of the Stoney and Thornton Model

Minutia Description and Survey

After proposing their set of model features, Stoney and Thornton performed a systematic study of epidermal ridge minutiae[22] using a ridge-based minutia description method.[51] The study was based on a survey of minutiae from the distal portions of 412 thumbprints (pairs of right and left thumbs, all from males, including 147 Whites, 56 Blacks, and 3 Asians). For each thumbprint, a centrally located focal minutia was chosen and neighboring minutiae were sampled.

The distal portion of thumbprints was chosen by Stoney and Thornton because prints of this area are commonly encountered and because of the absence of pattern type characteristics in this region. Regardless of the pattern type, ridges on the distal portions of the digits show similar ridge flow, conforming to the digital outline, flowing in an arch from one side of the finger to the other.

The focal minutia was selected in a systematic way. A minutia was sought in the most central portion of the ridge having a 5 mm radius of curvature. If there was a single minutia on this ridge, within 45° of the center, then this minutia was chosen. If more than one minutia was present, then the minutia closest to the center line was chosen. If there was no minutia present on the ridge, then successively more distal ridges were examined until a minutia was found.

Once the focal minutia was chosen, neighbor minutiae were sampled within the arc 45° on either side of the minutia, and with ridge counts of up to six ridges proximally and nine ridges distally. The pattern type of the print was also determined, along with measurements of the minutia and ridge densities.

For each neighbor minutiae, the type, orientation, ridge count, and angular distance from the focal minutia was recorded. The minutia types allowed were forks, ending ridges, and dots. Other "compound" forms of minutiae were considered as closely spaced combinations of these three basic minutia types.

Orientation for minutiae was defined in relation to the ridge flow by aligning ridges horizontally. If a minutia produced an extra ridge as one followed the ridges from left to right, the orientation was termed "positive." If a minutia resulted in the loss of a ridge, the orientation was termed "negative." The relative position of neighboring minutiae was described using the two variables: the number of ridges separating the minutiae (the ridge count) and the distance between the minutiae along the ridge flow (distance).

For the ridge counts, a convention was introduced to accommodate minutiae that occurred on the same ridge. This occurs, for example, when one branch of a fork terminates. Either the upper or lower branch could terminate, and either would have a ridge count of zero. Stoney and Thornton assigned either a "+0" or "–0" ridge count in these situations to describe the upper or lower relationship.

The distance along the ridges was measured in units of ridge intervals from one minutia, along its ridge, until encountering a transect line running from the second minutia to the first minutia's ridge, perpendicularly across the ridge flow.

Using this system, Stoney and Thornton concisely described neighboring minutia pairs using six variables: the orientations of the two minutiae, the types of the two minutiae, the ridge count, and the distance. In all, 2645 minutia pairs were sampled.

Statistical Analysis and Findings

Stoney and Thornton's statistical analysis of the 2645 minutia pairs revealed a number of significant findings, which they compared with the work of other investigators. They qualified their work, however, as strictly applying only to the epidermal ridges on the distal tips of the male thumb.

General Findings.   The method of minutia description was found to be acceptable to describe fingerprint variation. Ridge densities (number of ridges per centimeter) were found to be in excellent agreement with earlier studies by Kingston[20] and Cummins, Wait, and McQuitty.[55]

Minutia densities were found to differ from those reported by Kingston,[20] by Osterburg et al.,[21] and Dankmeijer et al.,[56] with the discrepancy attributed to differences in the size and location of sampling regions. The findings did support the generalization made by prior investigators that minutia density varies significantly among different areas within epidermal ridge patterns. In the distal region of the thumbprints, however, no difference in minutia density was seen among the various pattern types.

Distribution of the Number of Neighbor Minutiae.   The number of neighbor minutiae about the centrally chosen focal minutia was found to be normally distributed, with a mean of 6.42 and a standard deviation of 1.76.

Minutia Type Frequencies.   Minutia type frequencies were found to be independent of pattern type, which was in agreement with previous investigators.[57,58] The proportion of ending ridges to forks was found to be in good agreement with Roxburgh,[17] who had used a comparable sampling region, but differed significantly from proportions found by Kingston,[20] Sclove,[47] Okajima,[57] and Loesch.[58] These investigators had sampled area fingerprints other than the distal tips. The proportion of dots was found to be in agreement with Okajima[57] but differed from those found by Kingston[20] and Sclove.[47] Differences among the investigators were attributed to the variety of regions, pattern types, and fingers sampled.

Orientation Frequencies.   Frequencies of minutia orientations on the right and left thumbs were found to exhibit a mirror image relationship, with an excess of positive orientations on the left hand and an equal proportion of excess negative orientations on the right hand. Pooling of the minutiae from both hands resulted in a combined frequency of 0.746 for the preferred minutia orientation, which was in excellent agreement with Amy's value.[18]

Independence of Minutia Type, Orientation, and Distance.   Minutia type and orientation were found to be virtually independent of one another, with a correlation coefficient of only 0.065. The incidence of particular minutia types and orientations was found to be equal for corresponding positive and negative distances along the ridge flow, and independence was observed among minutia type, orientation, and distance along the ridge flow.

Linear Relationship Between Minutia Orientation and Ridge Count. A linear relationship was found between minutia orientation and ridge count, with the proportion of the dominant minutia orientation increasing proximally.

Relationship Between Minutia Type and Ridge Count.   Dot frequencies were not found to vary with ridge count, but the proportion of ending ridges and forks was found to vary significantly with ridge count, with the proportion of ending ridges decreasing proximally. Ridge counts of 1, 0, and −1 were found to show substantially greater proportions of forks than other ridge counts, a finding attributable to the geometrically based restriction on the allowable combinations of minutia types and orientations, given these ridge counts. After an adjustment for these three ridge counts, a linear relationship was observed between the ridge count and the proportion of ending ridges, with the proportion of ending ridges decreasing proximally.

Successful Linear Model. Modified linear models for minutia type and orientation frequencies allowed successful prediction of the observed frequencies on each ridge.

Distribution of Total Ridge Distance. Stoney continued development of his model by demonstrating that the occurrence of neighbor minutiae followed a gamma distribution.[53] This involved defining a new measure of minutia distance: the Total Ridge Distance (TRD). This was the total length of ridges occurring between two minutiae. The findings demonstrated an over-dispersed distribution of minutiae, supporting Kingston's observations based on quadrat sampling.[20]

Relationship Between Spacing and Orientation in Minutia Pairs. Stoney made one further observation regarding nearest-neighbor minutia pairs.[54] For minutiae with opposite orientations, mean distances were significantly smaller than for minutiae with like orientations. This finding was believed to be restricted to areas of the prints under study (distal tips of thumbprints).

Conclusion: Random Occurrence of Specific Minutiae Type and Orientation at a Specific Ridge Location. Based on the survey findings and subsequent analysis, Stoney concluded as follows: "Under ideal printing conditions, the random correspondence in minutia location, orientation and type when searching from one minutia to the next is expected with a frequency of less than 1.2%."[52] Stoney went on to stress that under non-ideal printing conditions, one must allow for greater range in minutia location along ridges and occasionally allow for differences in minutia type.

Discussion of the Stoney and Thornton Model

Stoney and Thornton proposed a set of desired features for a fingerprint model and attempted to meet many of these conditions using their survey of minutiae and subsequent data analysis. It is appropriate to judge the Stoney and Thornton model in relation to their proposed set of desired features.

    Their first required feature was that the ridge structure must be used to describe minutia location, recognizing the anisotropic nature of friction ridge skin by using a continuous variable along the ridge flow and a discrete variable across it. This condition was met.

The next related set of requirements was the description of minutia distribution using the same variables and accommodation of variations in minutia density along with ridge pattern elements and singularities. Stoney and Thornton effectively described the minutia distribution in the distal portion of thumbprints, but they assumed a constant minutia density and did not extend their study to include the pattern areas of fingerprints. Requirements to incorporate two opposing orientations of minutiae and three fundamental minutia types were met in the model.

Consideration of variation among prints from the same source — one of the most critical requirements — was not seriously addressed by Stoney and Thornton. Their tolerances for minutia position were derived from successive printings under ideal conditions: these tolerances are far too low to apply in actual fingerprint comparisons. Likewise, connective ambiguities were not factored into Stoney's ultimate 1.2% ceiling prediction.

Stoney and Thornton also did not meet their final requirement: providing a means to determine the number of attempted comparisons in order to assess the effect on the chance of false association. The significance of this omission is questionable, given the criticisms of Robertson and Vignaux.[59]

There are thus two fundamental limitations to the Stoney and Thornton model. First, the survey, and therefore the model, were of very limited scope, based exclusively on the distal (non-pattern) regions of pairs of thumbprints from 206 males. Second, no mechanism was provided to accommodate prints made under non-ideal printing conditions. Stoney and Thornton acknowledged these weaknesses and their work remains the only model to have attempted to describe minutiae within their ridge structure.

Similar to all the other fingerprint models proposed to date, the Stoney and Thornton model remains untested. What is missing is the use of the model to predict the frequency of occurrence of minutiae configurations, followed by the testing of the accuracy of the prediction.

Champod and Margot Model (1995–1996)

Based on the work in Champod's thesis,[11] Champod and Margot presented a statistical model that utilized computer-generated frequencies of minutiae occurrence and minutia densities.[60] Subsequently, this model was modified to reclassify certain additional, closely spaced minutiae as combined minutiae.[61]

Description of the Champod and Margot Model

Experimental Design

Champod and Margot designed a computer program to search for specific minutiae on fingerprint images. One thousand inked fingerprints were selected for the study, based on the quality and clarity of the inked print. The fingers included 321 ulnar loops from the right index finger, 365 ulnar loops from the right middle finger, 118 ulnar loops from the left middle finger, and 173 whorls from the right middle finger.

The inked fingerprint images were scanned at 800 dpi. Image processing algorithms were used to reduce the images to skeletons in where each ridge was represented by a single pixel line. The skeletal images were hand-verified vs. the original prints to ensure that the minutiae were accurately represented and that no connective ambiguities were introduced by the computer algorithms.

Nine minutia types were allowed. Ridge endings and bifurcations were considered fundamental minutia types, with seven additional compound minutia types (consisting of combinations of two fundamental minutiae). The seven compound types were defined as:

1. Island (*aka* short ridge), including the point as a special case (*aka* dot)
2. Lake (*aka* enclosure)
3. Opposed bifurcations, including the cross as a special case
4. Bridge
5. Double bifurcation, including the trifurcation as a special case
6. Hook (*aka* spur)
7. Bifurcation opposed with an ending

(Additional non-combined compound minutiae were defined in a later paper: interruptions, deviations, two ridge endings side-by-side, and ridge ending into a bifurcation.[61])

The compound minutiae were also subject to a maximum distance of separation between the two component fundamental minutiae. The program permitted these values to be determined separately for each compound minutia type.

The positions of minutiae were defined as the ending pixel on the skeleton for the ridge ending, the separation pixel for the bifurcation, and as the pixel in the middle of the segment that relates the fundamental minutiae in the compound minutiae.

Within the print, all minutia positions were recorded relative to the (classically defined) core of the fingerprint pattern. Cartesian coordinates and the number of ridges between the core and each minutia were used as indicators of position. Orientations of minutiae were only defined relative to other minutiae and only in areas where the ridge flow was in a constant direction. Orientation was defined relative to the vertical axis.

The compound minutiae were also characterized by their length; that is, the distance separating the two component fundamental minutiae.

Table 9.3   Champod's Upper Bound Frequencies for Minutia Types in the Three Statistically Different Regions of Fingerprints

Minutia Type	Delta	Out of Delta	Periphery
Ridge endings	0.420	0.571	0.658
Bifurcations	0.193	0.360	0.260
Short ridges (islands) and dots (points)	0.163	0.215	0.204
Enclosures (lakes)	0.059	0.063	0.022
Opposed bifurcations and cross	0.012	0.037	0.011
Bridge	0.092	0.041	0.021
Double bifurcation and trifurcation	0.112	0.086	0.011
Spur (hook)	0.128	0.068	0.052
Bifurcation opposed with an ending	0.066	0.062	0.009

Statistical Analysis and Findings

Minutia Density.   Champod and Margot found that the density of minutiae on the prints varied considerably, with higher densities in the core and delta regions. The number of minutiae was found to rigorously follow a Poisson distribution in the area above the core, and to have minor deviations from this distribution in the area under the core. The Poisson estimator λ, being based on density, varied with the position in the prints, but was found to be constant for a given positioning from the delta. This was consistent across all fingers.

Regional Frequencies of Minutia Types.   Minutia type frequencies were determined for each of eight 45° sectors about the core and within concentric regions divided by five ridge count intervals. It was observed that regions corresponding to the core or to the delta presented more compound minutiae than the periphery of the print.

Based on the findings, upper-bound frequencies for regional minutia types were calculated for each of the three areas: the delta area, the area outside the delta, and the periphery zone. (The periphery was defined as a ridge count of 15 or more from the core.) These upper-bound frequencies are presented in Table 9.3. With the exception of the occurrence of short ridges and dots (the two being considered one type), each type was found to be independent of the others, as well as of the number of minutiae found. The frequencies (Table 9.3) did not vary by finger, but were seen to vary by pattern type.

Relative Orientations of Minutiae.   Relative orientations were studied in 45° sectors about the core, excepting the delta region. The results showed that negative orientation was more frequent for ulnar loops on the right hand and that the reverse was true for the ulnar loops on the left hand. Separate

Table 9.4   Champod's Upper Bound Frequencies for Minutia Orientations in the Three Statistically Different Regions of Fingerprints

Minutia Type	Above Delta	Opposite Delta	Beside Delta
Ridge endings, positive	0.332	0.359	0.190
Ridge endings, negative	0.708	0.690	0.841
Bifurcations, positive	0.439	0.235	0.246
Bifurcations, negative	0.622	0.815	0.809
Other bifurcation types, positive	0.442	0.294	0.264
Other bifurcation types, negative	0.666	0.863	0.821

upper-bound frequencies for each of the minutia types having orientation were determined for each of the three non-delta quadrants. These frequencies are presented in Table 9.4.

The frequencies in Table 9.4 did not vary by finger or by ridge count. Some of the frequencies were pattern dependent, suggesting that orientations are influenced by the position of deltas. The orientation frequencies were found to be partially dependent on the type of minutia, but independent of the number of minutiae present.

Lengths of Compound Minutiae.   Lengths of each of the compound minutiae (other than the bridge and spur) were grouped into five intervals. The distribution within each of the intervals was determined and these distributions were compared in different regions of the fingerprints. Again, only the occurrence of short ridges and dots was found to vary with position on the print. The length variable for the other compound types was found to show regional independence. Each of the compound minutiae was independent of the number of minutiae and their relative orientations.

Conclusion

Champod and Margot found that their data and the statistical analysis confirmed and refined the validity of a calculation model used to express the probability of a configuration of minutiae.

Using their conservative, upper-bound estimates, they calculated the probabilities of occurrence of two minutia configurations under their model. One of the configurations had seven fundamental minutiae (five ridge endings and two bifurcations). This configuration was assigned a probability of 1/40,000. The second configuration had three fundamental minutiae and three combined minutiae (three ridge endings, one enclosure, one spur, and one opposed bifurcation). This configuration was assigned a probability of 1 in 1.42×10^9. It was noted that these calculations did not take into account the probability of the ridge arrangements; inclusion of this additional constraint would make the probability still lower.

Champod and Margot noted the relatively high significance of compound minutiae in these calculations. Similar high significance was later shown in two additional compound minutia types, although a third (two ridge endings side by side) was found to have a high frequency in the delta region.[61]

Several weaknesses of the model were acknowledged, including:

1. The position of the minutiae relative to the core must be known. If it is not, then different calculations need to be considered.
2. The model does not allow connective ambiguities and, if they must be accommodated, multiple weighted calculations would be necessary.
3. If the finger and position of the print on the finger is not known, then calculations of the number of possible positionings of the print on a suspect's hands must be considered.

The authors concluded that the study strongly suggested the possibility of evaluating fingerprint evidence in a probabilistic way.

Discussion of the Champod and Margot Model

Champod and Margot collected data far exceeding any prior study and analyzed that data in an innovative, effective way. The fundamental weakness of the model is its failure to focus explicitly on the minutiae within the ridge structure. The use of ridges is restricted to locating minutiae in concentric bands about the core, five ridges wide. This weakness in the model is acknowledged, and is one of the reasons that the calculations are presented as conservative.

At the same time, however, there are a number of other aspects (also acknowledged) that make the probabilities inappropriately low. These were listed in the prior chapter section: the need to know positioning relative to the core, the need to accommodate connective ambiguities, and the need to consider the number of possible positionings of the print as a whole.

Champod and Margot did not study variation in prints from the same finger and avoided defining tolerances for correspondence in minutia position and in compound minutia length. This was achieved by grouping minutia position and length variables into wide intervals — intervals that appear to substantially exceed comparison tolerances.

In contrast to Stoney and Thornton, who rigorously avoided defining compound minutiae, Champod and Margot explicitly define them and introduce the compound minutia length as a new variable. This is an innovative and important aspect of their model, and one that is made possible by their large data set. By comparison, Stoney and Thornton sampled less than one sixth the number of minutiae, and sampled these from the peripheral region that Champod and Margot proved to be substantially under-populated in compound minutiae.

One questionable aspect of the Champod and Margot model is the grouping of short ridges and dots into one compound minutia category. This category suspiciously stands out (alone) as non-independent in three of the statistical tests. Dots, as the extreme in a short ridge, are an unambiguous, single pore structure, and empirical observations strongly suggest that they do not occur independently. Many prints are seen where there are abundant dots, far more than would be possible given their overall frequency.

Unfortunately, once again, the Champod and Margot model, like all the other fingerprint models proposed to date, remains untested. To reiterate: what is missing is the use of the model to predict the frequency of occurrence of minutiae configurations, followed by the testing of the accuracy of the prediction.

Meagher, Budowle, and Ziesig Model (1999)

The most recent model for fingerprint individuality was developed as a specific response to challenges that fingerprint evidence does not meet the Daubert criteria for admissibility.

Description of the Meagher, Budowle, and Ziesig Model

Meagher, Budowle, and Ziesig utilized AFIS computer matching to inter-compare electronic fingerprint records. The records were a set of 50,000 rolled fingerprints, all from white males and all of the "left loop" pattern class. This restriction of pattern type increased the chances of fingerprints being similar because the general flow of the ridges in all the fingerprints in the set was the same. The size of the data set was restricted so that the experimentation could be completed in time for the Daubert hearing. Two experiments were conducted on this data set.

The First Experiment, Based on Inter-comparing Records of Rolled Fingerprints

In the first experiment, each of the 50,000 full fingerprint records was compared with itself and with each of the other 49,999 records. Two different fingerprint matching algorithms were used, resulting in two different scores for each of the comparisons. For each algorithm, the score from comparing the print to itself was used to normalize the other 49,999 scores. A third algorithm was used to combine the two scores for each print and to select (again for each print) the 500 most similar fingerprints from among the print's 50,000 scores. The distribution of these $500 \times 50,000$ non-matching scores was then compared to the distribution of the 50,000 scores that resulted from comparing each of the fingerprint images to itself. This was done by assuming normal distributions and applying a sample Z score.

When examining the Z scores for the non-identical prints, Meagher, Budowle, and Ziesig noted three comparisons with unusually high scores (6.98, 6.95, and 3.41). Investigation of these comparisons led to the discovery that they had resulted from comparisons of different prints from the same finger. That is, within the data set of 50,000 prints, there had unintentionally been included some rolled inked prints that had been made by the same finger on different occasions. The three scores that were unusually high were attributed to:

1. Comparing Print A of Individual 1 with Print B of Individual 1
2. Comparing Print B of Individual 1 with Print A of Individual 1
3. Comparing Print A of Individual 2 with Print B of Individual 2

From these results, it was apparent that another same-finger, different-print comparison was in the set; namely:

4. Comparing Print B of Individual 2 with Print A of Individual 2

This comparison was subsequently found to have a Z score of 1.79, well in among the scores of the non-identical prints. After discovery of these two pairs of prints from the same fingers, these prints were excluded from the analysis.

Meagher, Budowle, and Ziesig proceeded by noting that the largest remaining Z score for the non-identical print comparisons was 1.83 and that the smallest Z score for the comparisons of the same print with itself (under the hypothesis of equal means) was 21.7. For the two-sample test of means, this Z score is associated with a probability of $1/10^{97}$; thus, Meagher, Budowle, and Ziesig concluded that the probability of a non-mate rolled fingerprint being identical to any particular fingerprint was less than this value. They went on to state that, given a world population of 5.9×10^9, the approximate chance of any two rolled fingerprints on Earth being identical was $59/10^{88}$, a value obtained by multiplying their original probability by the world finger population.

The Second Experiment, Based on Comparing Subsets of the Records with the Same Complete Records

The second experiment conducted by Meagher, Budowle, and Ziesig closely followed the first, but simulated latent prints, constructed from the 50,000 prints, were used to compare against the same set of 50,000 prints. To construct the simulated latent prints, the central 21.7% of the whole rolled fingerprint was isolated. This area was chosen as it was the average area found in a set of 300 latent fingerprints. The simulated latent prints, each actually a subset of the original electronic fingerprint record, were then compared against each of the 50,000 full fingerprint records.

The same software was used to compare fingerprints, compute scores, and consolidate the scores. The same statistical analysis was performed.

As with the first experiment, examination of the Z scores from the non-identical prints revealed a number of unusually high scores. These included the four same-finger, different print comparisons discovered in the first experiment, here showing Z scores of 8.00, 7.58, 8.01, and 8.38. Additionally, another same-finger, different print pair was discovered, showing Z scores of 3.91 and 5.85.

Similar to the first experiment, these different prints from the same finger were excluded from the analysis. Meagher, Budowle, and Ziesig proceeded by grouping the Z score results according to the number of minutiae in the simulated latent print and a chart was prepared of Z score vs. minutia count. The highest Z scores for the non-identical print comparisons were plotted, along with the Z scores for the comparisons of the simulated latent prints with their corresponding original electronic record (under the hypothesis of equal means).

Meagher, Budowle, and Ziesig concluded by calculating probabilities that simulated latent prints with a particular minutia count would be identical to a subset of any particular fingerprint. For a simulated latent with a small number of minutiae (c.f. 4) they stated that the probability was less than $1/10^{27}$, decreasing with larger numbers of minutiae (c.f. 18) to $1/10^{97}$ (the same probability offered in the first experiment for complete rolled fingerprints).

Following their earlier analysis, Meagher, Budowle, and Ziesig compared the larger (4 minutia) probability with the world population, concluding that the chance of any two (small) minutia subsets from any (different) fingerprints on earth being identical was $59/10^{18}$.

Discussion of the Meagher, Budowle, and Ziesig Model

The Meagher, Budowle, and Ziesig model has been discussed by Stoney[62-64] and by Wayman.[65] The major issue with this model is that, with the exception of the excluded data, the Meagher, Budowle, and Ziesig experiments do not include comparing two different prints of the same finger with each other. All actual fingerprint comparisons have this aspect, and every fingerprint examiner knows that no two impressions from the same finger are exactly alike. There would never be an occasion to compare a single fingerprint with itself.

The model, therefore makes an extremely elementary, fundamental mistake. It contrasts scores of two types:

1. Scores from comparing individual, single fingerprints with themselves (high scores)
2. Scores from comparing fingerprints from different fingers (low scores)

The conclusions from the model stem from showing how unlikely it would be for scores from type 2 comparisons to be as high as those from type 1. What is missing are comparisons of another type: comparisons of different prints from the same finger.

Sparrow[66] has commented on this practice when used for the (much less critical) task of testing AFIS matcher accuracy:

> "One of the most obvious errors involves using one set of cards as the 'file set' (perhaps embedding them into a much larger existing database) and then reentering a selection of that same card set as searches. Clearly such a test does not assess a system's ability to match different images created from the same finger. It tests only the system's ability to match images, not fingers. It does not, therefore, test the system's ability to cope with either the spatial or topological distortions that occur from one image of a fingerprint to the next. Dealing with these various distortions is the very heart of the fingerprint matching problem."

Since fingerprints were first used as evidence it has been axiomatic that no two prints from the same finger are exactly alike. Meagher, Budowle, and Ziesig conduct their experiments as if the opposite is true: they assume that all fingerprints from the same finger will be identical. Indeed, when different (high-quality, professionally rolled) fingerprints from the same finger were (inadvertently) included in the data set, much lower Z scores were found.

In all, there were three instances uncovered where second prints of the same finger were included in the study. These three pairs of prints provided six comparisons. In the first experiment, three of the six comparisons showed suspiciously high Z scores, but still tremendously lower scores than those for the comparison of the same print to itself (6.98, 6.95, and 3.51 compared to 21.7). The Z scores for the other three "same finger/different print" comparisons were even lower, so low that they were well within the distribution of Z scores for prints from different fingers (1.47, 1.83, and 1.79). This means that once one includes different prints from the same finger, as opposed to comparing a single print with itself, one gets scores that can be indistinguishable from those found by comparing prints from different fingers. This renders the model worthless for documenting the individuality of fingerprints and demonstrates that, for the experiments as designed, the two populations are too close to distinguish.

In actuality, we do not know how many pairs of different prints from the same finger are present among the 50,000. Three pairs were uncovered, but only because of the unusually high Z scores. There could well be more.

Compounding and including this most fundamental error, the second experiment also employed the thoroughly discredited practice of using subsets of inked prints to simulate latent prints. Sparrow[66] has also commented on this conceptual error:

> "A much more common error is to create artificial latent marks by masking rolled images. Occasionally, the images are deliberately blurred (smudged or de-focused), and some areas are obscured. Then the newly created partial prints are entered as latent, with the original rolled images being incorporated into the file database. This approach fails to emulate the real world of operational fingerprint comparison in that no distortion of any kind is introduced — neither spatial nor topological. The search print is actually a piece of the matching file print image. Again, this tests the system's ability to match pieces of identical images, not different images made by the same finger."

It is remarkable that a study with such fundamental flaws was presented in court, especially with the internal inconsistencies of the "same finger/different print" comparisons. The defects were immediately recognized and fully explained in opposing briefs and testimony. Subsequently, Wayman provided a criticism, "When Bad Science Leads to Good Law."[65] In addition to pointing out the fundamental errors of comparing the images to themselves and the use of masked pseudo-latents, Wayman questioned the assumption of normality in the data.

> "The comparison of images to themselves lead, of course, to extremely high scores, which researchers called the 'perfect match' score. Because in life fingerprints are always changing, no real comparison of two *different* images of the same finger will ever yield such a high score. By adopting, as definition of 'in common,' the score obtained by identical images, the government very strongly biased any results in the *government's* favor.
>
> "Now the government did something worse: They looked at all the scores between different fingerprint images and declared them to follow a 'bell curve.' There are potentially an infinite number of curves that could fit the data, some better than others. There are simple tests available to show if the 'bell curve,' or any other curve, roughly fits the data. No such tests, which might have eliminated the 'bell curve' assumption, were performed, however. Now, the government simply pulled out a college-level textbook on statistical estimation and, based on the 'bell curve' assumption, found

the probability of two different prints being 'in common,' as previously and unreasonably defined, to be one in 10^{97}. This number, 10^{97}, is extremely large.... It is possible that in the entire future of mankind there will never be 10^{97} fingerprints. Yet, the government is comfortable predicting the fingerprints of the entire history and future of mankind from a sample of 50,000 images, which could have come from as few as 5000 people. They have disguised this absurd guess by claming reliance on *statistical estimation*."

Meagher, Budowle, and Ziesig also incorrectly applied their probability to the world population. After calculating their probability that a non-mate fingerprint would match any particular fingerprint, they multiplied this probability by the world population to arrive at "the approximate chance that any two fingerprints on earth" would be identical. This is a basic error. The point is often illustrated in basic statistics courses by calculating the probability that two persons in a classroom of, say 30, would have the same birthday. Although there is a 1/365 chance of a match between two people, there is a more than 70% chance that there will be one or more shared birthdays among 30 people. This is a minor point, however, given the far more fundamental conceptual errors in these experiments.

The Meagher, Budowle, and Ziesig model is extraordinarily flawed and highly misleading. It was specifically designed to "prove the uniqueness" of fingerprints in a Daubert hearing, and incorporates a profound ignorance of both forensic science and statistics. Perhaps the most remarkable aspect of these experiments is that they continue to be introduced in such hearings. Whether or not the courts ultimately feel there is any question about fingerprints meeting the conditions of Daubert, there can be no doubt that the Meagher, Budowle, and Ziesig model itself could not.

Conclusions

From a statistical viewpoint, the scientific foundation for fingerprint individuality is incredibly weak. Beginning with Galton and extending through Meagher, Budowle, and Ziesig, there have been a dozen or so statistical models proposed. These vary considerably in their complexity, but in general there has been much speculation and little data. Champod's work is perhaps the exception, bringing forth the first realistic means to predict frequencies of occurrence of specific combinations of ridge minutiae. None of the models has been subjected to testing, which is of course the basic element of the scientific approach. As our computer capabilities increase, we can expect that there will be the means to properly model and test hypotheses regarding the variability in fingerprints. The most difficult challenge will remain the growth and acceptance of scientific practices in the fingerprint profession itself. We can be encouraged by the dedication of fingerprint practitioners and by the many other progressive changes that are well underway. These include, most notably, the open debate in the professional literature, efforts toward standardization, increased training, and professional certification.

References

1. Ashbaugh, D.R., *Quantitative-Qualitative Friction Ridge Analysis*, CRC Press, Boca Raton, FL, 1999, 103.

2. Daubert *v.* Merrell Dow Pharmaceuticals, 509 U.S. 579 (1993).

3. Dalrymple, B., Fingerprints (Dactyloscopy) Identification and Classification in *Encyclopedia of Forensic Science*, Siegel, J. et al., Eds., Academic Press, New York, 2000, 872.

4. Ashbaugh, D.R., *Quantitative-Qualitative Friction Ridge Analysis*, CRC Press, Boca Raton, FL, 1999, 89.

5. United States of America vs. Byron Mitchell, U.S. District Court Eastern District of Philadelphia. Government Exhibit A in Daubert Hearing before Judge J. Curtis Joyner, July 7, 1999.

6. Ashbaugh, D.R., *Quantitative-Qualitative Friction Ridge Analysis*, CRC Press, Boca Raton, FL, 1999, 138.

7. Loesch, D.Z., *Quantitative Dermatoglyphics*, Oxford University Press, New York, 1983.

8. Moenssens, A.A., *Fingerprint Techniques*, Chilton Book Company, Radnor, PA, 1971, 262.

9. Kingston, C.R. and Kirk, P.L., Historical development and evaluation of the '12 point rule' in fingerprint identification, *Int. Criminal Police Rev.*, 186, 62, 1965.

10. Champod, C., Edmond Locard — Numerical standards and 'probable' identifications, *J. Forensic Ident.*, 45, 136, 1995.

11. Evett, I.W. and Williams, R.L., A review of the sixteen points fingerprint standard in England and Wales, *J. Forensic Ident.*, 46, 49, 1996.

12. Cowger, J.F., *Friction Ridge Skin*, Elsevier, New York, 1983.

13. Margot, P. and German, E., Fingerprint identification breakout meeting "Ne'urim Declaration", in *Proc. Int. Symp. Fingerprint Detection and Identification*, Almog, J. and Springer, E., Eds., Israel National Police, Jerusalem, 1996, 21.

14. Galton, F., *Finger Prints*, McMillan, London, 1892, 100.

15. Henry, E.R., *Classification and Uses of Fingerprints*, Routledge & Sons, London, 1900, 54.

16. Balthazard, V., De l'identification par les empreintes digitales, *Comptes Rendus, des Academies des Sciences*, 152, 1862, 1911.

17. Roxburgh, T., On the evidential value of finger prints, *Sankhya: Indian J. Stat.*,1, 189, 1933.

18. Amy, L., Valeur de la preuve en dactyloscopie I., *J. Soc. Stat. Paris,* 88, 80, 1946.

19. Trauring, M., Automatic comparison of finger-ridge patterns, *Nature*, 197, 938, 1963.

20. Kingston, C.R., Probabilistic Analysis of Partial Fingerprint Patterns, D. Crim. dissertation, University of California, Berkeley, 1964.

21. Osterburg, J. et al., Development of a mathematical formula for the calculation of fingerprint probabilities based on individual characteristics, *J. Am. Stat. Assoc.*, 72, 772, 1977.

22. Stoney, D.A. and Thornton, J.I., A systematic study of epidermal ridge minutiae, *J. Forensic Sci.*, 32, 1182, 1987.

23. Stoney, D.A., A Quantitative Assessment of Fingerprint Individuality, Ph.D. dissertation, University of California, Berkeley, 1985.

24. Champod, C., Reconnaissance Automatique et Analyze Statistique des Minuties sur les Emreintes Digitales. Doctoral thesis, Université de Lausanne, Institut de Police Scientifique et de Criminologie, 1995.

25. Meagher, S.B., Budowle, B., and Ziesig, D., 50K vs. 50K fingerprint comparison test, United States of America vs. Byron Mitchell, U.S. District Court Eastern District of Philadelphia. Government Exhibits 6-8 and 6-9 in Daubert Hearing before Judge J. Curtis Joyner, July 8-9, 1999.

26. Roxburgh, T., Galton's work on the evidential value of finger prints, *Sankhya: Indian J. Stat.*, 1, 50, 1933.

27. Pearson, K., *The Life and Letters of Francis Galton*, Vol. IIIA, University Press, Cambridge, 1930, 182.

28. Kingston, C.R., Probabilistic Analysis of Partial Fingerprint Patterns, D. Crim. dissertation, University of California, Berkeley, 1964, 12.

29. Galton, F., *Finger Prints*, McMillan, London, 1892, 107.

30. Bose, R.H.C., *Finger Prints Companion*, quoted in Roxburgh, T., Galton's work on the evidential value of finger prints, *Sankhya: Indian J. Stat.*, 1, 50, 1933.

31. Wentworth, B. and Wilder, H.H., *Personal Identification*, Richard G. Badger, Boston, 1918, 312.

32. Cummins, H. and Midlo, C., *Finger Prints, Palms and Soles*, Blakiston, Philadelphia, 1943, 143.

33. Gupta, S.R., Statistical survey of ridge characteristics, *Int. Criminal Police Rev.*, 218, 130, 1968.

34. Amy, L., Recherches sur l'identification des traces papillaires, *Ann. Med. Legale*, 28, 96, 1948.

35. Roxburgh, T., Galton's work on the evidential value of finger prints, *Sankhya: Indian J. Stat.*, 1, 62, 1933.

36. Galton, F., *Finger Prints*, McMillan, London, 1892, 91.

37. Amy, L., Valeur de la preuve en dactyloseopie II, *J. Soc. .Stat. Paris*, 88, 189, 1946.

38. Amy, L., Recherches sur l'identification des traces papillaires, *Ann. Med. Legale*, 28, 96, 1948.

39. Battley, H., *Single Finger Prints*, Yale University Press, New Haven, 1932, 9.

40. Cowger, J.F., *Friction Ridge Skin*, Elsevier, New York, 1983, 174.

41. Kingston, C.R., Probabilistic Analysis of Partial Fingerprint Patterns, D. Crim. dissertation, University of California, Berkeley, 1964, 61.

42. Locard, E., *Traité de Criminalistique*, Vol. 1, Desvigne, Lyon, 1930, 221.

43. Osterburg, J., An inquiry into the nature of proof: the identity of fingerprints, *J. Forensic Sci.*, 9, 413, 1964.

44. Santamaria, F., A new method for evaluating ridge characteristics, *Fingerprint and Identification Magazine*, 36, 3, 1955.

45. Aitken, C.G.G. *Statistics and the Evaluation of Evidence for Forensic Scientists*, Wiley, New York, 1995, 41.

46. Sclove, S.L., The occurrence of fingerprint characteristics as a two-dimensional process, *J. Am. Stat. Assoc.*, 74, 588, 1979.

47. Sclove, S.L., The occurrence of fingerprint characteristics as a two-dimensional Poisson process, *Commun. Stat.- Theoretical Methods*, A9, 675, 1980.

48. Cummins, H. and Midlo, C., *Finger Prints, Palms and Soles*, Blakiston, Philadelphia, 1943, 152.

49. Stoney, D.A. and Thornton, J.I., A critical analysis of quantitative fingerprint individuality models, *J. Forensic Sci.*, 31, 1187, 1986.

50. Federal Bureau of Investigation, An analysis of standards in fingerprint identification, *FBI Law Enforcement Bull.*, 46(6), 7, 1972.

51. Stoney, D.A. and Thornton, J.I., A method for the description of minutia pairs in epidermal ridge patterns, *J. Forensic Sci.*, 31, 1217, 1986.

52. Stoney, D.A., Local modeling of ridge minutiae, *J. Can. Soc. Forensic Sci.*, 20, 86, 1987.

53. Stoney, D.A., Distribution of epidermal ridge minutiae, *Am. J. Phys. Anthro.*, 77, 367, 1988.

54. Stoney, D.A., Observations on orientation and distances between nearest-neighbor minutiae, *Am. J. Phys. Anthro.*, 78, 309, 1989.

55. Cummins, H., Waits, W.J., and McQuitty, J.T., The breadths of epidermal ridges on the fingertips and palms: a study of variation, *Am. J. Anat.*, 68, 127, 1941.

56. Dankmeijer, J., Waltman, J.M., and De Wilde, A.G., Biological foundations for forensic identifications based on fingerprints, *Acta Morphologica Neerlando-Scandivanica*, 18, 67, 1980.

57. Okajima, M., Frequency of forks in epidermal-ridge minutiae in the finger print, *Am. J. Phys. Anthro.*, 32, 41, 1970.

58. Loesch, D., Minutiae and clinical genetics, *J. Mental Deficiency Res.*, 17, 97, 1973.

59. Robertson, B. and Vignaux, G.A., *The Interpretation of Expert Evidence*, John Wiley & Sons, New York, 1994, 95.

60. Champod, C. and Margot, P.-A., Computer assisted analysis of minutiae occurrences on fingerprints, in *Proc. Int. Symp. Fingerprint Detection and Identification*, Almog, J. and Springer, E., Eds., Israel National Police, Jerusalem, 1996, 305.

61. Champod, C. and Margot, P.-A., Analysis of minutiae occurrences on fingerprints — The search for non-combined minutiae, in *Proc. Int. Assoc. Forensic Sciences*, (IAFS), Tokyo (Japan), August 27, 1996.

62. Stoney, D.A. Direct testimony in United States of America v. Byron Mitchell, U.S. District Court Eastern District of Philadelphia, Daubert Hearing before Judge J. Curtis Joyner, July 12, 1999, 35.

63. Stoney, D.A. Cross examination in United States of America v. Byron Mitchell, U.S. District Court Eastern District of Philadelphia, Daubert Hearing before Judge J. Curtis Joyner, July 12, 1999, 235.

64. Stoney, D.A. Testimony in United States of America v. Hilerdieu Alteme et al., Federal District Court, Southern District of Florida, Daubert Hearing before Judge Lurana S. Snow, April 3, 2000, 9.

65. Wayman, J.L., When bad science leads to good law: the disturbing irony of the Daubert hearing in the case of U.S. v. Byron C. Mitchell, Biometrics Publications, National Biometric Test Center, San Jose State University, http://www.engr.sjsu.edu/biometrics/publications_daubert.html, 2000.

66. Sparrow, M.K., Measuring AFIS matcher accuracy, *The Police Chief*, April 1994, 147.

The Expert Fingerprint Witness

10

ROBERT J. HAZEN
CLARENCE E. PHILLIPS

Contents

0-8493-0923-9/01/$0.00+$1.50
© 2001 by CRC Press LLC

The fingerprint expert is unique among forensic specialists. Because fingerprint science is objective and exact, conclusions reached by fingerprint experts are absolute and final. Acceptance of fingerprint experts did not spontaneously evolve; it was scientifically and painstakingly developed over the past 80 years through the diligent efforts of innumerable identification officers. They established a heritage of exactness in their fingerprint identifications that is now routinely accepted and relied upon in courts of law. The professional status of the fingerprint expert is well earned and demands preservation. It is a standard of excellence by which all who participate in the scientific area of fingerprint identification are judged. It is the authors' hope that by studying this chapter, identification officers will further enhance their expertise as expert fingerprint witnesses and thereby stand ready to perform this vital service while at the same time maintaining and enhancing this priceless heritage.

A discussion of a recent (July 1999) hearing in a case (U.S. v. Byron C. Mitchell, U.S. District Court for the Eastern District of Pennsylvania) that raised the issue of fingerprint individuality in a *Daubert* context can be found in the Appendix to this chapter.

Definition of an Expert

An expert is generally defined as any person who is skilled in a specific science, trade, or occupation. Because of this particular knowledge, the expert is qualified to analyze or compare a stated set of facts and render an opinion based upon those facts. This opinion is permitted because of the expert's special knowledge, which the layperson generally does not possess.

Qualifications of the Fingerprint Expert

The fingerprint expert may acquire this expertise in a variety of ways. For the most part, however, expertise comes from experience gained through on-the-job training or by working as an apprentice for an experienced, recognized expert. The expert has also participated in formal classroom training in fingerprint classification and advanced latent fingerprint techniques.

Knowledge of the Fingerprint Expert

It is imperative that the expert be knowledgeable in all phases of the fingerprint science.

Fingerprint History

The fingerprint expert is often questioned on the witness stand relative to the historical development of the science. The expert must be knowledgeable regarding the fingerprint pioneers and their contributions to the development of fingerprint science.

Fingerprint Classification

The expert must possess a thorough understanding of the basic Henry fingerprint classification system and be able to explain and illustrate all phases thereof. This expert must also be aware that there are fingerprint classification systems other than the Henry system.

Latent Print Procedures

The expert needs a thorough understanding of all phases of latent fingerprint matters, including

1. Powder and chemical development of latent prints
2. Elements of the perspiration to which the different chemical developers respond
3. Formulas necessary for mixing chemicals
4. Comparison of latent and inked prints
5. Detection of latent prints by laser and other light amplification technology technologies

Scientific Publications

1. The expert must keep abreast of the latest developments in the fingerprint science by reading publications and periodicals, including the

FBI Law Enforcement Bulletin, Journal of Forensic Sciences, Journal of Forensic Identification, and *Fingerprint Whorld.*

2. It is especially advantageous for the expert to have written articles, papers, or books on the various phases of the fingerprint science.

Evidence Examination

The ultimate conclusion, which is possible in any evidence examination, is the appearance of the expert in a court of law for the purpose of presenting testimony relative to any phase of the examination. This testimony may result from a negative as well as a positive examination. It is therefore important that all correspondence, as well as the rough and complete notes, be retained for each and every phase of the examination. This process should begin when the evidence is initially received and end when final disposition is completed. The following are some of the forms and records the expert should keep.

Evidence Receipt Form

When evidence is delivered to the expert's department from another law enforcement agency, a letter from the head of that agency should accompany the evidence to be examined. From time to time, however, evidence will be delivered without a letter or a telephone request will be received. When this occurs, an evidence receipt form should be completed. A similar form can also be utilized to facilitate the handling of intradepartmental evidence. An example of an evidence receipt form appears in Figure 10.1.

Worksheet (Notes)

Handwritten notes made during the examination should be recorded on a specific form or worksheet (see Figure 10.2). Items that must be recorded on the work sheet include:

1. The exact time and date that the evidence was received
2. The specific and exact quantity, type, and condition of the evidence when it was received
3. The name(s) of the person(s) to whom the response is to be directed, as well as the name(s) of the person(s) who should receive copies of the report
4. Type(s) of examination(s) conducted on the evidence
5. Method used to develop the latent prints
6. Number of latent finger- and palmprints developed and on what specimens they were developed (unless obvious in photographs or on evidence, location of latent prints on each item must also be recorded)

7. Results of comparisons conducted
8. The number of latent prints identified with a specific individual and on what specimens the latent prints appear
9. The particular fingers identified
10. Complete names, known arrest numbers, social security numbers, and dates of birth of all persons whose prints were compared
11. Identity of examiner who noted (coexamined) the evidence and verified the identifications
12. Time and date the examination was completed
13. Method used to mark each piece of evidence (so expert can readily identify each item in court)
14. Final disposition of the evidence (In most jurisdictions, evidence must be returned to the contributing agency by registered mail. Registry number should be retained. Disposition of intradepartmental evidence can be documented using a special form.)
15. Name of contributor of evidence
16. Expert's reference numbers and contributor's reference number if received from another agency
17. Request for special handling or answer
18. Registry or certified mail number under which evidence was received
19. Full name, rank, and title of person making delivery (if evidence is hand-delivered)

If during testimony it becomes difficult to remember the facts, the expert should refer to the worksheet. It is important to obtain authorization from the judge before doing this. It should be pointed out, however, that continual reference to the worksheet can create the impression that the expert is inadequately prepared. Under the Jenks Act (Title 18, U.S. Code), the defense attorney may request to see and then cross-examine the expert from any worksheet referred to during testimony. It is wise to have a photocopy of the worksheet for consultation if the defense attorney conducts a cross-examination from the original worksheet. If handwritten, all notes should be legible.

Appearance and Clothing of Witness

A fingerprint expert is a salesperson selling the identification to the jury. The appearance and clothing of the expert are therefore important factors in this selling process. The expert's appearance and clothing create the jury's initial impression of the expert. The jury judges the witness from these outward signs given to them. Physical appearance, dress, and manner of testifying all affect the jury as they begin to determine the credibility and weight to be given to the expert's testimony. The expert witness does not have time to overcome an initial negative impression; the first impression must therefore be a positive one. Research shows that clothing and appearance are two of the more important forms of nonverbal communication.[1] Often, these non-verbal forms of communication are as important as the facts of the case.

John F. Molloy in *Dress for Success*[1] reveals that one's dress and appearance convey strong impressions about personal ability, prestige, and even character. Molloy has extensively studied the effects of dress on interpersonal evaluations. His results indicate that, especially in limited interactions such as courtroom testimony, seemingly slight variations in an individual's dress can significantly influence personal and professional evaluation by others. Molloy further states that while even the best attire will usually not result in significant over-evaluation, poor or inappropriate attire can cause a person's stature and abilities to be harshly devalued.

Molloy's research has shown that for maximum jury impact, the male expert witness should be neatly and conservatively dressed and readily identifiable as upper-middle-class. A blue or gray three-piece suit is appropriate. Hair should be neatly combed and short. The preferred dress for a female expert witness is a skirted suit of knee length; appropriate colors are blue, gray, and beige. Her hairstyle should be neat and short.

Some departmental policies may require experts to wear a uniform in court. It must be emphasized in these cases that weapons, handcuffs, keys, etc. should not be worn to the witness stand.

Experts should avoid wearing fraternal organization lapel buttons, tie pins, glaring jewelry, or other items that detract from testimony. In addition, items of this type could produce a less-than-positive association for some jury members.

Pretrial Conference with Prosecuting Attorney

It is absolutely necessary that the expert witness insist on a pretrial conference with the prosecutor. It is the prosecutor's responsibility to introduce and present the evidence for the jury to determine the guilt or innocence of the accused. This presentation of evidence cannot be accomplished without the help and guidance of the expert. The time for this initial assistance is during the pretrial conference.

Some sources suggest that if the prosecutor says he/she is too busy for a pretrial conference, the expert should imply to the prosecutor that he will not willingly testify at the subsequent trial.

Frequently, the prosecutor is an assistant district attorney. It is more diplomatic, but just as effective, to tell the prosecutor that if time is not granted for a pretrial conference, the district attorney will be informed of that fact. Usually then, the prosecutor will find the time for a pretrial conference. The following are suggested procedures for the pretrial conference.

1. The expert should familiarize the prosecutor with all the essential details known about the case so that both the prosecutor and the expert can review the testimony to be given. This is also an excellent time to check the evidence. The expert must make sure this is the same evidence that was originally examined. Also, the expert should check where the evidence was initialed, so that when called upon in court to identify the evidence, the initials can be indicated easily.
2. The expert can then advise the prosecutor of the preferred sequence of witnesses.
   a. Initially, testimony is given to the introduction and identification of the object, lift, or photograph showing the latent print. This testimony states the location of the object or latent print at the crime scene, the date found, and the circumstances surrounding the evidence's development and preservation. Although the person offering this testimony may have some training or experience in these practices, this witness does not have to be, nor qualify as, a fingerprint expert.
   b. Introduction and identification of the known fingerprints of the defendant follow. This testimony must be given by the person(s) who took the defendant's known prints. Although this person has knowledge and experience concerning the proper recording of fingerprints, it is not necessary that he/she be a fingerprint expert nor qualify as one in order to offer this testimony. The defendant's name should appear on the card as well as the signature or other personal identifying mark of the person taking the prints. Whenever possible, the known fingerprints used to establish the identity of the defendant should bear the current charge for which the defendant is being tried. Any data on the fingerprint card relating to a prior arrest must be brought to the attention of the prosecutor. Such data must be masked out. If this information inadvertently becomes known to the jury, it may be grounds for an immediate mistrial.
   c. The final witness is the fingerprint expert. The expert should offer the prosecutor a list of qualifying questions, designed to establish the expert's qualifications and to give the jury a better understanding of the fingerprint expert's testimony. The following is a suggested list of qualifying questions for the introduction of the fingerprint testimony.

- What is your name?
- By whom are you employed?
- Where are your official headquarters?
- What is your official title?
- What are your official duties?
- How long have you been employed in fingerprint work?
- What is an inked print?
- What is a latent print?
- How are fingerprints compared and identifications effected?
- What are the basic factors in the use of fingerprints as a means of identification? (Alternative: Why are fingerprints used as a means of identification?)
- What training and experience do you have that qualifies you as a fingerprint expert?
- Have you written and published any articles, papers, or books on fingerprint science? (Appropriate only if witness has authored something.)
- Have you seen exhibit _____ before?
- Where did you see it?
- Did you examine exhibit _____ for latent prints?
- What was the result of this examination?
- Have you seen this fingerprint card before?
- Where did you see it?
- Did you compare the latent fingerprint(s) on exhibit _____ with the fingerprints on this card?
- What was the result of your comparison?
- Do you have charted enlargements illustrating the identification(s)?
- Will you demonstrate these charts to the jury?

It is important for the expert to consider his/her answers to these questions. The following are suggested responses to some essential questions. These responses can be used as guides in answering some of the above questions.

Question: What are your official duties?
Included among my official duties are the examinations of fragmentary latent prints that may be either present or developed on objects associated with different types of crimes. I also evaluate photographs, negatives, and lifts to determine if latent prints appear either in or on them. I compare these latent prints with the inked prints of known suspects. I will, on occasion, examine the hands and fingers of unknown deceased individuals in an attempt to establish their identity. At the conclusion of

any examination that I have conducted, I will report my findings and, if requested to do so, testify to my findings in court.

Question: What is a known print?
Present on the palmar surface of the hands and fingers and the plantar areas of the feet of humans is skin that is far different from the skin that we have on the other areas of our bodies. Unlike our other skin, this skin is rough and corrugated, consisting of raised portions that are called friction ridges. These ridges do not go unbroken from one side of the hand, finger, or plantar area of the foot to the other, but rather are broken and noncontinuous. An example would be a single ridge that ends or two ridges that join together to form a single ridge. By spreading a thin film of black fingerprint or printer's ink over the ridge surfaces and then placing them in contact with a recipient surface, preferably white paper or cardboard, a permanent and lasting recording of these friction ridges are made. This recording is an inked fingerprint.

Known prints can also be produced using electronic scanners. These devices are known as "live-scan" systems. Live-scan prints are made by placing the finger on a flat transparent glass-like plate or platen. The friction ridge area is then scanned. The friction ridge information, depicting the precise ridge arrangement, is captured and stored by a computer. When needed, one or more "hard copies" of the known print can be electronically produced from the computerized information.

Question: What is a latent print?
Present on the tops of the friction ridges are very minute sweat pores that are constantly exuding perspiration. This perspiration adheres to and covers the summits of the ridges. When the friction ridges come into contact with a suitable surface, this perspiration is transferred to that surface, leaving a recording, or print, of the friction ridges. At times, this print will be entirely visible to the naked eye. An example is a print left on a highly reflective surface such as a piece of polished metal or a mirror. At other times, however, the print may be indistinct or invisible (e.g., latent prints left on a piece of paper, cardboard, or unfinished wood). In this instance, the latent prints must be "brought out" or made visible through some developmental process so that they can be photographed and thereby preserved.

Question: How are fingerprints compared and identifications effected?
The friction ridges are not all continuous, but are broken, forming various characteristics. These characteristics include ridge endings, ridges that divide (also called bifurcations), and small ridges called dots. A dot

may look much like a period at the end of a sentence. The characteristics in one print are compared with the characteristics in another print. When the characteristics in both prints are observed to be the same and occupy the same unit relationship, an identification has been effected.

Question: What are the basic factors in the use of fingerprints as a means of identification? (*Alternative:* Why are fingerprints used as a means of identification?)

The basic factors are that fingerprints are permanent and individually unique: that is, the fingerprints of no two individuals are the same. Every finger of every person bears a ridge arrangement that begins to form during the twelfth week of gestation. Barring accidental or intentional removal or destruction, this ridge arrangement is permanent for the life of the individual and will endure until decomposition of the body after death.

3. When listing membership(s) in professional associations in connection with establishing expert qualifications, the witness must know and be able to state requirements for membership and positive reasons for being affiliated with these organizations. If the attainment of organizational membership demands the passing of examinations and/or successfully undergoing professional and ethical investigations, be able to relate those requirements to the prosecutor and, ultimately, to the court and jury. Membership is indeed reserved for qualified professionals and not available to anyone simply for the payment of membership dues. Reasons for being associated with such organizations are that they provide the means by which forensic identification professionals can stay abreast of technical, professional, and legal developments within their discipline. This can be accomplished through personal involvement with other professionals, attending educational conferences, reading association journals and other publications, and through participation in association-sponsored workshops and other learning opportunities.

4. It is to the advantage of the prosecutor to have the expert's complete testimony presented. It will be most impressive to the jury to hear the expert's testimony; and if the outcome of the trial is appealed at a later date, the testimony is then a matter of court record. Often, the defense attorney will want to stipulate to the expert's testimony. The stipulation in all probability will be offered on the pretense of saving the court's time; it will in fact be offered so the jury will not have an opportunity to hear the expert's testimony. Although the stipulation is made in open court, in the presence of the jury, it is often difficult for the jury

to fully understand the meaning of this procedure. However, if the judge agrees with the defense attorney's motion for the stipulation, then the testimony will not be allowed.

5. It is recommended that the expert relate to the prosecutor the approximate number of latent cases he/she has previously examined, the number of comparisons made, and the number of previous testimonies as an expert. The prosecutor may want to bring out this background during direct examination. The expert should therefore be prepared to provide this information. The witness should also be able to logically explain how these numbers were derived. Previous experience conducting numerous latent print case examinations and extensive testimony experience are most impressive to the court. This experience also significantly aids in establishing the witness's credibility as an expert.

Pretrial Conference with Defense Attorney

If the defense attorney requests a pretrial conference, the expert can, if approved by the prosecuting attorney or judge hearing the case, grant the conference. If granted, this pretrial conference with the defense attorney should always be conducted in the presence of the prosecuting attorney or the prosecutor's representative. Notes taken should be recorded by an impartial person, not a representative for the defense. The expert should immediately request a copy of the notes to verify their authenticity.

There are several advantages to a pretrial conference with the defense attorney. Often, on the basis of the conference, the defense attorney may plead his client guilty. Also, this conference affords the expert an opportunity to evaluate the defense attorney. On the other hand, the defense attorney has the opportunity to evaluate the expert witness.

Charted Enlargements

While the fingerprint expert can testify to his/her opinions in court without a demonstrable exhibit, this testimony will be much more meaningful and convincing to the jury if it can be illustrated to the jury just exactly how the identification was effected. Accordingly, it is strongly recommended that at least one set of charted enlargements illustrating how the identification was made be prepared for each defendant being tried. If possible, charted enlargements should be prepared using the most incriminating latent print identification (e.g., a latent print from the murder weapon). The charts should be sufficiently large so that the jury members in the back row can clearly see the ridge characteristics. The jury should not have to wait until deliberations for its first good look at the exhibit.

The advantages of using charted enlargements include:

1. The jury learns more through seeing than through hearing.
2. Charted enlargements break up the testimony and make the case more interesting.
3. This demonstration makes the expert's testimony stronger.
4. The jury will be impressed by the amount of preparation.
5. According to surveys, the expert witness standing and illustrating before the jury was chosen as more knowledgeable than one who does not stand before the jury by a ratio of better than 5 to 1.[2]

Courtroom Methodology: Direct Examination

On the day that the expert is to present testimony, it is good policy to arrive at the courthouse early. It is important for experts to remember they are being observed from the moment they enter the courthouse, and any person may be a prospective juror. The message should be clear: the courthouse as well as the courtroom is the setting for a very serious and solemn affair. It is advantageous for the expert to look over the courtroom before testifying so that the exact location of the witness stand is known.

Swearing In

Swearing in can be done either singularly or as a group before the trial. During the swearing-in process, the expert should stand before the person administering the oath and should maintain a very serious and business-like manner. The expert should stand erect, raise his/her hand high, and look directly at the court officer administering the oath. After the oath has been given, the expert responds "I do" in a firm, distinct voice that conveys sincerity and seriousness of purpose and can be heard by all present. The witness should never take the so-called traveling oath, that is, taking the oath while walking toward the witness stand.

Assuming the Witness Stand

After being sworn in, the expert should walk to the witness stand in a very positive and confident manner. It is of great importance that the expert witness exude self-confidence at all times. A witness who appears nervous and unsure in demeanor is extending an open invitation for a vigorous cross-examination and is begging for a negative response from the jury.

When seated in the witness stand, the expert should sit erect but in a comfortable manner, with feet planted squarely on the floor and hands on lap. It is most important that clothing fit comfortably. If clothing is uncomfortable, the witness may be constantly moving, thus conveying the impression of nervousness.

Courtroom Communication

It should be noted that when talking to the jury, the expert must use easy-to-understand language. Technical jargon does not impress, but rather confuses. If, during the first few moments of testimony, the jury does not understand what is being said, they will simply not listen. Under optimum conditions, an individual's maximum listening capacity is only about 40%. Prior to actual testimony, it is an excellent idea for the expert to test responses to the basic qualifying questions on family, neighbors, or some other laypersons who have no knowledge of the fingerprint science. If they do not understand what is being said, the expert should modify his/her answers. The expert must be conscious of the quality and tone of voice. To emphasize a point, a pause is much more effective than raising one's voice. It is good to remember that a witness is a vocal performer when testifying. An expert's responses to questions in court should be succinct but thorough. If the jury appears interested, however, it is a good policy to go into some detail. The expert witness can observe the jury's nonverbal communication to determine their degree of interest. Pupil dilation of the jurors' eyes is an indication of interest. When answering the qualifying question, the expert can closely observe the jury to determine if their interest has been aroused. This can be noted very readily if their eyes are transfixed on their own hands and fingers as they take a close look at the friction ridges the expert is describing. to them.

Credentials

It has been said that when expert fingerprint testimony is presented in plain, easy-to-understand language, the jury will fully understand what is being said. However, some attorneys say this is not true. They do not believe that on the basis of direct testimony only, the jury can fully understand the fingerprint expert's testimony. What the jury can understand are the expert's credentials. It is felt that if there are two opposing experts presenting testimony at a trial, usually the one with the more impressive credentials will prevail. A fingerprint expert's credentials can be divided into three categories:

1. Education/training
2. Work experience
3. Professional recognition

Education/Training

1. College
2. Fingerprint courses
   a. FBI
   b. State bureaus
   c. American Institute of Applied Science course

Work Experience

The expert must be able to logically explain to the court and jury his/her work experience, including the following, and how this experience was gained.

1. Previous testimonies
2. Comparisons conducted
3. Cases examined
4. Crime scenes examined
5. Articles/books published on fingerprint science

Professional Recognition

1. IAI Latent Print Examiner certification
2. Supervision/management experience
3. Member/officer in professional organizations
4. Awards and honors received

Response to the Jury

It is very important for the witness to remember to address all responses directly to the jury. Eye-to-eye contact with the jury should be established when responding to questions from both the prosecutor and the defense attorney. Eye contact with the jury denotes both trustworthiness and competence. The expert who is uncomfortable with eye contact should merely look just over the tops of the jurors' foreheads. It will still appear as if the witness is looking directly into their eyes. An assistant U.S. attorney describes a case that clearly illustrates this point in which a father was charged with the rape of his daughter. The defendant, who was a very articulate person, took the witness stand and denied that he had committed the crime. But when making the denial, in lieu of looking the jury directly in the eye, the defendant looked down at the floor. The prosecuting attorney in his closing argument brought this fact to the attention of the jury. The prosecutor very strongly noted that although the defendant had denied committing this crime, in making this denial, the defendant had not looked directly at the jury but looked down at the floor instead. After a short deliberation, the defendant was found guilty. A poll of the jury brought out the fact that one of the major factors in their guilty verdict was that during his testimony, the defendant had not looked them in the eye.

Pause Before Answering Questions

Although the expert generally knows what the responses will be to questions on direct examination, the witness should allow a momentary pause before answering the question. This pause serves a twofold purpose:

- It gives the opposing attorney an opportunity to object to the question. Objections provide the witness with an excellent opportunity to collect thoughts and to formulate answers.
- If there is a momentary pause before an answer is given on direct examination, then, under cross-examination when there is also a pause before an answer, the pause is not as noticeable. If the response on direct examination is very quick, however, a momentary pause before the answer is given during cross-examination will be very noticeable.

Sometimes inadvertently, or by design, the prosecutor or the defense attorney may interrupt the expert before he/she has finished answering the question. If this happens, the expert should tell the judge and should ask for permission to finish the response.

Modification of Response

At times it may be necessary to modify a response. It is not mandatory to answer yes or no to a question just because the attorney demands a yes or no answer. The expert need only turn to the judge and advise that the question cannot be answered with a yes or no and that he/she would like permission to more thoroughly explain the answer. The judge rarely denies a request of this type. If the expert does not know the answer to a question, of course, then this should be acknowledged. In lieu of replying, "I do not know," the expert should give consideration to responding, "I have no personal knowledge." For an expert to continually answer, "I do not know" may give the appearance that the expert is not a very knowledgeable witness. The following are examples of questions that are difficult to answer with a yes or no:

Question: Have you ever made a mistake?
A suggested response is "In any field of human endeavor, there can be oversights. However, of one thing I am very sure. I have never made a mistake in presenting evidence in court."

Question: Are you telling this court that you have never told a lie?
A suggested response is "Never while under oath."

Mannerisms of Speech

Certain speech mannerisms can be very damaging. For example, the expert should not preface comments with, "I can truthfully say." The implication is that the rest of the time the expert is not telling the truth. Double negatives or double positives (i.e., "No I did not" or "Yes I did") are redundant and unnecessary. A simple yes or no suffices.

Comparisons in Court

If a request is made to conduct comparisons while in court, the expert should ask the judge for a recess and a room with adequate lighting where the examination can be conducted in private. The expert should ask for more time than will probably be needed. This ensures that the expert will have adequate time in case the difficulty of the comparisons has been underestimated. The expert can use the extra time to organize his/her thoughts before retaking the witness stand. Although the expert could have conducted the comparison in the courtroom in a matter of just a few minutes, it is wise to request the time. A quick courtroom comparison may encourage the jury to conclude that the witness is careless and less than thorough and that anyone can conduct latent print comparisons without difficulty. Fingerprint expertise is based on many years of training and experience. To maintain the integrity of the fingerprint profession, the expert should always counsel the court and jury that the science of fingerprints is a profession requiring exceptionally high levels of knowledge, skills, and abilities, which can only be attained through experience, education, training, and dedication.

Discussion of Case

The expert must be careful to discuss the case only with those persons who have a legal need to know. Those individuals include the expert's supervisor and the prosecutor. Talking indiscriminately can be disastrous: the person the expert talks to within the courthouse could be a prospective juror. During a recess at the trial, the defense attorney may send his/her representatives out into the hallways to observe and listen. If a member of the press or anyone else should ask the expert any questions, the expert should politely but firmly refer them to the prosecutor. Any statements that are given may be restated to improper persons, or even misstated. It is a sound policy to stand aloof from everyone except the attorney who retains you to testify.

Courtroom Courtesy

When in court, it is the mark of a professional witness to show respect for the court. The judge should always be addressed as "Your Honor," and the attorneys as "Sir" or "Ma'am" or by their surnames. The expert should always stand when the judge enters or leaves the courtroom. It is essential for the expert to remember that the purpose of being in court is to testify to the results of the examination conducted. The expert has no personal knowledge of the innocence or guilt of the defendant. If the expert appears very friendly toward the prosecutor and antagonistic toward the defense attorney, the jury will notice immediately and the testimony will no longer appear objective.

Courtroom Methodology: Cross-examination

Whether the expert is subjected to a preliminary cross-examination during direct testimony or after testifying is a matter of judicial decision. Cross-examination is an absolute necessity, as it affords the person against whom such testimony is given a full opportunity to show whether the conclusion of the witness is warranted by the facts. It is possible that the direct testimony is untrue, exaggerated, or presented in a manner to produce an erroneous impression.

Vulnerable Areas of Fingerprint Testimony

Most defense attorneys will not attack the validity of the latent print identification. Two critical areas of latent print testimony the defense attorney may attack are the age of the latent print and the source of the latent print.

Age of the Latent Print

The age of the latent print cannot be determined by a technical examination. If the latent print was developed on a nonporous surface, however, an age determination can be made if the expert can establish the last time the surface was cleaned. (By wiping a nonporous surface with a cloth, one effectively removes any latent prints that might be present.) This method of age determination can sometimes be effectively used. The following is an example of a trial in which the age of the latent print was determined by this method. The latent palmprint of the defendant was developed on the counter of the victim teller in the bank that had been robbed. The defendant's alibi was that he had been in the bank several days before to obtain change for a $20 bill and that he had left the latent palm print on the counter at that time. A custodial employee testified that she had cleaned the counter the previous evening, as she does on a daily basis. This testimony effectively established the age of the latent print as some time between when the bank opened and when the law enforcement officer developed the latent print. The defendant's alibi was thereby rebutted.

Source of the Latent Print

The source of the latent print is also very critical. If the defense attorney can illustrate to the jury that the defendant could have had legitimate access to the object or area where the latent print was developed, he/she can effectively dilute the weight of the latent print testimony. An example is if the latent print was developed on an entrance door to the bank that had been robbed. Obviously, anyone could legitimately touch an entrance door. If the latent print is from the vault door of the bank, however, and the defendant is not an employee of that bank, there is no legitimate reason for his latent print(s) being present on the vault door.

Transcripts of Prior Testimony

The expert should review transcripts of any previous testimony given in the case in which the expert is about to testify. If testifying in state or federal court, testimony will be recorded. Defense attorneys will often examine previous transcripts of expert testimony for any inconsistencies in the same area of testimony. An example is in stated qualifications. If any inconsistencies are noted, they can be used against the expert. If the expert does not satisfactorily explain these inconsistencies, the jury may give less credit to the expert's testimony.

Use of Books and Articles in Cross-examination

A defense attorney may attempt to cross-examine the expert from a book or article. The defense attorney must initially establish the book or article as being authoritative; this can be accomplished in any one of three following ways:

1. The easiest method is to have the expert admit that the book or article is authoritative.
2. The judge may take judicial notice that the book or article is authoritative.
3. Another expert may testify that the book or article is authoritative. (Of course, the defense attorney would not attempt to introduce the article or book unless it contained statements contrary to the expert's testimony.)

When the defense attorney reads a quote from a book, the expert should always ask to see the book unless personally familiar with the book. The expert should then read the quote. This is absolutely necessary for the following reasons:

1. The quote may have been taken out of context.
2. The quote may have been incomplete.
3. The publication may be outdated.

If the attorney does not have the publication, the expert should still insist that it be reviewed before an answer can be given to the question. If the quote is accurate, however, the expert should be prepared to answer the quote from the publication and to justify any disagreement with the publication.

Tactics of Defense Attorneys

1. Some defense attorneys will deliberately mispronounce an expert's name in order to disturb or upset him/her. The expert, in a polite but firm manner, should inform the attorney of the correct pronunciation of his/her name. At all times, the expert should maintain composure.
2. Defense attorneys may also at times ask three or four questions in rapid succession in order to give the expert little time to think. If this occurs, then the witness should ask the defense attorney to ask only one question at a time so that an answer can be given to that question, and then proceed to the next question. If the expert attempts to answer all questions at once, he/she may get caught up in the rapid pace of the questioning and make a mistake.
3. The fire-and-brimstone type of defense attorney will shout and be deliberately antagonistic in an attempt to intimidate the witness. The expert witness should react by answering the questions in a firm but polite manner, watching the reaction of the jury. The jury will generally identify with and be sympathetic to the expert. The defense attorney will then usually stop this line of questioning inasmuch as he is only hurting his client.

Completion of Testimony

After testimony has been completed, the expert should be excused in open court. The expert should leave the courtroom immediately and should always ask the prosecutor for permission before reentering the courtroom.

Conclusion

This chapter represents an effort by the authors to present some general guidelines for the reader's consideration in becoming a more effective expert fingerprint witness. The following suggestions may be helpful in enhancing one's skills as an expert witness:

1. Conduct mock-court sessions and obtain feedback.
2. Test answers to the basic qualifying questions on non-fingerprint persons and obtain feedback.

3. Dress the part.
4. Listen.
5. Think positively.
6. Remember at all times to be objective.
7. Watch the jury for nonverbal communication feedback.
8. Learn to effectively use silence.

Glossary of Commonly Used Courtroom Terms

Accusation   A formal charge filed by the state against a person

Accused   One who is charged with a crime. The person who is a defendant in a criminal case.

Admissible   Evidence of such a character that the judge or court allows it to be introduced.

Appeal   The removal of a case from a court of inferior, to one of superior jurisdiction, for the purpose of obtaining a review and retrial.

Arraignment   The initial appearance of the accused in the court where the charges against him are read and a plea is entered.

Arrest   Taking under real or assumed authority, custody of another, for the purpose of holding or detaining him, to answer a criminal charge.

Arrest warrant   The written order of a magistrate or judge that directs peace officers to arrest the person named who is accused of a criminal offense.

Bail   Security deposited that procures the release of a person under arrest by becoming responsible for his appearance at the time and place designated.

Bailiff   One who helps maintain order while court is in session. One who escorts inmates in and out of the courtroom and guards them during the proceedings.

Bench warrant   Process issued by the court itself for the arrest of a person, for contempt, failure to obey a subpoena, or where an indictment has been found.

Beyond a reasonable doubt   In evidence means fully satisfied, entirely convinced, satisfied to a moral certainty.

Change of Venue   The removal of a suit begun in one county or district to another county or district for trial.

Clerk of the Court   Custodian of the case records and physical items introduced into evidence. One who swears in witnesses.

Conclusive evidence   Evidence that is so strong and convincing as to over-bear all proof to the contrary and to establish the proposition in question beyond any reasonable doubt.

Confession   A voluntary statement by the accused that he/she committed a criminal act, including all the elements of the crime.

Continuance   A postponement of an action before the court.

Court reporter   The person who records testimony. One who records every word spoken (usually on a manual printer or on tape recording equipment), except discussions or comments that are ruled "off the record."

Cross-examination   The examination of a witness, by the party opposed to the one who produced him/her, upon evidence given by the witness in chief to test its truth, to further develop it, or for other purposes.

Deposition   An oral statement by a person under oath before an officer of the court (but not in open court) and recorded by a court reporter.

Direct examination   The first interrogation or examination of a witness on the merits by the party on whose behalf he/she is called.

Duces tecum   Subpoena requiring a party, who is summoned to appear in court, to bring with him/her some document or piece of evidence to be used or inspected by the court.

Felony   A crime of a graver or more atrocious nature than those designated as misdemeanors.

Grand jury   A jury that investigates alleged violations of the law and that returns an indictment against those it believes violated the law.

Guilty   The word used by a prisoner in pleading to an indictment when confessing to the crime of which he/she is charged, and by the jury in convicting.

Hearsay   Evidence not proceeding from the personal knowledge of the witness, but from the mere repetition of what he/she has heard others say.

Hung juries   A jury so irreconcilably divided in opinion that it cannot agree upon a verdict.

Hypothetical Question   A question asked of an expert witness and based on a combination of proved and assumed facts.

Impeachment   Adducing proof that a witness who has testified in a cause is unworthy of credit.

Incarceration   Imprisonment or confinement in a jail or penitentiary.

Indictment   An accusation in writing by a grand jury, charging that a person named therein has committed a criminal act.

Judge   A public officer, appointed or elected, who presides in a court of law to administer the proceedings and to render decisions on the questions of law.

Jury   A certain number of men and women, selected according to law, to inquire of certain matters of fact, and declare the truth upon evidence to be laid before them.

Jury box   The place in court where the jury sits during a trial.

Misdemeanor   Offenses lower than felonies and generally those punishable by a fine or imprisonment of 1 year or less.

Mistrial   An erroneous or invalid trial that cannot stand in law because of disregard of some fundamental requisite.

Nolo contendere   Latin for "I will not contest it." The name of a plea in criminal action having the same legal effect as a plea of guilty as long as the matter or proceeding objected to is improper or illegal.

Overrule   Refusal to sustain or recognize as sufficient an objection made in the course of a trial as to the introduction of particular evidence, etc.

Pardon   An act of grace that exempts the individual on whom it is bestowed from the punishment the law inflicts for the crime he/she has committed.

Perjury   A willful statement that is not true, made by a witness under oath in a judicial proceeding.

Plea   The answer to a criminal action brought against the defendant.

Preemptory challenge   A challenge against a prospective juror without cause, by the prosecution or the defense.

Preliminary hearing   A hearing given to one accused of a crime, before a judge or magistrate, to determine whether there is sufficient evidence to require the accused to answer the charges against him/her.

Prima facie **evidence**   Evidence that suffices for the proof of a particular fact until contradicted and overcome by other evidence.

Probable cause   A reasonable ground for belief in existence of facts warranting the proceedings complained of.

Prosecuting attorney   Public officer who is appointed or elected to conduct criminal prosecutions on behalf of the state or people.

Re-cross-examination   The last opportunity for the defense attorney to attack testimony. Questioning is restricted to points covered on re-direct.

Re-direct examination The opportunity for the prosecutor to question again after cross-examination, to rehabilitate areas of testimony that may have been damaged by the defense attorney's interrogation.

Relevant That which applies to the fact in issue.

Search warrants A written court order authorizing a law enforcement officer to search a named person or place.

Sequestering of Witness The exclusion of witnesses from the courtroom during a trial so that no witness will hear testimony of other witnesses.

True bill The endorsement on a bill of indictment by a grand jury when it determines that there is sufficient evidence to sustain the accusation.

Venue The county or geographical location in which a case is brought to trial and which is to furnish the panel of jurors.

Voie dire (1) The preliminary examination of jurors before trial at which challenges may be made to their sitting on the jury. (2) A preliminary examination to determine the competency of a witness or juror.

Waiver The intentional or voluntary relinquishment of a known right.

Warrant A writ from a competent authority in pursuance of law, instructing an officer to do an act and affording him protection from damages if he does it.

References

1. Burke, J.J. Testifying in court. *FBI Law Enf. Bull.*, 1975.
2. Kogan, J.D. On being a good expert witness in a criminal case. *J. Forensic Sci.* 23, 190, 1978.
3. Molloy, J.J. *Dress for Success.* New York: Warner Books, 1978.
4. Petersen, R.D. *The Police Officer in Court.* Springfield, IL: Charles C Thomas, 1975.
5. Tanton, R.L. Jury preconceptions and their effect on expert scientific testimony. *J. Forensic Sci.* 24, 681, 1979.
6. Black, H.C. *Black's Law Dictionary.* St. Paul, MN: West Publishing Company.

Daubert Hearings

EDWARD GERMAN*

During most of the 20th century in America, the admissibility of friction ridge evidence in the vast majority of American courts relied upon the 1923 "Frye" rule of "general acceptance in the particular field in which it belongs" (Frye v. United States, 293 F2d. 1013, D.C. Cir. 1923). So long as it could be shown that a scientific principle or discovery, such as the uniqueness and permanence of friction ridge formations, was generally accepted by other experts, it was admissible. Those few states not adopting the "Frye test" generally embraced Federal Rule of Evidence 702 (or a similar state rule) to ensure that expert testimony was relevant and based on reliable scientific theories.

Beginning in 1993, however, the admissibility of friction ridge identification has come under much closer scrutiny. In 1993, a civil case (Daubert v. Merrell Dow Pharmaceuticals, 113 S. Ct. 2786) ruled that the Federal Rules of Evidence superseded "general acceptance" tests for admissibility of novel scientific evidence; and that the rigid "general acceptance" test, which arose from Frye v. United States, is at odds with the liberal thrust of the Federal Rules of Evidence.

The Daubert ruling stated that:

- The trial judge must still screen scientific evidence to ensure it is relevant and reliable.
- "The focus, of course, must be solely on principles and methodology, not on the conclusions they generate."
- Factors the court should consider include:
  - Testing and validation
  - Peer review
  - Rate of error
  - "General acceptance"

---

* Included with the author's permission; originally prepared by the author and others for posting at http://onin.com/fp.

The 1999 decision Kumho Tire Co. v. Carmichael (131 F.3d 1433, 11th Cir. 12/23/97) added additional factors for a court to consider in determining the admissibility of a scientific theory or technique. Because the Daubert ruling impacted only "expert" testimony, prosecutors had the option of avoiding its more stringent requirements by entering fingerprint evidence as "technical or other specialized knowledge." Under Kumho, the court ruled that Daubert applies to all expert testimony, whether expert, technical, or specialized knowledge. Although Daubert/Kumho is not recognized as the standard by all American courts, it is the new yardstick by which most courts now measure the admissibility of scientific evidence.

During a four and one-half day hearing in July 1999, the United States Government presented strong and extensive defense in the first Daubert hearing seriously challenging the admissibility of fingerprint evidence. The U.S. v. Byron C. Mitchell Daubert/Kumho hearing held in Philadelphia (U.S. District Court for the Eastern District of Pennsylvania) was the first hearing of its kind in America in over 70 years. The government's experts were described in court records as follows:[1]

"The government introduced the testimony of two scientists, Dr. William J. Babler, an expert in the field of prenatal development of human variation, particularly friction ridges and their configurations, and Dr. Bruce Budowle, an expert in the field of genetics, genetics population, statistics, quality assurance standards, and validation of scientific methods. Dr. Babler gave an extensive presentation of his research and findings on the creation and development of the human friction ridge skin and friction ridges. Other evidence, which was presented by the government at the hearing also, supported Dr. Babler's opinions and findings.

The government also introduced the testimony of several highly qualified fingerprint experts, characterized by a defense witness, Dr. Simon A. Cole, as the "elite" in their field. Testifying at the hearing were Staff Sergeant David R. Ashbaugh of the Royal Canadian Mounted Police; Special Agent Edward German from the United States Army Crime Laboratory in Atlanta, Georgia; and Stephen B. Meagher, Supervisory Unit Chief in the Latent Fingerprint Unit of the Federal Bureau of Investigation in Washington, D.C. Also testifying was Donald Ziesig, an algorithmist employed at Lockheed Martin in Orlando, Florida. Ziesig is an expert in Automated Fingerprint Identification Systems, an expert in pattern recognition, and a former rocket scientist. Ziesig explained some of the aspects of Automated Fingerprint Identification Systems (AFIS) and the 50K × 50K Fingerprint Study. In the government's rebuttal case, the government produced the testimony of Pat Wertheim, another highly qualified fingerprint expert and rebuttal testimony from Dr. Budowle."[1]

The U.S. Government set presented evidence supporting three premises of the science of friction ridge (fingerprint) identification, as follows:[2]

PREMISE 1 — Human friction ridges are unique and permanent.
  The scientific basis for uniqueness and permanence begins with understanding friction ridge skin development. The sciences of biology, embryology, and genetics are keys to understanding this development. Fetal development of friction ridge skin has been extensively studied and documented. Factors affecting friction ridge variability include both genetics and the intra-uterine environment. Each unique ridge formation is caused by random growth.
  Friction ridges form during gestation and the final configuration and development is complete prior to birth. This configuration persists throughout life except when damage occurs to the basal layer of the epidermis.
  The proliferation of skin growth during gestation accounts for the variability in human friction ridges, thus establishing uniqueness. Friction ridges are unique to the individual ridge.
  The biological development of friction ridges establishes the scientific basis for uniqueness and permanence. Each friction ridge is unique.

PREMISE 2 — Human friction ridge arrangements are unique and permanent.
  As with a single friction ridge, the proliferation of skin growth during gestation accounts for the variability in human friction ridge arrangement. The aggregate of the ridges permits individualization.
  Pattern or class characteristic ridge arrangement is genetically based; unique ridge relationship is caused by random growth.
  Friction ridge detail represented in impressions is observed in three levels. Ridge paths may contain Level 1, 2, or all 3 levels as follows:
    Level 1 includes the general ridge flow and pattern configuration. Level 1 detail is not sufficient for individualization, but can be used for exclusion.
    Level 1 detail may include information enabling orientation, core and delta location, and distinction of finger vs. palm.
    Level 2 detail includes formations, defined as ridge ending, bifurcation, dot, or combinations thereof. The relationship of Level 2 detail enables individualization.
    Level 3 detail includes all dimensional attributes of a ridge, such as ridge path deviation, width, shape, pores, edge contour, incipient ridges, breaks, creases, scars, and other permanent details.

PREMISE 3 – Individualization, that is, positive identification, can result from comparisons of friction ridge skin or impressions containing sufficient quality (clarity) and quantity of unique friction ridge detail.

The friction ridge examination process must adhere to a standard scientific method to achieve accurate and reliable conclusions. The standard methodology consists of four elements: analysis, comparison, evaluation, and verification (ACE-V).

The two factors integral to a successful examination process are the quality (clarity) and quantity of friction ridge detail. These two factors are interrelated.

The four elements to the scientific methodology are as follows:

Analysis: the qualitative and quantitative assessment of Level 1, 2, and 3 details to determine their proportion, interrelationship, and value to individualize.

Comparison: to examine the attributes observed during analysis in order to determine agreement or discrepancies between two friction ridge impressions.

Evaluation: the cyclical procedure of comparison between two friction ridge impressions to effect a decision, i.e., made by the same friction skin, not made by the same friction skin, or insufficient detail to form a conclusive decision.

Verification: an independent analysis, comparison, and evaluation by a second qualified examiner of the friction ridge impressions.

Uniqueness and permanence of human friction ridges and human friction skin arrangements are the scientific bases, which permit individualization. Biological variation enables individualization to be recognized with the application of scientific methodology. That individualization is limited to one friction skin area to the exclusion of all others.

The scientific basis and method stated herein establishes friction ridge positive identification supporting individualization to the exclusion of all other friction skin ridge areas.

Friction skin ridge and ridge impression individualization results from ACE-V.

The government's case presented by Assistant U.S. Attorney Paul Sarmousakis during the four-and-one-half day July 1999 Philadelphia hearing included testimony about special AFIS research involving 50,000 fingerprints compared against each other, twins-print research, empirical knowledge of the uniqueness and permanence of fingerprints during the previous 100 years and various other supporting evidence. No single witness or piece of evidence provided the supporting proof of the validity of the science of fingerprints.

Presided over by the Honorable J. Curtis Joyner, the hearing was an overwhelming win for the most widely accepted forensic evidence in the world — fingerprints. Although additional Daubert hearings continue to occur in various jurisdictions, as of this writing, the 1999 Philadelphia Daubert hearing on fingerprints remains the premier model hearing and ruling for the science of fingerprints in America.

Appendix References

1. Government's Proposed Findings of Fact and Conclusions of Law, *U.S. v Byron C. Mitchell*, U.S. District Court for the Eastern District of Pennsylvania, No. 96-00407.

2. Daubert study materials prepared for SWGFAST (Scientific Working Group on Friction Ridge Analysis, Study and Technology) by Stephen Meagher, David Grieve, Patrick Wertheim and Edward German, August 1999.

Index

A

Abderhalden, E., 127, 182
Absolute identification, basis for, 331–332
Accidental fingerprint class, 290n
Accuracy, biometrics and, 277–278, 313, 316
Accusation, defined, 409
Accused, defined, 409
Acetic acid
    1,2-indanedione formulations, 199
    DFO formulations, 197
    ninhydrin formulations, 184, 185, 186
    prewash treatments with, 258
Acetone, 184, 243
Acetyl cholinesterase, 72
Acidic prewash treatments, 249, 258, 260
Acid phosphatase, 72
Acne, 84
Adhesive tapes, development of prints from,
    147–148, 158
Admissible, defined, 409
Adolescents, sebum composition of, 82,
    83–84
Adults, print residue composition, 82, 84, 86
AFIS, see Automated fingerprint
    identification systems (AFIS)
Age
    expert witness testimony and, 405
    latent print composition and, 85, 86
    sebaceous gland activity and, 74
    sebum composition and, 81–84
Alcohols, 1,2-indanediones and, 135,
    198–199
Aldehydes, sebum composition and, 80
Alignment, fingerprint, 302–303, 305
Alkaline papers, Ag-PD and, 257–258

Alkaline phosphatase, 72
Alkoxyninhydrin, 196
Alkyl ninhydrins, 195
Allergies, ninhydrin, 184n
Alloxan, 178, 181, 193, 194
Almog, J., 191
Alternate light sources, print detection by,
    152–153, 178, 190–191, 211
Aluminum foil, development of prints from,
    150
*American Journal of Microscopy and Popular
    Science*, 36
Amidation reactions, nanocomposites and,
    229, 230–233
Amido black, 38, 92, 143–144
Amino acids
    latent print composition and, 85, 178
    reaction with 1,2-indanedione, 199
    reaction with DFO, 196, 197
    reaction with ninhydrin, 177, 181–182,
    183
    reagents for detection of, 132–134
    secretion of by eccrine gland, 70–71, 73
    visualization of on paper, 178–179
Amino acid visualization treatment,
    178–179, 243
Aminoninhydrins, 135, 195
Aminopyrine, 72
Ammonia, 69, 73, 85
Amy fingerprint identification model,
    345–352
    false association and, 348–349, 351–352
    indistinguishable minutia arrangements,
    346, 350
    number and position of minutia and,
    345–348, 350

formation of fluorescent metal complex
by, 192
lasers and latent print enhancement, 152
ninhydrin analogues and, 136, 192
production of by ninhydrin-amino acid
reactions, 130, 131, 177, 180, 181,
182, 183
Ruthenium tetroxide (RTX), 127, 150
RUVIS, 152

S

Savannah River Technical Center (SRTC),
89–90
Scalp, sebaceous glands on, 68
Scanners, live-print, 286–289
early models of, 320
FTIR, 282, 286–287, 288
hologram-based, 286, 287–288
noise added to image by, 282
thermal-based, 286, 289
ultrasound-based, 286, 287
Scanning electron microscopy (SEM), 153,
186, 268
Scars, prints from fingers with, 290, 303, 330
Schmidt, H.S., 127, 182
Schnetz, B., 266
Scientific publications, expert witnesses and,
391–392, 406–407
Scientific Research and Development Branch
(SRDB), 85, 185
Search warrants, 411
Sebaceous glands, 66, 68
density of, 68, 73–74
origin of sebaceous lipids, 75–76
sebum composition and, 74, 76–80, 81
fatty acids, 76, 78
miscellaneous constituents in, 80
phospholipids, 78–79
squalene, 80
sterols, 79–80
variation in by age, 81–84
wax esters, 79
sebum production and, 74–75
Sebum
bacteriological changes in after excretion,
76
chemical composition of, 76–80
fatty acids, 76, 78
miscellaneous constituents in, 80

phospholipids, 78–79
squalene, 80
sterols, 79–80
wax esters, 79
origin of lipids in, 75
oxidation of after excretion, 76
production of, 74–75
variation in composition of by age, 81–84
adolescents, 83–84
newborns, 82
post-adolescents, 84
young children, 82, 83
Second Level Detail, 332
Secretory glands, dermal layer, 66, 68–69,
70–71
apocrine, 66, 68–69, 80–81
eccrine, 66, 68
anatomy, 69
composition of sweat from, 69–73
weight, 69
sebaceous, 66, 68
density of, 68, 73–74
origin of sebaceous lipids, 75–76
sebum composition and, 74, 76–80
sebum production process, 74–75
variation in sebum by age, 81–84
Selenium, 194–195
SEM, see Scanning electron microscopy
(SEM)
Semiconductor nanocomposites,
photoluminescent, 220–236
CdS/dendrimer nanocomposites,
224–233
CdSe nanocrystals, 233–236
CdS nanocrystals, 222–224
Semi-porous surfaces, silver physical
developers and, 255, 257–258
Sensing, AFIS, 283–289
from inked prints, 283–284, 285, 286
live-scanning and, 286–289
noise added to image by, 282
print distortion and, 281–282
Sequestering of witness, 411
Serine, 70
Seymour trace latent print method, 46
Shortwave UV illumination, 151
Silver colloids, need for in Ag-PD solution,
254
Silver fingerprint powders, 109
Silver halide crystals, 244, 245